PREVENTIVE
DIPLOMACY

PREVENTIVE DIPLOMACY

STOPPING WARS BEFORE THEY START

EDITED BY

KEVIN M. CAHILL M.D.

REVISED AND

UPDATED EDITION

A JOINT PUBLICATION

OF

ROUTLEDGE

NEW YORK LONDON

AND

THE CENTER FOR INTERNATIONAL
HEALTH AND COOPERATION

Published in 2000 by
Routledge
29 West 35th Street
New York, New York 10001

Published in Great Britain by
Routledge
11 New Fetter Lane
London EC4P 4EE

Designed by KS of Sun & Vine Design

Printed in the United States of America on acid-free paper.

10 9 8 7 6 5 4 3 2 1

Library of Congress Cataloging-in-Publication Data

Preventive diplomacy : stopping wars before they start
/ edited by Kevin M. Cahill—
Revised and updated ed.
p. cm.
Includes bibliographical references and index.
ISBN 0-415-92284-4 — ISBN 0-415-92285-2 (pbk.)
1. Diplomatic negotiations in internal disputes.
2. Pacific settlement of international disputes.
3. Diplomacy. 4. Conflict management. I. Cahill, Kevin M.

JZ6045 .P74 2000
327.2—dc21   00-062565

FOR MICHAEL J. O'NEILL

whose generous and wise counsel is rooted in
the passionate pursuit of truth and justice

CONTENTS

ACKNOWLEDGMENTS   X

ABBREVIATIONS   XI

INTRODUCTION BY KEVIN M. CAHILL, M.D.   XIII

PART I
OLD CONCEPTS/ NEW APPROACHES

CHAPTER ONE   3

A Clinician's Caution: Rhetoric and Reality
Lord David Owen

CHAPTER TWO   17

Peace and the Healing Process
John Hume

CHAPTER THREE   29

The Fundamentals of Preventive Diplomacy
Mohammed Bedjaoui

CHAPTER FOUR   51

The Challenge of Humanitarianism
Peter Hansen

CHAPTER FIVE   67

Developing Preventive Journalism
Michael J. O'Neill

PART II
PARTICULAR PROBLEMS IN PREVENTIVE DIPLOMACY

CHAPTER SIX   83

Women as Partners for Peace
Rosario Green

CHAPTER SEVEN   101

Neutrality or Impartiality
Alain Destexhe, M.D.

CHAPTER EIGHT   119

Changing Concepts of Displacement and Sovereignty
Francis Deng

CHAPTER NINE   143

Economic Sanctions as a Means to International Health
Lord Robert Skidelsky and Edward Mortimer

PART III
MAJOR ACTORS

CHAPTER TEN   165

Creating Healthy Alliances
Cyrus Vance and Herbert S. Okun

CHAPTER ELEVEN   173

The Peacekeeping Prescription
Kofi A. Annan

CHAPTER TWELVE   189

Reflections on the Role of the UN and Its Secretary-General
Boutros Boutros-Ghali

CHAPTER THIRTEEN   205

Observation, Triage, and Initial Therapy
Marrack Goulding

CHAPTER FOURTEEN 215

Establishing Trust in the Healer:
 Preventive Diplomacy and the Future of the United Nations
Jan Eliasson

PART IV
POTENTIAL PARTICIPANTS IN PREVENTIVE
DIPLOMACY

CHAPTER FIFTEEN 243

Early-Warning Systems: From Surveillance to Assessment to Action
Ted Robert Gurr

CHAPTER SIXTEEN 263

Localizing Outbreaks
Salim Ahmed Salim

CHAPTER SEVENTEEN 273

International NGOs in Preventing Conflict
Kenneth Hackett

CHAPTER EIGHTEEN 287

Emerging Infectious Disease: Threats to Global Security
Scott R. Lillibridge, M.D.

CONCLUSION 299
NOTES 301
ABOUT THE AUTHORS AND THE CIHC 319
INDEX 323

ACKNOWLEDGMENTS

This book was made possible by the generous contributions of many individuals and organizations. It is based on a symposium held at the United Nations and originally published in 1996. The text has been widely used in universities around the world, and has now been revised and updated for this edition.

All the participants accepted my invitation on short notice and came, all from busy schedules, many from long distances, and for no honorarium, because they shared my belief that the topic of preventive diplomacy demanded international attention, and that the timing was critical. The authors agreed to view their assigned topics through the prism of public health, and an evolving enthusiasm for this approach was very evident at our United Nations symposium. I know my colleagues realize the depth of my respect and gratitude for their efforts, and I hope that my editing of their manuscripts in a cohesive book fulfills part of my debt to them.

The Directors and staff of both the Center for International Health and Cooperation (CIHC) and the Department of Humanitarian Affairs at the United Nations generously supported the entire effort, willingly offering their resources and skills to assure success. I particularly acknowledge the gracious and wise advice of former UN Under-Secretary-General Peter Hansen. The Executive Secretary of the CIHC, Renée Cahill, made a complex and difficult task a pleasure. Eric Nelson and Amy Shipper of Routledge provided support throughout the reediting and publication process.

ACC	Administrative Committee on Coordination
CD	Conference on Disarmament
CIHC	Center for International Health and Cooperation
CIS	Commonwealth of Independent States
CMCA	Commission for Mediation, Conciliation and Arbitration (OAU)
DHA	Department of Humanitarian Affairs
DPA	Department of Political Affairs
DPKO	Department of Peacekeeping Operations
ECHO	European Community Humanitarian Office
ECOMOG	Economic Community Military Observer Group
ECOSOC	Economic and Social Council
ECOWAS	Economic Community of Western African States
EPIET	European Programme for Intervention Epidemiology
HEWS	Humanitarian Early Warning System
IACS	UN Inter-Agency Standards Committee
ICJ	International Court of Justice
ICRC	International Committee of the Red Cross
IFOR	NATO Implementation Force
IGADD	Intergovernmental Authority Against Drought and Desertification
IMF	International Monetary Fund
IOM	International Organization for Migration
MCPMR	Mechanism for Conflict Prevention, Management and Resolution (OAU)
MINURSO	UN Mission for the Organization of a Referendum in Western Sahara
NMOG	Neutral Military Observer Group
OAU	Organization of African Unity
OSCE	Organization for Security and Cooperation in Europe
PIOOM	Interdisciplinary Program of Research on Root Causes of Human Rights Violation (Leiden University)
RUF	Revolutionary United Front
SAM	Sanctions Assistance Mission
UNAMIR	UN Assistance Mission in Rwanda

UNASOG	UN Aouzou Strip Observer Group
UNAVEM	UN Angola Verification Mission
UNDP	UN Development Programme
UNEF	UN Emergency Fund
UNHCR	UN High Commission for Refugees
UNICEF	UN Children's Fund
UNITAF	Unified Task Force (Somalia)
UNOMUR	UN Observer Mission into Uganda and Rwanda
UNOSOM	UN Operations in Somalia
UNPREDEP	UN Preventive Deployment Mission
UNPROFOR	UN Protection Force (Yugoslavia)
UNSCOM	UN Special Committee
UNTAC	UN International Transitional Authority in Cambodia
UNTAG	UN Transition Assistance Group (Namibia)
WEU	Western European Union
WFP	World Food Programme
WHO	World Health Organization

INTRODUCTION

KEVIN M. CAHILL, M.D.

One of the supreme creations of the human spirit is the idea of prevention. Like liberty and equality, it is a seminal concept drawn from a reservoir of optimism that centuries of epidemics, famines, and wars have failed to deplete. It is an amalgam of hope and possibility which assumes that misery is not an undefiable mandate of fate, a punishment only redeemable in a later life, but a condition that can be treated like a disease, and sometimes cured or even prevented.

During a lifetime in the practice of medicine—in Africa, Latin America, and Asia, as well as my own country—I have seen the daily wonders of the healing arts: lives rescued from once-fatal cancers, epidemics miraculously cut short, and countless millions of people saved from communicable diseases like polio and smallpox. Indeed, the conquest of smallpox, one of history's deadliest scourges, is itself a triumph of prevention attributable not only to Edward Jenner's vaccine but to the skills and untiring efforts of thousands of public health workers over a span of two hundred years.

So it is only natural for me to think of clinical and public health models in contemplating the disorders now threatening the health of the world community as it emerges from the rigid alignments of the Cold War and gropes for a new organizing principle in a new age of high technology, global economic competition, and multipolar politics. For power balances, realpolitik, and the other blunt-edged tools of East-West confrontation simply do not fit the need now for far more subtle, creative, and prospective approaches to the problems of peace.

Wanton killing and brutality within supposedly sovereign borders, ethnic and religious strife, millions of starving or near-starving refugees, other millions of migrants fleeing their homes out of fear for their lives or in a desperate search for a better life, human rights trampled down, appalling poverty in the shadows of extraordinary wealth, inhumanity on an incredible scale in what was supposed to be a peaceful dawn following the fall of the Berlin Wall—these are the awesome challenges that face us, and they are quite different from the nation-state rivalries and alliances that preoccupied statesmen during most of this century.

They call for earlier diagnoses and new kinds of therapy. Underlying causes have to be attacked sooner rather than later, before they become fulminating infections that rage beyond rational control or political containment.

This is the defining principle of preventive diplomacy, which argues that social detection and early intervention should be as honored in international relations as crisis management and political negotiation. In its pristine form, the idea is simplicity itself; it is reason opposed to irrationality, peace preferred to violence. In the reality of a disorderly world, however, preventive diplomacy is incredibly more complex and, in some respects, controversial. People can disagree on how to define social health and political disease. The tensions between rights and obligations seem to be intractable. Conflict is often needed to achieve social progress, so it is not always and forever to be shunned. In cases of unrelieved injustice, even violence may be justified.

The challenges and hopes for preventive diplomacy are explored in this book by statesmen, diplomats, physicians, humanitarians, government officials, and other leaders, who have been serving on the front lines in the pursuit of a better world. The first edition of *Preventive Diplomacy* rapidly became a standard text in academic courses on diplomacy, conflict resolution, and international political science. It was also widely used as a basic document at the United Nations and at peace conferences around the world. The present revised and updated version is published with the hope that it will contribute to the emergence of a more benign international system that can reduce the violence and suffering that now blight the lives of far too many millions of our fellow human beings.

The overall theme is captured most succinctly, perhaps, by Jan Eliasson, Sweden's Secretary of State for Foreign Affairs and the United Nation's first Under-Secretary-General for Humanitarian Affairs. "Prevention of conflicts is a moral imperative in today's world," he writes. "It is a humanitarian necessity in order to save innocent lives. It is an economic necessity both for the countries immediately involved and for the international community, because of the exorbitant price of war and postwar reconstruction. It is a political necessity for the credibility of international cooperation, in particular for the United Nations."

The very breadth of this view of preventive diplomacy suggests that the term itself is far more restrictive than its purpose and conception. For diplomacy, as it has been practiced during most of a now-dying Industrial Age, has been centered on the idea of nation-states dealing with each other on a government-to-government basis with the help of professionals specializing in secret negotiations and political conspiracy. Now, however, international relations have been utterly transformed by the technological revolution, by better informed and more active publics, by the spread of market capitalism, the fragmentation of politics, and a veritable explosion of commercial transactions and nongovernmental activism. Even the supposedly bedrock principle of national sovereignty is being eroded.

The sources of human stress, community breakdown, and group violence are far too diverse and too deeply embedded in social change to be consigned to the windowless compartments of conventional diplomacy. Many problems do not move in a straight line but in endless gyres of cause and effect so that a fall in coffee prices, for example, triggers economic collapse in Rwanda, then enormous personal hardships followed by social unrest, genocide, and fleeing refugees, starvation, cholera, dysentery, and other diseases that overwhelm medical workers and relief organizations. The cycle of disaster involves many different disciplines, including medicine, so that prevention calls for a symphony rather than a solo performance by a single profession like diplomacy. It also calls for a new kind of diplomat. "Preventing conflict," observes Lord David Owen, a neurologist as well as a statesman, "requires different skills from resolving conflict, even though they cannot always be separated out. Yet diplomats, unlike physicians, have not fully developed a preventive ethos and a disciplined method of working."

Mohammed Bedjaoui makes a similar point, arguing that preventive diplomacy is the mission of a wide variety of protagonists, "from the statesman to the businessman, from the journalist to the international organization, and from the banker to the nongovernmental organization." World public opinion is itself concerned," he says, "and should be even more concerned, given what is at stake in the achievement of peace."

If that thesis is valid, then the orchestra clearly needs a knowledgeable and committed conductor capable of promoting preventive diplomacy around the world. In a powerful chapter, former UN Secretary-General Boutros Boutros-Ghali identifies prevention as an absolutely urgent priority for the United Nations. The military costs of peacekeeping operations are overwhelming the resources and distorting the primary mission of the world organization. In moving terms he cites the difficulties he faced with noncompliant patients, recalcitrant nations, and contestants who refused to cooperate in a prescribed regimen for peace: "There are no guaranteed vaccinations to prevent conflicts from starting and no miracle cures to end them once they have started." Nonetheless, he writes, an international diplomat "cannot abandon his principal duty any more than a conscientious physician can abandon a difficult case. The Secretary-General's duty is to use all the means available to him . . . to save succeeding generations from the scourge of war." In the endless striving toward that ideal, United Nations officials deal daily with emerging as well as existing conflicts all over the world. In complementary chapters, former Under-Secretary-General Marrack Goulding and current UN Secretary-General Kofi A. Annan detail the methods they have used in detecting, treating, and eradicating international violence. They emphasize the need for flexibility and adaptation in preventive diplomacy, and couch their impressions and advice in memorable medical metaphors.

I have long suggested that health and humanitarian issues should be the pragmatic as well as the symbolic centerpiece of American foreign policy, and that the methodology of public health, and even the universally understood semantics of medicine, provide an exceptionally solid basis for a new type of diplomacy.[1] But if preventive diplomacy is to replace traditional reactive diplomacy, there must be fundamental change in our national mind-set.

At present only problems that attain crisis proportion seem to attract the attention of politicians or diplomats. Our leaders simply are not attuned to incipient disorders at a time when prevention is possible. Public figures are obsessed with dramatic solutions, with a fire-brigade approach that assures a continuation of catastrophes. In preventive medicine one begins by searching for fundamental causes, for the etiology of a disease, and for techniques that can interrupt transmission before serious signs and symptoms become obvious and irreversible damage occurs. One should be able to adapt this approach to the epidemiology of conflict; Nobel Laureate John Hume details his efforts to patiently pursue peace in Northern Ireland using the methods of *Preventive Diplomacy*.

The origins of violence clearly lie in incubating prejudices and injustices that inevitably breed hatred and conflict. But how rarely are these evil forces exposed early enough, or fought with effective tools, before predictable disaster strikes? If a fatal disease threatens to spread, health experts devise control programs based on careful research and laboratory experiments, sophisticated statistical studies and models, and field trials and double-blind surveys that try to minimize biases and biologic variants that often contaminate the best-intentioned projects. When deaths do occur, scrupulous postmortem analyses are customary so that the errors and failures of the past become the building blocks for a better approach in the future.

Diplomatic exercises should be subjected to similar probes and autopsies. Nations, particularly great powers and international organizations, must become humble enough to learn from failed efforts rather than merely defend traditional practices. If there are new actors in world conflicts and a new global environment created by, among other factors, a communications revolution, then the therapeutics of international mediation must also change.

The international system is in transition so that the contours of the post-Cold War age are still far from clear. But already there are a number of fascinating trends that are central to the development of the preventive diplomacy idea. One is a tentative shift in the direction of individualism that focuses international attention on personal human rights rather than only on the rights and privileges of national sovereignty. Rosario Green documents the unique burdens borne by—and potential contributions of —women in conflict. Francis Deng, who addresses the agonizing problems of internally displaced persons, argues that when sovereign nations fail in their obligations to their citizens, the international community has the responsibility "to hold the states accountable" and, if necessary, to intervene to "provide the needed protection" and even to help find remedies for the underlying conditions that led to violence.

During the post-World War II years, as Deng observes, the cast-iron definition of sovereignty was corroded by a decolonization process that championed self-determination. More recently, the concept has been weakened further "by the internationalization of human rights and the wave of democratization that is sweeping the world." In international law now, he says, quoting Michael Reisman, "what counts is the sovereignty of the people and not a metaphysical abstraction called the state." Deng warns, however, that a countertrend has developed. Governments that feel threatened by these contemporary intrusions on sovereignty are reasserting their claims by arguing, among other things, that the concept of universal human rights is just "a Western ploy for interfering in the internal affairs of other countries."

Deng contends that human rights must be defended within countries not only after masses of people already have been displaced but before that happens. "Human rights violations are a major factor in causing displacement. . . . Safeguarding human rights in countries of origin is therefore critical, both for prevention and for the solution of refugee and internally displaced persons problems. . . . Preventive strategies are critical." Ted Robert Gurr, an academician with extensive field experience in disaster areas, seeking better predictive methods to deal with imminent conflicts, has devised workable statistical models for diplomats.

Robert Skidelsky and Edward Mortimer, who wrestle with the issue of economic sanctions in their chapter, note that the "fundamental ground" for sanctioning domestic state misconduct is that it may disturb international relations. "Where domestic policy is likely to impose costs on third parties, there is a clear case for preventive intervention," they say, noting the way that persecution, genocide, or civil war can create masses of refugees who then become wards of the international community or burdens for neighboring countries. But in a related point that again emphasizes the complexity of the issues involved, they ask whether the mistreatment of minorities is justification per se for intervention. Does a state have the right to wage a civil war, for example, to prevent its own dissolution by a minority group that is waving the banner of self-determination?

The authors concede that with the fall of communism and fascism there is much less ideological conflict about what constitutes a "healthy" nation-state so that it may be possible to develop widespread agreement on "norms" of domestic state behavior. But they warn that essentially Western "norms," based on liberal democracy and private enterprise, may not be accepted by other societies in Asia, Africa, and the Middle East. And even if some norms are "universally accepted," they add, "their disregard may not be acceptable as a ground for intervention."

Still another perspective on this baseline issue is developed by Alain Destexhe in a chapter that attacks the application of the neutrality principle in humanitarian interventions and conflict prevention. In a series of bristling criticisms, he argues that the kind of neutrality once practiced by the Red Cross and some international organizations may end up aiding the villains more than the victims. In a similar vein, the United Nations' Peter Hansen insists that a first step in preventive diplomacy should be to recognize that "humanitarian intervention is not only inherently political but that it now must become more politically engaged."

When humanitarian aid is almost the only international response to a crisis and when that aid makes no distinction between different categories of victim, Destexhe says, then all catastrophes are "reduced to their lowest common denominator—compassion on the part of the onlooker." In the process, humanitarian action masks blame and obscures the obligation to intervene in other ways. He recognizes that the international community cannot react to Russia's intervention in Chechnya in the same way that it might have acted in Rwanda and Bosnia. Instead of neutrality, however, he proposes an alternative principle—impartiality. "Whereas neutrality focuses on the warring parties, impartiality focuses on the victims as individuals . . . making no distinction between victims in regard to race, ethnic origins, political, philosophical, religious, or other beliefs." The rights of the victims and "the moral imperative of justice" would take precedence over the "excuses" of neutrality or sovereignty.

Another fact that is exerting a powerful influence on the emerging post-Cold War patterns of international relations is the swift and nearly complete dominance of the global economic system by an American-led, knowledge-based, free market capitalism. Like the emphasis on human rights, this has important implications for preventive diplomacy, which ultimately has to deal with root causes of human afflictions that are very often found in the grossly unequal distribution of economic benefits. "A virtually unipolar world power is emerging," writes Mohammed Bedjaoui, "with the promotion of a single, generalized type of economic organization, nationally as well as internationally, summed up in the market economy system." But he sees dangers in the contrast between the success of this system and the weaknesses in the former Soviet Union and, more generally, in the Third World, where threats to peace lurk in three interrelated problems: underdevelopment, over-population, and lack of democracy.

He notes, for example, that underdevelopment and overpopulation are "triggering a migratory movement toward the Northern Hemisphere, which the North is attempting to curb or at least to control, because it is a major socioeconomic danger to itself." The prevention of both internal and international tensions, he argues, "should begin with efforts to generate economic development and significant progress . . . in education and training." However, he adds that "new concepts of development, hinged upon liberalism and competition, inevitably engender economic and social Darwinism, the survival of the fittest, and the exclusion of the rest." As a result, some nations are "perpetually deprived states, always drifting and always abandoned to their fate," and ultimately, he says, "that is a dangerous situation."

Salim Ahmed Salim, who is engaged in hand-to-hand combat with conflict prevention problems as Secretary-General of the Organization of African Unity, also draws a straight line to root causes as the starting point for prevention. Among other factors, he cites the failure of majorities to share in political power, religious and tribal intolerance, and lack of education. He also says that "mass unemployment among the young creates a politically explosive situation that is almost bound to result in violence and anarchy."

Peter Hansen offers a similar analysis. "It is not the end of the Cold War that has precipitated the rapid erosion of social structures, ethnic and religious conflict, and micronationalism," he writes, "but rather the intensifying effects of population growth, environmental degradation, and economic disequilibrium, both nationally and internationally. The latitude for a growing number of states to reconcile contending interests from within has been substantially reduced. Political opposition, often preceded by gross maldistribution of resources, has been the result as well as the precursor to political unrest and upheaval." Quite often, he says, humanitarian action serves only "as a buffer" between political action and human survival, a role "foisted upon the humanitarian network" because the international community lacked the will ito address the root political causes of state crises."

It is this lack of will in the face of extraordinary suffering and social chaos that is so appalling. While the wealthy nations of the world ride the crests of technological advancement and market expansion, the poorer countries are left behind in the troughs of lagging development so that the separation between the haves and have-nots becomes more and more extreme. Just as we can see the deadly cycle of unsanitary conditions and contaminated water in diseases like cholera, so now we can also see the vicious circle of crushing poverty, inadequate education, and poor health, that drive societies toward destruction and set off the desperate migrations that Mohammed Bedjaoui talks about. This is a highly unstable condition with ominous implications for the entire international system.

After World War II the United States launched the Marshall Plan that provided massive economic aid to prevent the collapse of a war-shattered Europe. Now the challenges to political and social stability are much larger in both scale and complexity, but the international community seems to be incapable of rising to its responsibilities even though it will eventually pay the price if violence instead of peace opens the new century. The United Nations is hardly able to support itself, much less lead the way to a new world order, and the world's economic leaders are too preoccupied with their own narrow interests to do anything about it.

Much of the burden of preventive action meanwhile falls on a vast array of nongovernmental organizations, or NGOs, that provide humanitarian assistance, sponsor public health programs, promote human rights, monitor abuses, and perform other services all across the international front of social need. Their work involves a great many issues related to the cause of preventive action. One of the more difficult is the extent to which humanitarian assistance may or may not be used to influence political outcomes in a violent dispute.

As a matter of policy or practical necessity, NGOs have often found themselves delivering food through governments that were violating human rights, simply because these governments controlled the distribution system. As a result, opposition groups fighting for democracy and individual human rights have been effectively cut out of the aid loop. Other NGOs have fought to get aid through to opposition forces even when, sometimes, this has involved clandestine operations with guerrillas. As Destexhe notes, "sans frontieres" organizations believe they have a dual role to play, "to provide aid to victims in the field, but they also speak out as witnesses to intolerable events."

The number of NGOs has expanded dramatically in recent years, and they have performed spectacularly in many troubled areas where the major powers have been absent or ineffective. But they also have their "weaknesses," as Cyrus Vance and Herbert S. Okun point out in their chapter. "While espousing broad humanitarian principles," they write, "some [NGOs] have their own partisan religious or political agendas. Rather than promoting peaceful settlements of conflict or working to prevent potential conflicts, such agendas can continue or even stimulate violence."

Another point made by Vance and Okun, as well as by other critics, is that NGOs tend to become "increasingly dependent" on government financing as they grow larger. "This results in their not being able to go where the need for prevention is paramount or where a humanitarian need is great, but rather where governments want them to go." In the Vance-Okun view, competition for funds also means that NGOs have to act in ways that invite the kind of media attention that impresses financial backers, and this can distort priorities.

Kenneth Hackett, speaking from his perspective as head of an NGO, Catholic Relief Services, argues strongly that "conflict prevention depends not only on addressing the causes of the tensions but, more fundamentally, in repairing relationships and changing systemic problems in society." In his conception, economic development is not enough to build a cohesive society; what is needed is "integral human development" in all of its social, psychological, spiritual, and political aspects. He suggests that private voluntary organizations, or PVOs, believe the best way to promote long-term peace is to work "at the inter-mediate and grassroots levels to undercut the capacity of those who manipulate and perpetuate conflict." Instead of governments, the emphasis is on churches, schools, and health care institutions where trusting relations with people can be more easily developed.

The old idea of great economic development projects simultaneously lifting living standards and creating political and social stability has been discredited in many ways. Indeed, there are great uncertainties about what tools will or won't work in conflict prevention. In the search for answers, Lord David Owen suggests the same kind of postmortem examinations that physicians use to discover the causes of death and to uncover clues leading to the prevention or cure of disease. Disappointing results, he says, mean that even the principle of inter-vention now has to be "critically reassessed." "Just as the wise clinician understands that the body has an ability to heal itself," he observes, "so the wise politician knows that the body politic, too, has its own correct-ing mechanisms. If one intervenes to correct one factor, an imbalance will often appear somewhere else." Inaction in politics, as in medicine, can be damaging, he says, but intervention is capable of wreaking far more havoc than inaction. Although "do something" is a common cry, he adds, the frustrating fact is that often "the short-term remedy con-flicts with the long-term solution."

Owen calls for intensive postmortem investigations of the crises in Somalia, Bosnia, Kosovo, and Rwanda, which he calls "the biggest single humanitarian disaster since World War II." These spectacular demonstrations of institutional failure, which he dissects with surgical brilliance and with the perspective of his own special experience, are lit-erally a school for folly. Paradoxically, however, they also can yield important lessons for preventive diplomacy if the international commu-nity is willing to learn.

One of Owen's recommendations is that the world's major economic institutions, such as the World Bank and International Monetary Fund, be drawn into prevention efforts rather than left on the sidelines. "A predictive capacity of potential conflicts," he says, "is needed that is capable of reaching across from economic to political factors." Economic institutions that monitor these factors, he says, "must be mandated to work with the UN Secretary-General." Without the man-date, this kind of involvement will not happen. In an allusion to the pre-sent disconnect between economic and political action, he suggests pointedly that the World Bank explore why it and other institutions loaned "so much money to Yugoslavia with so little conditionality" during the Tito years.

Owen believes the whole issue of sanctions also should be studied intensively. He notes that sanctions against Iraq and Serbia took a long time to bite and affect the regimes and their leaders while they had a "dire" effect on the civilian populations. Evidence that strong financial sanctions selectively can hurt governments more than civilians, he says, needs to be explored. Action to control drug money, for example, has now made it "very hard for any government to evade the seizure of their financial assets."

Skidelsky and Mortimer advance a very interesting related idea: that the enormous premium that the global economic system now places on domestic stability in a country is a powerful instrument for applying political pressures to influence behavior. "If we think of the post-Cold War era in economic rather than political terms (the global market)," they say, "new forms of sanctions become possible at the subpolitical level." Loans made or backed by the World Bank and similar organizations have "strong conditionality clauses attached to them." These are aimed at insuring against commercial risk "but political risk is part of commercial risk, so that political conditions, like respect for human rights, can be made part of the conditions."

The emergence of private credit-rating institutions that rank the political risk of countries "points in the same direction." World trade rules and new monitoring agencies like the World Trade Organization are also "fertile ground for linking trade issues to legal conditions, including human rights guarantees." "Thus," the authors conclude, "the process of economic integration can be used to promote a common set of standards for doing business, which spill over into political standards."

The enormous impact—for good or ill—in our "CNN era" of instant communications is considered by the former president of the American Association of Newspaper Editors, Michael J. O'Neill. The dangers inherent in TV's need to summarize complex diplomatic issues into thirty-second "bites," the problems of compassion fatigue caused by a series of images of famine, war disease, and death are real problems that must be recognized as one tries to build public and political support for preventive strategies.

The absolute urgency of preventive strategies may be nowhere better appreciated than in the world of bacterial epidemics, emerging diseases, and the threat of bioterrorism. If fatal epidemics spread, or germs are purposely released, preventive measures must be in place or whole populations may perish. Dr. Scott R. Lillibridge, the chief of the Office of Bioterrorism for the United States, carefully considers these emerging medical and diplomatic problems.

Ideas like these crowd the pages of this volume and, taken together, bring great wisdom to the eternal search for a better world. There are no final answers; there cannot be in our finite and imperfect state. But in the presence of disease, there is common pain that makes no distinctions of race or religion or class or wealth. No matter where disaster strikes, all the strands of shared humanity converge in shared suffering. In medical practice, a tumor or a tubercular lesion or an arrhythmia present in an identical manner, and it makes no difference whether the patient is an ambassador or a street cleaner.

It is also true in medicine and public health that persuasion is more effective than coercion. In the case of AIDS, for example, attempts to curb the disease through legal enforcement have failed. Only persuasion, education, and cooperation have had any success in altering lifestyles that contribute to the problem. In the same way, force has proven to be a poor treatment for violence. Indeed, military intervention and sanctions often do more harm than good. And that is the attraction of persuasion, cooperation, and prevention in international relations— to stop wars before they start. Even if, as we must fully expect, that noble goal proves elusive, preventive diplomacy offers the best, and maybe the only viable alternative to the failed practices of the past. Even after conflicts have begun, this new diplomacy, based on a philosophy that focuses on root causes and promotes early involvement, can help de-escalate violence and hasten the restoration of peace.

The development of sanitation, vaccines, and, more recently, environmental controls has produced phenomenal progress against the enemies of health. In the case of human organization, the invention of liberal democracy and individual rights marked an historic advance beyond such ancient concepts as slavery and the divine right of kings. The United Nations, however imperfect or structurally handicapped, represents a tentative step toward a world society and away from the anarchy of unaccountable sovereign nations. And now there is the chance that the principle of prevention may take its place as a significant improvement over inaction or coercion in dealing with conflict.

That is greatly to be hoped.

PART 1

OLD CONCEPTS / NEW APPROACHES

Anyone working in public health knows that specific ailments may be caused as much by economic factors as by biologic agents, and that most epidemics have their roots deep in poverty, ignorance, and oppression, in corruption and incompetence. The paths of government and medicine inevitably overlap and intertwine. But most political leaders tend—as do we all—to compartmentalize life, to stay safely within their expected areas of comment, thereby denying society the fullness of their experience and vision. It takes courage, and unusual wisdom, to look beyond predictable solutions and devise imaginative answers to chronic problems. Such creativity and leadership distinguish the statesman from the mere diplomat.

Throughout this book there is an emphasis on the importance of humanitarian issues in preventive diplomacy; that focus obviously reflects my own background and bias. The humanitarian emphasis also reflects my belief that people of all classes, in all societies, all over the world, would better understand the efforts of politicians and diplomats if they could relate them to their own lives. I suggest this can be done by utilizing well-known methods of public health and the common metaphors of medicine. I also suggest that peacekeepers could better appreciate their own potential, and limitations, by comparing their techniques and results with those that have proved satisfactory in the ancient field of disease prevention.

Using this approach, the centrality of health in foreign policy can be better recognized, and the ultimate importance of each individual's physical and mental well-being may finally be accepted as essential ingredients in creating a stable political environment. Humanitarian concerns and crises are, increasingly, the bases for international interventions. Epidemics, starvation, genocide, and gross violations of human rights are no longer considered as merely the internal problems of sovereign nations.

In this section four internationally acclaimed masters—in politics, jurisprudence, and international humanitarian affairs—accepted the challenge to construct from their own experiences the foundations for a new diplomacy.

Lord David Owen opens with an overview drawn from his unique medical and political background. Nobel Peace Prize Laureate John Hume suggests universal lessons from a local conflict. The Chief Justice of the International Court in the Hague, Mohammed Bedjaoui, emphasizes, in an eloquent essay, timeless values and the necessity, especially in the poor countries of the world, that preventive diplomacy be based on development, education, and an evolving acceptance of human rights. Peter Hansen, a former UN Under-Secretary-General for Humanitarian Affairs, demonstrates the significance of humanitarian affairs in modern diplomacy. Finally, Michael J. O'Neill, to whom this volume is dedicated, assesses the terrible power—for good or ill—of the media in a new world order of instant communication.

K. M. C.

1

A CLINICIAN'S CAUTION
RHETORIC AND REALITY
LORD DAVID OWEN

The Greek Physician Herophilus observed some two thousand years ago that illness renders science null, art inglorious, strength effortless, wealth useless, and eloquence powerless. Conflict does much the same to the body politic. Conflict is cancerous in the way it erodes democracy and trust, brutalizes behavior, and destroys civilized values and constraints. Preventing is very different from curing illness, and preventive health has acquired over the centuries particular disciplines and skills. Preventing conflict also requires different skills from resolving conflict, even though they cannot always be separated out. Yet diplomats, unlike physicians, have not fully developed a preventive ethos and a disciplined method of working.

The second half of the nineteenth century and the first half of the twentieth century has seen in the developed world a dramatic fall in mortality rates, mainly attributable to the prevention of deaths from infectious diseases. Preventive public health measures to provide clean water supplies and improved housing have made, though it is not often recognized, a far more dramatic impact than clinical treatment. Prevention continues to do so through immunization programs. The WHO eradication-of-smallpox campaign was a striking success and we hope polio will soon follow. Yet, tuberculosis is returning. Drug therapy, particularly antibiotics, have played their part as have modern surgical techniques and chemotherapy. There has also developed a counter-movement to ill-judged medical interventions seen in the growth of lifestyle adjustments, homeopathic medicines, and a greater readiness to rely on the body's own defense mechanisms.

Realistic doctors are only too well aware of the inadequacies of their skills when confronting much illness. It is a salutary fact that as the population lives longer the vast bulk of modern illness is not cured but alleviated by the doctor's skills. The majority of doctors', nurses', and therapists' time is spent in helping patients to accommodate themselves to the facts of their illness. The largest element in all illness in modern society is the aging process itself—a largely irreversible process. Health services and the doctors are cast in the role of the providers of good health, yet, at best, for the bulk of illness all they can do is watch as the body wears itself out. The dramatic cure is the exception rather than the rule.

Much the same limitation affects politicians dealing with conflict within a nation or internationally. Violence is part of daily living; we can deplore its existence but we are not likely to be able to root it out from our diverse societies. The Cold War avoided a set battle between NATO and the Warsaw Pact—but there were surrogate battles between the United States and the Soviet Union, and many other conflicts that resulted in a hideous loss of life. Despite the UN providing a framework for international order and world peace, its first fifty years were sadly characterized by multiple wars. The possibility of the UN intervening in a conflict within a nation-state was virtually excluded after the Korean War. After the collapse of the Berlin Wall the UN authorized humanitarian interventions in Iraq, Somalia, Croatia, Bosnia-Herzegovina, Haiti, Rwanda, and, depending on one's interpretation of the Security Council Resolutions, Kosovo. Yet the disappointing results mean that even the principle of such interventions is now having to be critically reassessed. It also has become clear that we do not know enough about the multifaceted impact of economic and trade sanctions as well as differing forms of military intervention.

The doctor and the politician are not as different as perhaps both, and in particular the doctor, would like to think. Each is essentially involved in the practice of natural science. The physicist and engineer deal in absolutes. The clinician and the politician can only use science as an aid, and they are both intimately involved in human behavior. Inevitably in their decision making they fuse not only scientific and statistical evidence but also important elements of the behavioral sciences. Both have to relate their decisions to and identify with a multiplicity of human variables. The doctor is primarily involved with the individual, the national politician inevitably predominantly with groups of individuals, the statesman with groupings of nations. The skill of the good politician and the skill of the good clinician come not just from their ability to observe life, to understand and feel a concern for their fellow men and women, but also from knowing when to intervene and when to leave alone. The greatest mistakes in politics and medicine often derive from an inability to comprehend and anticipate the underlying trends and developments affecting individuals.

I have adapted an old prayer of Sir Robert Hutchinson, a nineteenth-century physician at the London Hospital, into a "Politician's Prayer":

> From inability to let well alone, from too much zeal for the new and contempt for what is old, from putting knowledge before wisdom, science before art, and cleverness before common sense, from treating individuals as statistics, and from making change in the body politic more grievous than the endurance of the same, good Lord deliver us.

Just as the wise clinician understands that the body has an ability to heal itself, so the wise politician knows that the body politic, too, has its own correcting mechanisms. If one intervenes to correct one factor, an imbalance will often appear somewhere else. The good clinician can never diagnose or treat any symptom in isolation: the whole man embraces his environment just as much as his ailment. In politics exactly the same factors have to be reckoned with, for an interventionist style of politics is an exposed one, and any action will be clearly related to the change it may introduce—positive or adverse. Inaction and immobility in politics, as in medicine, can exaggerate or perpetuate tendencies that already exist so that they become damaging. Intervention, on the other hand, is capable of wreaking far more havoc than inaction. The interventionist politician, like the interventionist clinician, therefore, has a duty to commission research and pay respect to the results of any such research. An intervention that is not based on as much factual evidence as is available is simply irresponsible.

Yet just as doctors and politicians can work only on the margin of human behavior and existence, society still thinks they have far greater power than in reality they possess. "Do something" remains a common cry. However, the frustration the doctor feels, as does the politician, is that so often the short-term remedy conflicts with the long-term solution. Both have to accept, albeit with resignation, the limitations imposed by the structures on which they operate: the human body and the body politic. In consequence the wisest course is often only a series of patching-up expedients. Careful research and observations can indicate worthwhile initiatives that are capable of ensuring that eventual benefits do accrue, but they may only rarely be dramatic or even directly attributable to their initiator. In an ideal world it would not sound horrifying or cause alarm if politicians and doctors admitted more freely and more openly that their decisions are often influenced and even dominated by the maxims of calculated neglect and masterly inactivity. But although they know that this may be the wisest course, they also know that it may be a course that opens them to bitter criticism and, in a crisis, to almost universal condemnation. Patients and parliaments want activism when faced with crisis.

In international politics calls for action are not new, as any reading of the reports from war correspondents from the Boer War and before will show. What is different today is the "CNN effect." The TV camera in Sarajevo recording minute by minute, hour by hour, day by day in real time from the battleground conveys an immediacy and has an impact that no newspaper, with its greater number of words qualifying and explaining, or even a radio commentary, carries. Although there is no CNN camera yet in the consulting room or operating theater, medicine is now dramatized on TV and patients' rights and medical litigation have ensured that doctors no longer agonize in private when facing choices of life and death.

Doctors call this triage, the inescapable three-way choice: who to treat, who will die, who can wait. It is worth examining the qualities of the individual surgeon whom a doctor will choose for themselves or their family. One will invariably find that high up is a known reluctance to wield the scalpel for its own sake. This proper caution over intervening medically or surgically is as much about understanding the natural history of disease as recognizing the dangers of upsetting the restorative nature of the body's defense mechanisms.

The general public has come to recognize even in the richest industrial nations that no system of public health care will provide wholly adequate resources. Some degree of rationing is accepted as inevitable, and this realization has heightened the question of how such choices should be made. As people realize that there will always be an unsatisfied medical demand, there is more questioning of whether rationing of facilities, or, more seriously, scarce medical and surgical skills, clearly public goods, can be justified on anything other than the basis of need. But who determines that need, the doctors or the politicians? Because these subjective judgments are so complex we are finding it hard to escape from a mixed health care system, part publicly organized providing on the basis of need, part privately organized on the ability to pay.

A similar questioning is occurring within the international community about conflict prevention and resolution as it becomes ever clearer that we will not devote to it the much needed financial resources. We will defend our own state but are wary of involving our troops within another state's territory. In the early 1990s the Stockholm International Peace Research Institute showed that of thirty major armed conflicts in the world only one was interstate, and that was between India and Pakistan. All the others were within states. Until the end of the Cold War the Security Council did not intervene in the internal affairs of a Member State. Now politicians and those who practice international diplomacy, after intervening in Iraq, Somalia, and the former Yugoslavia, are better aware of the perils of interventionism. As a result they are exhibiting a newfound sense of caution. In the United States this caution manifested itself after Vietnam with the often repeated message that the United States has no wish to become the world's policeman.

A new self-disciplined approach to UN intervention was first spelled out by President Clinton in a policy directive in April 1994, shortly after the last U.S. troops left Somalia. The world was put on notice that the United States believed that the Security Council could not respond to each and every crisis. Unfortunately the Rwanda crisis in the spring of 1994 was the moment when the Security Council policy of accepting that the United Nations could not be everywhere or do everything was first put to the test. The U.S. refusal to sanction further UN involvement had been strongly influenced by what had happened in Somalia and what was happening in Bosnia-Herzegovina. Another strong and related motivation was congressional resistance to paying for UN peacekeeping and a wish to control the spiraling U.S. deficit in their assessed contribution to the UN budget. Yet in both Somalia and Bosnia-Herzegovina the initial UN intervention saved hundreds of thousands of lives. In the autumn of 1992 both were seen as humanitarian interventions and were so described, but it was never going to be possible to keep such a limited mission beyond a few months. "The international community should discard the illusion that one can intervene in a country beset by widespread civil violence without affecting domestic politics and without including a nation-building component."[1]

The international community was under few illusions about the scale of the task if they were to intervene in Rwanda.[2] They did know about the highly volatile ethnic composition of the country, of how the minority Tutsi had exercised economic and political domination prior to independence, and how, since independence in July 1962, the majority

Hutu had ruled. Initially Rwanda achieved modest economic growth (1.6 percent increase of GNP on average from 1965 to 1980). Even so Rwanda had the highest population density in Africa and it was very vulnerable economically, with 80 percent of its exports being coffee and tea. When the International Coffee Agreement collapsed in 1987 and the coffee price fell to half its 1980 value, we knew this would have a particularly damaging effect on Rwanda. It was then that conflict prevention in the form of economic assistance could have worked, and we must examine the role of the Bretton Woods Institutions, the World Bank in particular, in any strategy for conflict prevention for the twenty-first century.

In October 1990 an exiled Tutsi-dominated Rwandan Patriotic Front (RPF) attacked into northeastern Rwanda. The Organization of African Unity (OAU) organized a Neutral Military Observer Group (NMOG) to monitor buffer zones separating the RPF and the Hutu government forces in July 1992 and in February 1993 to ensure resettlement in demilitarized zones. In June 1993 the United Nations agreed to an Observer Mission into Uganda and Rwanda (UNOMUR) and it was sent in to implement a peace agreement concluded at Arusha in August 1993. The OAU lacked the resources among its member states to carry through their political decision. In 1993 the UN Special Rapporteur observed that the situation was deteriorating with the Hutu government labeling all the Tutsi people as accomplices of the RPF. Following the RPF invitation in 1990, France sent its own soldiers and advisors. In October 1993 the UN Secretary-General persuaded the Security Council to establish an Assistance Mission for Rwanda (UNAMIR) to help implement the Arusha Accords. By March 1994 UNAMIR's strength was 2,539 people with twenty-four participant countries. Then, ten Belgian peacemakers were killed, and the Belgian government announced they would withdraw. This dramatically changed the picture just as when eighteen U.S. Army Rangers lost their lives on October 3–4, 1993, in Somalia, and U.S. forces went on the defensive until their withdrawal on March 31, 1994. It seems that public opinion in many troop-contributing countries will not accept such casualties from peacekeeping missions. Yet we need to counter this opinion by honoring more the sacrifices of those who lose their lives or hazard their health when serving in "blue berets."

The Security Council then faced an all too familiar choice: to reinforce or to reduce the UN commitment. The council chose to reduce. On April 21, with the United States in the lead, the UN Security

Council decided to cut UNAMIR from 1,700 people to 270 people. This was done against the open advice of UN officials and all the main humanitarian NGOs operating in the country. By the end of April the aid agencies estimated that some two hundred thousand people had been killed in Rwanda. The killing rate rose thereafter remorselessly to over five hundred thousand. On May 13 the UN Secretary-General recommended that the Security Council deploy 5,500 troops in a UNAMIR II. The United States took the lead again within the Security Council in urging that UNAMIR II be confined to the borders of Rwanda, and there was a slow build-up in troops. U.S. officials were said to have been instructed by the State Department not to talk of acts of genocide so as to avoid incurring an obligation to act under the UN's Convention on Genocide. None of the governments on the Security Council could have been in any doubt that by then what was occurring was the largest and most explicit genocide the world had seen since the German genocide against the Jews. Also, unlike the genocide in Cambodia, there was no likelihood of a veto in the Security Council preventing action.

Even so the Security Council was still not ready to deploy sufficient force to stop the Rwandan genocide, and some doubted that even a large force could stop what was happening. Why were the permanent members so reluctant? In part because it was happening on the African continent, which did not arouse as much public feeling as, for example, the former Yugoslavia. In part because, of the permanent members, only France had real interests in that part of the African continent. In part because the Security Council was not ready to provide the money and logistical support for the OAU and the surrounding African countries to participate in large numbers. The United States felt they had been humiliated in Somalia. The French and British felt they were fully committed to peacekeeping in Bosnia. The Russians were otherwise engaged, not least in Chechnya. China had no links and was anyhow hostile to the very concept of intervention in the internal affairs of a member state. The world's press and TV covered the horror of what was happening extensively, but there was never the same build-up of public pressure to intervene as had happened over the famine in Ethiopia or was evident over the plight of the Kurds in 1991 and the humanitarian crises in Somalia and Bosnia in 1992.

It is easy, on moral grounds, to deplore the decision to limit UN intervention, but it was not a decision taken lightly or out of ignorance but a decision bedded in realpolitik. Furthermore, it is the sort of decision that we can expect to be repeated. It is encouraging that President Clinton while visiting Africa a few years later did apologize and admit that U.S. policy had been wrong in not intervening in Rwanda. Politicians should take a leaf out of the medical profession's preventive discipline and institute a postmortem on the Rwanda genocide, a quite distinct investigation from the Rwanda War Crimes Tribunal. The findings of any such postmortem should examine the effect of the precipitate fall in the price of coffee in 1980 destabilizing the Rwandan economy. People may rightly say that there are numerous other countries politically vulnerable to a fall in coffee prices, but analysis may also show that of those countries few, if any, had the same combination of dependence on coffee exports and potential for ethnic instability. An important military-led reassessment of the Canadian General's plan for a UN Rwandan intervention force of five thousand well equipped and trained troops in April 1994 has been conducted by the Carnegie Commission on Preventing Deadly Conflict,[3] and this concluded that it could have halted the genocide but it would have had to be deployed quickly for there was only a three-week window of opportunity.

A predictive capacity of potential conflicts is needed that is capable of reading across from economic to political factors. This must be an open procedure and cannot just be built up by the UN Secretary-General or the Security Council. Existing economic institutions which carefully and routinely monitor such factors must be mandated to work with the UN Secretary-General, who should be charged with coordinating and publicly highlighting the implications of such research. Without a specific remit, the UN Secretary-General will not get the involvement of institutions like the World Bank or IMF, who see themselves as totally separate from the UN in New York. Also, any UN Secretary-General will be subjected to considerable pressure not to publish the findings, for fear that it will be a self-fulfilling prophecy, and the mere act of calling attention to a potential crisis will precipitate conflict.

Another area on which a Rwanda postmortem should focus is the links established between the OAU and the United Nations as the OAU observer group was deployed.[4] Could the observer group have been strengthened with some financial assistance or military logistical backup and equipment? If this help could not come from the United Nations, should this be the sort of specific action that the richer democracies should help finance? Could the economy of Rwanda have been buttressed at that time in 1992 with more international aid? We need to know exactly what financial help was asked for and what was refused.

Another issue that should be explored is if UN forces were never ready to be deployed in bulk, should they have gone in at all in 1993? Would it not have been wiser to have drawn the line not at increasing the size or the deployment pattern of an existing UN force but at the concept of moving in at all, given the limitations and hesitations over further involvement? Politicians must not fail to look back on Rwanda, which has been the biggest single humanitarian disaster since World War II. If we do not learn lessons here there will be little hope for rational prevention and resolution of human conflict in the twenty-first century.

The UN General Assembly commissioned in 1999 a retrospective analysis of the flawed "safe haven" policy in Bosnia-Herzegovina adopted by the Security Council. I have made a contribution to this with an account of my own personal odyssey.[5] The Dutch government has established a commission to consider the circumstances that led to the massacre of seven thousand Muslims in Srebrenica in June 1995, an episode very well described by two Dutchmen.[6] The Carnegie Endowment Fund sponsored a commission out of the Aspen Institute in Berlin which reported in 1996 on the breakup of the former Yugoslavia. The Security Council should consider in the light of these studies early in the twenty-first century what disciplines can be adopted in the future to curb the unreal nature of so many of the UN Security Council resolutions. The World Bank should explore the Tito era and offer to see why the World Bank and other institutions lent so much money to Yugoslavia with so little conditionality, either in terms of real market reforms, greater openness, or democratic reform in Yugoslavia. Intellectuals from the West were praising the dissident Djilas, but their governments did little to reinforce his message.

After the end of the Clinton administration in 2001 it should be easier to conduct a retrospective analysis of the full extent of U.S. involvement in all the military aspects of the Somalia peacekeeping exercise. This needs to be independently documented to counter the propaganda and scapegoating that has so far pushed all the blame onto the UN itself.

On the 1999 war in Kosovo there will be many studies to determine why NATO was unable to prevent the war, what went wrong with the preventive diplomacy, particularly the Rambouillet Conference, and how the eventual settlement was made, as well as the effectiveness of NATO air power.

In the implementation of sanctions policy there is also much to be learned from retrospective analysis. Sanctions against both Iraq and Serbia took a long time to bite on their regimes, during which time the

effects on the civilian population were dire. A study published in the
Lancet of December 2, 1995, on the health of Baghdad's children
showed a strong association between economic sanctions and an
increase in child mortality and malnutrition rates, the under-five mortality rate rising fivefold.[7] It claims that since August 1990, 567,000
children in Iraq have died as a result of economic sanctions, which the
Iraqi government refused to alleviate by exporting oil in exchange for
food and medicine, denouncing this as an unacceptable interference in
Iraqi sovereignty. In a more extensive survey in 1999 UNICEF documented the continued impact of economic sanctions and Iraqi policies
on infant and child death rates.[8] Iraq now has an under-five mortality
rate comparable to those of Haiti or Pakistan, and "there would have
been a half million fewer deaths of children under five in the country as
a whole during the eight year period 1991-1998."

Figure 1
Iraq—Under-Five Mortality Rate Disparities

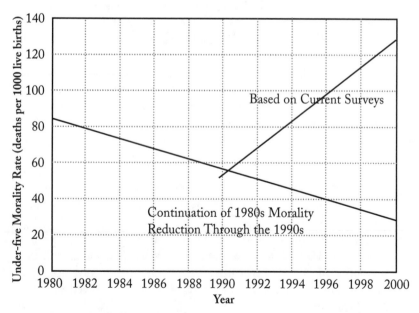

*The chart shows the large disparity between the mortality rates based on recent
surveys and what would have been the situation if the mortality trend in the
1980s had been continued through the 1990s.*

We need to examine carefully what financial measures and mechanisms are available to ensure a quicker impact on such governments and, if possible, where we can reduce the burden of sanctions on their civilian populations. President Mitterrand once remarked that the lesson of sanctions is that they are put on piecemeal, bite too slowly, and stay on too long. Sanctions against Serbia had their effect gravely weakened by the black market established with neighboring countries. One of the reasons why neighboring governments did not clamp down on those black market activities was that their own economies were suffering serious damage, and the UN Charter provision for alleviating the effect of sanctions on the surrounding areas was never invoked by the rich industrial nations. Oil and other goods flooded across from Macedonia, and later Albania, to Serbia, rendering much of the work of the Sanctions Assistance Monitoring (SAMs) teams null and void.

One of the many reasons why sanctions are imposed in a haphazard way is that their application is often controversial within the Security Council and it is easier to apply them little by little, but we have to question whether this manner of implementation is not discrediting sanctions. Would the Security Council not be better off applying the discipline of an all-or-nothing approach to sanctions? There are humanitarian arguments for this line of thinking, for it appears that in Iraq and Serbia hardship inflicted on innocent people was cumulative, hurting children and older people more as the years went on, while giving time for elites to develop a black market.

Admittedly, the propaganda effect of sanctions was heightened by their governments wanting and ensuring bad publicity for the Security Council actions and using the suffering of their children in their battle with the rest of the world to have sanctions lifted. There is an argument for moving to a strong, full sanctions package immediately and in particular using financial sanctions at the start, because it appears that financial restrictions hurt governments more than their civilian population. However, we need more evidence on this. We saw in 1986 that the actions of private banks in Switzerland in withholding credit from South Africa was a powerful factor in persuading the white South African regime to negotiate with the African National Congress and end apartheid. Had financial sanctions been used earlier in South Africa there might not have been the thirteen-year period between the first mandatory sanctions on arms being applied in 1977 and opening of the path to negotiations in 1990. Financial sanctions can have their effectiveness massively enhanced by the legislative powers UN Member States took in the 1980s to monitor and control drug money. It is now very hard for any government to evade the seizure of their financial assets. It was noticeable that the threat of financial sanctions, to take effect at the end of April 1993, was the key factor in convincing President Milosevic to accept the Vance-Owen peace plan.

Just as a little medicine can have no curative value, so a minimalist sanctions package can often have little damaging effect on the economy of a country and can even, as we saw in Rhodesia in the 1960s and early 1970s, by encouraging import substitution and self-sufficiency, bolster economic performance in the medium term. The world needs to consider these factors very carefully before embarking on any new sanctions strategy. It has been noticeable that, for example, over Nigeria in the 1990s there was much heart searching and serious questioning of the effect of applying sanctions, and now that democratic government has been established it would be worth reflecting on whether the reluctance to cross the sanctions threshold had been correct. Sanctions must not be imposed just to satisfy public opinion in Security Council countries. A maritime or land-based blockade of all goods has to be counterbalanced by food aid and medical supplies best supplied from the start by UNHCR and WHO. Inevitably much of such food aid will feed the armies. By 1995 it was estimated that more than 50 percent of the food going into Bosnia-Herzegovina went to feed the three armies and it was also continuously traded on the black market.

The other self-discipline that needs to be applied relates to the differing forms of military intervention. It is not an easy area in which to establish clarity but politicians should perhaps again learn a lesson from the therapeutic application of poisons and radiotherapy in the treatment of cancer. Military intervention always will be a dangerous operation, even more so if the task of peacekeeping has any elements of enforcement. The United Nations has developed special peacekeeping techniques for monitoring and observing cease-fire agreements. The parties to a dispute have to be agreed on the UN force coming in and what the UN force's main tasks are before it arrives in the area. We need to recognize that there is no such thing as a surgical intervention in a civil war, either to stop it or control its aftermath. NATO's involvement on the ground to implement a negotiated settlement in Bosnia-Herzegovina and in Kosovo carried with it the danger that as the political settlement remained elusive, NATO troops would start to be seen to be part of the problem rather than the solution.

The arrival of any external military force will change the dynamics of that war. If it is announced in advance that the force will stay only for six weeks or a few months, then the parties may only play for time until the force exits. Limitations on the force easily can encourage one or other of the fighting parties to await withdrawal. It is also unwise to spell out to the fighting parties that the intervening forces will never impose a settlement. In both Somalia and Bosnia-Herzegovina the parties soon knew that the United Nations would not impose a settlement and, for much of the time, felt they might leave. Although an exit strategy for the United Nations is often thought by troop-contributing countries to be essential, usually the less it can be talked about the better. Timetables may concentrate minds, but not always in the most helpful way. In Kosovo NATO had learned its lesson and from the start made it clear it was not on a fixed timetable.

Can there ever be a purely humanitarian intervention? After the experience of the humanitarian military intervention in Bosnia-Herzegovina, there will be a legacy of hostility within the Security Council to believing that such an exercise, with its initial restrictive mandate, can ever be repeated. Their skepticism is understandable but regrettable. In terms of lives saved, either from malnutrition or hypothermia, during the winter of 1992–93, the Bosnian humanitarian operation was an unqualified success. Its restricted mandate worked for the first few months and became impossible only after the Bosnian Serbs had rejected the Vance-Owen, UN-EU peace plan. That was the time, as I argued, at the end of May 1993, to have withdrawn the UN forces from exposed ground and used NATO air power to impose a settlement that NATO would then have had to implement. Over two years later, in September 1995, that is, in effect, what was done with the crucial help of the Croatian armed forces. But by then the ethnic cleansing had continued at such a rate that partition was all that was left. In Kosovo it was crucial to get the refugees back before the winter of 1999. The lesson is that a strictly humanitarian intervention can probably only be sustained for six months or a year.

Humanitarian interventions depend absolutely on the UN, NATO or other intervening forces like the Economic Commission of West African States Ceasefire Monitoring Group, which operated in Sierra Leone, being seen at all times to be acting impartially. Peacekeeping is greatly helped if one is able to rely on the cooperation of all the parties. But in the absence of being able to act impartially, a strictly humanitarian intervention becomes unsustainable. Also, if the Security Council cannot maintain the self-discipline to be impartial, it is better not to launch a strictly humanitarian intervention, for that will undermine the credibility of the force. Nation building and restoring civil order takes years, not months, and can necessitate fairly large force levels. To conduct oneself with impartiality is not the same as being neutral. UN commanders must be free to criticize abuses and to authorize their forces to fire back when fired on.

In the case of NATO and other regional organizations, when intervening under the authority of the UN Charter it is even more necessary to establish a reputation for impartiality. It was a tragedy in Bosnia-Herzegovina after Dayton that NATO was not able to unify Mostar with the help of the EU. In Sarajevo the exodus of Serbs was encouraged from Pale but with a more active NATO role might have been avoided.

In Kosovo, having bombed Serbia as well as Kosovo, NATO faces a difficult task in establishing that it is there to protect and persuade Serbs to remain. The most dangerous period will be when the KLA become impatient for independence and find NATO blocking that since there is unlikely to be Security Council support without at least an overall Balkan settlement being put in place.

Another limiting factor is that military intervention to peacekeep, to peace enforce, or to assist humanitarian relief will involve casualties, and troop-contributing countries must be able to carry public opinion in their own countries when faced by such an eventuality. Troop-contributing countries must also be able to influence Security Council resolutions to ensure they are based on the realities on the ground. For all these reasons Security Council Member States should be obliged to make an effective contribution to a UN Rapid Reaction Force during their time as members of the council, something discussed by the Carnegie Commission.[9] In that way rhetoric and reality may be matched better than at present, because UN interventions fail where rhetoric bears little relation to reality. It is very important that the French and British governments have now earmarked forces for a UN rapid reaction capability which must be built up to be ready to act quickly, which the Rwanda experience shows is so essential.

In all cases of a military humanitarian intervention we have to be ready, as part of the price of rapid deployment, to cut one's losses and leave. Intervention cannot always be sustained, and knowing when to leave is as important as knowing when to enter.

2

PEACE AND THE HEALING PROCESS

John Hume

Politics can be a healing profession and is a critical element in preventive diplomacy. The use of medical terms and examples helps us appreciate both the complexity of the challenges we face and the importance of our efforts.

In one of the most famous pieces of political oratory, the Gettysburg Address, Abraham Lincoln spoke at the end of bloody civil war about binding the wounds of the nation. This is probably the most famous example of medical analogies being used to describe problems being suffered by, or processes being proffered to, the body politic.

It is not uncommon to hear people despair about the cancer of sectarianism or racism. References are made to paralysis, situations hemorrhaging, crippling effects, pain, hurt, trauma, fractures, mental scars, and prognoses in many political commentaries, not only in situations where violence is, or has been, waging. Over the years I have often talked of Ireland's need for a "healing process" and cautioned against notions of "instant cures." On numerous occasions I have found myself advising people to diagnose and treat causes of our political condition instead of scratching or picking at symptoms.

Medical or health analogies are particularly understandable in the context of a dysfunctional polity. They probably proliferate especially in circumstances where such political dysfunctionalism manifests itself in violence creating trauma that is all too real and literal. The medical profession has to treat the consequences of such violence. In our own situation it has done so with distinction, dedication, and determined cooperation spanning all levels and branches of the profession and associated professions. From my perspective, the political profession has to identify, isolate, and treat the causes of such conflict. Unfortunately a comparable concerted effort involving all politicians to match the response to challenge by the clinicians has not yet been brought about—yet!

This can be explained partly by the fact that violence itself generates secondary political malignancies and complications. As Martin Luther King, Jr. said, "Violence as a way of achieving justice is both impractical and immoral. It is impractical because it is a descending spiral ending in destruction for all. The old law of an eye for an eye leaves everybody blind. It is immoral because it seeks to humiliate the opponent rather than win his understanding, it seeks to annihilate rather than convert. Violence is immoral because it thrives on hatred rather than love. It destroys community and makes brotherhood impossible. It leaves society in monologue rather than dialogue."

Recognizing that violence can only frustrate what we want to further and end up destroying what it starts out claiming to defend, we must see if we can isolate violence itself. In Northern Ireland the effects of violence were preventing and undermining successful treatment of our underlying problem. Only by securing total relief from violence could we progress from monologue to the dialogue that is needed to treat our problem and help us toward the healing process. Securing relief from the harrowing and debilitating secondary condition or symptoms does not constitute a cure. Nor does it lessen the need to go on to deal with the underlying problem. We need to be resolved rather than reluctant about moving on to the other phases or episodes of treatment and care without which we cannot have a healthy outcome.

I can understand fears, misgivings, and nervousness about the process ahead. It will be uncomfortable for all of us but we have no alternative course to stability. People want cures but we do not like undergoing operations, just as people want to go to heaven but nobody wants to die. It is surprising what some people will tolerate in terms of toothache before submitting to a dentist.

I suppose we all have a particular phobia about losing something. In our situation those in all traditions have an innate fear about having to give something up even if it is only vestigial. Anyone planning a successful intervention should be sensitive to such fears without being completely constrained by them. Feeding fears will not build the confidence and comfort necessary for us to undergo and undertake the appropriate interventions and exercises.

As you can tell by now, I am given to the idea that politics is concerned with healing the wounds of society, just as physicians heal the wounds of individuals. Given the attitudes of many people toward politics and its practitioners, this might seem an exaggerated or downright presumptuous claim. Nevertheless, I would argue strongly that healing is what politics should be about.

Politics in my view is essentially about creating hope for a better future, which, of course, implies creating a substantively better present. To do so involves dispelling many illusions about the purpose and capacities of political power. For instance, notions that war is a legitimate and effective extension of politics or that violence is an effective means of political change have to be undermined and discredited. But the idea that we can make the world better is the foundation of all constructive human endeavor. Hope allows people to think that they can improve their quality of life and that their grievances can be addressed. It sustains democracy. Without the possibility of democratic change, violent, xenophobic, and nihilist reflexes have free rein.

People actively involved in politics, as well as the ordinary citizen, also need hope to carry on their activities. That is possible because of free will. There is no predestination in politics. Nothing in politics is inevitable. Peace or war, poverty or prosperity, all result from more or less conscious decisions and actions of human beings. We can create circumstances in which wars are more or less likely and more or less unthinkable. We can make decisions that affect the general level of prosperity or the distribution of wealth. We may not always know what the impact of decisions will be, but we do know that political leaders have a moral and political responsibility for their actions and inactions.

As a result, even if there are profound reasons to be pessimistic about the future of the world, or any part of it, it would be ultimately irrational to despair. Because we are able to improve conditions, we are morally bound to try to do so. If there is any plausible chance of putting an end to a conflict or of improving the material conditions of citizens, it would be unacceptable not to take the necessary initiatives.

Given the limits on human knowledge, one must be careful not to allow good intentions and the duty to act to aggravate a particular situation. The fact that it is not always possible to know in advance whether a particular course of action will be beneficial or harmful is not a sufficient motive to inspire political paralysis. We do not make wars or conflicts any more acceptable by walking away from them. The "let them get on with killing each other" school of thought merely ignores problems rather than solves them.

Furthermore, in a global society where our various countries are interlinked and interdependent, the slogan "an injury to one is an injury to all" is now more valid than ever. Events in part of the planet distant from wherever we happen to be often have direct effects upon us. This is not simply a matter of having our consciences aroused by CNN or the BBC, important though that is; it is the emergence of a global concept of solidarity. For example, wars in Africa and Eastern Europe lead to global and sudden movements of population that have implications for countries thousands of miles from the war zones as well as for neighboring countries. The Mexican currency crisis had profound implications for the stability of the world financial system, as do the continuing problems of debt in the Southern Hemisphere. Military tensions between neighboring peoples have serious consequences for the rest of the world. For instance, the way in which Russia resolves its war with Chechnya will have an impact on the security architecture and defense policies of the whole of Europe. Put simply, nowhere nowadays is really a long way from anywhere else.

We have an individual and collective responsibility to devote our efforts to resolving the numerous violent conflicts throughout the world. Even if the odds on saving and regenerating any particular society may be highly unfavorable, it is still necessary to strive for justice and peace. Politics may, therefore, be seen as the triumph of persistence over experience.

Of course, conflict and division is the foundation of politics, just as disease and injury is an essential prerequisite for the medical profession. If there were no divisions and difference of opinion in society, there would be no need for politics, just as there would be no need for doctors if there were no illness. But just as no doctor welcomes disease or injury for the sake of it, no politician should welcome conflict. To do otherwise is to betray the trust our fellow citizens put in us.

There are a number of similarities between medicine (in which as a layman I include surgery) and politics, which I would like to consider. There are also significant differences, which I will also examine.

First, medicine and politics have a common interest in healing. While medicine heals individuals, politicians have to deal with the defects of society. While medicine tackles disease and injury, politicians battle the problems of poverty, unemployment, and, in much of the world, violence. Of course, it would be naive to believe that there is no connection between individual illnesses and the social ills that politicians have to address.

Second, medicine and politics have a common awareness of the limitations of their knowledge and powers. Despite the great progress made over the years, there are still diseases that cannot be cured, and there are still great social evils we have yet to overcome. Indeed, the great successes of the past are not irreversible. No advance is permanent. Each step forward has to be fought for again and again. It is not realistic to expect miracle cures. We cannot resolve immediately all the problems we face. But we can play a part in paving the way for eventual long lasting solutions.

That is why we have to take a long-term approach, playing our part in developments whose beneficiaries will be future generations. We have to do our best to make breakthroughs, to build on existing achievements, and to prepare the future. We cannot necessarily offer the promised land but we should be pointing in the right direction.

As far as the differences between medicine and politics are concerned, the major one is the respectful gap between achievement and aspiration in them. While the medical profession has a solid record of achievement, politics and politicians often fail to live up to their aspirations. The outline above of the nature of politics obviously contains a degree of aspirational thinking on my own part rather than being simply a description of politics as it is today. That is not necessarily a criticism since politics is the realm par excellence of aspiration, and without it we would still be living in caves.

The problem occurs when politicians decide that their role is simply to articulate and reflect the divisions in society. In a divided society such as ours in Ireland, every public representative is, to a greater or lesser extent, a reflection of the deep divisions that exist. That is inescapable but one does not have to resign oneself to such a limited role or, even worse, make it one's raison d'etre. There is a challenge to extend ourselves to leadership rather than to content ourselves with spokespersonship alone.

Unlike doctors, politicians do not have to swear an oath to do no harm. It probably would not solve anything if we did, given that the divisions in our society mean that oaths are contentious in themselves. But I believe that the real purpose of politics, and the justification of political leadership, is to find ways of overcoming such divisions. Our moral duty is to find a way in which the people of our divided island can agree on how to share it and to begin the process of healing. Our experiences offer lessons for other troubled societies.

A further substantial difference between politics and medicine is the relative weight given to diagnosis. A doctor uses the symptoms to diagnose the illness; too many politicians use the symptoms to ignore the underlying political problems. The cycles of violence which have so disfigured our history perpetuated themselves because they were seen as the problem, not as a symptom of a general political failure to create adequate political institutions. In the divided island of Ireland only institutions that will accommodate the different traditions on the island can guarantee a peaceful and democratic future. We need institutions that allow for the expression rather than the suppression of difference.

I have spent many years stressing the need for a serious diagnosis of the nature of the problem in Ireland, for which I have received much criticism. Indeed, I would argue that without an adequate definition of the problem and some degree of consensus on the diagnosis it is impossible to treat it. Without some minimum degree of agreement on the nature of the problem, we would be restricted to the political equivalent of using leeches. But I was, and remain, convinced that the progress made so far toward a peaceful island has been greatly facilitated by the gradual development of a minimal consensus on diagnosis, though quite naturally the prescriptions remain extremely diverse.

I would also like to point out one other major difference between politics and surgery. We operate without anaesthesia, even though some political leaders see themselves as amateur anaesthetists. It is not the job of public representatives to provide unjustified reassurance to their supporters. It is our job to tell our supporters that we have serious problems to overcome and that this can be done only if we are all prepared to engage in a radical reexamination of our presuppositions and prejudices and inherited hatreds. We should refuse to even offer the prospect of pseudoanaesthesia; it is our duty to inform and convince our fellow citizens of the need to take an active part in the creation of a new dispensation in our divided Ireland. This is perhaps the equivalent of the important role of health education and awareness programs.

Bearing this in mind, I would like to emphasize a certain number of principles that have been important in the peace process so far, and indeed form the basis of the success so far achieved in silencing the guns. These principles will continue to underpin our strategy in the future.

First, we must address the problem of difference. There are three options in the face of difference: to pretend it does not exist, to combat such differences, or to accommodate them. We have seen the failure of the Stalinist attempt to pretend that difference either does not exist or is an irrelevance. We all have been sickened by the efforts of the warlords in former Yugoslavia to eradicate difference by killing and ethnic cleansing. In Ireland, the eradication of difference has been a regrettable part of our history.

We also have suffered from the activities of those who thought that being Irish or British was a matter of life and death, and who were prepared to make sure that it was. It seems to me therefore that the only rational, human, and realistic course of action is to try to seek arrangements that will allow different traditions to live together while preserving their identities.

The only sensible way forward is to accept difference as inevitable and see it as a basic and natural principle of human society. Indeed, with advances in DNA analysis, we have scientific proof that difference is universal. We must cherish the diversity of cultures that exist in Ireland, and seek to preserve them and the equilibrium between them.

In this respect, we can draw a great deal of inspiration from the existence of the European Union as living proof that a solution can be found. The European Union is the greatest example of conflict resolution in human history: countries that had spent centuries invading, occupying, expelling, and massacring each other came together freely to put aside their past hatreds. They came together to work in their common interests and to ensure that war could no longer be a way to settling their differences—this in itself would have been remarkable. But the fact that these countries will preserve their identities is even more encouraging. It proves that it is possible to establish institutions that allow for common policies without submerging the variety of cultures and traditions which are real riches. The experience of the European Union therefore affords a good many lessons for those of us who still have to deal with the consequences of difference being perceived as a threat, both in Ireland and further afield. Without seeking to impose a particular political blueprint, I am convinced that there is much that can be adapted from the European Union for our eventual domestic use.

The second principle is that force, or the threat of force, is not a useful method of dealing with difference. Indeed, it often reinforces identities that might otherwise be only a minor part of a person's life. The use of force also generates more force, creating the vicious cycle of an eye for an eye. The use of violence merely makes problems more intractable, as I have indicated earlier.

Third, differences can be accommodated only by dialogue and agreement. The basis for the cease-fires in Northern Ireland by both loyalists and republicans is the acceptance of this principle. Those organizations previously involved in violence now agree that only through negotiation can a suitable settlement be worked out. Neither side can force the other to accept the unacceptable. The peace has held because of the common commitment to agreement. It is time we moved on to serious talks on the content of an eventual political accord supported by all traditions in Ireland.

Fourth, we must be imaginative about political structures. No one should be scared of political change per se, though clearly change must be brought about by agreement. But change is as fundamental to human society as diversity. Without it, stagnation is inevitable. Stagnation itself is a cause of conflict, just as its biological equivalent causes degeneracy and disease.

It is also necessary to ensure that political institutions are adapted to the needs of citizens rather than mold the citizen to suit the purposes of the institutions. In a divided society it is therefore vital that the institutions reflect the needs and aspirations of all sections of society. Creating institutions that can command the consent of all citizens of whatever identity is not a simple task, but there is no doubt that it can be done. In many countries there are complex political arrangements that are not easy to understand as an outsider but that command the support of the overwhelming majority of their citizens.

We should not be afraid of complexity and diversity in our political systems. Complexity and diversity are increasingly recognized by scientists as the crucial organizing factors in the natural world. Why shouldn't it be the same in the social and political world? If anything, society and the political system should be even more complex than the natural world. We should not be worried about creating complex political structures if their purpose and effect is to create an inclusive system capable of securing the allegiance of all citizens of all traditions. What we should denounce are systems, simple or complex, that serve to exclude citizens of any or all traditions from the decision-making process.

Where does this leave us? The most urgent requirement now is to overcome the obstacles to comprehensive all-party negotiations. Though we have succeeded in putting a stop to violence, we have yet to make the peace. There is a long way to go before a political settlement can be concluded to which all sections of our divided people can give their allegiance. Such a settlement will be necessary if our people are to look forward to a future where all our energies are devoted to overcoming the massive political, economic, and social challenges facing our society. We have to ensure that the conflict which has so disfigured our society becomes and remains a distant and tragic memory.

To achieve this goal will take a great deal of effort. It will require all of us to examine our traditional assumptions and preconceptions. It will take a lot of hard thinking and tough talking. It will require serious negotiations in which all relevant parties to the conflict engage in the overriding task of finding new political arrangements that reflect the interests and aspirations of all traditions in Ireland.

The keys to the eventual political understanding for which all our people are crying out can therefore be easily identified: the need for a speedy beginning of all-inclusive negotiations, and the recognition that an acceptable political system can be created only by agreement. There is no place for any form of duress, physical or moral, within the creation of new, genuinely democratic institutions. Nor is there any room for the type of thinking that is dominated by notions of victory and defeat. The successful creation of an Ireland at peace and striving for prosperity can only be a victory for all traditions, just as violence, conflict, and the absence of peace are a defeat for us all.

It is also clear that the need for agreement on the future of Northern Ireland is generally accepted by all parties and by both the Irish and British governments. The Downing Street Declaration made this clear, as have subsequent comments by the various parties and the two governments. The task is now for the divided peoples of Ireland to work out an agreement on the ways in which we can share our island.

Both the British and the Irish governments have made it clear that they accept the right of the people in Northern Ireland to define their own future political institutions and that their wishes will not be over-ridden by either state. The British government, for instance, has made it clear that it has no selfish or strategic motive to hold on to Northern Ireland against the will of its people. It is up to us, the people of Ireland, North and South, unionist and nationalist, to map out an agreement. Having said that, it is important that the opportunity to create political agreement in Ireland for the first time is seized as rapidly as possible. We therefore believe that all-inclusive talks must continue. We do not think it is helpful to impose preconditions on such talks, since the whole purpose of negotiating is to surmount the difficulties that the preconditions undoubtedly reflect. We prefer to address the underlying conditions from which preconditions emerge, concentrating on the problem rather than the symptoms.

The crucial task is to take the gun out of Irish politics once and for all. The only way we can do that is to tackle the problems of division, mistrust, and hatred which led people to resort to violence in the first place.

Since the cessation of violence, the major preliminary question has been answered. Groups formerly committed to the use of force have made it clear that they are prepared to enter into negotiations on the understanding that they are determined to use exclusively peaceful and political methods to pursue their objectives. That is the major touchstone for all-inclusive negotiations. We believe that no serious government or political force in these islands could fail to seize this unprecedented opportunity.

While we are convinced that all-inclusive negotiations are the only possible route to peace, we do not underestimate the difficulties involved in bringing about a successful conclusion. Clearly, the parties involved have considerable difference of opinion, which will not be changed overnight. Our history of violence and conflict has left many wounds that will not easily heal. The extent of poverty and deprivation has alienated many people of all traditions from the political process. We do not have a culture of negotiation and agreement.

But we are totally convinced that an eventual political agreement is feasible and can be brought to fruition. Three reasons can be cited: the underlying common interests of our citizens, international support for the peace process, and the emergence of political agreements in other divided societies throughout the world.

Despite our political differences, our traditions have a common interest in peace and in economic prosperity. There is a vast area of economic and social policy where our divided peoples are united and where we can work together without compromising on deeply and sincerely held convictions. We can spill our sweat and not our blood and so build the necessary trust to heal our deeper divisions. As a peripheral region of the European Union, we have a common interest in adopting a united approach to our European partners, just as we have such a common interest in our relations with the rest of the world. We have a common interest in developing our economic position within the global economy and in establishing fair patterns of trade in international markets. The more we get used to pursuing our common interests, the more we can address our political divisions.

Second, the support and goodwill of our friends in the European Union, the United States, and the Commonwealth is an asset of enormous value. The interest shown in the peace process in the outside world is very helpful in building confidence among our peoples and in combating the tendency to think in narrow and self-defeating terms. Seeing how diverse peoples throughout the world have ordered their affairs is a useful corrective against an excessively Anglo or Hibernocentric view of the world.

Finally, the emergence of peace processes in divided societies in other parts of the world is a massive boost for confidence in the possibility of negotiated agreements. For instance, in South Africa the work of Nelson Mandela and F. W. de Klerk has produced an agreement far more successful than anyone thought possible. We will have to find our own way, just as South Africa did. The real lesson we take is that, given sufficient determination and imagination, political structures that respect diversity and difference and reconcile former enemies are possible and indeed the only path to peace. Just as with many medical interventions and treatments, we cannot guarantee that there is absolutely no risk. But without taking a course with its element of possible risk there may be no hope of recovery.

Yitzhak Rabin's efforts for peace offer a good example. He grew from being a brave soldier to being a brave statesman. He embraced in the Middle East the profound value of what Olof Palme tried to tell the Cold War world—we can only truly be secure with each other, not against each other. With Shimon Peres, Yasser Arafat, and others he took risks for peace, just as he took personal risks in war. Indeed, a public exhortation of the need to take risks for peace were among his last words at the peace rally where he was assassinated.

As we think of this man who has helped to build peace in the Promised Land and offered us hope and help for peace in that region, we can usefully reflect on some words from another assassinated leader. Martin Luther King, Jr. said, on the eve of his death, "I have seen the promised land. I may not get there with you. But I want you to know that we as a people will get to the promised land."

On an earlier occasion Martin Luther King, Jr. offered counsel that is valuable for the motivation and morale of clinicians and politicians alike and relevant to frustrations now being experienced: "We must accept finite disappointment, but we must never lose infinite hope." He also challenged all of us to reach beyond the confines of our given orthodoxies or our local and subjective perspectives and to embrace mutual acceptance and human solidarity. He offered a most meaningful interpretation for health and wealth in this world and at the same time tried to rally us above notions of narrow nationalism. With words that are a most appropriate reference for preventive diplomacy, the unending struggle to stop wars before they start, Martin Luther King, Jr. said, "As long as there is poverty in the world I can never be rich even if I have a billion dollars. As long as diseases are rampant and millions of people in this world cannot expect to live more than twenty-eight or thirty years, I can never be totally healthy even if I just got a good check-up at Mayo Clinic. I can never be what I ought to be until you are what you ought to be. This is the way our world is made. No individual or nation can stand out boasting of being independent. We are interdependent."

3

THE FUNDAMENTALS OF PREVENTIVE DIPLOMACY

MOHAMMED BEDJAOUI

> Mankind must put an end to war or war will put an end to mankind.
> —John Fitzgerald Kennedy

> In time of war, who will sow the fields?
> —Antonio Machado
> L'Espagne en paix

When, at the end of World War I, President Woodrow Wilson expended so much imagination and effort in launching the League of Nations—the first universal organization for peace—and then gave the world his celebrated Fourteen Points, which I regard as the first charter of preventive diplomacy, the United States disowned his work: America was apparently isolationist. Is this still the case today?[1]

Now leading politicians from both parties strongly denounce peacekeeping operations launched by the United Nations, claiming they have endangered American interests, depleted American resources, and may cost American lives. They tell us that the American people will not accept American losses in the name of irresponsible internationalism, adding that it is just as unacceptable to give aid to foreign countries with the taxpayers' money.

Preventive diplomacy today requires all of us to distance ourselves from our own immediate interests, to sanction sacrifices in human life and money. Preventive diplomacy is more than ever needed to save our world, to prevent, especially in America, a fatal isolationism. What is preventive diplomacy? One generally accepted definition recognizes that this kind of diplomacy serves three purposes: it aims (1) to prevent disputes arising between states or between governments and minority parties within states; (2) to prevent an existing dispute from being transformed into an open conflict; and (3) if a conflict breaks out, to ensure that it spreads as little as possible.[2] In this respect, it is much like preventive medicine, the purpose of which is to prevent illness before it occurs.

Preventive diplomacy is not a contemporary invention. It has always, or almost always, existed in all human societies. To give a princess in marriage to a neighboring monarch, to make a political and military alliance between two or more monarchies, to exchange one portion of territory for another, to conclude a treaty of one kind or another, were different ways of safeguarding national interests and perpetuating advantages. But such diplomacy was deployed by a state to serve its own ambitions and not necessarily to preserve regional peace. In centuries gone by, a state did not hesitate to conduct a preventive war to serve its own interests. However, it was more often the case that the action taken by the state, in its attempt to protect its own interests, did not at the same time coincide with the desire to maintain peace in its own region. For convenience, let us call this former diplomacy "traditional preventive diplomacy."

This traditional preventive diplomacy has certainly not disappeared in our day. Large nations undertake various forms of action, whether covertly or overtly, directed at other nations, in order to obtain from them an advantageous commercial position or favorable terms of trade. Those nations favor the eventual emergence of a friendly political forum; they propel into power men likely to serve their interests in the future. This is a preventive strategy that is still common.

But a completely different type of preventive diplomacy is emerging in the contemporary world. The maintenance of world peace occupies an essential place in it; in principle, the systematic pursuit of immediate selfish national interests is banished therefrom, and the basic constituents of this contemporary preventive diplomacy are based on the universality and global nature of problems. These are some points that differentiate traditional preventive diplomacy from contemporary preventive diplomacy.

The fact is that the world has become a small village. Telecommunications make light of frontiers. Pollution does not respect maritime or land boundary delimitations. The economies of all countries are heavily dependent on the world economy. Weather does not stop at national boundaries. The world financial and stock market system recognizes no national sovereignty over a specific geographical area. Transnational companies are, by designation and by function, corporations that operate in the global market. Furthermore, war is no longer, in contemporary international law, an exclusive competence of the sovereign state; it is prohibited by Article 2, paragraph 4, of the United Nations Charter, except in self-defense.

This interdependence of nations is a sign of the times. Like the economists, the political pundits, or the lawyers, the geographers now teach us that each geographical space acts upon all the other spaces in the world. It is the "world system" described in France by Professor Roger Brunet's team in his *Géographie universelle*. No country can live as an autarchy today. The kick given to a citizen of Santiago de Chile by a henchman of Pinochet was felt by everyone on the planet. Proximity is no longer merely a geographical notion. Geography is deceptive. Today all countries are neighbors. Peoples, nations, organizations, and public opinion are only slowly, too slowly, becoming aware of this, which is why preventive diplomacy is experiencing failures. A fundamental truth must be tirelessly reiterated: What affects one country affects the others. And this nascent truth of today will be an absolute truth tomorrow as mutual dependency becomes reinforced.

All of this endows contemporary preventive diplomacy, its motives, its aim, its means of action, and its purposes, with a particular quality. The basic data on international affairs have radically altered. Preventive diplomacy must broaden its horizon in order to build on the planetary scale. This diplomacy, therefore, becomes particularly delicate, and even tenuous. It becomes a school seeking to discipline the immediate interests of the state for the benefit of world peace and its beneficial effects, which are more certain but much more remote from us all.

In other words, this contemporary preventive diplomacy, which cannot but be collective (and this is another area of differentiation as against traditional preventive diplomacy), has the drawback for the state that it does not quickly make it aware of all its advantages. It is, therefore, not surprising that the state is not always wholly motivated to undertake preventive action which it does not see as directly beneficial to itself, whether within an alliance or in the United Nations, or in relation to a distant country. Thus there is already the fear that, contrary to traditional preventive diplomacy, contemporary preventive diplomacy, whose essential aim is to preserve world peace and which is, therefore, global, universal, and collective, is not particularly motivating for those states—and there are many of them—whose vital interests are not directly challenged by the threat of a conflict that seems to them geographically and politically remote. This is why contemporary preventive diplomatic action is sometimes so hesitant.

The first alarming and overwhelming reports by the American State Department on ethnic cleansing in the former Yugoslavia were made public from 1991 onward. A disastrous intercultural and interreligious conflict in Bosnia and Herzegovina flared for four years, during which irreparable damage was inflicted on the eminent dignity of man, without the countries of Europe managing to engage in preventive diplomacy capable of circumventing the conflict or, at least, limiting its terrible consequences. In Kosovo, the sixth Republic in the former Federal Republic of Yugoslavia, the ashes smoldered for another three years before exploding in flames. No action to prevent the conflict between the Serb minority and the huge Muslim majority was undertaken until after NATO bombs were dropping and hundreds of thousands were displaced.

Today, after the civil war in Rwanda, which claimed over a million lives, an internal conflict of the same kind poses a serious threat to a neighboring country, Burundi. A campaign of preventive diplomacy has been halfheartedly launched under the auspices of the United Nations, but with what paucity of means and what indifference of world opinion! This is the way of the world. This is the way of international affairs. Traditional preventive diplomacy, or close diplomacy, apprehends danger and makes a concrete response to it. The measures are tangible and the national interests to be protected are clearly perceived by politicians.

This is not the case of contemporary preventive diplomacy, which is a diplomacy of distance, in space and in time. By this, I mean that Burundi, for example, seems too far removed, geographically, from this or that European or American capital, and their problems simply do not exert an irresistible hold on our attention and force us to set in motion measures of preventive diplomacy. Geographical distance makes it impossible to assess the importance and urgency of an intervention. Moreover, a great deal of virtue would surely be required of a state becoming involved, for such a state cannot easily foresee the impact and repercussions of such action until a long time has elapsed. In particular, the feeling that preventive action serves its higher interests is rarely perceived by that state as self-evident. At most, it may vaguely appreciate that it is contributing to political peace in a region that is very distant, and that its action may affect the peace of the whole world. Furthermore, this remote state will have to act in the framework of an international institution, such as the United Nations, which further dilutes the feeling of responsibility. Collective preventive diplomacy does not immediately attract support. Lastly, any action of this kind implies expenditure, which the most virtuous state is not always able to meet.

THE GEOPOLITICS OF PREVENTIVE DIPLOMACY

The major risk areas for world peace appear to be situated in the East and South. But so far this is only a subjective determination of the areas of turbulence; it has yet to be proved. Before one proceeds to this proof, it should be recalled that a conflict may involve two or more states or it may be internal.

THE DANGERS IN THE EAST

The beginning of the modern era was marked by the fall of the Berlin Wall and the end of the Cold War. But this new era does not offer any clear pointers. It is essentially characterized by uncertainties. The Cold War had gradually developed rules of play observed by the two super-powers; they knew from experience how far they could go in throwing down challenges to each other. The striking characteristic today is the fact that these rules of play have fallen into disuse but have not been replaced by others, at least not yet. This is true to such an extent that there is a remarkable degree of improvisation in the running of international relations. This uncertainty factor naturally renders analysis and forecasting, and consequently the pursuit of preventive diplomacy, much more difficult than in the past.

Western military strategists were highly skilled at identifying their enemy and knew him inside out for the past half century. Now they are seeking him out. He is no longer in the East, it would appear. But is this quite certain? The sudden collapse of communism and the rapid disintegration of the USSR constituted a major historical break. The fantastic imperial power of the Soviets disintegrated. It is hard, in the history of mankind, to find a major event comparable in its suddenness, scope, and in the depth of its repercussions.

But after the Soviet collapse its nuclear power remains all the more dangerous in that it is no longer controlled by a strong, centralized political power. It is here, indeed, that one of the great risks lies. When the two warmongering blocs still existed, they certainly represented a danger to the very survival of mankind, paralyzed by a latent nuclear peril. However, man had learned to live in the shadow of the nuclear threat; this threat ultimately came to form part of the human condition. And while the death-dealing system was being created, while the universal government of death, this thanatocracy, thus enveloped the world, the spontaneous instinct of self-preservation prescribed the survival of the human species by a balance of terror and nuclear deterrence.

Today, the change is radical. Our world is learning to live with the leadership of *The One without the Other*, to borrow the suggestive title of a work by André Fontaine.[3] A virtually unipolar world power is emerging with the promotion of a single, generalized type of economic organization, nationally as well as internationally, summed up in the market economy system. But this world leadership is under threat—and this is a paradox—from the weakness of the former Soviet camp. Politically, economically, and socially, that camp is disintegrating. But it is also leading to a dangerous dispersal of its nuclear weaponry. The West is doing everything it can to maintain control of this formidable arsenal and to prevent illicit transfers to various countries.

But the risk in the East is not merely nuclear. The unprecedented social and economic disorder in Russia and in the countries of Eastern Europe is a source of upheavals, retrograde steps, or an obscuring of respect for human rights. The dangers in the East are, for that reason, many and varied. Preventive diplomacy is essential there, perhaps more than elsewhere, for the stakes are beyond measure. The United States has already set the pace, as it clearly perceives its interest here in impelling the former Soviet camp toward liberal democracy and the market economy. Hence the recurrent loan of billions of dollars that Russia has obtained from the World Bank and International Monetary Fund.

THE DANGERS IN THE SOUTH

The destabilizing threats in the South that are responsible for probable consequences in the North, are a simple but essential triptych. These dangers are made up of the following:

- underdevelopment;
- overpopulation;
- lack of democracy.

The first two, namely, underdevelopment and overpopulation, are triggering a migratory movement toward the Northern Hemisphere, which the North is attempting to curb or at least to control, because it constitutes a major socioeconomic danger to itself. The United States and Canada are closing their doors to Latin America—or opening them slowly and reluctantly —and Europe is doing the same with respect to Africa. The third aspect, the lack of democracy, is a curse for the South, implying a politico-cultural danger for the North, among other things owing to the violation of human rights and the spread of various brands of fundamentalism.

Some years ago, underdevelopment, the population explosion, and the lack of democracy in the Southern Hemisphere were deemed by the North to be purely domestic affairs, a part of the internal life of each of the countries concerned, and, in any case, for the West, remote topics. Today, on the contrary, and more clearly than in the past, underdevelopment, overpopulation, and the lack of democracy are beginning to arouse a great deal of interest and considerable anxiety in the North and are also attracting a small amount of aid.

In former times the threats were considered real only when they came from one enemy and that enemy was strong. Today, the threats have changed; they can come not only from the enemy but from the associate, not only from the strong but from the weak. The weakness of the South is a threat to all. In fact, the underdevelopment and overpopulation of the South are triggering an undesirable and dangerous South to North migratory flow, coupled with disturbances in political relations resulting from the fundamentalist intolerance engendered by the lack of democracy. What is more, it is clear that disturbances in the South can endanger the investments and, more generally, the economic interests of the North.

So what should be done? What are the vectors of effective preventive diplomacy? While remaining skeptical about their real chances of success, I should like to cite several: if the world has changed, and if the parameters of international relations are more flexible and less easy to pin down, a number of major constants nevertheless remain. It is easy to discover what they are by pondering the causes of the tensions and crises—not the circumstantial causes, but the deep-seated ones. These causes include deficient economic levels (underdevelopment), inadequate cultural levels (illiteracy or inadequate education), and, as a direct result, a very rough acceptance of human rights in the broad sense. Quite simply, this means that the prevention of internal or international tensions should begin with efforts to generate economic development and promote significant progress in the instruction, education, and training of men and women as citizens.

PREVENTIVE DIPLOMACY TO PROMOTE DEVELOPMENT

Each day that passes shows that His Holiness Paul VI was right in asserting that "development is the new name of peace." I do not wish to offend anyone when I say that the page of si vis pacem para bellum has faded somewhat today. Poverty cannot be eradicated by weapons. There is a constant need to stress the obvious point that there is a close relationship between development and peace. This has been dramatically noted by two well-known North Americans, Nobel Peace Prize Laureate Lester B. Pearson, former Prime Minister of Canada, the author of the celebrated UN report that bears his name, entitled *Partners in Development*,[4] and Mr. Robert McNamara, former U.S. Secretary of Defense and former President of the World Bank, and the author of a well-known work, *One Hundred Countries, Two Billion People*.[5]

In June 1972, when receiving a human rights award in London, Lester Pearson told his audience that there could be "no peace, no security, nothing but ultimate disaster" once a few rich countries, whose population was only a small minority of the world's peoples, were alone in having access to the new, formidable, and terrifying world of science and technology as well as to a materially high standard of living, while the vast majority of people lived in deprivation and need, cut off from any possibility of complete economic development.

For his part, Robert McNamara considered that the North-South economic gulf represented a profound seismic fissure running through the earth's sociological crust. It might—it would—occasion thunderbolts and violent tremors. If the rich nations do not do a better job of bridging that gap between the affluent northern part of the planet and the deprived Southern Hemisphere, "ultimately nobody would be safe, however great our stockpiles of weapons."

The existence of a mutual causal link between development and peace can be demonstrated in two stages:

- underdevelopment is a threat to international peace and security,
- development is a factor for peace.

To avoid linguistic pitfalls, we should try to understand the current use of the terms underdevelopment and peace. Underdevelopment is not historically or geographically inevitable. It is not a delayed-action phenomenon, which can be attributed to purely national factors, such as internal constraints of all kinds, the incompetence of those in power, or the corruption of local leaders. Admittedly, these factors play a part, and sometimes a great part—I am sorry to say—in national underdevelopment. But one must beware of invoking them as alibis to disguise another more decisive reality: underdevelopment is a structural phenomenon linked to a specific type of international economic relations, and to a certain international division of labor. Underdevelopment is not inevitable, any more than war is. Underdevelopment is the product of an unequal system of domination and exploitation. In essence, this system thwarts the prospects for prosperity of two-thirds of mankind.

There are also many false faces of peace. Dynamic peace is a ceaseless activity geared toward the banishment of all the social ills that generate tension, violence, and war. It cannot, therefore, be a resigned acceptance of injustice or exploitation. It is nonviolence compared to the violence of underdevelopment. It is clear that the objective of peace with development cannot be attained by the acceptance of a link between peace and underdevelopment.

Nor is peace merely the absence of war. The threat of a generalized war must not at any time lead us to overlook the reality of regional conflicts and aggression, of which any particular region in the Third World continues to be the victim. The affirmation that our planet has lived in peace since the end of World War II must be vigorously called into question. It is too easy to overlook the fact that, although fifty years have passed without a third world war breaking out, the world has nonetheless registered some 150 armed conflicts in geographical areas of underdevelopment. When the rich arm the poor and we witness an "aberrant militarization of poverty," the developing countries not only become simple pawns on the world chessboard, without any independent decision-making power of their own, but commit themselves into the bargain to military expenditure that paralyzes their development efforts.

However, it must also be noted that the tensions from which the Third World countries suffer do not all fall within this category, and many of them sometimes have endogenous causes—alas. Particular to underdeveloped countries are an abundance of tribal or religious conflicts, which, moreover, are a clear manifestation of a state of underdevelopment.

One must, therefore, first agree on what peace is, or at least on what cannot be seen as peace. It must be emphasized that:

1. The simple absence of war is patently not enough to constitute peace.
2. Also, an examination of the international situation reveals that this absence of war is in no way general. Above all, the absence of war in one region or another should not lead one to conclude ipso facto that there is peace in the world.
3. In reality, peace is indivisible. Peace within the frontiers of the developed world alone is not necessarily peace in the world. True peace does not automatically ensue from a readjustment of the relations between the superpowers.
4. One cannot speak of peace in a world that is still the scene of various phenomena of domination.
5. Similarly, one cannot seriously speak of peace in a world that continues to live by the maxim *si vis pacem para bellum* and which bases its security on the balance of thermonuclear terror. Since the end of the Cold War this situation has altered somewhat, but we are still waiting

for the "peace dividends" which could serve the interests of development.

6. Peace, much more than war, is a total, complex phenomenon, which
cannot be achieved by any recipe. Hence, the answer to the question
as to what should be done to establish peace is that no first step toward
a satisfactory solution can be found without seriously challenging the
system of international relations, which is a specific source of war
solely by virtue of the fact that it has been established by and for the
benefit of a small number of states and therefore to the detriment of
all the rest.

UNDERDEVELOPMENT: A THREAT TO INTERNATIONAL PEACE AND SECURITY

The primary merit of the United Nations is to have learned the lesson
of the failure of the League of Nations by making room for world economic problems. Hence, the United Nations Charter, unlike the
Covenant of the League of Nations, makes room for economic problems, devoting two chapters to them. This is certainly a significant difference between the two international organizations.

A second merit of the United Nations is that it not only has assumed
responsibility for economic problems, but it also has made them the
precondition for the maintenance of peace—an authentic and forceful
but also revolutionary way of emphasizing these economic problems.

There is, however, a very serious shortcoming in the United Nations
Charter—underdevelopment as a threat to peace is not subject to the
jurisdiction of the Security Council. Some time ago, a resolution tabled
before the European Parliament in Strasbourg, as well as motions by the
Chamber of Deputies and Senate in Belgium and the Parliament in
Luxembourg, invited the governments of the EEC countries to appeal
to the Security Council, as a matter of urgency, to consider the problem
of famine in the world as a serious threat to international peace and
security. In fact, it may seem mentally unsatisfying that the slightest
frontier skirmish may bring about a session of the Security Council,
whereas the extermination by famine of some fifty million human
beings each year would not have the same effect. However, the provisions of the Charter allowed the Security Council to declare itself
incompetent to deal with such matters.

Nevertheless, the characterization of famine as a threat to peace has
become a reality before other bodies. For example, various manifestations of the economic aspect of peace problems can be found in the res-

olutions of the United Nations General Assembly. In the "Universal Declaration for the Definitive Eradication of Famine and Malnutrition," adopted by the General Assembly on November 16, 1974, it is stated that: *"peace entails . . . an economic aspect contributing . . . to the eradication of under-development, offering a definitive solution to the food problem for all peoples."*

DEVELOPMENT—THE BEST CONTRACEPTIVE

It has been maintained that the cause of Third World underdevelopment is its alarming overpopulation. This shows a certain confusion between cause and effect. In order to gloss over the negative consequences for the Third World of the current international division of labor, underdevelopment is attributed to the runaway increase in population. The reverse seems to me to be true: overpopulation results from underdevelopment. The initial cause of the terrifying increase in the world's population resides squarely in underdevelopment. The Third World is prolific because it is underdeveloped, not underdeveloped because it is prolific. Josué de Castro used to say that "the poor man has an empty table, but a fertile bed."

The facts are there: the more the Third World sinks into underdevelopment the faster its population increases. It can be seen, on the contrary, that as the countries of the North continue to develop, their population continues to go down.

The developed countries cannot fail to take an interest in the crisis now prevailing in what is known as the developing world, because, if they do so, they would obviously ruin their own economies. The United States is possibly the only country with a sufficient autonomy of resources and enough of an internal market to be able to do without the resources and markets of the Third World. But one simply cannot possibly contemplate the problem of development from anything other than a global standpoint. What is more, the promotion of Third World development, by its action upon global consumption, would in itself constitute a powerful factor for relaunching the whole world economy.

President Truman, in his "Point IV" of 1949, told the American people that experience showed that its trade with other nations became more significant as those nations developed, and it remains true today. It is patently obvious that the bankrupting of developing countries, their collapse under the burden of international debts, the sudden outbreaks of violence that occur and that could become even more serious, the tensions that could be provoked by that violence with respect to supplies of raw materials, basic commodities, energy, and so on, cannot but affect the rest of the world in a great many ways. This means that preventive diplomacy would do well to focus upon the struggle against underdevelopment. But what results have been obtained until now?

THE SEVERE DISAPPOINTMENTS OF PREVENTIVE DIPLOMACY IN THE AREA OF DEVELOPMENT

In spite of all its efforts, the United Nations has not been able to disseminate development. The North-South dialogue has not taken place. Development aid is inadequate and poorly targeted. In a number of countries in the Southern Hemisphere, people are dying of hunger. A World Covenant on Food Security, guaranteeing a minimum level of nutrition, ought to have long since sanctioned the fact that that security must constitute a collective responsibility of mankind. Within the framework of the right to development of all the world's peoples and of all human beings, I proposed more than fifteen years ago having essential world food resources given the status of a common heritage of mankind. It was perhaps just a dream—it has still not materialized. However, one should beware of spurning other people's dreams.

The intention to base peace upon the development of the world's peoples finds expression in Article 1 of the Charter of the United Nations. But the failure of the United Nations to bring about development places even more emphasis upon the looming threat to peace itself. This fact must be taken together with the United Nations' failure to achieve a satisfactory settlement of the insistent problem of the choice between armed peace and disarmament. The world knows that there is no peace without development, and no development without peace.

PREVENTIVE DIPLOMACY THROUGH WORLD-WIDE EDUCATION

It seems strange and incomprehensible to a great many peoples and states when they are told that preventive diplomacy can be—prosaically but effectively—reduced to a campaign against illiteracy in the world. Above all, this is an approach that is alien to a number of countries in the Northern Hemisphere, who could well wonder not only why illiteracy in a foreign country is a source of internal and even external tensions, but above all in what way that distant situation might affect them or even be of any concern to them at all. It is legitimate for foreign investors to ask why they should open schools in the countries where their intervention takes place. Their natural impulse is rather to invest in profitable economic projects—if possible, those giving an immediate return. There is, however, one truth that has been neglected for too long and that needs to be given its rightful place.

A revolutionary truth is haunting us at the present time: that there is no better investment than an investment in human beings. Even the World Bank now invests in education and realizes that it is the best form of preventive diplomacy, the most powerful strategy to promote development. Victor Hugo told us that "a school that opens is a prison that closes." At the present time, one might add that "a school that opens is a factory that opens." As president of the World Bank, Mr. James Wolfensohn, himself a former banker, gave a vigorous impulse to promote education and social progress in the countries of the Third World. He considered the human and social dimension of economic development to be of fundamental significance.[6]

At the celebration of the fiftieth anniversary of the United Nations, I was mindful of the resolution adopted in 1945 by the founding fathers of that organization in a bid to "promote social progress and better standards of life in larger freedom."[7] No one will deny that education is one of the most propitious instruments for the attainment of those objectives, so much so that the Universal Declaration of Human Rights adopted three years later, in 1948, devoted its longest provisions to the individual's right to education. The right to education was subsequently just as forcefully enshrined in the United Nations Covenant on Economic, Social, and Cultural Rights of 1966, and more recently, in the United Nations Convention on the Rights of the Child of 1989, to cite only a few of the most important universal legal instruments in this field.

School, college, and university, the key vehicles for the transmission of knowledge, are, therefore, without the shadow of a doubt, instruments of economic development, instruments of freedom, and instruments of peace. Unless I am mistaken, knowledge and learning are the only possessions which can be given away at no cost to the giver: when two people exchange the only idea they possess, each of them ends up with two ideas. For this reason, knowledge and learning are riches that cannot prosper in a vacuum: they can be increased only if they are exchanged. Consequently, any undertaking or initiative aimed at facilitating the promotion of exchanges and cooperation in the field of education must be welcomed and encouraged.

Knowledge is the key to social progress and education is the principal vector of knowledge. As such, education should be considered one of the engines of the economic development of states and an instrument for the self-fulfillment of their peoples. As traditionally conceived, the right of every individual to education is, thus, a human right whose translation into practice is the responsibility of each state individually. However, the provision of primary, secondary, and higher education for all presupposes not only a very heavy financial burden that many countries are unable to bear, but also a relatively long time to be put into practice. It will, therefore, come as no surprise that the individual's right to education varies in substance from one country to another. The full exercise of that right requires the assistance and cooperation of the developed states, within a framework of preventive diplomacy.

I do not think there is any need for me to dwell excessively on the importance of education in preparing the future of present generations. I will give the last word to Jean-Jacques Rousseau: "Plants are fashioned by culture, men by education."

PREVENTIVE DIPLOMACY AND HUMAN RIGHTS

The state of underdevelopment of a good many countries can be compared to the condition of an invalid with a wasted body, consumed by disease, and deprived of both food and medical attention. It is this invalid whom we are asking to respect human rights within the framework of preventive diplomacy. Can he do as we ask? When an underdeveloped state is lacking in every kind of necessary resource, it is by definition incapable of protecting the first human right, the right to life, with all it implies in the way of rights to social protection, work, health, education, and so on. There is thus no point in giving the invalid a transfusion of blood or of glucose if one is unable to treat his various organs affected by disease. It is equally pointless to instill human rights by transfusion into a debilitated social fabric if one cannot remedy the primary, deep-rooted causes of the diseases affecting that social fabric. The primary cause is economic underdevelopment. Let us sow the seeds of development and we shall reap human rights. In other words, there is an indissoluble link between underdevelopment and the violation of human rights, and at the same time there is a definite equation between development and the observance of human rights.

In such a context, preventive diplomacy will encounter tremendous problems. To succeed in ensuring the observance of human rights, it must engage in a vast preventive campaign against underdevelopment. The struggle for the promotion of human rights cannot be limited to artificially tacking human rights onto an underdeveloped social fabric, as one might attach an artificial limb to a living human body. This means that, although it is desirable not to ignore any of the successful foreign experiments in the area of the observance of human rights, it is nevertheless true that imitation is not a good political recipe. Moreover, it is a political recipe that cannot automatically be adapted to local conditions, particularly in circumstances of underdevelopment. If, for instance, we had to opt for one type of democracy or another, the worst solution would be to copy what has been conceived in another country with a view to applying it in our own. Institutions that are the product of the soil, of history, of the environment, and of all these converging forces cannot be transplanted without prejudice to the citizen. There are people and nations that, sprung from the fierce struggles for independence, aspire to something other than abstract formalism. They are brimming with strength and vigor, for they were born in suffering and are not taken in by the mirage of fanciful democracies.

This gives the measure of the unsuitability of the message relating to "standardized" human rights, which does not take any account of a certain relativity in this field. Indeed, the message on human rights put out by Europe or the West, which is to say a region of the world privileged in material terms by comparison with those at whom this message is aimed, who sometimes live in subhuman material and moral conditions, risks seeming singularly detached from reality. Such a message will appear abstract, and, sometimes, even ideological, with calculated deliberate choices, presuppositions, and political ulterior motives. Such a message, therefore, necessarily loses credibility.

Furthermore, this message on excessively "standardized" human rights is transmitted by different channels propelling everyone toward standardization without taking local conditions into account. What is good for the West is not necessarily good for the rest of the world. And among these different channels, which act as relays and transmitters, are the global economic players. They lay down global strategies. And with a view to total control of this global market, they endeavor—for the most part successfully—to condition our needs, to standardize our tastes, to standardize our habits as consumers, in short, to impregnate us with a standardizing culture, for national, cultural, or linguistic barriers all constitute obstacles to profitable expansion of markets.

Our world, therefore, has imposed upon it a dominant or ambient culture, with a standardized lifestyle, visible in clothes, music, drinks, cooking, or leisure activities. We are witnessing the global conditioning of mankind, with a view to leveling and standardizing our reflexes as consumers. What this clearly means is cultural integration, from which Western society suffers as much as other societies. For Western society is increasingly perceived merely in its material reflections which—to Westerners as to others—transmit an increasingly adulterated cultural message.

In all this, it is overlooked that our world, which although in some respects has become a global village, possesses great social and cultural diversity. At the same time, we live in different civilizations, centuries, and periods, depending on where we are. The diversity of culture, development, and power, in addition to the diversity of geography and climate, characterizes our world.

The model of development transmitted to the underdeveloped countries by the transnational companies is peculiar to the industrialized countries and ill-adapted to the basic socioeconomic needs of the developing countries. The transnational corporations create a type of development that not only does not meet real needs but also creates superfluous ones. They modify the patterns of consumption in the host countries. They implant in the poor countries the consumer habits of the rich countries, thus entailing the wastage of the meager resources of the countries concerned. A "civilization of the digestive tract" is thus being created. The whole planet is conditioned to consumption. The assault of this lifestyle is ostentatious. Traditional wisdom and the simple lifestyle forming the basis of certain national cultures are being destroyed.

Yet, the perception of the rights that are the prerogative of all men is not globally uniform. It is conditioned, in space and in time, by many factors, historical, political, economic, social, cultural, and religious. Hence, the actual content of these rights will be defined in various ways. Hence also, the modalities of their realization will vary.

A uniform system of values cannot be imposed tyrannically and lastingly in a highly pluralistic world. This uniformity is neither necessary nor desirable, for an international consensus can and must be minimalist. A number of irreducible values must be identified. But these values may have a different profile among themselves and with respect to other values, depending on their cultural context. What is important is not the profile of these values, but rather the fact that these irreducible values are found in every culture. It is in the interests of every nation to help to identify this core of humanitarian ethics and to tolerate the many different ways in which this core is expressed.

We have not yet developed a broad consensus, of the whole planet, all systems and ideologies taken together, as to what the supreme permanent inalienable common values might be. However, cultures and religions all recognize that the human being has an irreducible moral dimension. Values such as respect for life, duties toward future generations, protection of the environment, and the duty to help and protect the weak at all levels, from family to global, via the national level, may and must constitute the ethical core for which a broad consensus exists.

We must establish human rights acceptable to a whole range of cultures and ideologies. These norms must be founded on the principle of the uniqueness, indivisibility, and the pluralist nature of the human species. In determining human rights, the uniqueness of the human species and the diversity of cultures must be taken into account simultaneously and together. The importance of Resolution 31/130, adopted by the United Nations General Assembly over thirty years ago, has not been properly taken into account. It proclaimed the universal, indivisible, and interdependent nature of human rights. This implies paying equal and simultaneous attention to the attainment of all rights, be they civil or political, economic, social or cultural, individual or collective.

How are permanent common values (though not eternal or absolute ones, let it be said) to be attained? The solution would be to seek common denominators. To achieve this, what is required is simply to set out from the identity of the object: man. It is the right to be man. This implies protecting his dignity. Human dignity must be defended against the attack of poverty and of underdevelopment. What counts is to apprehend the uniqueness of man through his dignity. Gandhi said, "We are all cast in the same mold; to despise a single human being is to despise the divine which is in us." Through the diversity of cultures and of values, unity and that which does not vary must be sought. This unvarying factor is human dignity.

The "conclusion of the conclusion" is that human rights, in that they have a meaning other than as an instrument of mutual propaganda and subversion, must simultaneously be defined by a twofold assertion: they may be universal only in the diversity of cultures. The international consensus on the fundamental rights peculiar to the human species must be identified and, at the same time, cultural differences must be more strictly respected, and, hence, also the determination and concrete expression of those rights.

PREVENTIVE DIPLOMACY AND SECURITY

There are some golden rules for ensuring security. What is more, they are very straightforward, which does not mean that they are easy to apply on all occasions and under all circumstances.

1. The first golden rule of security is to free one's adversary from his fear. To do so, it is imperative, as soon as a conflict begins to take shape, to rebuild confidence—necessary for all, beneficial for all.

2. The second rule seems to be that it is an elementary duty to guarantee one's own security, but not to make it an obsessive, unhealthy, and excessive political concern. I am mindful of Goethe's thought that: "Der ist schon tot, der um seiner Sicherheit willen lebt," or, "He who lives for his security alone is already dead."

3. The third golden rule is that one must never lose sight of the fact that, in the age of ballistic missiles, it is a delusion to think that one can protect the inviolability of a frontier. It must not be forgotten that the most secure boundaries are those that separate two friendly countries. One must, therefore, begin by building up cooperation and confidence, and friendship must be encouraged to flourish.

4. The fourth golden rule is to see world peace as an indivisible whole. The Conference for Security and Cooperation in Europe (CSCE), which issued its Final Act more than twenty years ago in Helsinki, seemed to have made a correct assessment of that obvious political imperative. We would now do well to issue, with all speed, a "Helsinki Final Act for the South" or else organize a conference on security and cooperation in the Mediterranean area with, as its guiding principles, the following points:

   • mutual recognition of existing boundaries;
   • necessity to progress toward democratization throughout the region;
   • policy of progressive disarmament;
   • campaign against terrorism, pollution, and drugs.

At the same time we should press for other Helsinki-type agreements in all the sensitive areas of the world.

5. The fifth golden rule is that security and cooperation are a united couple who do not believe in divorce. One cannot carry on without the other. Cooperation is the indispensable corollary of security. The major states are well aware of this—those states whose geostrategical evaluations are always closely bound up with their economic interests.

PREVENTION AS A MATTER OF NECESSITY, DIPLOMACY AS A GESTURE OF HUMILITY

The expression "preventive diplomacy" has now gained full acceptance, but it must not be allowed to lead us astray. It does not mean that preventive work aimed at the maintenance of international peace and security is a matter for diplomats alone. It is true that traditional preventive diplomacy perhaps involved a greater contribution by diplomats. Prince Von Metternich, who was Foreign Minister of Austria for thirty years and who, by preventive diplomacy, gave Marie-Louise in marriage to Napoleon I, stood alone at the heart of the Congress of Vienna of 1815. Talleyrand, for his part, became a diplomat who was indispensable whatever the circumstances, as he served in succession the French Revolution of 1789, the Directorate, the Consulate, the Empire under Napoleon, the Restoration under Louis XVIII, the Revolution of 1830 and Charles X, the Revolution of 1848 and Louis-Philippe!

Contemporary preventive diplomacy, focused upon the maintenance of world peace, also, quite naturally, enlists the services of diplomats in order to exploit all their talents to the full. However, contemporary preventive diplomacy relates to and implies a role for other protagonists, from the statesman to the businessman, from the journalist to the international organization, and from the banker to the nongovernmental organization. World public opinion is itself concerned, and should be even more concerned—given what is at stake in the achievement of peace.

According to the wisdom of the Far East, a date is not selected for the commemoration of a major event until the astrologers have been consulted—because it is believed that by the exercise of their skills, they can avoid undesirable astral encounters and seek out those that are favorable. They accordingly select and recommend the most propitious day for a wedding, an official visit by a head of state, a surgical intervention, an international conference, a business contract, or the conclusion of a treaty between states. However, preventive diplomacy is not a divinatory art, even though the diplomat involved in such work is generally armed with an astrologer's intuition because, in order to succeed in a negotiation, he has to calculate his chances, establish a strategy, prepare his tactical approach, enter into negotiations at the right time, and make the necessary concessions at a given moment. The wise diplomat knows that one cannot and must not manage the affairs of the world without the necessary rationality and without a minimum of anticipation. As President Adolphe Thiers was wont to say, "to govern is to anticipate future developments."

In the French language, a *diplomate* is a man whose job it is to deal with interstate relations and international relations, representing his country and asserting that country's interests. Moreover, as the sphere of his activities implies that considerable matters are at stake, matters that can lead to nothing less than such crucial alternatives as peace and war, the diplomat has become by extension, in the mind of the public, a man endowed with tact and skillfulness in his relations with other people. However, in that same French language, the word *diplomate* also means—by the influence of degeneration or delight?—a sort of pudding made from cake and custard, decorated with crystallized fruit! This means that, whether promoted to the rank of an empire builder or reduced to the condition of a delicious dessert, the diplomat, already short-circuited by his ministry (which frequently supplants him as travel has become easier and faster), seriously challenged by the expansion of the services made available by telecommunications and computer networks, assumes with a certain humility his mission in the preventive diplomacy of today.

He is aware of the importance of the human element, as institutions are worth no more than the worth of the people staffing them, but is also conscious of the importance of the institution, to whose interests he must always give way. At present, peacekeeping questions are a matter for the primary responsibility of the Security Council, which in practice refers to each of the states that constitute it and, in particular, to each of the five permanent members.

As they currently approach world affairs from the standpoint of the requisite preventive diplomacy, statesmen, diplomats, and international bodies, such as the Security Council, the General Assembly or certain specialized agencies that are competent in this area, are of course well aware that the time has come to start thinking of a safer and more equitable world, with less deprived peoples and a greater degree of fairness in the internal distribution of wealth.

However, they are working on a new economic and social web of international relations, constituted by a new liberal order. Now liberalism, which runs counter to the whole ideology of development advocated for the past half century by the United Nations General Assembly, is quite naturally animated by the cardinal principle of nondiscrimination. However, the whole of "development law" is based upon the contrary principle of positive discrimination, aimed at giving an advantage to Third World countries and helping them to make up for time lost in terms of development.

That "preferential revolution" has miscarried and has gradually been supplanted by programs for the reform of the relevant national economies, which are like so many "shock treatments" administered to bodies that have grown frail. Under those circumstances, it is not surprising that the predicted boost to development has not yet materialized, at any rate in most countries of the world. It is to be feared that the United Nations, whose efforts over the past fifty years have yielded no more than very mediocre results, might be reduced to playing an even more marginal role, whether or not it is converted to the philosophy of unfettered liberalism.

The new concepts of development, hinged upon liberalism and competition, inevitably engender economic and social Darwinism, the survival of the fittest, and the exclusion of the rest. Today, however, liberalism—combined with the disappearance of communist ideologies—could greatly facilitate a transfer of the resources once devoted to weaponry to the various spheres of economic and social development.

However, for the time being, the disastrous state of the world places certain states of the international community in a particular category, to which we are alas becoming accustomed, of perpetually deprived states, always drifting and always abandoned to their fate. Ultimately, that is a dangerous situation.

Quite apart from questions of options or philosophies of development, it must be agreed that the United Nations, which is struggling with a severe financial crisis, does not have the resources to sustain a preventive diplomacy focused upon development. The international financial institutions are perhaps better endowed, and so can make a contribution to that preventive diplomacy. They could doubtless do better, just as other international financial circuits could. However, when an official from the United Nations Development Programme proposed to the Social Summit of the United Nations in Copenhagen that a tax, representing a very modest levy, should be imposed upon the tremendous daily movements of capital throughout the world, he was given a very chilly reception.

In preventive diplomacy focused upon development, the activity of the United Nations remains confined to cooperation rather than direct, operational action. In its first half century of history, the United Nations has given the impression of a major weakness in matters of coordination. We have heard of overlapping efforts, a proliferation of institutions, organs, and the like, and of a more or less generalized paralysis.

Has the Organization now got off to a new start? This question can be discerned implicitly in all the actions of the United Nations. Can it be that the restoration of the state, a necessary undertaking, has also given the United Nations an opportunity to restore its capacity for coordination, intervention, or efficiency? In other words, can it not be seen as a blessing, ultimately, because a twofold objective will have been attained, namely, the restoration of the United Nations through the restoration of the state?

The contribution of the United Nations to the restoration of the state does, of course, raise a certain number of major questions. There is something in the air surrounding all those questions, something like a reappearance of the Wilsonian ideology that surfaced just after World War I—a vision of a world at peace, consisting exclusively of democratic states, resulting from free elections. But how far can the United Nations take its contribution to the restoration of the state? The problems are complex, and it is difficult to see how it can carry through the reconstruction of the state by substituting its own authority for the fragile and contested authorities of some states.

But by making that effort, the United Nations is assuming a mission fraught with implications for its future, the future of the states, and the future of international relations. It will have to shoulder even heavier responsibilities, insofar as the criteria employed by the United Nations to restore the state are criteria borrowed from a political philosophy that some people would describe as exclusively Western. There are two difficulties. The first is the very real risk of seeing the application of those criteria come to naught, leading to the failure of the United Nations' mission; and the second is the need to ask oneself—in advance —about the legitimacy of those operations if they are carried out only in accordance with Western criteria.

THE CHALLENGE OF HUMANITARIANISM

PETER HANSEN

Humanitarian assistance can and should serve as an essential ingredient in an overall prescription to prevent conflict. Different stages of actual or potential conflict may influence the prescription's mode of application and eventual results; but in the final analysis, the key elements in any prescription to prevent conflict must include humanitarian activities as part of an overall remedy.

In considering this essential humanitarian element as a factor in conflict prevention, we should begin first of all with a fundamental issue, namely, the politicization of humanitarian assistance. The myth that humanitarian assistance is not inherently political is old and increasingly unhelpful. A more positive approach as one looks toward the future is to accept the political nature of humanitarian assistance and to determine how best that reality can be put to humanity's best use in the context of conflict prevention.

Indeed as a first step, one may need to accept that humanitarian intervention is not only inherently political, but that it now must become more politically engaged. And yet in suggesting this, one must wonder why there has traditionally been such resistance to acknowledging the relationship between political process and humanitarian assistance. I will first suggest that the isolation of humanitarian intervention in the traditional or narrow sense from a broader conflict-prevention prescription does not address maladies of the real world. Second, I will argue that the general reluctance to accept this fundamental interrelationship and the rapidly evolving nature of emergencies and emergency requirements are forcing the humanitarian network[1] to become increasingly involved in activities frequently central to the political process. Third, I will suggest the need for reconciling the seeming political and humanitarian paradox, and outline three phases in which humanitarianism can be a force in overall efforts to deal with conflict.

The potential dangers that exist for many in taking the humanitarian network down this route are evident, particularly for those who hold tightly to the importance of protecting the "humanitarian mandate." Here, I shall conclude by arguing that conflict resolution and mitigation can be reconciled with the practicalities of providing neutral and impartial humanitarian assistance.

On one level, humanitarian assistance always has been enmeshed in a web of politics. It can be argued that the very decision to provide relief aid is replete with political implications and consequences. No one can deny that negotiations to gain access to affected populations or even to provide assistance have been essentially part of a political process, one that has resulted on more than one occasion in compromises that actually have politicized the relief process.[2]

On another level, whatever the reality, humanitarian assistance is increasingly perceived even by those who are beneficiaries of relief as neither neutral, impartial, nor "apolitical." More and more, the humanitarian process is seen to be driven by motives that are linked to ethnic preferences, historical alliances, and the interests of donor states. Here, Bosnia-Herzegovina and Rwanda are but two tragic examples.

The purpose of this chapter is, however, not to decry the inevitable, though not always acceptable, perceived or real links between political process and humanitarian action. To the contrary, it suggests that maybe the international community has to see the world of humanitarian action more proactively engaged in the realm of politics, and that although impartiality and neutrality are prerequisites for determining how relief aid, per se, is provided, they should not serve as the sole basis of the humanitarian network's value system.

This chapter concludes with the belief that the same humanitarian imperative that drives the relief process should be used wherever possible to play an active role in conflict prevention. Without this dimension, humanitarian organizations will be providing merely brief succor to ever more enduring conflict-related suffering and disruption.

FROM DISASTER RELIEF TO HUMANITARIAN ASSISTANCE: THE DEFINING MOMENT

It was late July 1992, and five thousand metric tons of relief goods waited off the port of Kisimayo for eventual delivery to camps of displaced persons in Somalia's Lower Juba area. These goods would not, however, be unloaded until specific instructions to do so were received from the Special Representative of the UN Secretary-General. However, that remained uncertain, because the Special Representative intended to use the delivery of those goods as an instrument to lever concessions from the local warlords who controlled that very important Somali port.

The implications of the Representative's strategy were clear. Rarely in recent humanitarian operations had relief assistance been used so blatantly as a weapon in the arsenal of political bargaining. And yet, this obvious interpretation revealed a more subtle set of dynamics at play, an emerging interrelationship between politics, conflict resolution, and emergency relief, which was changing conventional assumptions about the purported neutrality and impartiality of humanitarian assistance.

This emerging reality is in seeming contradistinction to what has been described as "the ideal of humanitarian service . . . expressed since antiquity in the form of samaritan work."[3] The roots of humanitarian service have been sown not only in the ideals of the good samaritan, but also in a certain otherworldliness reserved for those whom one might wish, but does not have time, to emulate.

As opposed to the incident in Kisimayo, this heritage is part of the false divide between what one might refer to as the real world and the world of "disaster relief" and humanitarian assistance.[4] It is this false divide which accounts in no small part for the conceptual constraints placed upon humanitarian assistance and continues to be sustained by at least three fundamental issues: (1) the perception that disasters and emergencies are aberrant phenomena; (2) the traditionally state-centric approach to disaster relief; and (3) political processes in the guise of neutrality.

THE ABERRANT PHENOMENA

It is a commonplace to suggest that today the international community finds itself involved in more humanitarian emergencies than at any time over the past three decades. In Sub-Saharan Africa alone, the international community is directly involved in attempting to assist at least twenty-five million people in twenty-some emergency-affected countries. However, as these humanitarian commitments increase, it is worth reflecting upon the true nature of at least one of the phenomena faced more and more by the international community, namely, complex emergencies.

Complex emergencies are not new phenomena, though the term is relatively new to the humanitarian community. The magnitude of their impact and indeed their very complexity give them a high profile in the media and in policy-making circles. Such attention reflects both the scale of many of today's emergencies but also their political nature. Lebanon and Liberia are recent examples that come to mind.

While it is quite understandable why terms such as *complex emergencies* are needed, there is, nevertheless, a conceptual danger in using such terms without a full appreciation of their perceptual implications. In resorting to such categories as "complex emergencies," the international community continues to isolate a humanitarian event from its broader social context. For the past twenty years, a host of emergency categories has emerged, such as natural, man-made, sudden onset, protracted or drought-led famine, joined now, more and more, by a new and seemingly more pernicious type of event, the complex emergency.

For some, this relatively new category reflects the consequences of the post–Cold War "new world disorder." However, too much has been made of the impact of the end of the Cold War on the upsurge in ethnicity and religious violence, micronationalism, and political unrest. Too little attention has been paid to what in reality has been a thirty-year trend in increasing disaster vulnerability, impoverization, and social unrest.

It is not the end of the Cold War that has precipitated the rapid erosion of social structures, ethnic and religious conflict, and micronationalism, but rather the intensifying effects of population growth, environmental degradation, and economic disequilibrium, both nationally and internationally. The latitude for a growing number of states to reconcile contending interests from within has been substantially reduced. Political opposition, often preceded by gross maldistribution of resources, has been the result as well as the precursor to political unrest and upheaval.

The use of the term *complex emergency* is merely a protraction of the false divide between humanitarian crises and the societies within which they occur. For decades, emergencies and disasters have been regarded as aberrant phenomena, divorced from "normal life," when, in fact, emergencies and disasters to a significant extent reflect normal life—the ways that societies organize themselves and allocate resources. Therefore, what we witness today under the rubric of "complex emergencies" is the continuation and intensification of radical social adjustment and in some instances implosion.[5]

The implications of treating the two as separate are twofold. First, it is increasingly difficult to maintain the pretense that humanitarian responses can be isolated from fundamental social adjustment. In the past, critics of the international relief network complained that emergency relief was always too little too late, and normally too late. Now a criticism that cannot be ignored is that emergency relief, all too often isolated from a broader context, has unwittingly prolonged the very factors that have led to some of today's worst humanitarian crises, be they in Bosnia, Angola, or Rwanda.

Second, because emergencies continue to be perceived and addressed as "aberrant phenomena," the full scale of response and solutions is limited to the inadequate armory of the relief network, namely, those that deal with disasters and emergencies. Hence, causation and response are too often restricted to the conventional capacities of a relatively ill-equipped component of a much wider community.

STATE-CENTRICITY AND HUMANITARIAN RESPONSE

The continued perception that disasters and emergencies are "aberrant phenomena" is consistent with the inherently state-centric approach that underscores humanitarian response. Although the erosion of sovereignty will be explored in the following section,[6] it is worth noting at this stage that the sovereign state has been the traditional guardian at the gate of humanitarian action.

States have had a vested interest in maintaining the distinction between normal life and aberrant disaster incidents. Nowhere does this become more evident than in Amartya Sen's study of the 1943 great Bengal famine. Between 1.5 and 4 million people died from starvation while, paradoxically, sufficient food supplies were available. Few governments would be willing to admit that this level of mortality was due to government ineptitude, and yet, at central as well as local levels, incompetent government was the principal agent of disaster.[7] More fundamental, however, is the fact that the structure of the Indian society at the time, the ways that resources were allocated, deprived those many millions of their "entitlements."

Historically, governments of disaster-affected states have been the main conduits through which relief assessments and information, as well as relief provisions, have passed. The machinery of state, though perhaps less so now, was more often than not the principal if not the sole determinant of the effects of a disaster and of who were and were not "victims."[8] In this way, not only was there a mechanism that directed the relief process, but one that also limited the impact that humanitarian response would have upon reforms that might well have prevented future disasters.[9]

The emphasis upon the central role of the state is not to denounce that role nor to propose an alternative. It is instead to suggest that the state, faced with a host of contending pressures, is normally adverse to seeing or accepting the full implications of disasters or emergencies, and, therefore, is more inclined to ignore the political implications of either.

A GAME OF CONVENIENCE

It has been a political convenience to see humanitarian assistance as apolitical. It is a game played not only by governments but by humanitarian organizations as well. Of course, governments are the first to accuse humanitarian organizations of playing politics, but that is not the issue. More fundamental is the fact that governments feel that it is wrong for humanitarian organizations to do so, perhaps because to do so is to expose the true cause of humanitarian crises, namely, the particular structure and dynamics of the state and society themselves.

Humanitarian organizations in one sense allow this game to be played out, for they, too, need the protection that comes from maintaining the fiction. The language of humanitarian negotiations is intended to separate humanitarian activities from the political in order to allow practical concessions to be made without undercutting political positions. A humanitarian organization can press for a government to allow relief flights to go through an area that, in effect, is controlled by a group in violent opposition to the government because the activity is humanitarian, thus separated from politics. In playing this game, the government makes no overt political concession by "authorizing" access. The humanitarian organization does not force the government into making such concessions, while the opposition authority who has actual control of the area is not granted any political recognition.

CHANGING CONTEXT, CHANGING NEEDS

The perception that emergencies and disasters are aberrant phenomena in large part continues. That states still continue to be the principal factor in defining emergency and disaster causation and response also remains essentially unchanged, as does the politically convenient—for both the state system and the humanitarian network—popular perception of emergency and disaster relief as apolitical in nature. And yet, while these remain relative constants, the fact of the matter is that the contexts in which humanitarian assistance is provided as well as the very nature of humanitarian assistance itself are changing. The question remains whether those who espouse traditional assumptions about emergency and disaster relief will be able to make the paradigmatic adjustment necessary to respond effectively to changing contexts and needs.

EXPANDING BOUNDARIES OF HUMANITARIAN ASSISTANCE

The boundaries of humanitarian assistance are expanding in several ways. In a growing number of instances, humanitarian action has served as a type of vanguard for the international community's response to states under siege. Such states may have "collapsed," as in the case of Somalia in the early 1990s, or the ability of states to exert their authority within internationally recognized boundaries (for example, Sudan) may have been undermined. Some states may have emerged from the trauma of violent change, such as the case of Rwanda, while others, for example Angola, struggle to steer between change and social disintegration.

In these and other instances, humanitarian action has served—normally quite unintentionally—as the buffer between political adjustment and human survival. This difficult role was reflected in many of the humanitarian initiatives in what were called the New Independent States, where assistance provided to vulnerable groups at the same time served to safeguard social services normally performed by state machinery.

Quite often, however, this role as buffer has been foisted upon the humanitarian network as a result of the international community's lack of political will to address the root political causes of state crises. One could well argue that Rwanda is a painfully obvious case in point. After the frustrations arising out of the peace-enforcement intervention in Somalia, and with the immediate future seeming to reflect powerful states' increasingly narrow interpretation of national interest, humanitarian intervention appears to have been an unfortunate alternative to political action. As one observer remarked, "In practice, crisis management seems to mean humanitarian relief."[10]

There is a further element that reflects the ever broadening boundaries of humanitarian assistance, and that is the assumption that humanitarian response can pick up the pieces created by international activities that may negatively affect social structures. In that respect, it is interesting to note the assumptions that seemed to underlie the 1994 devaluation in the Communaute Financiere Africaine (CFA) Zone. As the World Bank rightly noted, as a result of the devaluation, "the social needs of genuinely vulnerable groups in francophone west and central African countries will need particular attention in the immediate future." The assumption was therefore that the responsibility for deal-ing with the vulnerabilities created by structural adjustment measures to stabilize CFA nations would be that of the humanitarian network.

Thus, if one looks at the areas and types of intervention in which humanitarian organizations are increasingly becoming involved, there is a pattern worth noting. On the one hand, it is reflected in a growing tendency to assume that humanitarian assistance can provide a safety net for mitigating the effect of measures that have enduring social con-sequences. On the other hand, it is a pattern where humanitarian inter-vention is more and more linked to supporting social structures and governance, those that exist and those that are emerging.

REDEFINING HUMANITARIAN NEEDS

Disaster relief had initially been easy to define. When the infamous Bay of Bengal cyclone struck East Pakistan in 1970, the relief requirements were standard and predictable. Feeding centers, short-term potable water programs, temporary shelter, and clothing assistance, as well as local medical interventions, were the basis of the response to one of the greatest disasters ever to attract international assistance since the end of World War II.[11]

The definition of humanitarian assistance thirty years later lacks that same predictability. The humanitarian network finds itself involved in a variety of activities designed not only to provide survival needs to disaster- and emergency-affected peoples, but also to social structures and even governance. Assistance proffered to individuals has expanded. For example, trauma programs frequently go hand in hand with other urgent forms of relief for vulnerable groups. But even a greater depar-ture is reflected in the type of "humanitarian assistance" relief organiza-tions provide in a broader societal context.

Humanitarian assistance now often includes measures to stabilize state institutions, structures, and services without which more people would cross the threshold into desperate vulnerability. Activities that fall into this category are not those of rehabilitation or development; they are part of a burgeoning package of essential requirements when both society and governance are "victims" in urgent need. Such vitally needed requirements may include programs to house the military, to establish police or security forces, to provide for burial and grievance, to establish systems for property rights and compensation claims, to provide for mass trauma reduction, justice and prison systems, local credit schemes, support for recurring costs, demining, demobilization, as well as for rec-onciliation programs.

The problems presented by this widening spectrum of needs and requirements are at least three. In the first place, the mandates of many international and indigenous institutions in the humanitarian network must be adjusted to enable them to meet the new requirements. Either through greater "command and control" coordination mechanisms or through clear delineation of mandated responsibilities, humanitarian organizations must know who will be responsible in a humanitarian crisis for such concerns as internally displaced people, demining, and development of security and police programs. Second and closely related, the international community and the institutions that form part of the humanitarian network will just have to accept that the types of activities required to support traumatized societies and fragile national and local authorities often will be politically sensitive (for example, building prisons, providing barracks for former guerrilla forces), and yet these activities must be funded.

A third problem that must be addressed concerns the funding mechanisms of donors. Although the spectrum of humanitarian activities grows wider, the funding instruments upon which it depends do not seem to have adjusted commensurately. This is not to raise the issue of resources, though that is surely a legitimate concern, but rather to point to the fact that donor mechanisms seem to be trapped in a conception of disaster and emergency relief of an earlier era. Because so many of the activities that now appear on the humanitarian spectrum are neither conventional relief nor standard rehabilitation or development, support for essential activities seems very often to fall between stools.

Without specific solutions to these problems, the capacity of the humanitarian network to respond effectively to changing contexts will be seriously undermined. One of the "victims" will be a humanitarian impact upon the management of conflict.

INSTRUMENTS OF CHANGE

Increasingly the types of activities being undertaken by the humanitarian network reflect political as well as value choices. Support for a form of governance and for particular approaches to assist a traumatized society are clearly both. Such choices are made for various reasons. Perhaps the alternative is worse than what one has chosen, or, possibly, there was no choice at all. Maybe the emotional context surrounding a particular situation (for example, the aftermath of genocide or ethnic cleansing) established a clear choice, or a choice emanated from identification with a particular value system (for example, democracy).

In any event, values and political process become entwined in the world of humanitarianism, and this has particular relevance in the context of conflict management. In an era when conflict has become a prime agent of emergencies, the humanitarian network can be a potent force in conflict prevention. Yet, in so saying, humanitarianism should be regarded as but one element in a cohesive international effort to stem or thwart the impact of conflict. And, even here, humanitarian intervention in the realm of conflict prevention must not violate those fundamental principles that are essential to the humanitarian mandate.

HUMANITARIAN INTERVENTION AND CONFLICT PREVENTION

Throughout this chapter, reference has been made to the close relationship between politics, humanitarianism, and conflict prevention. The evidence is clear that the three are entwined, but at the same time one cannot stress too strongly that the role of humanitarian intervention is not actively to promote political objectives. In using humanitarian activities as a force to support conflict prevention, resolution, or mitigation, one has to be mindful of the dangers of crossing too far into the realm of political intervention.

Hence, humanitarian organizations in a conflict-prone country can use their resources, for example, to develop projects that indirectly foster interethnic harmony, but should be extremely wary of being used to support distinct political groups, even if they seek to promote interethnic harmony directly. The latter actually is ultimately the role of the local society itself, but as such can be supported by human rights organizations that have specific responsibilities for such activities.[12] Humanitarian organizations cannot afford to be placed in a position in which the distribution of resources may be seen as favoring one group over another.

This said, there are at least three broad types of activities where humanitarian organizations can have a direct impact upon conflict prevention.

PRECRISIS PREVENTION ACTIVITIES. In Rwanda, in late August 1994, hundreds of thousands of potential refugees were poised to seek asylum from southwestern Rwanda (an area that the French military temporarily occupied as "Zone Turquoise") into eastern Zaire. Should such a flood of asylum seekers have occurred, it not only would have placed extreme burdens upon humanitarian organizations and the local and national authorities in Zaire, but would have placed the lives of many thousands of Rwandan refugees at risk. The answer was to find some mechanism to persuade the potential refugees to stay in place and not to make the trek across the border.

Various humanitarian organizations made enormous efforts to provide the sort of food and nonfood assistance that might have led those
hundreds of thousands to stay on their side of the border. Unfortunately,
without sufficient political support and support from the French forces
at the time, the very brave effort of the humanitarian organizations ultimately could not constrain the movement, and, as had been feared, over
one million Rwandese fled their country to camps hastily established in
Zaire's Goma and Bukavu areas.

This example shows the potential that humanitarian intervention
can lend to crisis prevention and in a related way to conflict prevention.
For had the humanitarian effort worked, it is quite likely that a considerable number of Rwandese, who as refugees in Zaire today look with
hostility and fear upon the government in Kigali, might well have been
integrated into their home areas in Rwanda. This example of potential
crisis prevention also brings to the fore another important element. Had
there been closer cooperation and indeed agreement between the military forces in the Zone Turquoise and humanitarian organizations, it is
quite likely that the potential would have been transformed into a true
conflict-prevention and life-preserving reality.[13]

Moving away from an example of what one might call dramatic
potential, one should also note that there are a variety of practical day-
to-day activities that in relatively small ways can address some of the
problems that otherwise might lead to open hostilities. Measures to
ensure balance in local services, be they medical or clean water, can have
a positive impact upon communities. Joint participation in decision
making about project proposals can be useful in bringing potentially
conflicting parties together on a functional basis.

Equally as important is the early-warning perspective that
humanitarian organizations can give in anticipating conflict. Here, the
humanitarian network—with its field-based contacts—should be able
to provide information that would sensitize a wider international community to the prospects of violence and possible solutions.

IN THE MIDST OF CONFLICT. Conflict situations have more and more
become the operational testing ground of the humanitarian network. In
the first instance, humanitarian organizations may be immersed in providing standard types of relief. Nevertheless, in the midst of conflict, the
humanitarian network must work closely with others to see what measures can provide stability once peace—no matter how fragile—is
restored. Such measures may begin with a planning process that
includes relevant national and local authorities as well as interested

international organizations and NGOs about immediate postconflict requirements.

Planning might be translated into appeals and resource mobilization efforts to ensure that requirements are lined up and ready to introduce quickly. Such measures will have to be coordinated carefully with other components of the system, possibly peacekeeping forces and those international entities involved in political affairs and development. The point is simple: the humanitarian network must organize as early as possible the types of emergency assistance that will sustain the new-found peace.

In tandem with such initiatives is what the UN has referred to as "humanitarian diplomacy." The purpose of humanitarian diplomacy is twofold. First, its most obvious objective is to ensure access to affected populations by promoting such mechanisms as corridors of tranquillity and zones of peace. However, a second and equally important objective is to build bridges between parties in conflict,[14] while trying through humanitarian assistance to at least maintain pockets of stability in areas surrounded by conflict.

A telling example of what is needed to mitigate ongoing conflicts can be drawn from Somalia in 1993 when "disaster relief specialists wrote an economic recovery program for Somalia—a task well outside their expertise—because no one else was available. Given that so much of the economy revolved around the plunder of food aid, the failure to develop a plan to restore the economy to normal was a grievous error and emblematic of the mission's failure to address anything beyond exigencies."[15]

Here is a situation where, in retrospect, the prescription for dealing with conflict now appears readily apparent, but where, at the time, the international community failed to understand the interrelationship between development, humanitarian intervention, and Somalia's political economy. This is an important example of the need to develop broad-based and coherent strategies to stem conflict and of where humanitarian activities can only have an impact as part of a more harmonious overall plan.

POSTCONFLICT RECOVERY. A recent international colloquium on postconflict reconstruction strategies concluded that "once peace has been restored to a war-torn society . . . the over-riding goal of the international community should be to assist in national efforts to ensure that conflict and chaos will not recur. This goal must be met over and above needs for relief, rehabilitation and resumption of development."[16]

The fact of the matter is that this abiding goal can be effectively pursued with the assistance of the humanitarian network. Even if the immediate requirements for a newfound peace situation have been met, the threat of a return to conflict is ever present. The energies of humanitarian organizations must focus on specific means to ensure that legitimate governance is supported and that broad social needs are covered. Implementation time must be driven with the energy of a relief operation, while the substance of such interventions will be more in the nature of rehabilitation or in the sorts of unusual activities noted earlier in this text.

Returning to Rwanda in 1994–95, there was a clear case for greater attention and resources to be devoted to what at the time were called "stabilization activities," such as immediate assistance to government institutions and developing justice systems. Rapid support for the government was seen by many as the surest way to defuse the high level of hostility that several key officials in the government had for the international community, an hostility that was spilling over into the government's perception of refugees in neighboring countries as well as IDPs within Rwanda itself.

However, the situation was complicated by several important considerations. Although humanitarian organizations were well aware of the need to press for stabilization activities, the donor community was uncertain whether such measures were "development" or "relief." The distinction was important to them, because it determined the "pockets" from which the funds would be drawn and would also affect the timing. Many donors were also worried about the implications about the types of projects requiring funding, including the building of prisons and the support to civil service salaries. Perhaps, in some donor circles, a further concern was investing in a government whose attitudes toward its own peoples seemingly remained uncertain and in a government whose very stability remained untested.

With all these considerations, the fact of the matter nevertheless was that by not making appropriate investments in stabilization activities sufficiently quickly and substantially, the international community did little to promote postconflict recovery that could have been an additional buffer against a return to conflict.

If these broad approaches reflect useful humanitarian contributions to conflict management, then considerable emphasis will have to be given to the ways that these approaches relate to the activities of other actors, particularly amongst political and development partners.

An important breakthrough in this regard is the establishment of what has been called "the framework," or the regular consultative process mechanism between three major UN departments, namely, the Department of Peacekeeping Operations, the Department of Political Affairs, and the Department of Humanitarian Affairs. This process should allow for analysis of potential conflict situations to enable the UN system to respond appropriately. The framework experiment is at an early stage, and its actual utility can only be assumed. However, its potential importance cannot be exaggerated.

And yet, whatever actions the UN system may devise to thwart or stem conflict, the effectiveness of the international response normally will depend upon the reactions of the UN Security Council. It is important to note that the Security Council since April 1991 has used its authority increasingly to support humanitarian requirements.[17] And now humanitarian organizations will have to see if the Security Council's support can eventually be translated into resources from assessed contributions that can be used for humanitarian activities related to conflict management.

However, although the possibility of utilizing assessed contributions for humanitarian purposes will be important and the support to date for humanitarian activities is gratifying, the Security Council and Member States in general will need to deal with a far more fundamental issue.

Earlier in this chapter, it was mentioned that humanitarian affairs all too often were used as an alternative to decisive political intervention. The international community, and, in this sense, the Security Council must make a more concerted effort to address the causes of potential conflicts and the means for resolving ongoing conflicts. Humanitarian assistance has indeed a role to play in conflict management, but it can never do so alone or without the commitment of Member States to remove political constraints hampering the provision of humanitarian assistance.

PROTECTING THE HUMANITARIAN MANDATE

In April 1994, the Inter-Agency Standing Committee (IASC)[18] was presented informally with a draft document "The Protection of Humanitarian Mandates in Conflict Situations." The thrust of the effort was to determine best how humanitarian organizations could protect the fundamental principles of neutrality and impartiality while accepting that "humanitarian action is not to be seen in isolation, but as part of a comprehensive response to complex emergency situations." As the draft so clearly stated, "Given the inter-related causes and consequences of complex emergencies, humanitarian action cannot be fully effective unless it is related to a comprehensive strategy for peace and security, human rights and social and economic development, as proposed within the framework of the Agenda for Peace."[19]

This proposed IASC policy statement by implication accepts the important role that humanitarian assistance can play in building peace without sacrificing humanitarian principles. More specifically, neutrality and impartiality must be the fundamental principles that guide the provision of humanitarian assistance. No potential recipient must ever feel that urgently needed relief depended upon factors such as ethnicity, race, religion, political persuasion, or political convenience.

Nevertheless, one must not perpetuate the illusion that humanitarian assistance is anything but profoundly political. Indirectly or directly, its impact affects the very structure and fabric of a recipient society. Perhaps it is this very home truth that leads many to sustain the myth that relief is essentially "apolitical."

Whatever reluctance there might be to accepting this reality, the day-to-day burdens being borne by the humanitarian network are clear evidence that humanitarian assistance is indeed becoming increasingly engaged in central political processes. This is apparent not only from the context in which humanitarian organizations now operate, but also from the broadening spectrum of needs that humanitarian organizations are required to fill.

As the political nature of humanitarian assistance inevitably becomes more apparent and overt, the international community and certainly the humanitarian network as part of that community must accept the potential benefits of politically engaged humanitarianism. The realm of conflict management offers one area in which the benefit of such engagement should be felt, for here the potential impact of humanitarian assistance may be able to influence conflict prevention, mitigation, and resolution.

Yet, this assumption is based upon very important prerequisites. The first is that one must accept that humanitarian involvement in conflict management is not "value free" but rather "value loaded." It assumes that for the most part there are alternatives to conflict, and that stability is normally preferable to radical change pursued violently. For many around the world, this is a politically weighted statement. However, it is an assumption that humanitarian organizations will have to ponder as they lend their potentially considerable weight to conflict management.

One also must assume that any humanitarian effort in conflict management must be made as part of a more broad-based initiative, including where relevant, peacekeepers, the development community, and those who seek to promote human rights. Humanitarian organizations cannot act as a substitute for political will, but can have considerable impact upon common and agreed objectives such as stemming conflict.

However, that said, there invariably will be times when humanitarian organizations become uneasy partners in such broad-based initiatives. In particular, when relief aid is used and seen to be used as a "reward" or incentive for adopting particular political positions, most humanitarian organizations will see this as a fundamental breach of their humanitarian mandates. There is a profound difference between the calming influence of effective humanitarian intervention and the use of humanitarian aid as "stick and carrot."

As one looks toward the future, it is clear that the international community must never relinquish the principle that humanitarian assistance must be provided to all in need, in a neutral and impartial manner. Nevertheless, the very act of providing assistance is inherently political, and the political dimension of humanitarian assistance can and should serve as an important element in an overall effort to prevent conflict. Herein lies the essence of an approach that is a departure from the remedies of earlier times.

5
DEVELOPING PREVENTIVE JOURNALISM
MICHAEL J. O'NEILL

It may seem odd to talk about preventive journalism[1] in the same breath
with preventive diplomacy when it is well known that the media are
more devoted to controversy and conflict than to tranquility, and that
war is routinely defined as news while peace is not. What is good for the
world, in other words, is not necessarily good for the news business. As
Shakespeare put it so eloquently, bad things have to happen to important people or the groundlings won't buy tickets.

Because of its sibling attachment to misfortune, news is constantly
generating hostile feelings in the people it touches, from presidents and
foreign ministers to the innocent victims of a street crime who are suddenly caught in television's gaze. The general public is also surprisingly
negative, influenced in part, it seems, by those unedifying mob scenes
when TV reporters swarm all over an embattled Monica Lewinsky or
terrify a bewildered survivor of a terrorist bombing. Although journalists see themselves as champions of the common weal, their fellow citizens put them down in the popularity basement with lawyers and
politicians.

Traditional diplomats like George Kennan have an even lower opinion of reporters than the public, but their own world of elite policy-
making and secret negotiation has been reduced to ruins by the same
communications revolution that has also enhanced the role of the
media. This has driven international relations out from behind closed
doors and onto television screens and moved public opinion into the
center ring of policy-making so that journalism and diplomacy are more
closely linked than ever before. Not only do the media deliver and
sometimes even select the messages being passed back and forth
between statesmen and the public, but television has become a major
arena of policy debate and a frequent catalyst of public action. "Any discussion of changes in the diplomatic system must begin with the most

potent and far-reaching transformation of all: the collapse of reticence and privacy in negotiation," says Abba Eban. "The intrusion of the media into every phase and level of the negotiation process changes the whole spirit and nature of diplomacy. The modern negotiator cannot escape the duality of his role. He must transact business simultaneously with his negotiating partner and his own public opinion. This involves a total modification of techniques. Whether this is a favorable development or not is irrelevant; it is certainly irreversible."[2]

For better or worse, the whole idea of preventive diplomacy depends crucially on effective communication from the smallest units of global society to the highest. Television, newspapers, the Internet, and a whole galaxy of new electronic wonders are absolutely essential to pick up and relay the first signs of trouble in order for people to take timely action in their own defense. Even more important, perhaps, an early-warning approach to news coverage is needed to generate the critical mass of public knowledge, emotional engagement, and support required to inspire sluggish institutions to take note and possibly even to act in crises like the ones in Iraq or Yugoslavia.

The communications revolution, which is a common denominator of change in both journalism and diplomacy, is the defining fact of our age because it has collapsed time and space and extended living experience to the farthest reaches of the earth, to the illiterate as well as literate, to poor peasants as well as city elites. The volume of human interactions, global commerce in information and data, and wrenching social disruptions are outracing human nature. Great transitions that once took centuries are now compressed into decades, years, or only months. Just think of the millions of peasants now streaming off the land into the overcrowded cities of China—a short march in time but another long march in history. Everything is happening too fast and on too vast a scale for rational containment; political systems and social institutions—including journalism and diplomacy—are everywhere running behind the curve of change. As the historian William H. McNeill has warned, all of humankind is now in "a kind of race between the rational, disciplined, co-operative potentialities of humankind, and the urge to destroy, which also lurks in every human psyche."[3]

What the electronic acceleration of history means is that troubling new trends must be caught at much earlier stages if there is to be any chance of altering their course and affecting their outcomes. Whether it is exploding populations and vast intercontinental migrations, ethnic rivalries and religious conflict, endemic poverty, or a painful redefinition of labor by computers, problems cannot be left to fester until they are turned into disasters and then uncontrollable violence. The traditional politics of reaction and crisis management needs to give way to a new system that assigns its highest priority to social detection and prevention. Preventive politics. Preventive diplomacy. And yes, preventive journalism. A systematic and continuing effort to patrol ahead for causes before they become results, to attack problems in the deepest recesses of society before they grow into political strife and then explosions, and to reduce the incidence of folly and surprise, which have been our too constant condition, is needed.

One of the greatest threats to peace now, for example, is an unpublicized cause on its way to calamity—the seething discontent of hundreds of millions of people left behind in the onrush of new technology. Like a giant centrifuge, the whole international system is concentrating wealth and power in the industrial elite and separating out the poor and weak.[4] The value of labor is measured by education; the success of nations depends on technology and trained talent. Because commerce moves faster than education and cultural accommodation, the globalization process is inherently divisive and destabilizing. "Inequality," says the French thinker Jacques Attali, "will cleave the new world order as surely as the Berlin Wall once divided East from West."

What is happening is eerily reminiscent of the social repercussions of the Industrial Revolution that governing elites failed to recognize or prevent before cascading disasters, took charge of the twentieth, century. Now international corporations roam the earth in pursuit of profits, and governments scramble for national advantage in an economic free-for-all while showing little concern for those being crushed by the very global capitalism they celebrate. If the new millennium is to be more peaceful than its predecessor, today's leaders need to take preemptive action so that blind self-interest does not again take the world into the abyss.

The preventive process has to begin not with politicians and diplomats huddled around a crisis that has already appeared on the evening news but with people on the front lines of life where new crises are being incubated. It has to begin at the molecular level of society, with sociology, or the science of "nonlogical actions," as Vilfredo Pareto defined it.[5] And nowhere was this more cruelly evident than in Yugoslavia, which Richard Holbrooke has called "the greatest collective security failure of the West since the 1930s."[6] The tragedy was not "foreordained" by ancient ethnic hatreds as so many have claimed, he said, but deliberately created by criminal leaders who used television to fan latent hatreds into flames. The former U.S. ambassador to Belgrade,

Warren Zimmermann, underlines the same point in his memoirs. "Those who argue that 'ancient Balkan hostilities' account for the violence that overtook and destroyed Yugoslavia," he writes, "forget the power of television in the hands of officially provoked racism. . . . The virus of television spread ethnic hatred like an epidemic throughout Yugoslavia. . . . An entire generation of Serbs, Croats and Muslims were aroused by television images to hate their neighbors."[7] Another witness was Noel Malcolm, author of *Bosnia: A Short History*, who reported that after watching Belgrade television he could understand why ordinary Serbs would think they were under attack from Ustasa hordes or fundamentalist jihads. He said "it was as if all television in the USA had been taken over by the Ku Klux Klan."[8]

Slobodan Milosevic's campaign of hate began in that extraordinary year, 1989, when a mesmerized world was watching the Soviet Union crumble and the Cold War abruptly cease to be. Yugoslavia did not make the evening news shows; there was no public outcry to disturb self-congratulatory Western statesmen. Even two years later, when the mushrooming crisis was clear for all to see, Secretary of State James Baker still argued that there had to be "a greater sense of urgency and danger" to get any action.[9] A normal response for diplomats who are trained to end crises, not to prevent them. Political leaders never face a problem they can avoid or postpone. And the media find the precursors of war too untelegenic for even the twenty-four-hour news channels. So prevention, which works best before opinions harden and danger becomes acute, was not really tried. Milosevic's mutilation of Yugoslavia continued unchallenged.

This changed in the summer of 1995 when in four days of savagery Serbian troops massacred more than seven thousand Bosnian Muslims in Srebrenica. With the help of emotion-laden media coverage, including stomach-turning scenes of carnage, the atrocity sent shock waves through Europe and the United States. After Srebrenica, said Holbrooke, "The United States could no longer escape the terrible truth of what was happening in Bosnia. A surge of sentiment arose from ordinary Americans who were outraged by what they saw on television and from senior government officials who could no longer look the other way."[10] Western emotions kept rising until the full force of NATO, with U.S. bombers leading the way, was finally brought to bear on the crisis.

Another classic example of the media's impact on diplomacy was Kurdistan just after the Gulf War when President Bush was compelled to do a U-turn with his own policy. The TV screens then were filled with images of women and children screaming for scraps of bread and calling out for help that didn't arrive. As the tragedy was paraded before millions of viewers, public demands for action rose like a storm. France's foreign minister said the world had to intervene. Britain's prime minister, John Major, urged creation of a safe haven inside Iraq. President Bush resisted for days and *Newsweek* ran a headline that asked: "Where Was George This Time?" Finally, he buckled and rushed troops into Northern Iraq.

Mistreatment of the Kurds was an old problem; what was new was the power of mass media coverage to mobilize public opinion across national borders and force a multilateral international response. A similar pattern has appeared in many other areas. Famine in Africa only became a major issue in the West after news pictures belatedly reached Western viewers. For some of the same reasons, Somalia became a center of attention while Sudan and Rwanda did not.[11]

Television is the most visible new force in international relations but it is only part of a much broader and more profound technological revolution that is remaking the global system for the new millennium. This is forcing a radical change in the whole axis of the relationships between peoples. The channels of diplomacy that used to run directly from government to government under the jealously-guarded management of foreign ministries are now broad freeways of interaction connecting societies at every level of social, economic, technological, and political interest. Thousands of individuals, corporations, special-interest groups, NGOs, government agencies, and international organizations are busy dealing directly with their foreign counterparts without the help, thank you, of diplomats. Human rights, the environment, and other issues have become global movements. And statesmen bypass conventional diplomacy to deal directly with foreign publics through the media. When Jordan's late King Hussein wanted to counter a U.S. statement on the Middle East, he didn't call his ambassador or foreign minister; he telephoned CNN to make sure his views would be heard in Washington.

All these complex phenomena dramatize the need for wrenching institutional change. During the very years when global communications, technology, and economics were remaking the whole international system, foreign policy professionals barely noticed. The words "economics" and "technology" do not appear in the index of Henry Kissinger's magisterial book, *Diplomacy*. Intellectually, he acknowledges the new state of affairs. "Never before," he writes, "has a new world order had to be assembled from so many different perceptions, or on so global a scale. Nor has any previous order had to combine the attributes of the historic balance-of-power systems with global democratic opinion and the exploding technology of the contemporary period."[12] But little was done when he was in office, or afterward, to fit America's foreign policy culture to the new reality.

Although officials appreciate the need for so-called public diplomacy, they consider it peripheral to their central functions of political reporting, negotiation, and palace watching. In Moscow, the professionals meticulously tracked every twist and turn in the Kremlin. They even became boosters for Mikhail Gorbachev's perestroika and Boris Yeltsin's historic fight against the communist party. But they utterly failed to pick up the undercurrents of change deep within Soviet society. Like Western journalists who based much of their reporting on a few dissidents, the experts were taken by surprise when the Berlin Wall fell without giving them proper notice.

Joseph S. Nye, Jr., and Admiral William A. Owens attribute the surprise mainly to "outmoded thinking" that failed to recognize the enormous implications of the communications revolution. Granting a necessary continuing concern for military and strategic threats, they argue that American policy makers should also recognize that "information power" is a major force in international relations that needs to be understood and put fully to work to project democratic ideals around the world. They claim this would be particularly helpful in combating demagogic leaders who have fomented so much of the communal, ethnic, and religious strife that has defiled the post–Cold War period. "Information campaigns to expose propaganda earlier in the Rwanda conflict," they suggest, "might have mitigated the tragedy."[13]

In addition to making better use of modern communications to combat propaganda and to influence both domestic and foreign public opinion, a new communication age diplomacy must also develop a better early-warning system than the traditional political reporting that has failed so spectacularly in places like Russia. Observers need to get out into the field, work in villages, follow social and economic trends at ground zero and spot the earliest signs of stress that signal future crises. If closed societies were an excuse for superficial reporting in the early years when the KGB, the Stasi, and other security forces brutally suppressed contacts with foreigners, there is little excuse now when most of the information barriers have fallen.

The same point about reporting can be applied to journalists. They, too, should be searching past today's news to discover the hidden pockets of misunderstanding, the undetected human tensions that will become headlines tomorrow, next week, or a year from now. It is no longer enough for reporters to stand on the sidelines of history, merely recording the scenes passing before them while another unseen world throbs with warnings they do not hear.

The fact is that many of the most fateful issues facing the world lie beyond the reach of conventional journalism because it is a system that specializes in action and confrontation rather than in the more subtle forces of change. Whereas it is superb at covering riots, it is ill-equipped to uncover the causes of riots in time for society to avoid or prevent them. Yet this has to be one of the critical tests of a journalistic tradition—its ability to probe deeply into its own society and into other societies so that citizens can form timely and accurate judgments for their own protection.

This kind of journalism would be a powerful force in the cause of preventive governance and preventive diplomacy. By reporting on problems in their first stages, the media would bring public pressure to bear on officials to move sooner rather than later to find solutions. At the same time, diplomats following a sophisticated conflict-prevention strategy would be searching out early dangers that the media could then pick up and publicize. In this way, without even a hint of collaboration, both institutions would be focusing attention on problems before they became crises and, with the help of news coverage, mobilizing public support for action. There is a natural synergy between journalism and diplomacy that is much more important now when people, who are often as quickly informed as their leaders, are more directly involved in international crises than ever before.

As in the case of diplomacy, however, journalism would have to change its ways. And this involves many complex issues, including the fact that the profession has itself been changed by the communications revolution in which it is both a participant and a casualty. Six phenomena are especially relevant.

First is the persistence of a journalistic tradition that is superficial, poorly informed, and essentially reactive, focusing on action rather than the less visible but often more important forces of social, economic, and cultural change. Second is the worldwide explosion in news and information, including multiple outlets and activist reporting in many countries where all information formerly was censored and manipulated. A third, seemingly contradictory phenomenon is a sharp cutback in full-time foreign correspondents and a preoccupation with domestic news in the absence of Cold-War dangers. Fourth is the wildfire spread of new technologies that, on the one hand, are democratizing communication but, on the other, are neutering the journalist gatekeepers who traditionally apply standards of accuracy and balance to protect the public against dangerous distortions of news. Related to this is a fifth problem: the destructive invasion of journalism by Hollywood values that glorify entertainment and celebrity and trash old-fashioned ideas of truth, objectivity, and public responsibility. And finally there is the high cost of a preventive journalism that profit-chasing multimedia corporations and chain-owned newspapers seem unwilling to pay.

As far as journalistic tradition is concerned, Max Frankel of the *New York Times* has underlined a key failing. "The political, social and economic forces that shape our lives are much less expertly covered even as they have become vastly more complex and global in scope," he says. "We are simply not well enough staffed and equipped to cover most important news or to make important news interesting to mass audiences. . . . It takes extraordinary talent to dramatize the undercurrents in human affairs, and much more money than our market economy will naturally provide."[14]

Henry A. Grunwald, former editor-in-chief of *Time* magazine and former U.S. ambassador to Austria, notes that one reason cited for the failure of reporters to predict the fall of the Soviet Union is that they paid too much attention to government officials and "did not pay enough attention to 'civil society'—the many forces and people who move events quite independently of governments." The press made a similar mistake in Iran, he says, "when it concentrated on the shah and disgruntled intellectuals rather than on mullahs and bazaars."[15]

By contrast, the core idea of preventive journalism is to start a story at the beginning of the news chain instead of the end. Rather than depend on the central switchboards of public action—a prime minister's office, a few government offices, city hall, and police headquarters—reporters would reach down into neighborhoods to discover all the daily life teeming beneath the political surface, to explore the smaller cells of human stress that often tell larger stories than acts of state. Journalists need to get closer to people the way humanitarian workers do. It is no compliment to the journalism profession that NGOs are constantly in the field while most foreign correspondents only parachute in when some tragedy is sufficiently mediagenic to make the news shows. Problems need to be caught in their cribs if the public is going to be alerted in time to take corrective action.

For preventive journalism to work, however, correspondents have to be much better educated than before in foreign languages, history, economics, and social change. Ethnic, racial, religious, and cultural turmoil are now playing a more germinal role in global crises than traditional conflicts between states, yet these are the very intangibles that conventional journalism, like realpolitik diplomacy, is least able to deal with. Reporters, used to covering celebrities, politics, and wars, have neither the mind-set nor the knowledge to cope with highly nuanced cultural shifts, tangled ethnic trails, strange new cults, and religious conflicts in distant nations. In the United States the media are not sure footed even about a homegrown Christian coalition, much less evangelicals in Russia, liberation theology in Latin America, or Falun Gong in China.

The second phenomenon is an astonishing increase in international news and information of all kinds because of rapid advances in electronics, the opening up of closed societies, the explosive expansion in international commerce, and the multiplication of globe-circling communication companies. In many countries, once-fettered local journalists—trained or untrained, responsible or irresponsible—have become the terriers of press freedom, constantly harrying officials about everything from incompetence to corruption. In Russia, Boris Yeltsin was a hero in 1991 but a few years later could hardly get a good night's sleep because of roughriding media critics. In Central Europe, government officials almost everywhere are crying foul over what they call reckless and sensationalist reporting. In Japan, journalists who used to cross a street to avoid meeting a government scandal are no longer so accommodating. Indeed, hundreds of reporters have been murdered or imprisoned for exposing drugdealing, corruption, and other offenses against humanity.

Local reporting, of course, helps to balloon the volume of international news. It provides more foreign access to local sources and information. Global news services like the BBC pick up local stories and send them around the world. Indigenous national and regional TV networks relay news in the native languages of viewers. And constantly proliferating electronic networks are flashing masses of news and data from corporation to corporation and nation to nation so that in a very real sense everyone is awash in information. But media volume and frenetic activity are not the same as quality.

The irony is that as the information tide has risen, business reporting is booming but general foreign coverage has declined. A third element bearing on preventive diplomacy and the media is the fact that the major news organizations have been cutting back on full-time foreign correspondents and, except for dramatic exceptions like war and misery, the newspaper space and TV time devoted to foreign news in the

United States has been declining. Alvin Shuster, summarizing an International Press Institute survey, made several points, including:

• Print and broadcast media are cutting back correspondents overseas, mainly because of costs. They depend increasingly on wire services, temporary stringers, and "parachute" coverage in which home-based reporters quickly drop in and then out of foreign stories.
• Asian newspapers are increasing their coverage of foreign news, in part because of the economic boom that has stimulated local interest in other countries.
• American newspapers, except for a few national papers, have reduced staffs at home and abroad. The television networks have cut back even more drastically. (A large U.S. newspaper can field more full-time reporters in a single city than a major network can muster around the world.)[16]

Another related concern is the superficial and episodic nature of much of the coverage that ultimately does make its way into newspapers or onto TV screens. James F. Hoge, Jr., Editor of Foreign Affairs, notes that in the case of Western-dominated global news operations, most reporters are poorly schooled in non-Western cultures, are spread too thin, and are too much on the run from one assignment to another "to make up the deficiencies." More and more, he says, cost-conscious broadcasting networks are relying on freelance video footage and commentary. In some instances, the freelancers have had "dubious connections and lax standards" that have resulted in "doctored news events and slanted commentary."[17]

Making matters even worse is a fourth threat to quality in the new media world: trained journalists simply do not have the control they used to have over the way news is gathered and presented. Whatever their shortcomings may be in practice, their ideals of fairness and objectivity serve the public interest, but their influence has been shrinking. One reason is that communication technology has been democratized, which is to say that it is now so ubiquitous and so easy to use that just about anybody can be his own publisher or broadcaster. Statesmen in Moscow or Taipei or wherever create their own photo ops. Politicians interview themselves on their own TV shows. Lobbyists produce TV infomercials and e-mail avalanches on cue. Special interest groups ring the globe with "save the environment," "stop nuclear testing," and other messages. No one even knows how many people have launched pages on the Internet. Bill Kovach, curator of the Nieman Foundation at Harvard, observes that "it seems anyone and everyone, from the phone company to a computer hacker in Oslo, is in the business of making news available."[18]

Minicams, video recorders, microwave relays, dish antennas, cable, satellites, and computers mean news crews can deliver instant action pictures from anywhere in the world, often raw footage and even rawer reporting shot into living rooms untouched by editorial judgment or factual evaluation. Instant emotions flash through optical cables and over the Internet, fact or fiction, nobody knows. Local TV stations import reports directly from every kind of source without any guidance from experienced network news divisions. The number of cable channels, narrowcast programs, and talk shows multiply almost out of control with unpasteurized rumors and gossip masquerading as news. Still other electronic networks linking corporations, financial markets, advocacy groups, government agencies, and who knows what else are carrying great masses of news and information in real time, and they also are operating outside of journalism.

Related to these developments is a fifth factor, in some ways the most serious barrier of all to a preventive journalism: the corruption of classic news values by a culture of entertainment, by technology that informs by image and emotion rather than by explanation and reason and by the casual blurring of the lines between fact and fiction, between what is real and unreal, between natural occurrence and synthetic event, so that truth becomes relative and our links to certitude are broken. These tendencies are on display in many areas of the world but they are especially pronounced in the United States where phoney TV docudramas, fanciful biographies, staged events, and the unlabeled welding of news to commercial hype have created a dispiriting climate of artistic and journalistic fraud.

News events are routinely converted into TV movies, suitably mangled for emotional impact, and then news shows broadcast fake news interviews to promote the movies, in a seamless circle of falsified fact. As Michiko Kakutani observed despairingly in the *New York Times,* "We are daily assaulted by books, movies and television docudramas that hopscotch back and forth between the realms of history and fiction, reality and virtual reality" and, she added, this happens "with impunity."[19] Why? Because in television's never-never land entertainment is more important than reality, and entertainment, in turn, is defined by a Hollywood culture steeped in emotional exploitation, social nihilism, and moral relativism. If there are no rules in life, if everything is relative, then how can anyone say that something is right or wrong, true or false? As entertainment is fused with news, therefore, we lose contact with the actuality which classic journalism tries to discover and report. And the general public, which has a right to be honestly informed, loses its ability to think clearly about the policy judgments it must make in its own behalf.

Finally, there is the problem of cost. Preventive journalism is an expensive proposition. A TV station can assign one reporter to city hall and pretend it is covering a great metropolis. It takes a battalion of reporters to track neighborhood life in the same city. Even more expensive are foreign bureaus and correspondents. As Richard Lambert of the *Financial Times* has observed, the rush of business news organizations to cover the world "helps to plug the gap left by the contraction of international reporting by television and newspapers." But it is hardly a replacement. "Sound political leadership depends on the support of informed citizens," he says. "That in turn requires a steady and consistent view of both local and international events—and one that is not just confined to the business pages."[20]

Thanks to colossal failures of imagination and entrepreneurial courage most newspaper owners stood by while other industries—entertainment, communications, computers, or what have you—took over the playing fields of the new information age. Now they are fighting high structural costs and declining circulation levels on a narrower economic base than many of their competitors. This does not encourage heavy investment in foreign news that, in any case, is not in great reader demand.

To recite this litany of problems is to invite doubts about the chances for progress. Still, these same problems are also a source of hope. For many editors are arguing that the very survival of newspapers in the electronic age will depend on providing large quantities of serious news, not less—more substantive, penetrating, and comprehensive reporting, not the sound-bite journalism of *USA Today* or the striptease exhibitionism of the London *Sun*.

A more thoughtful journalism is the one form of journalism with which television cannot compete. The readership might be smaller, but it would be more selective, more attentive. The coverage would be more valuable to this audience because it would not be available elsewhere. Also, I happen to believe there is a way to ameliorate the cost problem by developing highly specialized reports for niche audiences willing to pay premium rates. Some of their profits could then be used to subsidize more intensive general coverage aimed at sophisticated readers—the "attentive classes" in Hoge's phrase—who want to follow international affairs in some detail.

Of course, there is another formidable obstacle. Like diplomats, newspapermen and women are notoriously resistant to change. They were almost the last to see how they would be affected by the communications revolution, so institutional reform may seem remote. But what is remote when time has collapsed and today is already yesterday, and tomorrow is today, and the future is tomorrow; when the Berlin Wall seemed forever, then crashes and is now forgotten? We are living in an age when what seemed probable to experts never happened, and what seemed impossible became a daily surprise. Nothing, it seems, is more certain than surprise.

Preventive diplomacy and preventive journalism are abstractions. They are like the horizon where the sun rises and sets; it is always out of reach—only a mythical line between sky and sea. And yet for centuries, this same line has helped to guide mariners safely across trackless oceans.

PART 2
PARTICULAR PROBLEMS IN
PREVENTIVE DIPLOMACY

As one looks toward the future, it is clear that we must develop new approaches to old problems. The very act of providing assistance is at least partially political, and that dimension can and should serve as an important element in an overall effort to prevent conflict. Such an approach is a departure from the remedies of earlier times; challenges may seem overwhelming but new opportunities exist.

In this section particular problems in preventive diplomacy are analyzed by four experts with exceptional field experience. Rosario Green discusses the role of women in conflict prevention and resolution. Alain Destexhe explores the philosophy and methodology of humanitarian organizations during conflicts, and the need for a reinterpretation of neutrality and impartiality. Francis Deng considers the world's response to an ever escalating number of refugees, especially those displaced within the borders of their own nations. Robert Skidelsky and Edward Mortimer cite historical and current examples, and inherent dangers, of economic sanctions as a tool of preventive diplomacy.

WOMEN AS PARTNERS FOR PEACE

ROSARIO GREEN

I have come, you see, to a strange fork in the road. It is so very odd to look back and see the path that I have tread, now overgrown and distant, and wonder, what if?... I stand at the crossroads of life, with what could have been behind and what must be ahead.

—J. Nozipo Maraire in
Zenzele: A Letter for My Daughter

Peace is a human aspiration, yet peacemaking and peace-building have largely been the affairs of men and carried out through a male perspective. This chapter proposes the need to introduce a gender-sensitive vision to preventive diplomacy and the contribution that women and men, working in partnership, can make to these endeavors. It accepts the notion that "Preventive action, as early as possible, is the least complex, most humane and most cost-effective path for the international community to take in resolving disputes."[1] Conflict must be managed before it erupts into full-scale warfare.

According to the 1998 Human Development Report, "it is estimated that nearly 100 million people are in the middle of civil strife and hunger" and some "50 million have been forced to flee their homes," although "the number of conflicts worldwide fell from 21 in 1996 to 18 in 1997."[2] The prevalence of internal strife over traditional interstate military confrontation has brought to the fore, with greater emphasis than it ever did before, the need to reexamine the causes, characteristics, and consequences of conflict. Such an effort calls for the introduction of a gender perspective throughout this process in a twofold way: by tending to the needs of women as subjects and by incorporating them as full-fledged actors in peace endeavors. In accordance with the health and medical metaphors that inspire this book, this twofold approach presents women both as patients and as healers.

Women have begun to demand greater participation in the prevention and solution of conflicts based on their own experience, both as victims of warfare and as guarantors of survival in times of turbulence. "Women want peace in their societies and in their homes. They are at the center of peace movements because they know the effects of militarism, genderized violence in war-torn societies and conflict-prone families."[3]

This chapter does not attempt to define the well-known concepts of preventive diplomacy, conflict resolution, or postconflict peace-building. Rather, it aims to enrich them by incorporating the gender perspective. The Balkans, Somalia, Rwanda, Liberia, Sierra Leone, the Middle East, and the Democratic Republic of Congo (former Zaire) are among those cases in which countless civilians, female and male, have paid the price of failure to curb conflict. They demand that we search for innovative ways to strive for peace. Women and men must sit together on the side of peace, for war strikes all indiscriminately.

A DIAGNOSIS OF CONFLICT

The Nairobi Forward-Looking Strategies for the Advancement of Women, proclaimed in 1985, states, "Peace includes not only the absence of war, violence and hostilities at the national and international levels, but also the enjoyment of economic and social justice, equality and the entire range of human rights and fundamental freedoms within society."

In 1995, the Fourth World Conference on Women went further when it stated that "Recognizing that the achievement and maintenance of peace and security are a precondition for economic and social progress, women are increasingly establishing themselves as central actors in a variety of capacities in the movement of humanity for peace. Their full participation in decision-making, conflict prevention and resolution and all other peace initiatives is essential to the realization of lasting peace."[5]

The Platform for Action also recognizes that peace is inextricably linked to equality between women and men and to development. With the view of fostering the conditions for a world free of instability and violence, it recommends the implementation of cooperative approaches to peace by addressing gender equality: "The equal access and full participation of women in power structures and their full involvement in all efforts for the prevention and resolution of conflicts are essential for the maintenance and promotion of peace and security. Although women have begun to play an important role in conflict resolution, peacekeeping and defense and foreign affairs mechanisms, they are still underrepresented in decision-making positions. If women are to play an equal part in securing and maintaining peace, they must be empowered politically and economically and represented adequately at all levels of decision-making."[6]

In studying the underlying causes of conflict, it has become evident that discord has all too often resulted from an unfair and unjust distribution of political and economic power. From this perspective conflict covers a wide range of nonmilitary aspects: the increase in poverty and marginalization, the unwillingness or the incapacity of the state to respond to the basic needs of the population or to meet expectations that are broadly perceived as legitimate, the lack of credibility in the administration of justice, the absence of effective state protection from lawlessness and crime, and the lack of access to political participation, among others. All these elements are inextricably intertwined because participation in economic decision making is determined by the overall distribution of political power.[7]

The position of women in this context is particularly vulnerable. Figures speak volumes: women earn one-tenth of the world's income and own less than one-tenth of the world's property. Women represent 60 percent of more than 1 billion adults who have no access to basic education. Women comprise 70 percent of the world's 1.3 billion of absolute poor. Women within poor countries and communities are more impoverished than men. In African countries, for example, women account for more than 60 percent of the agricultural labor force and contribute up to 80 percent of the total food production but receive less than 10 percent of the credit to small farmers and 1 percent of the total credit to agriculture. In many ecologically fragile zones, especially those in war-torn areas and in communities undergoing economic and social disintegration, women and their children comprise 75 percent of the affected and displaced people.[8]

These figures tell not only of injustice against women but also of their resourcefulness. Throughout history women have been the key elements for the smooth functioning of societies. By virtue of their role in caring for their families and providing for their basic needs women ensure society's survival and continuity. In order to do so, they often develop the capacity to organize and to make decisions affecting their households and their communities outside formal institutional frameworks. All these reasons stress the urgent need for the full integration of women in the solution of political, economic, and social problems underlying conflict.

The United Nations Development Programme acknowledges that

"societies have made real progress over the past 30 years in achieving more equitable distribution between women and men of the benefits of development," and yet, it also affirms that "human development achievements of women fall below those for men in every country. Progress in building women's capabilities has been significant, but there is a serious delay in creating real opportunities for women."[9]

Indeed, although progress in this direction has been made in several areas, it is lagging behind in others. "The strategic importance of women's participation around issues of universal human rights, democracy and sustainable development is no longer in doubt. In areas, though, such as culture, ethnic strife and conflict resolution. . . women are just beginning to enter the debate."[10] Opportunities for success in peace efforts would be greatly enhanced by incorporating the gender dimension both in the way conflict is diagnosed and in the medicine prescribed to treat the disease or prevent a relapse.

The approach to preventive diplomacy, conflict resolution, and post-conflict peace-building would be enriched by including both the impact on women of "poverty, human rights abuses and underdevelopment—critical factors contributing to the breakdown of societies and the outbreak of violence,"[11] and the female perspective in tackling these problems. In this endeavor, partnership between women and men cannot be stressed enough: "The world needs a new vision that can galvanize people everywhere to achieve higher levels of cooperation in areas of common concern and shared destiny."[12]

It is a recognized fact that "women bring different experiences, perceptions, priorities to the decision-making process—which leads to different decisions being made."[13] The new vision proposed does not require new institutions nor special methodologies; it simply strives to involve all parts of civil society, half of which is female, thereby strengthening existing capacities and ensuring better coordination when resolving conflicts of mutual concern.

Regarding this issue, one particularly important strategic objective of the Platform for Action is the goal of promoting women's contribution to a culture of peace. Paragraph 146 of this document recommends that governments, international and regional intergovernmental institutions, and nongovernmental organizations "promote peaceful conflict resolution and peace, reconciliation and tolerance through education, training, community actions and youth exchange programmes, in particular for young women" and "consider establishing educational programmes for girls and boys to foster a culture of peace, focusing on conflict resolution by non-violent means and the promotion of toler-ance."[14]

The well-being of civil society, like that of the human body, is dependent upon the satisfaction of needs. Failure to meet human needs, be they physical, socioeconomic, ethno-cultural, political, or spiritual will inevitably impinge upon the development of certain actors and lead to social tension if unattended. An early diagnosis of society's needs is a basic tool for the timely identification of prospective conflicts. This does not imply that the mere recognition of conflict ensues its resolution, but it can serve as a yellow light, which is key in preventive diplomacy. This is similar to the detection of symptoms in the human body, which can lead to a precise identification of the disease, thereby providing vital information for the prescription of treatment.

Making the interests of women an integral part of the totality is cer-tain to have an impact on how humankind approaches conflict. Ignoring the grievances of women is comparable to ignoring half of the body's pain indicators. Neglecting the input of women in preventive diplomacy is analogous to blocking half of one's natural antibodies from fighting off diseases.

The unique contribution of the female perspective is supported by surveys and public opinion polls. Biology is by no means destiny, but women are different from men. This is not to say that one sex is better than the other, but that women and men need new ways of working and living together to bring out their respective strengths. Although it could be argued that the following characteristics are hardly sex-specific, some experts contend that more value should be placed "on women's caring, women's intuitiveness, women's empathy, women's attention to details, women's tendency to solve problems peacefully and through teamwork, women's ability to listen, women's strength in the face of adversity, and so on."[15] It is a fact, however, that these traits have not usually been ranked high among the qualities of decision makers, and yet they could prove of extreme usefulness for gaining confidence between contending parties and promoting consensus for change.

Women and men are perceived to interact differently. For instance, it is a shared idea that women are socially conditioned to be more peace-ful than men, an expectation that is tied to the responsibilities that come with motherhood, caregiving, and nourishing. In contrast, the tradi-tional value system that supports war is commonly thought to depend on male values. In this context, the term "gender" is of use, as it refers to the different cultural constructions of male and female identities, to which different roles, expectations, and, especially, values are socially assigned, whether they are real or perceived.

Because of the space in which women have traditionally interacted, there is evidence that they emphasize matters that benefit the community's development, and are keener, as Inger Skjelsbæk states, to stress "family matters, environment, equality between the sexes, child policies and sexual policy."[16] They have also shown influence in fostering change through the enactment of law. "Frequently, it has been the work of women in movements for change who have led the way to social legislation that has remedied unfair or harmful practices."[17] However, "they cannot make a difference unless they constitute a critical mass,"[18] meaning that at least a 30 percent participation of women in politics is required to incorporate female values. This reasoning is the centerpiece to assert that the participation of more women in decision-making positions can have an impact in the political agenda, bringing new chances for equality, development, and peace. It also questions the traditional concept of power and security and, as a consequence, introduces development as an important element of conflict avoidance and of preventive diplomacy.

Empowering women is therefore a means to opening the door to new development possibilities, both at the personal and national levels, but also to balancing the differences of power in society, with positive results in terms of fighting structural violence and promoting democratic values. With this aim, the United Nations Expert Group Meeting on Political Decision Making and Conflict Resolution: The Impact of Gender Difference (Santo Domingo, Dominican Republic, October 7–11, 1996) recommended that a transformation of the concepts of power, security, and participation was desirable to ensure an equal participation of women and men in decision making and conflict resolution.

Whether it is true or not that conflict resolution is based mainly on female values—such as a higher ability to listen and to empathize—it is quite desirable that the twenty-first century be an inclusive period that allows more women to participate in development and, therefore, in the construction of peace and in the definition of what constitutes conflict and how it can be prevented. The educational role of women adds a potential for a transformation of their families and societies toward peace. Women need better opportunities not only to reach their goals but also to contribute to their societies.

WOMEN AS PATIENTS

A gender-sensitive diagnosis provides a very dramatic vision of the ills of society at the end of the last century. As patients, women can be seen as victims of violence and bearers of the brunt of economic exclusion, social neglect, and political marginalization.

An expanded definition of peace incorporates both the absence of war and direct violence as well as the absence of structural violence. It stresses that violence in personal, national, and international spheres stems from the same roots and should be seen as an expression of the same social evils. It leads to the conclusion that sustainable peace cannot be achieved without eliminating violence at all levels, including violence against women.[19]

Violence is an underestimated phenomenon, widespread and tolerated. It leads to many circles of disrespect for the life and integrity of others.[20] "Violence against women exists in various forms in everyday life in all societies. Women are beaten and mutilated, burned, sexually abused and raped."[21]

In the United States, a woman is beaten every eighteen minutes; between three and four million are battered each year, but only one in one hundred cases of domestic violence is ever reported.[22] In India, five women are burned in dowry-related disputes each day, according to official figures, although the number estimated by activist groups is much higher.[23] In Colombia, about 20 percent of the patients in a Bogotá hospital were victims of marital violence.[24] Divorce petitions on grounds of violence in countries as diverse as Canada, Egypt, Greece, and Jamaica are further evidence of the magnitude of the problem of domestic violence and of the fact that it is becoming one of the main grounds for divorce in many countries.[25]

In situations of war, women, alongside men, have been victims since time immemorial. "Armed conflicts are leaving behind a growing number of civilian casualties, an increasing proportion of which are women."[26] "Civilian fatalities have climbed from 5% of war-related deaths at the turn of the century to more than 90% in the wars of the 1990s. As a result many of the casualties are women and children, with an incalculable impact on human development."[27] Some women have been combatants at the side of men, and many have been forced to leave their homes with their dependent children in search of safety. Between 75 and 80 percent of the world's fifty million refugees and internally displaced persons in more than one hundred countries are women and their children.[28]

None of the evils of war are alien to women. Rape and other forms of torture, starvation, and death have befallen them. Those who survive, oftentimes under physical duress and suffering from the psychosocial effects of post-traumatic stress disorder, still have to bear the burden of caring for their children. Compounding this, some of these children are born as a result of rape. The mother is confronted with caring, protecting, and nurturing the child despite the emotional scars of rape.

The special needs of women are frequently neglected and their voices silenced. However, the female perspective was instrumental in defining crimes against humanity, particularly when it involved sexual violence.

The acknowledgment of the long-lasting consequences that rape has on women in situations of armed conflict resulted in the wide participation of women's groups prior to and at the time the Conference of Plenipotentiaries on the Establishment of an International Criminal Court was held in Vienna in July 1998. In the preparation process, the Women's Caucus for Gender Justice played an important part to introduce a women's agenda. As a result, the Statute of the International Court includes as a crime against humanity forced pregnancy, and as war crimes, rape, sexual slavery, enforced prostitution, enforced pregnancy, enforced sterilization, and any other act of sexual violence, in agreement with international law (Geneva Conventions).

The influence of a female perspective was also in place in the cases of Bosnia-Herzegovina and Rwanda. After several resolutions of the Security Council referred to the massive, organized, and systematic detention and rape of women, in particular Muslim women, in Bosnia and Herzegovina, a commission of experts to investigate violations of international humanitarian law was established. This acknowledgement resulted in the establishment of an ad hoc war crimes tribunal in 1993, as a subsidiary body of the Security Council. The tribunal's governing statute expressly refers to rape in terms of a crime against humanity. In the same manner, in November 1994, the ad hoc war crimes tribunal for Rwanda was established and included rape among the crimes to prosecute. In other cases, however, the response of women's groups has been milder, as it is now being registered in regards to the situation of Afghan women. Women are also particularly affected by land mines: "More than 110 million active mines are scattered in 68 countries, with an equal number stockpiled around the world. Every month more than 2,000 people are killed or maimed by mine explosions."[29]

The assumption that refugee and displaced women have few capacities or skills is widespread. In Burundi, for example, internally displaced women were found to play no role in camp decision making. When the Representative of the UN Secretary-General on Internally Displaced Persons asked to meet with the spokespersons of a camp housing several thousand women and only twenty-five men, solely men came forward to discuss the problems of the camp.[30] How is it possible for men alone to voice the full reality of the situation in the camp and convey the needs of the community as a whole?

In refugee situations, participation of women in the daily activities of the collective center camp or within the household of the host family where they have been accommodated is crucial to their self-esteem, and should be secured. Refugee women from Bosnia-Herzegovina, however, found that, while living in collective centers in Slovenia, where meals were catered, they had been deprived of one of their last vestiges of control as women in refugee situations—that of cooking, for themselves and their children.

There are other cases in which female vulnerability has been critical, or in which women's potential has not been fully tapped. To consider issues related to health care, education, land tenure, income distribution, and political participation as alien to conflict prevention and resolution is tantamount to reducing social and political strife to a military equation. To ignore women's possible contribution in these fields is tantamount to self-limiting the possibilities to remedy the social ills that breed conflicts.

The unpaid work of women in homes and in the fields goes unrecognized, even though no national economy could survive without it.[31] In Africa, as already mentioned, although women produce 80 percent of the food consumed and at least 50 percent of the export crop, they have virtually no access to credit. In Central America, where 25 percent of all agricultural workers are female,[32] the rights of women to property were not appropriately considered in the peace-building initiative in El Salvador.

Despite the fact that women have made some progress in the developing world over the last two decades, the absolute number of women living in poverty in that part of the world has grown.[33] Currently, more than 564 million women live in absolute poverty in rural areas, which constitutes 60 percent of the world's one billion rural poor.[34] Certain human development indicators reveal that poverty is increasingly and disproportionately affecting women. This phenomenon has been referred to as the "feminization" of poverty, hinging on two interrelated facts: women bear a disproportionate share of poverty worldwide, and women shoulder an unequal burden in coping with poverty at the household level.[35] As stated in the UNDP 1995 Human Development Report, "Development, if not engendered, is endangered."[36]

Women are the primary health care providers for families worldwide. This entails a greater role for women in the developing world, where 75 percent of all health care takes place within the family.[37] They care not only for their own children, but are oftentimes responsible for the infirm and the elderly of their extended families. And yet, their role is hardly ever recognized and definitely never recorded.

Regarding education, figures again speak for themselves. A third of the adults in the developing world are illiterate; of these, two-thirds are women.[38] Educating women would also have an impact on the entire family. Teaching women and enlisting their contribution in fields such as nutrition, family planning, reproductive health, and the prevention of HIV/AIDS and other sexually transmitted diseases would enhance their own role as educators. If women were educated further, their input to economic and social development, to peace and security, to democracy, would greatly advance what has so far been an imperfect accomplishment of humankind.

According to the UNDP 1995 Human Development Report, although the gender gap is still quite large, it has begun to narrow in the past twenty years in terms of human capabilities (standards of living, levels of education and health, and so on). However, in terms of empowerment (income, parliamentary seats, professional and managerial jobs) it is still gigantic.[39] Although equality between the sexes has long been incorporated in the legal framework of most countries, this has not been translated into full female participation in politics and decision making. The existence of international laws and electoral rights at the national level has allowed women to vote and to be elected, but has yet failed to open the door to positions of responsibility for a substantive proportion of women.[40] Therefore, "a large share of the world's women remains voiceless and powerless."[41]

The scant representation of female decision makers in the economic and political fields at the local, national, regional, and international levels is the consequence of structural barriers and ingrained attitudes. Governments, private corporations, academic and research institutions, intergovernmental entities, including the UN system and the media, have failed to fully draw upon the wide range of women's talents as peace- and policymakers, business leaders, diplomats, and top opinion shapers.[42]

In 1994, women held a mere 1 percent of chief executive positions worldwide, only 10 percent of parliamentary seats, and just 6 percent of cabinet positions. One year later, female professionals and technical workers comprised 38.9 percent of the total, but female administrators and managers made up only 14.0 percent. As of December 1997 the percentage of women in parliament only reached 11.8.[43] Numbers in the United Nations were not more encouraging. Of the fifty-three presidents of the General Assembly chosen by the Member States up to 1998, only two were women: India in 1953 and Liberia in 1969. In 1995 only seven permanent missions out of 185 Member States and two Observers were headed by women. Among the 240 delegates holding ambassadorial rank, only 11 were female. Women represent only 22 percent of the total diplomatic staff of missions, not a very impressive increase from 1949 when they represented 16 percent of the total.

Despite the great expansion of the UN role and functions in peacekeeping missions since their inception in 1957, until 1992 only 1.1 percent of all participating personnel were women.[44] In both numbers and culture, "one of the most striking characteristics of militaries is that they are almost exclusively male."[45]

WOMEN AS HEALERS

Often women struggle for change in the world with weapons and words, as activists in favor of social reforms and justice. However, seldom do women sit at peace talks, peace negotiations, or other conflict resolution forums. Nevertheless, there are different instances in which women have sought their own means in search of solutions to conflicts.

Women's participation in nongovernmental activities related to peace has gone through various stages throughout this century, providing numerous examples of female initiatives, actions, and programs. These initiatives have demonstrated that women's approaches to peace, security, and other global problems are often different from or more innovative than those of men.

In Europe and North America many women have concentrated their propeace efforts in the area of disarmament. Some observers go as far as giving substantial credit to women and their organizations for mustering the political support that led to the negotiation and later ratification of the nuclear-test-ban treaty in 1963. In 1980 three Danish housewives launched a campaign against the stationing of cruise missiles in their country. Six months later the petition they had circulated had been signed by half a million women in Scandinavia and the weapons were never admitted on that territory.

In other cases, women have created their own channels to seek reconciliation between parties in conflict. For example, in Cyprus, despite the political division of the island, women from both sides have held joint meetings and seminars aimed at establishing a dialogue at the community level.[46]

At an international conference entitled "Women, War and Peace," sponsored by Women in Black and Women's Peace Movements, in January 1995, complaints were voiced about the fact that even though Israeli women had participated in the war, they were not included in the formal peacemaking process. Lilly Rivlin, a writer and filmmaker living in New York, said on the occasion: "I realized that though Israeli women have been excluded from the formal peace process—and their resentment was made clear—they had also created a parallel peace process with Palestinian women, one that is more humane and allows for feelings and issues that are not part of the formal negotiations. This cannot excuse the exclusion of women from the formal process. They belong in the center of discourse alongside men. But at least, as the peace develops diplomatically, this space created by women may allow for the cross-cultural exchange so vital for a life of co-existence."[47]

According to a female perspective, peace-building comprises any activity aimed at the replacement of armed violence and coercion in situations of conflict by nonviolent, justice-seeking behavior. Peace-building in this perspective entails the creation of new social spaces and relations.[48] Women who had joined guerrilla forces in El Salvador, for instance, played an important role in the formulation of peace strategies based on respect for human rights and the full democratization of the political system. More recently, in Sierra Leone, groups of women marching for peace were fired upon when they braved armed fighters. Women in that country were a driving force behind the military government's decision to hold elections[49] and they "withstood weeks of intimidation." The women of Bosnia also have had a high priority—to see the war criminals brought to trial. They have been willing to testify, for they are convinced that there cannot be peace without justice."[50]

In refugee camps in Central America women's capacity to develop self-reliance through education and income-generating projects proved vital, not only to alleviate the dire living conditions and to boost the morale of other refugees, but also to ease the burden on the host country. This proved beneficial to their communities when they were repatriated. In Rwanda it soon became evident that the distribution of food and medical supplies would have benefited greatly from a more active participation of women, if only because they were many and idle, not to mention the increase in their self-esteem, in addition, by feeling that they were part of the solution.

In keeping with the health metaphor, in humanitarian relief as well as in peace and development programs, it is equally important to send the right doctor or, at least, to obtain a second opinion. A female interlocutor is more likely than her male counterpart to obtain the trust of a woman who has been raped. Similarly, for cultural and religious reasons, many women are reluctant to see male health care practitioners or psychosocial counselors. Women talking to women, however, can bring the female component to preventive diplomacy, conflict resolution, peacebuilding, development, and democracy.

In many countries of Latin America women previously uninvolved and uninterested in politics became active mostly through their roles as grandmothers, mothers, daughters, sisters, and wives while searching for information on the fate of their missing children and beloved. At a time when military dictatorship had silenced all political activity, only they took to the streets, thus becoming mobilizers of public opinion and catalysts for change. Through this process, "a collective female space and a uniquely female set of images were created."[52] Through their participation, many women underwent an important transformation. They learned about human rights and the legal means to protect them. Many of them joined nongovernmental organizations and became advocates for peace and democracy. They also developed networks of mutual support. Their legacy was vital in building the consensus for a return to democratic rule.

In other countries as well, women risked their lives for peace. In the Philippines, women, some of whom were nuns, prevented tanks from attacking rebelling troops trying to overthrow dictator Marcos, by creating a human barrier and forcing them to stop. In Croatia, in 1991, mothers and wives of soldiers went to the streets to demand an end to hostilities.

The testimonies of women who were part of peace operations under United Nations responsibility provide significant insights into their roles in this area. According to their experience, the involvement of women in these activities does not just fulfill the objective of increasing female participation toward the goal of gender equality, but also gives the opportunity that a particular female perspective be brought to the programmatic output as well as to the work environment. Women have shown to be essential in building trust and confidence, and in establishing lines of communication so needed in the processes of reconstruction and reconciliation. They are more inclined to socialize with local families, which allows them to have a firsthand feedback. They also have contributed with a new approach in regard to violence in the family and confrontation issues. In certain occasions, they have even been seen as role models for local women.[53]

These findings support the idea of the importance of fostering a broader involvement of women, particularly young women, in peace-making and peace-building activities. An equal participation of women could contribute to ensuring that a female perspective is also in place. In Namibia, for example, women reached groups that men had found difficult to address and participated in different community projects. This is deemed to have had a positive impact on women's participation. Because the electoral process involved a great deal of political reconciliation and mediation related to human rights, it was necessary to convince representatives from the contending parties to meet face to face—most of them for the first time—and to agree on a code of conduct for the elections. This took a great deal of persistence and cajoling, but women were willing to volunteer their time and efforts to attain the desired goals.[54] The same could be said of certain police work, such as going to the scene of a domestic dispute. Often, women were given this assignment and succeeded—they seemed to have a higher potential for calming a volatile situation.[55]

In South Africa, in the process led by the United Nations Observer Mission, the level of participation of women was even greater. First, the mission itself was headed by a woman. Second, women comprised approximately half of the staff of the mission, including its top positions.[56] This proportion, however, shifted toward male predominance as election day approached and governments sent their monitors.

The peace mission in El Salvador also incorporated women in positions of responsibility. Some were involved in policy making. Approximately half the regional offices were headed by women. Many more played important roles in the substantive professional areas of human rights, electoral assistance, and programs for the socioeconomic reintegration of ex-combatants and of those segments of the population most affected by the war.

War does not elude women, though peace often does. Even though women suffer extensively from war and more civilians die than soldiers, it is assumed that peace will "trickle down" to women from all-male high-level deliberations.[57] In Eritrea, where thousands of women fought side by side with men in the rebel army that gained that country's independence from Ethiopian rule in 1991, they later had to return to the deeply traditional and patriarchal society they had temporarily left when they joined the People's Liberation Front. "But if women who were guerrillas had hoped that fighting and dying in the war would change their status in Eritrean society, they have discovered instead that society's traditions die hard."[58] Women were crucial in war; in peace, however, their demands could be ignored. Peace did not quite "trickle down" to them the way they had expected.

In 1998 the UN Commission on the Status of Women studied the measures needed to accelerate the implementation of the strategic objectives of the Platform for Action on "Women and Armed Conflict," taking into account the Commission's convened conclusions on human rights of women and violence against women and female children. The Commission organized its recommendations[59] according to five strategic objectives: 1) ensure gender-sensitive justice; 2) address specific needs of women affected by armed conflict; 3) increase the participation of women in peacekeeping, peace-building, pre- and postconflict decision making, preventing conflict, postconflict resolution and reconstruction; 4) prevent conflict and promote a culture of peace; and 5) address disarmament measures, illicit arms trafficking, landmines, and small arms.

Regarding the increasing participation of women in peacekeeping, peace-building, pre- and postconflict decision making, the Commission recommended to governments and international and regional intergovernmental institutions the adoption of policies and measures, affirmative action included, with a view to increasing "women's participation and leadership in decision-making and in preventing conflict."[60] It also recommended to give full support to women's nongovernmental organizations, in particular at the grassroots level, to prevent conflict through early warning and peace-building. Likewise, the Commission emphasized the need of mainstreaming "a gender perspective into peace-promoting activities at all levels, as well as humanitarian and peace-building policies," and of encouraging the "participation of more female personnel at all levels."[61]

Toward the goal of preventing conflict and promoting a culture of peace, the Commission recommended "to ensure women's participation in the elaboration and implementation of strategies for preventing conflict."[62]

This chapter contends, therefore, that only resolved and energetic participation of women in preventive diplomacy, conflict prevention, and postconflict peace-building activities will ensure that they will continue to share responsibilities and be much more committed to a peace constructed in partnership with men, as opposed to one that benefits women as well, but to which they have been only passive witnesses.

FINAL REMARKS

As we look to the future in our aspiration for peace, it is hoped that women will play a greater role in all its aspects, from the identification and articulation of needs, values, and interests, to the representation of positions at the negotiating table. It is also hoped that women will remain vigilant to avoid yet another broken peace. Preventive diplomacy will find in women strong advocates and steadfast allies. Their potential, however, has to be first acknowledged and translated into figures.

So far, in the foreign services, the military, and the police of most countries, women are still a small minority. Therefore, they are practically excluded from decision making in those areas that are crucial in the processes for peace. This has so far precluded the possibility to reach a "critical mass," where one sex is no longer in a significant minority and can function naturally in these areas, thus enabling it to make its unique contribution both at the national and the international levels.

Peacemaking is a conflict resolution approach that attempts to transcend incompatibilities that impede human progress.[63] It does so by emphasizing common interests and goals over contradictory positions. Although the sexes are not really at war, much work needs to be done to develop a greater commonality of interest and goals between women and men.

The object of peace-building is to lay the foundations for democracy and to create a material environment that forestalls conflict. In this sense, it constitutes the "practical implication of peaceful social change through socioeconomic reconstruction and/or development" aimed at "reducing inequity and injustice."[64] Fuller participation of women and men in reconstruction, development, equity, and justice will result in a stronger and more stable peace.

Today, United Nations peacekeeping missions include more non-military/civilian components for preventive diplomacy, conflict resolution, peacemaking, and postconflict peace-building.[65] One might expect talented women to rise in civilian institutions, just as many talented men have done in the military; women, however, usually have not risen to the top in civilian peacekeeping positions either.[66] Peacekeeping operations should include more women at all levels. Women as peacemakers; women as bridges to women in societies at war; women as peacekeepers, keeping in touch with female victims and their children; women in peace-building, closing gaps between the female and male components of a society, healing the body politic.

A new way of thinking is, therefore, required in the future. A way of thinking that will overcome ingrained prejudices and misconceptions "in which the stereotyping of women and men gives way to a new philosophy that regards all people, irrespective of gender, as essential agents of change."[67] Only then will women and men be able to build an effective partnership for the prevention of conflict and the promotion of a healthier society.

NEUTRALITY OR IMPARTIALITY

ALAIN DESTEXHE, M.D.

The construction of a new world order and the evolution of the United Nations after World War II have been guided by the principle: Never again! The Nazis' unprecedented crimes became a benchmark for an international community founded on certain basic values: opposition to genocide, the search for world peace, and respect for human rights. However, over the years, that determination has been replaced by pragmatism. The United Nations, rendered powerless as a result of superpower hostility, found its role restricted to the provision of development aid. The end of the Cold War raised again the idea of an international community based on shared values, administered by international institutions, and defended by democratic countries. In the face of an increasing number of crises, the UN is now called upon regularly to encourage negotiation, to interpose itself, and to assist people at risk. However, the window of opportunity that seemed to be opening with the end of the Cold War is rapidly closing, and the idea that the UN could be the guarantor of world peace is far from being realized. The honeymoon period and the dreams of a "new world order" seem to be over. The major powers have made it clear that they will neither sanction the UN to be the world's police force nor take on the role themselves, not even the United States.

Fifty years after the creation of the UN and five years after the end of the Cold War, the international community showed its true colors: in Rwanda, it failed to react to the first indisputable genocide since that perpetrated against the Jews; in former Yugoslavia, it failed to react to the return of war and "ethnic cleansing" at the heart of Europe. Under the pretense of neutrality, its only response was humanitarian aid.

THE SHORTCOMINGS
OF THE "NEW HUMANITARIANISM"

There has been an unprecedented enthusiasm for humanitarian work throughout the world during recent years, yet it is far from certain that this is always in the victims' best interests. The end of the Cold War ushered in a "new humanitarianism," or "emergency ethic," that has become increasingly prevalent. There was an end to the practice of judging individual victims from an ideological perspective, seen as "good" or "bad," depending on which sphere of influence they were from (communist or noncommunist). Now, they became simply fellow human beings deserving of compassion. However, we were too quick to forget that Cold War values were also combined with realpolitik and that it was moral outrage converted into action that, above all, helped to counter totalitarian thinking. From Afghanistan to Angola, from Nicaragua to Cambodia, no one major Western power used humanitarian aid as its sole weapon against the Soviets, the Cubans, or the Vietnamese: political or military interventions were key components in a strategy of containment in which humanitarian aid played only a minor role.

However, the recent examples of Bosnia and Rwanda demonstrated that this "new humanitarianism" has moved a stage further and can rebound on those it is intended to help. These fellow human beings, fighting to defend values we share, have become "victims" to be assessed in terms of their immediate suffering; hungry mouths to feed, if they survive. Protesting that it was essential to remain neutral, Europe, and later the UN, provided humanitarian aid as their only real response to Serb aggression in Bosnia; the same response, based on the same claim to neutrality, was proffered in Rwanda—when the genocide was over and it was too late to influence the situation. Here the massive deployment of aid to the huge number of refugees became the focus of the world's attention, disguising the culpable failure of the international community to come to the assistance of the Tutsi people. In Bosnia humanitarian aid, elevated to the status of official policy, encouraged and fostered aggression while convincing public opinion to accept both the fait accompli by the stronger party and an "ethnic" reading of the conflict.

A BRIEF HISTORY OF NEUTRALITY

From a humanitarian point of view, the principle of neutrality cannot be separated from the history of the Red Cross. The movement was founded by Henry Dunant in 1863, in reaction to his horror at the slaughter he witnessed at the battle of Solferino.[1] This led him to define the principle enshrined in the first Geneva Convention for the protection of wounded soldiers and to set up the neutral Red Cross agency to care for them. Subsequent Conventions extended this neutrality to other noncombatants: civilians and prisoners of war. The almost universally acknowledged Geneva Conventions remain the cornerstone of the Red Cross, a movement that has seen an enormous expansion in membership over the years. The Geneva Conventions represent a fundamental stage in the history of humanitarian action, first, because they enshrine the principle of neutrality applied to noncombatants, and second, because of the importance of the International Committee of the Red Cross, universally recognized for its total respect for the principles of neutrality and impartiality.

Dunant did not invent the concept of neutrality. Indeed, since the earliest times there have been many examples of neutral behavior during conflicts and of bilateral agreements aimed at respecting the wounded, civilians, and prisoners. But it was Dunant who had the genius to see that the principle enshrined in a convention would be universally respected. His wish has been realized; the four Conventions now in force, signed in 1949, have now been ratified by 165 countries, almost every country in existence today. Thanks to Dunant, the Red Cross is an agency backed by international law, to which it can refer when calling on warring parties to respect a certain number of basic rules in regard to the treatment of the wounded, both prisoners and civil populations.

However, despite this undeniable progress, the Red Cross principle of neutrality was soon brought into question and the difficulties that it presents have not been resolved. First, the principle of neutrality certainly could be applied to pitched battles between the armies of European countries that shared much the same ideology. But it was rendered null and void when, in the name of civilization, the white man attacked "barbarians." Then humanitarian law ceased to apply. The British, for example, after the battle of Omdurman, in the Sudan, did nothing to assist fifteen thousand wounded enemy soldiers. Yet this was 1898, thirty years after Britain had signed the first Geneva Convention.[2] The principle of neutrality was conceived with a civil war in mind, or a war of two opposing comparable forces. What relevance did it have in a war of aggression or in a case of systematic genocide such as that perpetrated by the Young Turks against the Armenians? Chateaubriand, the French writer, gives the answer: "Such a neutrality is derisory for it works against the weaker party and plays into the hands of the stronger party. It would be better to join forces with the oppressors against the oppressed for at least that would avoid adding hypocrisy to injustice."

Second, although the Red Cross is a private institution, it has always depended on national governments to enforce respect for humanitarian law. In order to avoid embarrassing Convention signatories, it has constrained itself to the discrete silence that is an essential part of the Red Cross image. In fact, over several decades the International Committee for the Red Cross (ICRC) has limited itself to transmitting protests from one party to another during a conflict without ever commenting on their validity. Meanwhile, many national Red Cross organizations, far from being apolitical or neutral, seem to have taken on the role of faithful government helpers.

The Red Cross grew up at the end of the nineteenth century, in a period of liberal ideas. Lenin and, to a greater extent, Hitler confronted it with regimes that were fundamentally opposed to the values on which it is founded. Forced to decide between respect for humanitarian principles and the universality of the movement, the Red Cross has always chosen the second alternative, persuaded—and not without reason—that only thus could it continue to play the role of a neutral intermediary in conflicts. The Red Cross has never broken off relations with a country's government; not with Mussolini, not with Lenin, and not with Nazi Germany, not even when Jews were expelled from the German Red Cross.

Although this was not clearly understood at the time, it was when faced with the "Final Solution" that the limits of humanitarian action really showed themselves. The Red Cross, as well as the Allies and the Vatican, knew about the terrible reality of the Nazi extermination camps. And today it is still reproached for never denouncing them and keeping silent about the largest-scale genocide in the twentieth century. Worse still, despite everything, the Red Cross tried to assist those held in the death camps by handing over aid packages for them, without any control whatsoever, to the German authorities. No matter the reasons the Red Cross presents as justification for its silence, the stance it took represents a black page in the history of the movement.[3] One result has been that the role played by the ICRC in other domains (prisoners of war, tracking down and reuniting family members, and so on) has received less attention than it deserves. Neutrality might have been an issue in regard to the German and Allied armies, but how could it be evoked in the face of the Nazi extermination camps? Organizations that aim to be "sans frontieres" ("without borders") were founded on lessons learned from that experience. The inhuman must not be humanized; it must be denounced and it must be fought against. Such organizations consider that they have a dual role to play: they provide aid to victims in the field, but they also speak out as witnesses to intolerable events.

The Biafra crisis was another important stage in the evolution of the humanitarian movement. On the one hand, it again underlined the limits of the Red Cross's "neutral" approach. It was unable to achieve an agreement between the two parties in order to allow food to get through to the Biafran enclave. It was a group of churches that finally decided to disregard the objections of the Nigerian government and the Red Cross and launched an air bridge to the encircled Biafran secessionists.[4] The churches thus invented the modern concept of humanitarian intervention, while making a significant breach in the principle of sovereignty that has so often been used as an excuse for nonintervention, and that is still invoked today.

The stance taken by the Western powers during the Biafran crisis foreshadowed the treatment of the Bosnian crisis, when all the major powers played the humanitarian card without ever looking for a political solution. France, for example, openly encouraged Biafra to secede, but it neither recognized the secessionist government nor provided arms to allow it to stand against Lagos. Unfortunately, Biafra's leaders soon learned that pictures of their starving children were the best weapon for ensuring an international response and famine became inseparable from the conflict itself.[5] When the time came to sum up, it was clear that the amount of humanitarian aid provided was always ridiculously small in comparison with the scale of the tragedy, although sufficient to allow the great powers to maintain the illusion of an international commitment. The world was convinced that it had flown to the rescue of Biafra: television images were proving more convincing than reality.

The guerrilla-style conflicts of the 1980s are an even clearer illustration of the limits to neutrality. The Red Cross and UN agencies, refused access to guerilla zones, had to choose between maintaining a presence that provided support exclusively to the government side or withdrawing completely. "Sans frontieres" organizations were much better suited to provide assistance in that period of guerilla wars. They could intervene clandestinely in most of these conflicts via neighboring countries, in defiance of international law and the niceties of national sovereignty. Unlike the Red Cross, this type of organization does not rely on humanitarian law but on the backing of public opinion aroused by witness accounts of massacres and aggression. Most of the larger-scale conflicts of the 1980s were indirect consequences of the growing influence of the USSR and her allies in developing countries, which became the battlefields where the Cold War was fought by proxy. As a result, consciously or unconsciously, humanitarian aid became a powerful instrument in the anti-Soviet struggle throughout the world as more than 90 percent of refugees during this period were fleeing from "progressive" regimes allied to the USSR. Humanitarian assistance was provided both to populations that could only be reached by the clandestine intervention of "sans frontieres" organizations, and to those in refugee camps set up on the borders of neighboring countries, which also served as sanctuaries for the guerrillas. It was at this time that the UN High Commission on Refugees (UNHCR), working in such refugee camps, developed into one of the most important agencies in the aid system.

If it was during the 1980s that the serious flaws in the concept of humanitarian neutrality became very apparent; it was in former Yugoslavia and in Rwanda that they came to be seen at their most perverse.

BOSNIA: THE "PLACEBO" EFFECT

The war that was fought in Bosnia for over three years claimed two hundred thousand victims, most of them civilian, and turned four million people into refugees and displaced persons. This conflict, the first on European soil since 1945, began in April 1992, the day the Republic of Bosnia-Herzegovina was recognized by the European Community (EC) and the United States. When Bosnian Serb forces, with the support of the Yugoslav federal army, quickly seized almost 70 percent of the new republic's territory, the Western powers appeared to acquiesce in this fait accompli, confining their response to reopening Sarajevo airport and deploying Blue Helmets in an attempt to help those most in need.

Although newspaper editorials had forecast war in Bosnia months before it finally broke out, there were no attempts to try to prevent it. The populations of Bosnia's towns and villages forced to leave their homes were not only the principal victims of the combat, but also the target of the whole pitiless conflict. Europe, reduced to the role of a charitable though powerless witness, raised no obstacle to ethnic cleansing in Bosnia, which was at times carried out under "humanitarian protection."

In fact, in a war being waged with the ultimate aim of excluding and expelling a large part of the population, humanitarian workers faced an impossible dilemma. There were two choices. Either they assisted people to evacuate so that they could be protected, which inevitably helped to achieve the objectives of ethnic cleansing, or they refused to ally themselves with such inhumane acts and left people to endure even more terrible suffering. The major preoccupation was no longer to provide material assistance but to protect the people, which has never been in the mandate of humanitarian organizations, but should have been included in that of the Blue Helmets. Thus, humanitarian action was reduced to feeding the mass of refugees. UNHCR representatives, delegated by the UN and EC to coordinate aid in the former Yugoslavia, had to decide countless times during the conflict which was the lesser of two such evils. Trying to protect refugees without having the power to prevent them from becoming refugees in the first place not only undermines humanitarian principles but actually aggravates the problem.

Paradoxically, humanitarianism, while siding with the victims, also became an arm of the aggressors. The Serbian army quickly realized the advantages to be gained from opening up "corridors of ethnic cleansing" for those they were expelling and bringing them to the "humanitarian front line." Indeed, on several occasions, the UN Protection Force (UNPROFOR) directly contributed to the enforcement of ethnic cleansing by "helping" in the exchange of population. In some ways, the humanitarian effort unintentionally served to help achieve Serbian military objectives because the ethnic cleansers were only too happy to hand over responsibility for the victims of their crimes to the international community.

The distribution of aid was subject to the acquiescence of the Serbs who opened and closed the tap to the aid pipeline as and when it suited them, but never without deducting a substantial levy. For more than a year, the encircled towns and villages of eastern Bosnia received no aid at all as UNPROFOR convoys never used force to get through.

Humanitarian arguments are used to explain the failure of governments to make clear strategic decisions. But the real question is whether humanitarian work should have been entrusted to UN troops in the first place. When peacekeepers are sent into the middle of a war, they may be expected to use their weapons. If relief work is impeded by violence, then the obvious role of armed UN troops is to protect relief convoys and oppose the people who are obstructing them. Unlike Somalia, in Bosnia the humanitarian problems were not the result of a general breakdown of order but of Serbian aggression. If force had any role to play in relieving human suffering in Bosnia, it should have been used to protect the population against the armed thugs who were massacring, raping, looting, and driving away people from their homes. But that was never the intention.

Many NGOs wish governments would leave humanitarian work alone and concentrate on the roles proper to them, which are political and military. In Bosnia humanitarian problems had political causes that governments failed to acknowledge and deal with. UNPROFOR was used in a humanitarian role as the alibi for the international community's disastrous cop-out, making it appear something was being done while failing miserably to react in the politico-military sphere, the only arena for resolving the root causes.

FROM "TOTAL WAR" TO "TOTAL HUMANITARIANISM"

World War II taught Western democracies that no spoon is long enough for supping with the devil. "Never again!" cried Europe in unison, and a whole generation grew up under the influence of this, rejecting all ideas of racial purity and territorial ambition. But this belief system was shattered the first time that Europe was again confronted from within by a racist policy based on religion and ethnic group. From that moment, history was forgotten and all the certainties and idealism flew out of the window; the countries of Europe started to behave as if they had learned nothing. Admittedly, there seemed only a small risk of the conflict spreading and becoming more generalized. Admittedly, Milosevic, or Karadzic, is not Hitler. Nevertheless, the Bosnian disaster flouted all the ideals on which the European democracies were founded in the aftermath of World War II, and no real attempt was made to defend them.

It was Winston Churchill who developed the concept of a "total warfare" against Nazism, enforcing land, sea, and air blockades that even prevented food getting through to Occupied Europe. The deterioration in health that inevitably resulted was seen as a weapon in this form of total war where politics forced humanitarianism off the stage. Although this concept posed a dilemma from a humanitarian point of view, the Allies were convinced that it was justifiable. In Bosnia, we passed from one extreme to the other, from the concept of "total war" to that of "total humanitarianism"; people were provided with food but not protection, and no real political pressure was put on the aggressor. The logic of humanitarianism prevailed over the logic of a politics that did not dare exercise its prerogatives for fear of endangering humanitarian efforts in the field. The question of what would have been the best course of action from the victims' point of view was made totally subordinate to that of how the international community could avoid involving itself in military intervention. Certainly food got through to Sarajevo most of the time and the impressive humanitarian effort saved the life of tens of thousands of people throughout the area. Certainly the presence of the Blue Helmets on the ground had a moderating effect. But what about Vukovar, Gorazde, and Srebrenica? Should we really be congratulating ourselves that fifty years after the creation of the UN we were unable to stop that kind of slaughter?

Despite the sop it offered to European public opinion, in the short term, humanitarianism achieved little. In the longer term, it served as an alibi for political impotence. Finally, in September 1995, under strong pressure from an American government that finally decided to involve itself more actively, air strikes were directed at Serb military targets and the Dayton Agreement led to the establishment of a NATO-led international task. But it was all too late to avoid the inevitable: the separation of Bosnia into separate, ethnically based ministates, that may yet divide even further. When they were confronted once again with Milosevic's intransigence, this time in Kosovo, Europe and the United States utilized the hard lessons learned from Bosnia.

RWANDA: FROM INDIFFERENCE TO COMPASSION

What took place in Rwanda between April and July 1994 was a genocide: an exceptional event in twentieth-century history. The term was first coined in 1944 by Raphael Lemkin[6] and is the basis of the UN General Assembly's convention committing member countries to punish and prevent genocide.[7] This convention, passed in 1949, defines genocide very specifically as those "acts committed with intent to destroy a national, ethnic, racial, or religious group." By applying it too generally, this specific meaning has been so watered down, taken out of context, and misused by those seeking to draw attention to other horrors that the real intention behind this particular crime has been lost and the word genocide has become synonymous with any act of mass murder. In fact, only three instances of mass slaughter the twentieth century can correctly be called genocide: the massacres of Armenians under the Ottoman Empire in 1915 and 1916, the extermination of the Jews and Gypsies under the Nazis, and the 1994 slaughter of over half a million Tutsis by Hutu militias in Rwanda.[8]

When the massacres first began in Kigali, the world turned its back and the UN decided to pull out its main body of Blue Helmets. Yet the death toll was increasing daily, and within four weeks it was estimated that over half a million people had been killed. But the genocide could have been stopped early on if two moves had been made. The UN could have used its troops to protect the churches, hospitals, schools, and other places where Tutsis were desperately seeking refuge, and the UN could have clearly recognized the Rwandan Patriotic Front (RPF) as the legitimate government of Rwanda and broken off relations with the government that initiated the genocide. Such measures would have changed the course of Rwanda's history, but they were not implemented. Again, the Security Council of the United Nations decided to remain neutral and not to take sides with the RPF.

By the end of June 1994 the crisis in Rwanda was seen exclusively as a humanitarian catastrophe affecting hundreds of thousands of (Hutu) refugees, arousing international compassion, and completely distracting attention from the genocide that had more or less run its course because there were no more (Tutsi) victims available for slaughter. As the RPF troops advanced, the architects and instigators of the genocide organized a mass exodus of the Hutu population into rapidly erected refugee camps in Goma (Zaire) and Tanzania, or into the French-controlled security zone within Rwanda. The former government planned this deliberately so they could claim that the RPF might have won the land, but not its people.

Humanitarian aid poured into the camps, fueled by the generosity of a public moved by television pictures of cholera victims in Goma. However, although such aid may be well intended and based on sound principles, as has already been pointed out, it can never be totally neutral. In this case, as so often elsewhere, it represented almost the only source of food, equipment, and jobs in the camps and thus became a major stake in the power struggle for control over the refugees. Humanitarian workers were continually confronted with the same problem: how to aid the victims without getting caught up in the power game being played by their oppressors, or in this case militias who were acting as the strong arm of the politicians in the camps.

The problem was (is) that the refugees settled commune by commune in the camps under the direction of the local leaders who had accompanied them. But this situation posed a major ethical problem inasmuch as these leaders, who were also implicated in the genocide, retained their authority over the refugees and passed on instructions to them from the former government-in-exile. It is with such people that the aid agencies have to collaborate.

It is useful to draw a parallel here with the way in which the Khmer Rouge were able to gain power over Cambodian refugees by manipulating humanitarian aid. At the beginning of 1979 the Khmer Rouge, who were responsible for the massacre of a million of their fellow Cambodians, fled before the advancing Vietnamese army. Using force and propaganda, they took with them hundreds of thousands of civilians into refugee camps in the frontier area with Thailand, where they experienced dreadful famine. The international community mobilized, although more slowly than would happen today, and thousands of lives were saved. But the humanitarian effort also fed the Khmer Rouge and inadvertently helped them to establish their control over the refugee population, enabling them to continue the conflict for a further decade.

It is clear that the international relief effort in Rwanda has created a similar vicious circle, fed by aid that could at worst grow into a future conflict and at best ensures that the Hutu refugees remain in the camps. This is the result of treating the Rwandan crisis as a purely humanitarian matter when it was first and foremost a political issue. Other measures could have been taken, for example, early deployment of human rights observers in Rwanda, increasing the amount of aid distributed directly through Kigali, reestablishing the justice system as quickly as possible, and organizing a Nuremberg-style trial for the main instigators of the genocide. If the right conditions had been provided, many humanitarian organizations were convinced that most of the refugees would have returned home. Instead, it is very likely that the world will have to assist two million refugees for a period that could stretch into years, war may well break out again, and further aid will be required for future victims. Political inaction thus risks a much stronger negative effect on the situation than the positive effects of the marvelous outpouring of solidarity that swept the world in 1994.

Humanitarian action provided a way of responding to the crisis while continuing conveniently to overlook the fact that a genocide had taken place, until the situation had evolved to the point where it could be ignored completely. In a world where humanitarian aid seems almost the only international response to a crisis, aid that neither can nor will make a distinction between different categories of victim, all catastrophes are treated alike and reduced to their lowest common denominator—compassion on the part of the onlooker. Certainly all victims merit our care and consideration, whether they be Tutsis suffering as a result of genocide or their murderers forced to become refugees and struck by cholera. Humanitarian action is at the service of all victims: it seeks to care for and feed them and does not take sides. But goodwill on its own is not enough and humanitarian aid is useless if it is not accompanied by political action and efforts to achieve justice.

Humanitarian action transforms any dramatic event—crime, epidemics, natural disasters—into catastrophes for which it seems that nobody is ever given the blame. Humanitarianism also masks the obligation and the necessity to intervene in other ways and acts as a defense against any possible future accusation of nonassistance to persons in danger. There are only a handful of individuals who might risk speaking out in the middle of a catastrophe, when donations are rolling in, to point out that giving food and drink to people who have lost everything in the wake of horrendous massacres is only the least that can be done. Unfortunately, any kind of debate along these lines is usually pursued when it is too late to be anything other than theoretical. It only can be usefully carried on while a crisis is occurring and some practical resolutions can be reached. Leave it too long and those who should be accused of mass murder have succeeded in rehabilitating themselves politically and become parties to the debate.

In short, confronted with the first unquestionable genocide since the Nazi Holocaust, the world reacted with indifference. It was the sight of hundreds of thousands of refugees pouring out of Rwanda and the subsequent cholera epidemic that aroused compassion and led to a purely humanitarian intervention. This was a convenient cover-up for nonintervention at the political or military level and allowed Western governments to look good because they appeared to be doing something. The refusal of the UN and the principle countries that should have been involved to take a firm stand against the former criminal regime in Rwanda allowed them to remain neutral in the face of the planned extermination of a population. But the concept of neutrality has no sense when a genocide is being carried out.

THE LIMITS OF HUMANITARIAN ACTION

Humanitarian action has acquired a monopoly on morality and international action in ongoing wars of a local nature. But if it is not coupled with political action and justice, it is doomed to failure: it can work as a palliative, not as a panacea. Even worse, when held up to the limelight by the media for its work during a major crisis, it becomes little more than a plaything of international politics, a conscience-saving gimmick. There is an enormous disparity today between the principles and values proclaimed by our democratic societies on the one hand, and the measures taken to defend them on the other. In summary, although we may take great satisfaction in commemorating past victories over tyranny, the historical lesson was not sufficiently well absorbed to move us into action against the first indisputable genocide since World War II in Rwanda or the return of ethnic cleansing to the heart of Europe.

For the international community to claim neutrality is a shaky defense of inaction. To be neutral is defined in the dictionary as "not assisting either party in the case of a war between other states."[9] The Red Cross is more specific: "In order to maintain the confidence of all parties, the Red Cross withholds from taking sides in hostilities and never takes sides in political, racial, religious or philosophical controversies." This is a radical interpretation of neutrality that suits the very specific mandate of the Red Cross (especially in regard to prisoners of war). However, if applied generally by the international community, NGOs, the UN, and individual states, there may be disastrous consequences for populations in danger.

A claim of neutrality may make sense in the context of fratricidal civil wars or countries such as Somalia, Liberia, or Afghanistan that are falling apart at the center and are sometimes referred to as "failed states." But it makes no sense at all in the case of genocide, where neutrality is reduced to the weakest possible definition of "indifference"[10] and succeeds only in removing every distinction between the victims and those who victimize them. A number of humanitarian organizations have found a very comfortable refuge in neutrality on the intellectual level, which provides them with an excuse not to question the sense or the consequences of humanitarian action. Indeed, neutrality can become a refuge large enough to accept inhuman policies.

Whether working at the heart of conflicts, the course of which they influence, or where faced with governments and totalitarian parties that are void of any scruple, humanitarian organizations are always faced with two recurring and related questions in the long term: first, to use the expression of William Shawcross, "how to feed the victims without also providing aid to their tormentors,"[11] and second, how to avoid humanitarian aid involuntarily having a negative effect on the victims instead of improving their situation. These questions often take on a sharper meaning in extreme crisis situations. It is self-evident that humanitarian action saves human lives. But it also risks a series of induced and secondary consequences that are extremely important. In Somalia food and other resources provided by the humanitarian organizations helped keep the conflict alive because gangs of armed bandits also benefited from it. Such aid often helps to prolong and modify the course of a conflict in other ways, because humanitarian organizations require authorization from the warring parties in order to have access to victims and this renders them vulnerable to blackmail, manipulation, and all sorts of other pressures.

ALTERNATIVE REACTIONS

DIAGNOSIS

A doctor's duty toward a sick patient is first to establish a diagnosis before undertaking a treatment and this principle should be applied just as systematically by the international community when faced with a crisis situation. We have too often seen a cure attempted before any serious analysis of the situation has been carried out. This results in a rash and unreflective prescribing of the type that largely explains the failures in international responses to Rwanda and the former Yugoslavia. Intervention should be a question of timely reaction motivated by political rather than humanitarian intentions. When the UN has to deal with a deadly conflict, it should analyze what is at stake for the parties involved, particularly the civilian population, and then base its response on a clear distinction between two kinds of conflict.

On the one hand, there may be a clear-cut, unilateral aggression by a very much stronger party against another. Recent examples of this would be Bosnia and Rwanda. In such cases, the UN cannot remain neutral. It must stand with the victims and the "weaker side" against the aggressor, and military intervention should at least be seriously considered. However, given that this might entail a risk of involvement over a long period, urgent consideration should also be given to other possible actions, including the use of diplomatic or economic sanctions. What is important is that the international community show a clear signal that it will no longer stand by helplessly in the face of massacres and the slaughter of civilians.

In Bosnia, during the spring and summer of 1992, a choice had to be made between allowing Serbia's Milosevic and Karadzic to seize territory and practice ethnic cleansing, or supporting the multinational government led by Bosnia's President Izetbegovic. The second alternative is the only one worthy of honest consideration. In Rwanda, as soon as it became obvious that Habyarimana's regime and his armed forces were conducting a genocide, the only morally responsible choice was to support the forces of the RPF, who could have halted the genocide. In cases such as these, it should be clear which is the right choice to make.

On the other hand, the conflict may take the form of a general breakdown in civil order with no clear-cut issues, no central authority in command, and an increasing number of warring factions and militias out of control. This would describe the situations in Somalia, Afghanistan, and Liberia. The UN must recognize that very little can be done to prevent or stop this kind of conflict and that its role is to avoid the ultimate collapse of the state and the prolonged suffering of civilians. Every diplomatic measure must be considered, and the earlier the better; the art of preventive diplomacy should be practiced far more often. Humanitarian assistance must, of course, be maintained impartially throughout the course of this type of conflict.

Most crises are a complex mixture of both models and there are some conflicts that do not fit neatly into either description; therefore, diagnosis is even more essential. Other political considerations complicate the situation even more. It is clear that it is not possible to react in the same way to Russia's intervention in Chechnya as to, for example, an attack on Belize by Guatemala. The principal point that must be recognized is that the international community and the UN failed in Rwanda and Bosnia because of a refusal to define and categorize the crises before responding to them.

IMPARTIALITY

Neutrality is a highly problematic concept. The official Red Cross definition is the following, "it means not taking sides—military or ideological—in hostilities or engaging at any time in controversies of a political, racial, religious or ideological nature." This is a radical definition. This definition presumes that no distinction is made between, for example, a racist authoritarian regime and democratic forces, between victims and their executioners. It also presumes that the crimes committed cannot be qualified because the parties to a conflict will never agree on the meaning of terms such as genocide or crimes against humanity. This definition of neutrality seems dangerous as it takes no account of the necessary distinction between criminal and other politically motivated actions, or the level of gravity of the acts committed.

There is an alternative to neutrality that does not pose these kinds of problems and that is impartiality. Whereas neutrality focuses on the warring parties, impartiality focuses on the victims as individuals. In this sense, impartiality means making no distinction between the victims with regard to race, ethnic origin, political, philosophical, religious, or other beliefs. In humanitarian terms, it primarily means to stress equality of all those who are in distress, with the only priority given based on the acuteness of the need for help. It does not mean reserving judgment of a political nature, but rather recognizing the validity and rights of an individual in distress. Were this concept to be emphasized by the international community and its official bodies (UN, and so on) in situations of deadly conflict, the rights of the victims would pass before that of any such ambiguous concept or excuse of neutrality or sovereignty. There would then be greater freedom to react in a variety of ways, and countries could no longer refuse to do more than provide an exclusively humanitarian response.

JUSTICE

It is essential that those responsible for formulating, instigating, and carrying out genocide, crimes against humanity, or ethnic cleansing be brought to trial. Justice is not only a moral imperative but a political necessity: ensuring that justice is seen to be done will discourage others from carrying out further mass crimes. Justice is necessary not only for the victims, but also for international order. There is an enormous potential in the world today for crises with an ethnic dimension. The greatest threat to society internationally is the rebirth of racist ideologies, with their racial hierarchies that reject and exclude all others. From Burma to Sudan, the Caucasus to the former Yugoslavia, Bosnia, and Zaire, such racism is flourishing. Only the threat of punishment for mass murder will make leaders think twice before playing the ethnic card to tighten their slackening grip on power. The special tribunal for former Yugoslavia will be the first test of international determination; the second will be that based in Arusha, Tanzania, to deal with those who planned and organized the extermination of the Tutsis in

Rwanda—if the countries sheltering these criminals can be persuaded to hand them over. Justice must play a more important role in international relations and could become a powerful instrument of preventive diplomacy.

CONCLUSION

Humanitarian action sometimes shows humanity at its most noble, providing assistance to victims, fellow human beings trying to regain control over their own destiny. When the international community, supposedly still acting in the name of humanity, reduces human beings to the status of mere biological organisms by providing food in the place of the military and political support they so desperately need and ask for,[12] then it must stand accused of complicity in a massive crime against humanity: nonassistance to people in danger. It must be stated one more time that passing food through the window when nothing is being done to get the assassin out of the house is not a humanitarian act. When hostages are taken, the first priority is to overcome the hostage-takers, not to feed the hostages while they are eliminated one by one.

To sum up, humanitarian problems are always the result of some more profound problem and cannot be solved by humanitarian means alone. In cases of aggression, crimes against humanity, and genocide, the international community can no longer invoke neutrality and be satisfied with an exclusively humanitarian approach, rendering it an accomplice to the most criminal regimes. If humanitarian assistance is to be worthy of its name, it must work in parallel with efforts to meet the demands of justice and respect for human rights.

8

CHANGING CONCEPTS OF
DISPLACEMENT AND SOVEREIGNTY

FRANCIS DENG

Displacement in all its manifestations, internal and external, has become a global crisis of grave and escalating magnitude. Since the end of the Cold War, the number of people displaced within the borders of their own countries has soared to an estimated twenty to twenty-five million, and the number of refugees is now estimated at over eleven million. Statistics indicate that although the number of refugees appears to be declining, the internally displaced populations worldwide seem to be increasing, a trend that suggests a correlation: as the right of asylum is restricted by governments, potential refugees join the ranks of the internally displaced. These are people who have been forced or obliged to flee or to leave their homes or places of habitual residence, in particular as a result of or in order to avoid the effects of armed conflict, situations of generalized violence, violations of human rights, or natural or human-made disasters.[1]

Nearly always, internally displaced persons suffer from conditions of insecurity and destitution, and they are acutely in need of protection and survival services. Whereas refugees have an established system of international protection and assistance, those who are displaced internally fall within the domestic jurisdiction and, therefore, under the sovereignty of the state concerned, without established legal or institutional bases for their protection and assistance.

This chapter has had to reconcile the basic theme of the book, which is preventive diplomacy, and the fact that displacement is an event that has already taken place. The concept of curative prevention is an attempt to resolve this paradox. It is based on the premise that displacement poses a challenge to the international community to develop norms, institutions, and operational strategies for preventing internal displacement, addressing its consequences once it occurs, finding solutions that would ensure people's safe return, reintegration into existing social services, and opportunities for self-reliant development.

It was to address the mounting crisis of internal displacement worldwide that the Secretary-General of the United Nations, at the request of the Commission on Human Rights, appointed me as his Representative on Internally Displaced Persons in 1992, initially for one year, to prepare a comprehensive study of the problem, its causes and consequences, relevant international legal standards and institutional arrangements, the degree to which they provide adequate coverage, and what needs to be done to remedy any gaps that might exist. The mandate has since been extended, first for two years following the submission of the comprehensive study, and subsequently for two three-year terms in 1995 and 1998, through to 2001. In addition to ongoing studies, I have embarked on a program of country visits to see the conditions of the displaced on the ground, to dialogue with governments and other pertinent actors on their behalf, and to report annually to the Commission on Human Rights and the General Assembly and, of course, to keep the Secretary-General informed.[2]

Displacement is not the disease, but a symptom of a public health epidemic with deep-rooted causes. Treating the symptoms or easing the pain through humanitarian assistance is only a first step toward the challenge of diagnosing the disease and attacking it from its root causes. A comprehensive strategy in response to the crisis of displacement must build on the three phases of the problem—causes, consequences, and solutions. Addressing the causes requires going beyond the mere fact of conflicts, communal violence, or human rights violations to appreciate the even deeper root causes. These are often reflected in the traumas of nation-building, involving crises of identity, historical denial of democratic liberties and fundamental human rights, and the deprivations of poverty and severe underdevelopment. Consequences relate to the humanitarian tragedies that result from violent conflicts, gross violations of human rights, and the sudden massive displacement they generate. Remedies envisage both a response to the emergency needs of the situation and a search for lasting solutions. In other words, the corresponding themes of response would be prevention; protection and assistance; and a secure process of return or permanent settlement in another area, rehabilitation, reintegration, and sustainable development. Action at these three phases must aim at balancing sovereignty, responsibility, and international accountability.

Discharging the preventive responsibilities of sovereignty must begin with addressing the root causes of displacement. As Mrs. Sadako

Ogata, UN High Commissioner for Refugees, has correctly observed, "Whether we speak of refugees or of internally displaced persons, it is clear that there will be no end to their plight until the international community has found ways to deal effectively with the root causes of forced displacement, so as to prevent or alleviate conditions before people flee."[3] Recent years have witnessed a strategic shift in the operational principles of the UNHCR. The new approach "is proactive and preventive, rather than reactive. Instead of focusing purely on countries of asylum, it is equally concerned with conditions in actual and potential refugee-producing states. And as well as providing protection and assistance to refugees, it seeks to reinforce the security and freedom enjoyed by several other groups: internally displaced people; refugees who have returned to their own country; war-affected communities and those who are at risk of being uprooted."[4]

Once displacement has occurred, priority then shifts to providing the affected population with protection and assistance. These functions should normally fall under the responsibilities of sovereignty, but in conflict situations the state often lacks the political will to discharge those responsibilities. Involving the international community to fill the vacuum of state responsibility means negotiating access against the obstacles of defensive state sovereignty. As Mrs. Ogata remarked in 1992, "How to secure the protection of the internally displaced and ensure their access to humanitarian assistance is one of the most important challenges facing the international community. Meeting this challenge will require the development of institutional and practical mechanisms."[5] There have since been important developments in both these areas, which will be highlighted in the course of this chapter.

MAGNITUDE OF THE CRISIS

Displacement is generally a consequence of conflict, which, in turn, is a symptom of deeper societal problems. Conflict occurs when two or more parties interact in pursuit of incompatible objectives, which may involve material or immaterial values. Various forms and degrees of conflict are pervasive features of normal life and, for the most part, are negotiated and resolved by the parties or by third-party mediators. Governance is primarily a function of preventing, managing, and resolving conflicts. The kind of conflicts that generate internal displacement, however, are generally of a more severe nature, involving deadly violence. As a result of these conflicts, much destruction to life and property is pervasive throughout the world; governments have disintegrated and entire regions have been destabilized, with devastating humanitarian consequences; and masses of uprooted populations in the affected countries survive on emergency relief supplies, displaced within their own countries or forced across international borders as refugees.

It is often argued that the internally displaced should be considered and treated like refugees who have not crossed international borders. The analogy is compelling. And yet, the border factor is crucial in legal and institutional terms to qualify one as a refugee who is thereby entitled to receive international protection and assistance. Even more significantly, while the refugee is outside the national framework of conflict and political persecution, the internally displaced, who would be a refugee if he or she had crossed international borders, remains trapped within those borders, a potential victim not only of conflict, but also of the persecution emanating from it and alienated from the government that is supposed to be a source of protection and support for citizens.

Overwhelmingly, such persons live in a hostile environment, often deprived of such survival needs as food, shelter, and medicine, frequently subjected to roundups, forcible resettlement, arbitrary detentions or arrests, forced conscription, and sexual assaults. Some of the highest mortality rates ever recorded during humanitarian emergencies have come from situations involving internally displaced persons. According to surveys conducted by the U.S. Centers for Disease Control, the death rates among internally displaced have been as much as sixty times higher than those of nondisplaced within the same country.[6]

Compounding the crisis is the nature of the conflicts in which the population is often caught up. Internal conflicts are frequently marked by few or no accepted ground rules. These wars, as former UN Secretary-General Boutros Boutros-Ghali observed in his Supplement to an Agenda for Peace, are "often of a religious or ethnic character and often involving unusual violence and cruelty."[7]

> They are usually fought not only by regular armies but also
> by militias and armed civilians with little discipline and
> with ill-defined chains of command. They are often guer-
> rilla wars without clear front lines. Civilians are the main
> victims and often the main targets. Humanitarian emergen-
> cies are commonplace and the combatant authorities, in so
> far as they can be called authorities, lack the capacity to
> cope with them. The number of refugees registered with the

Office of the United Nations High Commissioner for Refugees (UNHCR) has increased from 13 million at the end of 1987 to 26 million at the end of 1994. The number of internally displaced persons has increased even more dramatically.[8]

"Today's belligerents," a Foreign Policy Association study points out, "are more and more willing to use humanitarian access, life-saving assistance, and even civilians themselves as weapons in their political-military struggles."[9] The challenge posed by the situation of internally displaced persons and refugees is both to allow them to flee from danger and to ensure their right to remain. As Mrs. Ogata observed, "We must prevent refugee flows, not by building barriers or border controls but by defending the right of people to remain in peace in their own homes and their own countries."[10] The mere fact that people are forced to leave their homes to escape from conflict or persecution implies the violation of fundamental human rights, among them "the right to life, liberty and security of person, the right not to be subjected to torture or other degrading treatment, the right to privacy and family life, the right to freedom of movement and residence, and the right not to be subjected to arbitrary exile."[11] Curative prevention, which means securing the right to remain at home in peace, the right to protection and assistance during displacement, and the right to return home safely and reintegrate into a secure life therefore requires ensuring respect for the human rights of every person. This depends on the willingness of states to accept responsibility for their own citizens and the role of the international community "to foster responsibility as well as accountability of states as regards the treatment of their own citizens."[12]

Much has been written and said about the need for early warning and preventive measures. It is also increasingly acknowledged that most conflicts that have resulted in gruesome humanitarian tragedies have not been the result of lack of early warning, but rather because of lack of the political will on the part of the international community to act in appropriate time. As the former UN Secretary-General Boutros Boutros-Ghali noted in his Supplement to an Agenda for Peace, "Experience has shown that the greatest obstacle to success in these endeavors is not, as is widely supposed, lack of information, analytical capacity or ideas for United Nations initiative. Success is often blocked at the outset by the reluctance of one or other of the parties to accept United Nations help."[13]

Early warning and prevention essentially mean understanding the sources of potential conflicts and addressing them in time to abort their explosion into violent confrontation. Once a conflict has actually broken out, there is then the immediate need to address its humanitarian consequences while also seeking an end to the hostilities by addressing the issues that led to the conflict in the first place. The success of the effort means restoring peace and creating conducive conditions for reconstruction and development. These are essentially functions of governance that normally fall within the purview of domestic jurisdiction and therefore national sovereignty.

Although the response of governments to displacement generated by natural causes may sometimes be grossly inadequate, on the whole, it is sympathetic and supportive to the victims. Likewise, displacement caused by interstate conflicts generally elicits supportive response from the government of the affected population. In contrast, response to a displacement caused by internal conflicts, communal violence, and systematic violations of human rights is nearly always complicated by the cleavages involved. These cleavages often take the form of an identity crisis, whether based on race, ethnicity, religion, culture, or class. What this means is that the government or any other controlling authority concerned and the affected population identify themselves in divisive terms that undermine solidarity and support. The government or the controlling authority, rather than view the victim population as citizens for whom there is a moral and legal duty to protect and assist, tend to see them as enemies, or part of the enemy, with whom they are at war. In such a situation, which reflects a national identity crisis, the victim population falls into a vacuum of the moral and legal responsibility normally associated with sovereignty. It is to fill this vacuum that the international community is often called upon to step in and provide the needed protection and assistance.

It must be noted, however, that although this notion of identity crisis is pervasive, the degree varies from country to country. And so does the response of governments and other controlling authorities. There are situations of ethnic conflict in which the government still identifies the victim population as their people to whom they indeed provide food and medical supplies, sometimes in cooperation with rebel forces with whom the affected population is ethnically identified. Unfortunately, this appears to be the exception; the pattern is tragically one of denial of solidarity with the victim population on the basis of exclusive identity symbols.

THE CHALLENGE OF SOVEREIGNTY

There are two aspects to the challenges posed by internal conflicts for sovereignty. One is to establish and apply an effective system of conflict prevention, management, and resolution; the other is to provide protection and assistance to those affected by conflict. In both cases, the state may not be capable or willing to provide adequate solutions or remedies, especially because the government is nearly always a party to the conflict. And because it is partisan, the government often acts as a barrier to access by the international community to provide protection and assistance to the needy and to help in the search for peace. Such resistance to outside involvement is justified by the invocation of national sovereignty.

Since its inception, sovereignty has developed through several overlapping phases, which may not be neatly delineated historically, but which nonetheless signify an evolution. The first, represented by the Treaty of Westphalia in 1648, is the initial phase when the sovereign reigned supreme domestically and in relations with the outside world. The second, following World War II, marks the erosion of sovereignty with the development of democratic values and institutions internally and with international accountability on the basis of human rights and humanitarian standards. With the greater promotion of these values following the end of the Cold War, the third phase emerged as a reactive assertion of sovereignty by governments whose domestic performance renders them vulnerable to international scrutiny. The fourth is the current pragmatic attempt at reconciling state sovereignty with responsibility.

GENESIS OF SOVEREIGNTY

Sovereignty in legal and political theory was initially conceived in Europe as an instrument of authoritative control by the monarch over feudal princes in the construction of modern territorial states. It was believed that instability and disorder, seen as obstacles to a stable society, could only be overcome by viable governments capable of establishing firm and effective control over territory and populations.[14] The sovereign, as the lawmaker, was considered to be above the law. Indeed, law, according to the "command theory" of the leading positivist jurist, John Austin, is "a rule laid down for the guidance of an intelligent being by an intelligent being having power over him."[15] Law is thus considered the command of the sovereign who is habitually obeyed by his subjects.

The power of the sovereign is supposedly not limited by justice or any ideas of good and bad, right or wrong.[16] "For Austin . . . any legal limit on the highest lawmaking power was an absurdity and an impossibility."[17] Even in contemporary literature, it is still argued that "sovereignty is a characteristic of power that relegates its holder to a place above the law. A sovereign is immune from law and only subject to self-imposed restrictions."[18] Although the form of government might vary from monarchy, to aristocracy or democracy, it is considered essential that governments maintain order through an effective exercise of sovereignty.

On the other hand, the basic proposition of international human rights law is that "to qualify for the name of government, a government . . . has to meet certain standards, all of which involve restraints on the use of power; no torture, no brutalization; no seizure of property; no state terror; no discrimination on the basis of race, religion, or sex; no prevention of people leaving a particular country, and so on."[19] The limits of the "tyrannical" concept of sovereignty postulates three major premises: (a) "'humanity' is the raison d'etre of any legal system"; (b) "the international system . . . since the Peace of Westphalia, has not been fulfilling what should be its primary function, namely, the protection and development of the human dignity of the individual"; (c) "any proposed 'new world order' should be structured so as to maximize benefits not for States but for individuals living within States, all the way from freedom of speech and elections, on the one hand, to freedom from hunger and the right to education on the other hand."[20]

These principles impose on the international community a correlative responsibility for their enforcement. Herein lies the paradox of the supposed supremacy of sovereignty and the legitimizing function of the international order. That paradox was indeed inherent in the settlement of Westphalia from which time "sovereignty created both the territorial state and the international system."[21]

EROSION OF SOVEREIGNTY

The post–World War II era represents the second phase of the erosion of sovereignty. The application of the right to self-determination, which provided the basis for the process of decolonization, expanded the process of erosion. One of the effective measures in contravention of the narrow concepts of absolute sovereignty was that of international sanctions against South Africa. It was undoubtedly the combination of internal and external pressures that eventually culminated in the collapse of apartheid. The increasing internationalization of the human rights agenda and the wave of democratization that is sweeping the world are among the contemporary challenges to sovereignty.

The demands for democratic values, institutions, and practices have devolved the classic notion of sovereign will and authority to the people who are increasingly intolerant of the dictatorship of unaccountable government. More and more, it is recognized that it is the will of the people, democratically invested in the leaders they elect freely or otherwise accept as their representatives, that entitles authorities to value and uphold the sovereignty of a nation. As Michael Reisman has written,

> It should not take a great deal of imagination to grasp what an awful violation of the integrity of the self it is when men with guns evict your government, dismiss your law, kill and destroy wantonly and control you and those you love by intimidation and terror. When that happens, all the other human rights that depend on the lawful institutions of government become matters for the discretion of the dictators. And when that happens, those rights cease. Military coups are terrible violations of the political rights of all the members of the collectivity, and they invariably bring in their wake the violation of all the other rights. Violations of the right to popular government are not secondary or less important. They are very, very serious human rights violations.[22]

In the context of international intervention in Haiti, Reisman argues that "in modern international law, what counts is the sovereignty of the people and not a metaphysical abstraction called the state. If the de jure government, which was elected by the people, wants military assistance, how is its sovereignty violated? And if the purpose of the coercion is to reinstate a de jure government elected in a free and fair election after it was ousted by a renegade military, whose sovereignty is being violated? The military's?"[23]

The area of humanitarian intervention has witnessed the greatest erosion of sovereignty, mostly with the consent of the states, but at times through forceful enforcement. Nevertheless, mechanisms and procedures of implementation of the wide array of human rights and humanitarian standards remain undeveloped and grossly inadequate.

REASSERTION OF SOVEREIGNTY

The more the international community has been assertive, the more vulnerable governments have reacted defensively against the erosion of state sovereignty. This indeed marks the third phase of the evolution of sovereignty. Governments that are threatened by the erosion of narrow concepts of sovereignty and are defensively trying to reassert it use the argument of cultural relativity and characterize the universality concept as a Western ploy for interfering in the internal affairs of other countries.

Even among the supporters of a more liberal interpretation of sovereignty, its erosion has been viewed with ambivalence. Former United Nations Secretary-General Javier Perez de Cuellar, while acknowledging "what is probably an irresistible shift in public attitudes towards the belief that the defense of the oppressed in the name of morality should prevail over frontiers and legal documents," added the question, "Does intervention not call into question one of the cardinal principles of international law, one diametrically opposed to it, namely, the obligation of non-interference in the internal affairs of States?"[24] In his 1991 annual report he wrote, "The case for not impinging on the sovereignty, territorial integrity and political independence of States is by itself indubitably strong. But it would only be weakened if it were to carry the implication that sovereignty, even in this day and age, includes the right of mass slaughter or of launching systematic campaigns of decimation or forced exodus of civilian populations in the name of controlling civil strife or insurrection."[25]

In place of exclusionary notions of sovereignty, de Cuellar called for a "higher degree of cooperation and a combination of common sense and compassion," arguing that "we need not impale ourselves on the horns of a dilemma between respect for sovereignty and the protection of human rights. . . . What is involved is not the right of intervention but the collective obligation of States to bring relief and redress in human rights emergencies."[26]

RECONCILING SOVEREIGNTY WITH RESPONSIBILITY

Reconciling sovereignty with responsibility, the fourth phase of the evolution, has become the operative principle. Former Secretary-General Boutros Boutros-Ghali, in *An Agenda for Peace*, wrote that "the time of absolute and exclusive sovereignty . . . has passed," that "its theory was never matched by reality," and that it is necessary for leaders of states "to find a balance between the needs of good internal governance and the requirements of an ever more interdependent world."[27]

In another context, Boutros-Ghali elaborated his views on sovereignty by highlighting the need to rethink the concept in the contemporary global context, "not to weaken its essence, which is crucial to international security and cooperation, but to recognize that it may take more than one form and perform more than one function." Boutros-Ghali goes on to postulate an intriguing concept of universal sovereignty of individuals and peoples: "Underlying the rights of the individual and the rights of peoples is a dimension of universal sovereignty that resides in all humanity and provides all peoples with legitimate involvement in issues affecting the world as a whole. It is a sense that increasingly finds expression in the gradual expansion of international law."[28]

Living up to the responsibilities of sovereignty becomes in effect the best guarantee for sovereignty. As one observer commented, "Governments could best avoid intervention by meeting their obligations not only to other states, but also to their own citizens. If they failed, they might invite intervention."[29]

This was indeed the point made by the Secretary-General of the Organization of African Unity, Salim Ahmed Salim, in his bold proposals for an OAU mechanism for conflict prevention and resolution. "If the OAU, first through the Secretary-General and then the Bureau of the Summit, is to play the lead role in any African conflict," he said, "it should be enabled to intervene swiftly, otherwise it cannot be ensured that whoever (apart from African regional organizations) acts will do so in accordance with African interests."[30]

Criticizing the tendency to respond only to worst-case scenarios, Salim emphasized the need for preemptive intervention: "Pre-emptive involvement should be permitted even in situations where tensions evolve to such a pitch that it becomes apparent that a conflict is in the making." He even suggested that the OAU should take the lead in transcending the traditional view of sovereignty, building on the African values of kinship solidarity and the notion that "every African is his brother's keeper." Considering that "our borders are at best artificial," Salim argued, "we in Africa need to use our own cultural and social relationships to interpret the principle of non-interference in such a way that we are enabled to apply it to our advantage in conflict prevention and resolution."[31]

It is most significant that the Security Council, in its continued examination of the Secretary-General's report, An Agenda for Peace, "[noted] with concern the incidents of humanitarian crises, including mass displacements of population becoming or aggravating threats to international peace and security and concluded that under certain circumstances, there may be a close relationship between acute needs for humanitarian assistance and threats to international peace and security, which trigger international involvement."[32]

The crisis of internal displacement fits into this model in that it combines human rights with humanitarian concerns, and protection with assistance. Internal displacement is also a challenge to sovereignty in that providing the citizens with physical security and their basic survival needs are among the prerequisites for legitimacy and therefore recognizable sovereignty in the framework of international relations. These are among the principles that have guided the implementation of my mandate as Representative of the Secretary-General for Internally Displaced Persons.

The normative principles of my dialogue with governments are built on the premise that national sovereignty carries with it responsibility for the security and welfare of the citizens. When a state lacks the capacity to ensure the protection and welfare of its people, it is expected to call on the international community to supplement its efforts. The essence of the state responsibility, however, is accountability, both domestically and internationally. If states fail to live up to their obligations toward their citizens with the result that large numbers of people fall victim, their physical and social integrity violated or threatened and their very survival endangered, then the international community has the commensurate responsibility to hold the states accountable and obtain access to provide the needed protection and assistance and help in the search for remedies to the conditions that had caused the violent confrontation in order to restore a just and lasting peace.

INTERNATIONAL RESPONSES

The plight of the internally displaced has begun to receive significant attention from the international community. Because of the magnitude of the crisis, the inadequacy of the response system, and the urgent need for international remedies, a number of nongovernmental organizations, supported by concerned governments, urged the Commission on Human Rights to take action. Concerted action began with the consideration by the Commission of a report prepared by the Secretariat on the subject of internal displacement.[33] It was then that the Commission requested the Secretary-General to appoint a representative to study the problems. The study was to cover the root causes of internal displacement, the relevant international legal standards, the mechanisms for their enforcement, and any additional measures the United Nations might take to improve the situation of the internally displaced. In preparing the study, I undertook field visits to five countries and engaged in a dialogue with the governments. Since then, in-depth studies of the legal and institutional dimensions of international protection and assistance for the internally displaced, country visits, on-the-ground inspection of the conditions of the displaced, and dialogue with governments have been the core activities of the mandate. As we shall see in the following sections, these have brought about a number of tangible results.

LEGAL STANDARDS

The development of appropriate legal standards for the protection and assistance of internally displaced persons has been a main objective of the mandate since its inception. The need to examine the applicability of existing international human rights law, humanitarian law, and refugee law by analogy to the protection and assistance needs of internally displaced persons was a principal reason prompting the Commission on Human Rights to request the Secretary-General to designate a representative on internally displaced persons.

In particular, the commission requested an identification of existing laws for the protection of internally displaced persons, possible additional measures to strengthen the implementation of these laws, and alternatives for addressing protection needs not adequately covered by existing instruments. The following year the Commission noted that the compilation of existing rules and norms and the questions of general guiding principles to govern the treatment of internally displaced persons, in particular their protection and the provision of relief assistance, were among the tasks requiring further attention and study. Working with a team of international legal experts, this exercise resulted in the preparation of a compilation and analysis of the legal norms pertaining to internal displacement, consisting of two parts.

The first part of the compilation examined the relevant provisions of international law once people have been displaced. The study concluded that while existing law covers many aspects of relevance to the situation of internally displaced persons, there nonetheless exist significant gaps and gray areas as a result of which the law fails to provide sufficient protection. In addition, emphasizing the need for better implementation of the relevant norms, the study made recommendations for addressing the identified gaps and gray areas with a view to ensuring a more comprehensive normative framework for the protection and assistance of the internally displaced.

The second part of the compilation and analysis employed the same methodology of considering international human rights law, international humanitarian law, and refugee law by analogy to examine the legal aspects relating to protection against arbitrary displacement. The study found that many provisions in international law point to a general rule according to which forced displacement may be undertaken only exceptionally, on a nondiscriminatory basis and not arbitrarily imposed, but that this protection largely is only implicit. Accordingly, the study concluded that the legal basis for providing protection prior to displacement could be strengthened significantly by articulating a right not to be arbitrarily displaced.

Together, the two parts of the compilation and analysis of legal norms provided the basis upon which to return to the question of general guiding principles to govern the treatment of internally displaced persons. In 1996 the Commission called for the development, on the basis of the compilation and analysis, of a comprehensive normative framework of protection and assistance for internally displaced persons. This exercise resulted in the formation of Guiding Principles on Internal Displacement, which were presented to the Commission on Human Rights in 1998.

The stated scope and purpose of the Guiding Principles is to address the specific needs of internally displaced persons worldwide by identifying the rights and guarantees relevant to their situation and thereby providing guidance to all relevant actors: the Representative in carrying out his mandate; states when faced with the phenomenon of internal displacement; all other authorities, groups, and persons in their relations with internally displaced persons; and intergovernmental and nongovernmental organizations.

The Guiding Principles consolidate the numerous relevant norms which are at present too disperse and diffuse to be effective in ensuring the protection and assistance of internally displaced persons. Reflecting and consistent with international human rights law and international humanitarian law, the Guiding Principles set forth the rights and guarantees relevant to the protection of internally displaced persons in all phases of displacement: protection against arbitrary displacement; protection and assistance during displacement, and during return, resettlement, and reintegration. In particular, they pay special attention to the needs of internally displaced women and children, who typically comprise the overwhelming majority of any internally displaced population.

The Principles specify that children, especially unaccompanied minors, and expectant mothers, mothers with young children, and female heads of household shall be entitled to protection and assistance required by their condition and to treatment which takes into account their special needs. A number of specific provisions elaborate upon this principle.

In the short time since they were submitted to the Commission on Human Rights, the Guiding Principles have gained considerable international recognition and standing among states, the UN system, regional organizations, and NGOs as a useful tool for addressing situations of internal displacement. The Commission on Human Rights has welcomed the use of the Guiding Principles by the Representative in his dialogue with governments and intergovernmental and non-governmental organizations and has requested that he continue efforts in this regard. The Commission also has taken note with appreciation that UN agencies, regional organizations, and NGOs are making use of the Guiding Principles in their work and has encouraged the further dissemination and application of the Guiding Principles.

INSTITUTIONAL ARRANGEMENTS

On the issue of institutional arrangements, it is widely acknowledged that there is a gap in the coverage because there is no one organization, or collection of organizations, mandated to take responsibility for the internally displaced. At the same time, there is no political will to create a new organization with that mandate. Nor is it likely that an existing institution will be mandated to assume full responsibility for the internally displaced. Under the present circumstances, the residual option is that of a collaborative arrangement among a wide variety of agencies and organizations whose mandates and activities are relevant to the problems of internal displacement.[34]

The prerequisites for such a collaborative arrangement are that these agencies focus attention on the needs of the internally displaced and toward that end ensure better coordination among themselves. With regard to the first issue, it is encouraging that international agencies are now giving more attention to the question of internal displacement than ever before. The UNHCR, for instance, has played a significant role in a number of in-country situations, including Bosnia and Herzegovina, and Tajikistan and Chechnya. The UNHCR is increasingly confronted with the problem of internally displaced persons, whether in the context of repatriation operations when displaced persons are intermingled with returning refugees, or in its efforts to prevent refugee flows by protecting and assisting people before they are forced to cross a border.[35]

Other agencies also realize this challenge and are heeding the call for collaborative involvement. The largest category of beneficiaries of World Food Programme (WFP) relief aid are now internally displaced persons. The UNDP has recently reorganized its financial allocation procedures, allowing for greater programming flexibility that permits more involvement with situations of internal displacement. Two other agencies, UNICEF and WHO, have also enlarged their involvement with internally displaced persons. The International Organization for Migration (IOM) has expanded its activities with regard to the return and reintegration of internally displaced persons. The main organs of the United Nations, such as the General Assembly, and the governing bodies of UN agencies, in particular the Executive Committee of the High Commissioner for Refugees' program, have endorsed this trend. The High Commissioner for Human Rights has also focused her attention on the problems of internal displacement and has targeted the operations of human rights field monitors toward protecting the displaced.

In addition, the International Committee of the Red Cross (ICRC) has focused increased attention on the subject of internal displacement. In October 1995 it organized a symposium in which the specific situation of internally displaced persons in the context of armed conflict and the activities of the ICRC were discussed. The twenty-sixth International Conference of the Red Cross and Red Crescent, which took place in December 1995, adopted a resolution on the Principles and Response in International Humanitarian Assistance and Protection, the first part of which concerns internally displaced persons and refugees. The resolution calls on states to ensure access to internally displaced persons for neutral, impartial, and independent humanitarian organizations, and to renew their support for the provision of food aid and other supplies to longstanding situations of internal displacement. It also invites the movement and national societies of the Red Cross and Red Crescent to enhance their capacities to provide services to the internally displaced, including protection and assistance, and to strengthen their cooperation with the United Nations.

The increased involvement of regional organizations is also an encouraging development. The Organization for Security and Cooperation in Europe (OSCE), for instance, has become gradually more involved with the plight of the internally displaced in Tajikistan, Bosnia and Herzegovina, and the Caucasus. Its role has focused on both prevention and protection. The Conference on Refugees, Returnees, Displaced Persons, and Related Migratory Movements in the Countries of the CIS and Relevant Neighboring States, which took place in May 1998 under the auspices of UNHCR, IOM, and the OSCE, represented an important step toward developing preventive and remedial approaches to displacement. The Organization of American States (OAS) has undertaken a preventive approach as well. Its efforts to promote democratic development in the hemisphere are serving as a framework of prevention against displacement. The Inter-American Commission on Human Rights has begun more systematic monitoring and reporting on situations of internal displacement and has called upon the OAS to establish structures to promote greater attention to situations of internal displacement.

Following a meeting I held with the OAS Inter-American Commission on Human Rights, the Commission decided to appoint a Rapporteur to focus its work on internal displacement. The OAU has also begun to devote more attention to the problem of internal displacement. In particular, it has focused on preventive efforts. A Mechanism for Conflict Prevention Management and Resolution, established in 1993, has emphasized that in seeking to resolve conflicts, it hopes to defuse conditions that could give rise to internal displacement. The OAU has also become involved in regional approaches for resolving problems of displacement.[36] In October 1998 the OAU cosponsored with UNHCR and the Brookings Institution Project on Internal Displacement a workshop on Internal Displacement in Africa, and in June 1999 the OAU Commission on Refugees invited the representative to present the Guiding Principles at its thirtieth session.

Emphasis should also be placed on the important role played by NGOs in assisting and protecting the internally displaced. Frequently, NGOs are in more direct contact with displaced populations and have closer relationships with the local authorities than do international agencies, who tend to work with the central government. NGOs, furthermore, are able to define and implement strategies that provide crucial assistance to the internally displaced, and tend to be more flexible in implementing integrated policies that address both protection and assistance. NGOs have also engaged in preventive strategies ranging from early warning to conflict resolution.

Correlative to the increased involvement of various agencies and organizations is the urgent need for coordination or a central point to assign institutional responsibility in emergency situations. In the last few years some institutional progress has been made in this area. There now exist coordinating mechanisms that promise to bring coherence into the international system. The focal points in these structural arrangements are the Emergency Relief Coordinator (designated as the reference point in the United Nations system for requests for assistance and protection for internally displaced persons), and the Inter-Agency Standing Committee, its working group. A similar coordinating structure is reflected at the field level through the Resident Representatives of UNDP or, in cases of complex emergencies, the Resident Coordinators or Humanitarian Coordinators who chair Disaster Management Teams (DMTs) composed of UN operational agencies and sometimes NGOs and coordinate humanitarian assistance for internally displaced persons.

The High Commissioner for Refugees has observed that the success of international involvement will depend on three key factors: "The first is a well structured division of work, on which coordination must proceed among organizations and institutions with the required expertise and ability to avoid duplication of efforts and fill gaps instead. The second is the ability of the international effort to mobilize and develop local capacities and responsibilities. The third . . . is their firm foundation in common and consistent human rights standards."[37]

Nor should the institutional challenge be seen merely in the context of the displacement that has already occurred. Human rights violations are a major factor in causing displacement as well as an obstacle to safe and voluntary return home. Safeguarding human rights in countries of origin is therefore critical, both for prevention and for the solution of refugee and internally displaced persons problems. If the increasing problem of internal displacement is to be contained and reduced, preventive strategies are critical.

United Nations human rights bodies have an important role to play in this regard. Preventive measures currently relied upon include dialogue with governments, urgent appeals, public statements, emergency meetings, the deployment of human rights field staff, machinery for the protection of minorities, and the extension of technical assistance. Commission reports addressing the root causes of mass exoduses also exemplify efforts at prevention. Human rights treaty bodies, moreover, have been requested to examine measures they might take to prevent human rights violations, and several have adopted emergency procedures and undertaken missions to countries for preventive purposes. The establishment of the post of United Nations High Commissioner for Human Rights has added momentum to the development of preventive strategies. Human rights field staff deployed under her auspices are playing a valuable preventive role. Human rights advisory services and education projects are valuable tools for the promotion of human rights and prevention of violations.

All these measures, however, are at an early stage of development and human rights bodies should be encouraged to increase their capacities for prevention. Mechanisms for minority protection in particular need to be strengthened as many displaced persons are members of minority groups who have been subjected to forcible expulsion, resettlement, and other persecution because of their ethnic or other origin. Promising initiatives include the adoption by the United Nations of the Declaration on the Rights of Persons Belonging to National or Ethnic, Religious and Linguistic Minorities and the establishment of a working group by the Submission on Prevention of Discrimination and Protection of Minorities to develop strategies for minority protection and to prevent conflict.

At the national level, promotion and protection of human rights through the establishment of effective national institutions to monitor and promote them is the safest guarantee against involuntary displacement. My country mission reports as Representative of the Secretary-General have emphasized the importance of supporting preventive techniques aimed at empowering the population at the grassroots level. Very often, local communities have built up effective strategies for mitigating the impact of displacement. The coping strategies that displaced populations themselves have developed should be carefully examined by NGOs and international agencies, because such mechanisms are essential elements of prevention and protection.

Irrespective of the level at which preventive strategies are pursued, efforts must be made to ensure that they do not interfere with the freedom of movement. There is a need to reconcile strategies that encourage people to remain within their own countries with those that safeguard the right to leave and seek asylum from persecution. Under no circumstances should the desire to forestall large-scale population displacements take precedence over assuring the security of displaced populations.

COUNTRY VISITS

Country visits remain the cornerstone of the mandate on internal displacement. Since becoming representative, I have visited thirteen countries—Azerbaijan, Burundi, Colombia (twice), El Salvador, Mozambique, Peru, the Russian Federation, Rwanda, Somalia, Sri Lanka, the Sudan, Tajikistan, and the former Yugoslavia. Missions create new awareness of the problems faced by the internally displaced among the key actors inside the country, including government officials, those who work with the displaced, and the public at large. The dialogue with governments is based on the premise that internal displacement falls within the domestic jurisdiction and therefore the sovereignty of the states concerned, but that sovereignty carries with it the responsibility to provide for the security and well-being of those residing in their territories.

In order for country visits and dialogue to achieve the most effective results, they need adequate preparation. Background studies about the country, the conditions of the internally displaced, and the activities of the international and local organizations are essential for making effective use of the limited time available during the visit itself.

The program of a country visit is indicative of the potential of this awareness-raising effect: it normally begins with a briefing by the UN representative, followed by meetings at the highest level of the government hierarchy, including the head of state and/or government, pertinent ministers, government officials with responsibilities for the internally displaced, representatives of specialized UN agencies and of the donor community, national human rights bodies, and human rights and relief and development NGOs, community leaders, and representatives of the displaced population and displaced persons. These meetings are then followed by on-site visits to displaced populations and dialogue with provincial and local authorities, including military commanders, civilian administrators, relief workers, local leaders, and the displaced themselves. The third phase is one of debriefing the local, provincial, and national authorities as well as international agencies about the on-site visits and the findings and recommendations for remedial measures.

Often these activities are accompanied by media coverage, the effect of which is to bring the problem to the fore, open it up for discussion, and make it a challenging and more pressing subject for policy analysts and decision makers. Government and nongovernmental agencies are challenged to rethink their policies, strategies, and priorities. Visits may motivate the convocation of a seminar or other forum where the government and NGOs participate together (sometimes for the first time), and they may trigger greater international support or donor assistance. They become catalytic in the sense that they open up spaces for increased dialogue between those concerned and they generate the momentum necessary to introduce reforms.

Country visits, however, are bound to have a very limited impact unless there is appropriate follow-up information and continued dialogue to ensure that recommendations are carried out. Four main sources of follow-up information can be identified: information provided by UN agencies in the field, information provided by other human rights bodies and mechanisms of the United Nations, information provided by the government, and information provided by NGOs. In addition, dialogue and cooperation are essential among all concerned—governments, international agencies, and NGOs. Follow-up missions also remain a potential source of assessing progress.

Country visits are not the only form of dialogue that should take place with governments. The problem of internal displacement affects far more countries than can be covered through missions. Internal displacement is a global phenomenon warranting a more extensive system of on-site monitoring and much more frequent contact with governments and other pertinent actors. Information on internal displacement is also provided by other special rapporteurs of the Commission and the human rights treaty bodies. NGOs, governments, and UNDP resident representatives have also made available information on internal displacement. An important development in this regard is the establishment of a database for systematically collecting, receiving, and analyzing information on internal displacement. This project, long advocated by the Representative, has been outsourced by the IASC to the Norwegian Refugee Council's Global IDP Survey.

The creation of the mandate of the Representative of the Secretary-General in 1992 was a measure aimed at studies that would make recommendations on what the United Nations could do to address this mounting crisis. Much work has been done on understanding the legal and institutional frameworks of protection and assistance for the internally displaced. Although the prospects for legal reform are promising, the issue of institutional arrangements is far more complex. For the moment, the only viable option is to utilize existing capacities in the international system. In this collaborative framework the mandate of the Representative of the Secretary-General has evolved into a catalytic role aimed at advocacy and awareness raising.

The Quest for Strategy

In virtually all dialogue with the governments and relevant actors, effort is made to link the immediate challenges of protection and assistance with the need to find lasting solutions, which in time draws attention to the causes generating the conflict that triggered displacement. This is, of course, a sensitive area in which reactions from governments are mixed. There are those who claim that it is outside the mandate of the Representative and those who acknowledge the need for peace as the real solution to the humanitarian tragedies of war. Objectively, there is no way the circular link between war, its human tragedies, and the need for solutions that address the root causes can be avoided.

In view of these anomalies and uncertainties, there is still a need for developing a strategy that would address effectively and comprehensively the crisis of internal displacement, both generically and contextually. As argued at the outset of this chapter, such a strategy should approach the displacement problem in its three manifest phases: causes, consequences, and remedies. The corresponding responses would be to develop measures for preempting and preventing displacement, to provide adequate means of protection and relief assistance during displacement, and to seek durable solutions through voluntary and safe return, resettlement, rehabilitation, reconstruction, and self-reliant development.

Ultimately, because conflict is at the core of displacement, emphasis needs to be placed on conflict prevention, management, and resolution in that order of priority. It should also be acknowledged that not only is displacement a consequence and, therefore, a symptom of conflict, but conflict itself is a symptom of deeper societal ills, generally rooted in ethnic, religious, and cultural diversities, disparities, and gross inequities or injustices. It is in the fertile soil of understandable and justified grievances that the virus of violence incubates and eventually explodes. Unless checked in time, this can turn into a chronic condition in the body politic and, as recent developments have shown, can be even terminal to the survival of nations.

Among the characteristics of the soil in which the virus incubates are poverty, scarcity of resources, maldistribution of the little there is, policies repressive of legitimate demands, gross violations of human rights and fundamental liberties, and a sense of hopelessness and despair. Under those conditions, governments or dominant authorities become perceived as tantamount to foreign bodies, implanted into a resistant body politic that is eventually forced to reject them.

To the extent that conflict represents a symptomatic warning of underlying and potentially more serious problems, it can play a positive role if constructively responded to. Indeed, the upsurge in violent conflicts following the end of the Cold War indicates that many latent conflicts were repressed through the awesome power of the bipolar control mechanisms of the two superpowers, driven not so much by ideals of right and wrong as by ideological alignments and strategic considerations. Repressive, unrepresentative governments and regimes were backed and supported by the superpowers because of their strategic or ideological stand with little or no regard to their domestic legitimacy. With the withdrawal of this support following the end of the Cold War, governments or regimes with the propensity to repress, oppress, and plunder became exposed to internal and external scrutiny and a more determined opposition that they can no longer contain, because they lack the capacity to exercise effective and decisive control over the situation.

This chaotic and often tragic conflict situation paradoxically offers countries and the international community the opportunity to review the normative and operational principles governing domestic jurisdiction and international relations. Foremost of these should be the stipulation of the normative standards of responsibility associated with sovereignty. Rather than a means of barricading governments and regimes against international scrutiny, sovereignty should be recast in response to its contemporary challenges as embodying the will of the people, represented by those they choose through free and fair elections or otherwise accept as their legitimate representatives. Sovereignty must also be viewed as an instrument for ensuring the protection and welfare of all those under its jurisdiction.

A concept that provides the core for formulating such a normative framework remains the human dignity of the individual and the group within the domestic jurisdiction. This concept is provided for in the charter of the United Nations, the International Bill of Rights, and all the human rights and humanitarian principles enunciated in many legally and morally binding documents, including now the Guiding Principles on Internal Displacement. Rather than a means of barricading governments and regimes against international scrutiny, sovereignty should be normatively postulated as an embodiment of the democratic will of the people and a tool for ensuring the protection and welfare of all those under domestic jurisdiction. The incorporation and embodiment of these human rights and humanitarian norms into the Guiding Principles on Internal Displacement is both a preventive and curative prescription. Governments and other custodians of national sovereignty should see the standards not only as a guide, but also as a yardstick for evaluating their own performance.

Conflict prevention, management, and resolution clearly pose paradoxical challenges for both change and stability. The gross inequities of the status quo need to be scrutinized and moderated, if not eliminated. But preserving a legal order that is protective of and responsive to reasonable standards of human dignity must be seen as an overriding goal. It is with these normative principles in mind that governments and the international community are called upon to address the mounting crisis of internal displacement, to prevent it by addressing its root causes, to respond to its human rights and humanitarian tragedies when they occur, and to strive to end it by creating appropriate conditions for safe return or alternative resettlement and restoring normal life in the community and the nation at large.

In conclusion, it should be reiterated that the international community has made considerable progress in responding to displacement, in particular with the development of the normative framework, in the form of the Guiding Principles, and enhancements of institutional arrangements at both the international and regional levels. However, much more remains to be done to give these legal and institutional developments meaningful impact on the ground, and above all, to make governments more responsive to the responsibilities of sovereignty for protecting and assisting their own citizens or else risk undermining their legitimacy both domestically and internationally. The glass is half-full, but that implies that it is also half-empty.

9

ECONOMIC SANCTIONS AS A MEANS TO INTERNATIONAL HEALTH

LORD ROBERT SKIDELSKY AND EDWARD MORTIMER

The traditional aim of preventive diplomacy is to ensure the maintenance of peace. This chapter examines the role of sanctions as an instrument of preventive diplomacy. It excludes consideration of the use of sanctions to support other objectives of a country's foreign policy—for example, the sanctions the United States imposed on Cuba. Here the one purpose of sanctions is taken to be the promotion of behavior conducive to peace.

It also excludes the use of military and diplomatic sanctions, and concentrates on economic sanctions. Economic sanctions, as traditionally defined, are the use of economic instruments to secure behavior desired by the sanctioning authority. They usually involve the imposition of, or threat to impose, economic costs on the sanctioned state. They are seen as one link in a chain of graduated pressure short of war, more powerful than diplomatic pressure, less powerful than military preparations. They can thus be used to prevent, contain, or eliminate undesired behavior; such behavior being defined here as behavior which endangers or breaches the peace, or otherwise imposes unwanted costs on the world community.

The chief instruments of economic sanctions are boycotts, embargoes, and capital controls. Boycott restricts the demand for the exports of the target country—like the oil boycott imposed on Iraq in 1991. Embargo restricts exports to the target state—like the oil embargo against Serbia. Capital sanctions restrict or suspend lending to, and investment in, the target state, and may involve the freezing of foreign assets and restrictions on international payments. A complete set of economic sanctions means a prohibition of all trade and capital flows between sanctioner and sanctioned, enforced by blockade and other measures.

Sanctions can be likened to forms of preventive medicine, whose purpose is to maintain public health and prevent the spread of infections. Preventive medicine can be used to secure immunization, to act on early-warning signals, or to localize or contain disease. When a general breakdown in health actually occurs, we have moved beyond preventive medicine into the realm of radical intervention designed to restore health. The outbreak of large-scale violence, like a major war, is analogous to a general breakdown in public health.

Traditionally, sanctions have chiefly been used for the last—and weakest—of the preventive purposes: to contain and bring to an end localized violence. However, there is increasing interest in using them to prevent the genesis of conflict. Pressure has been applied to governments to create domestic conditions (democracy, freedom, land reform, redistribution of wealth, and so on) in order to *entrench* health. The abuse of human rights might count as an early-warning signal of danger ahead, triggering off preventive interventions. Such extensions of preventive diplomacy imply intervention in the domestic affairs of sovereign states. The rationale of such interventions is twofold: (a) to prevent civil violence that may spill over into interstate conflict; and (b) to prevent humanitarian disasters (refugees, famines, epidemics) that become a charge on the world community. In 1992 there were 460,000 people killed in twenty-nine (mainly civil) wars, eighteen million refugees in UN care, twenty-five million categorized as "internally displaced." With worry about the ecological security of the planet, and the commitment of the Rio Conference to "sustainable economic development," the scope for interventions into domestic affairs has widened even further.

The medical analogy is seductive. If the aim of preventive medicine is to promote and maintain public health, can one not see the aim of preventive diplomacy as to promote and maintain a peaceful and harmonious international society? However, there are serious problems in applying the model of medical intervention to diplomacy.

First, there is far less agreement about what constitutes political health than physical health. Is a permanently peaceful world a healthy one? Many have doubted it. Although few, perhaps, now accept Mussolini's dictum that "war is to man what childbirth is to woman," many would argue that violence is justified if conditions are unjust and no peaceful means for the redress of grievances are available. Terrorists see themselves as freedom fighters. The relationships between peace, material prosperity, freedom, and well-being, all of which may be taken as indicators of political health, are problematic, as will be shown later in this chapter.

Preventive diplomacy is inevitably drawn, like preventive medicine, into defining and promoting healthy conditions of life. This involves establishing norms for state behavior that go beyond the traditional aim of punishing and reversing acts of aggression. If self-sustaining conditions of health can be established, this will be far less costly, in the long run, than interventions to cure disease.

A fundamental assumption of preventive diplomacy is that healthy states are more likely to seek peaceful resolution of conflicts than are unhealthy ones. Bad states seek to externalize domestic conflicts—to transfer the costs of misrule from their own people to outsiders. Thus the establishment of just domestic conditions may be seen as a guarantee that appropriate norms of international behavior will be followed. Intervention to secure these conditions can then be justified in the name of international peace. But the diagnostic basis of such health-building projects is much weaker than in medicine. We know, for example, that many infectious diseases are caused and carried by bacteria, and we can immunize individuals (and societies) against them. But we don't understand very well the causes of international violence and have, therefore, a very hazy idea of how to prevent it. There is no clear evidence that some kinds of domestic constitution are more conducive to peaceful international behavior than others. What is an unhealthy lifestyle for a state? Politics may, perhaps, be likened to a vaccine against war, and the idea that democracy is the peaceful form of the state, autocracy the warlike form, is powerful a priori. But it is not strongly supported by the facts. Even some fascist or fascistic powers were nonaggressive in their external relations (for example, Franco's Spain). The analogy between immunizing a society against smallpox and immunizing it against violence is somewhat far-fetched.

As a result of the collapse of fascism and communism there is now much less ideological conflict about the healthy form of the state than earlier this century. It may even be possible to secure widespread agreement on norms of domestic state behavior. Broadly, these would cover political, civil, economic, and social rights and the accompanying obligations on states to observe or promote them. Francis Fukuyama has argued that the world is converging on the norms of liberal democracy and private enterprise: hence the end of history. Given this, the conditions for using sanctions may be more auspicious than at any time this century; specifically, there will be far less opposition than in the past to

U.S.-led international coalitions using economic sanctions to prevent, contain, and resolve regional conflicts.

However, this may be doubted. Western victory in the Cold War may have removed one source of norm conflict, but will Asia, Africa, and the Middle East conform to Western standards of "political" health? The history of sanctions shows that norms accepted by different groups of countries (for example, the Arab League in sanctioning Egypt in 1979 for making a separate peace with Israel) can vary enormously. States that remain theocratic in their internal organization (like Iran) are unlikely to subscribe to the secularist norms of Western liberalism and democracy. Should we be in the business of sanctioning Iran? The general point is that since agreement on standards of political and social health is lacking, mandates for sanctions are likely to be weak expressions of power rather than moral authority. This means there will still be plenty of sanction breakers, unless the use of sanctions is restricted to a rather narrow range of state misconduct.

Second, even if some norms of domestic state behavior are universally accepted, their disregard may not be acceptable as a ground for intervention. Domestic and international norms conflict. The postwar international order is based on the principle of national sovereignty: China says the issue of the future of Taiwan is an entirely domestic matter. The Brezhnev doctrine (which allowed Soviet military intervention in the internal affairs of the Soviet satellites to protect their socialism) was widely seen as a cloak for imperialism. Interventions into the domestic affairs of states to secure civilized standards are likely to be viewed in the same way. The reason is that they are not based on scientific knowledge, as are medical interventions, and are likely to be viewed as expressions of power. The idea that self-government is better than good government is resonant because genuine agreement about what constitutes good government is lacking.

The fundamental ground for sanctioning domestic state misconduct is that it may well disturb international relations. Where domestic policy is likely to impose costs on third parties, there is a clear case for preventive intervention. Persecution, genocide, or civil war within states can produce masses of starving people and floods of refugees who become wards of the international community, as well as incite neighboring states to intervene on behalf of persecuted coreligionists or coracials. Similarly, ecological damage (cutting down rain forests) can have global consequences. But is ill-treatment of minorities—or in the case of minority rule, majorities—within a state a ground for preventive intervention per se? Even today there is a reluctance to intervene in domestic affairs unless spillover effects are probable. But there is no secure basis for calculating their probability. Preventive diplomacy remains stuck in this gray area.

Finally, even if universal norms of state behavior were to be agreed upon, the question of how best to secure these norms is problematic. There is a strong Western (predominantly Anglo-American) tradition stretching back to Adam Smith and Cobden that free trade in itself promotes state convergence on peacekeeping norms of behavior. But sanctions represent a breach of freedom of commerce. We will return to this issue later. Even if certain kinds of behavior are deemed worthy of sanctioning, the problem of what sanctions work, and in what circumstances, remains. But the effectiveness of sanctions remains problematic. (This is separate from the problem of securing enough agreement to put a plan of sanctions into operation.) The general idea of sanctions is to raise the costs of unacceptable behavior. They may either operate *ex ante*, deterring certain kinds of behavior (and rewarding others), or *ex post*, punishing them. But we have very little idea of what the effects of sanctions will be, either *ex ante* or *ex post*, because many evasive or adaptive strategies are open to sanctioned states. A brief glance at the history of economic sanctions will make these points clearer.

ECONOMIC SANCTIONS IN PRACTICE

LEGAL AND CONCEPTUAL BACKGROUND

Economic sanctions have been developed since early this century to express the opinion or enforce the will of the international community on an increasingly wide range of issues.[1] They have had a checkered history; this is reflected in the conflicting views about their purposes and efficacy. The use of economic policy to achieve political goals was standard in premodern times, but it disappeared in the nineteenth century, when trade was separated from politics: Russia raised loans on the London market during the Crimean War. It was revived by the League of Nations in the framework of peacekeeping after World War I and has been extensively applied since. The poor results achieved by sanctions in the interwar years (especially in Abyssinia in 1935) led to the view that economic sanctions were ineffective; but more recent experience, especially in Rhodesia in the 1970s, South Africa in the 1980s, and Iraq,

Haiti, and Yugoslavia in the 1990s has led to a reassessment.

Article 16 of the League Covenant and Article 39 of the UN Charter provide the legal bases for sanctions. In the League of Nations system, waging unlawful war was the only ground for sanctions, but Chapter VII of the UN Charter speaks of a "threat to the peace," giving a wide latitude of interpretation to the Security Council. The Council can define wrongdoing in the context of "new norms of decolonization, non-discrimination and human rights."[2]

League sanctions were intended to deter would-be rule breakers, or failing that, to bring rapid compliance by punitive effects. The rosy period when economic sanctions *on their own* were expected to have devastating results ended with the failure of sanctions to stop Italy's conquest of Abyssinia in 1935.

The UN Charter allowed domestic situations, such as apartheid in South Africa, to be brought under a sanctions order in the name of a threat to peace. The enforcement of agreed standards depends on agreement at least among Great Powers about the standards to be upheld and the means to be used. This was largely lacking in the Cold War, so condemnation and sanctioning were highly selective. Only the Security Council can mandate sanctions, but the General Assembly can recommend them. Until the end of the Cold War, mandatory UN sanctions were imposed in only two cases: against Rhodesia and South Africa. This reflected universal detestation of white minority rule. Since the end of the Cold War, mandatory sanctions have been imposed on Iraq, Yugoslavia, Libya, Haiti, Liberia, Somalia, Rwanda, Sierra Leone, and the Unita faction in Angola.

Regional organizations like the Organization of American States, the League of Arab States, or the Organization of African Unity can declare their members in violation of rules and recommend appropriate measures. Between the two extremes of self-help and mandatory Security Council enforcement under Chapter VII of the Charter there is a wide range of sanctioning possibilities of varying legitimacy.

PREWAR EXPERIENCE: ABYSSINIA/ETHIOPIA

Italy's invasion of Ethiopia in October 1935 led to the automatic application of sanctions under Article 16 of the League of Nations Covenant. It comprised an embargo on the export to Italy of the implements of war; the restriction of financial dealings; the prohibition of imports from Italy; and a ban on a wide range of exports from, and reexports to, Italy. Sanctions on oil, iron, steel, and coal imports to Italy were proposed, but abandoned as ineffective because the United States and Germany were not members of the League. Mussolini completed his conquest of Ethiopia in May 1936 and sanctions were abandoned on July 15.

Obviously sanctions did not deter or prevent his unlawful behavior. They were inconvenient but not crippling. The ban on the export of strategic raw materials to Italy was effective by December 1935, but Italy had stockpiled these, as well as oil. Italy's exports dropped by 50 percent in the first six months of 1936, making it difficult for it to pay for imports, regardless of source. The failure of sanctions was due partly to the gaps in the sanctions system, but the sanctionists also seriously underestimated the effects of sanctions in strengthening support for the regime, and the potential for internal adaptation to the needs of a war economy. The sanctionists incurred some of the costs of going to war with Italy, without reaping any of the benefits (victory). Politically, sanctions had the effect of driving Mussolini into alliance with Hitler. Partly for this reason, Britain and France agreed to lift them, arguably without giving them enough time to take full effect.

COLD WAR EXPERIENCE: RHODESIA AND SOUTH AFRICA

Following the Unilateral Declaration of Independence (UDI) by Rhodesia on November 11, 1965, Britain imposed an escalating set of economic sanctions, which culminated in a total ban of Rhodesian exports to and imports from British territories, and an embargo on all financial dealings of British subjects with Rhodesia. The Commonwealth and other countries followed Britain's lead. The United States and France imposed oil embargoes in December 1965, and France restricted the import of tobacco and sugar. Prime Minister Harold Wilson predicted the collapse of the rebellion "within a matter of weeks rather than months." When the collapse failed to occur, Britain took the matter to the Security Council in December 1966 and it voted to impose mandatory sanctions on December 16. The ground for collective action was that UDI was a "threat to the peace." Mandatory sanctions banned the export of petroleum, arms, ammunition and military equipment, vehicles, and aircraft to Rhodesia, and imports from Rhodesia of key commodities making up 59 percent of her export trade. These were intensified in May 1968 to include a total ban on Rhodesian trade (except for a few humanitarian items), an embargo on capital dealings, and the severance of all communications. But South Africa and Portugal continued trading and air links, Britain and the United States vetoing the extension of mandatory sanctions to these countries. The Pearce Commission of 1972 reported that black Africans were willing to pay the price of suffering the main burden of sanctions to achieve majority rule. Guerrilla warfare began in 1972 and was intensified by the collapse of the Portuguese empire in 1975. South Africa signaled it wanted a settlement. By 1976 Prime Minister Ian Smith of Rhodesia was prepared to accept a transitional multiracial government and majority rule within two years. The Muzorewa government was installed in 1978. In December 1979 a settlement was reached at the Lancaster House Conference. Robert Mugabe became Prime Minister of an independent Zimbabwe on April 18, 1980. Security Council sanctions were lifted on December 21, 1979.

Sanctions did not end UDI on their own. Rhodesia had a subsistence agricultural sector and was potentially self-sufficient in food; considerable mineral resources, including chrome ore and gold; an industrial base that could be rapidly expanded to utilize unused capacity; hydroelectric power. Its weaknesses were its landlocked position and dependence on foreign transport routes; dependence on foreign trade for 38 percent of its national income; the concentration of its export earnings on tobacco, and two markets (Britain and South Africa); its need to import petroleum amounting to 28 percent of its total energy requirements; and the numerical insignificance of its white population. The African population took the brunt of sanctions, with worsening unemployment, which fueled guerrilla forces.

Tobacco and sugar exports suffered, but Rhodesia diversified into wheat and maize, exporting these, plus beef and beef products, via South Africa, together with minerals, especially asbestos, nickel, and chrome. From 1971 to 1977 the United States imported chrome ore from Rhodesia under the Byrd amendment, because otherwise it would have had to import it from the USSR. Sanctions gave strong incentives to import substitutions and manufacturing. Manufacturers concentrated on the home market. New consumer products were developed, led by textiles and clothing. Foreign exchange control was a serious problem, and the tourist industry was heavily hit in the 1970s. Sanctions evasion was also a serious problem for the sanctioners, with petroleum the vital commodity.

Rhodesia was able, with difficulty, to adapt to life under sanctions. But developments in the 1970s posed more difficult problems. The international recession following the oil price shock of 1973–74, the collapse of Portuguese rule in Angola and Mozambique, and the escalating level of guerrilla warfare had devastating effects on the economy and white morale. White emigration rose to a flood after 1975, with 41,246 (out of a population of 250,000) leaving between 1976 and 1979. The withdrawal of South African support for UDI was probably decisive. Even if economic sanctions helped to create a situation that eventually ended the rebellion, the ability of 250,000 white settlers to defy the world community for fifteen years is hardly striking testimony to their efficacy. Sanctions in this case cannot be said to have prevented conflict, even if in the long run they helped the right side in the conflict win.

Did sanctions bring apartheid to an end in South Africa? Except for a ban of arms sales in 1977, South Africa was never subjected to mandatory UN economic sanctions but rather to a steadily escalating array of sanctions recommended by the United Nations and imposed by groups of nations (the Commonwealth, the EC, OAU, and so on). Although the precise contribution these sanctions made to the end of white minority rule remains controversial, it seems reasonable to conclude that it was an important one, though perhaps not decisive. The South African economy was not brought to its knees or to the verge of collapse. But the gradual tightening of sanctions, and especially their application by countries in Europe and North America from which white South Africans expected a degree of support and understanding, helped convince the South African government and its domestic supporters that they had no friends in the world and that their attempt to maintain white supremacy was ultimately doomed to failure. It gave extra cogency to the arguments for change put forward by relatively friendly foreign leaders such as Ronald Reagan and Margaret Thatcher, who opposed or sought to minimize sanctions but were clearly fighting a losing battle on this issue—the former against Congress, the latter against other leaders in the Commonwealth and EC—so long as the apartheid regime continued.

Insofar as sanctions on South Africa did contribute in this way, they may be considered a successful example of conflict prevention. Violence was not avoided altogether in South Africa, but few doubt that there would have been violence on a much larger scale and over a much longer period if State President F. W. de Klerk had not made up his mind, under strong pressure from the South African business elite, to negotiate a peaceful and orderly transfer of power to the ANC through free elections in which people of all races would take part on equal terms.

IRAQ. Iraq's invasion of Kuwait in August 1990 was a textbook case of aggression, which drew an immediate response from the Security Council. Within five days the Council had voted to impose the most comprehensive and most rapidly applied sanctions regime in UN history. All trade and financial transactions with Iraq and Iraqi-occupied Kuwait were prohibited; the overseas assets of both countries were frozen; and, for the first time, a sanctions-monitoring committee was set up to oversee implementation.

But these sanctions did not prevent conflict. To have done so, they would have had to be imposed or at least threatened before Kuwait was invaded. Neither the Security Council collectively, nor any of its members individually, made any attempt to use sanctions preventively in this sense. Nor were sanctions deemed sufficient in themselves to compel Iraqi withdrawal: this was done by military force. Yet again sanctions proved to be not an alternative to the use of armed force, but a useful adjunct to it.

The sanctions on Iraq by now have remained in place, however, for a decade after the liberation of Kuwait, in order to compel Iraqi compliance with cease-fire conditions imposed by the UN, mainly in the area of disarmament. In this they appeared by 1997 to have been largely successful, although the UN Special Committee (UNSCOM) was not yet able to certify full compliance. Further U.S. and U.K. military action was taken in December 1998 in an unsuccessful attempt to compel Iraqi cooperation with UNSCOM. The sanctions are still in force, and the United States is unlikely to agree to their being lifted so long as Saddam Hussein remains in power. His removal is thus an unofficial objective of sanctions for at least one permanent member of the Security Council. Only if and when it is achieved will an assessment of sanctions' role in bringing it about become possible.

Meanwhile, there can be no doubt that sanctions have inflicted crippling damage on Iraq's economy and substantially inhibited its rearmament. They have thus served to contain a regime that has twice in the recent past waged aggressive war (against Iran in 1980 as well as Kuwait in 1990). This must be considered a successful example of conflict prevention—but only in a context where force had already been used.

As always, the primary victim has been Iraq's civilian population, parts of which are suffering terrible hardship. Efforts to alleviate this through waivers for food and medical supplies, and by allowing Iraq to sell limited quantities of oil to finance the purchase of such goods, have been largely defeated by the Iraqi regime's predictable determination to turn sanctions to its own advantage. It seeks to do this by inflaming popular feeling within Iraq against the sanctions-imposing powers, by eliciting humanitarian sympathy around the world, by exploiting the black market (and probably also manipulating the world oil market) for financial gain, and by using its control over foreign exchange and other scarce commodities to reward its supporters and so maintain itself in power. It is thus at least possible that sanctions have strengthened rather than weakened Saddam Hussein's hold on power, at any rate in the short term.

Insofar as the real object of sanctions is his removal, it must be asked whether this objective could not have been achieved more swiftly, and at a lower cost in human suffering, by the direct application of military force—which a group of states did not scruple to use in April 1991 in order to protect a part of the Iraqi population from Saddam's anger, even though this involved a clear violation of Iraq's territorial integrity and has resulted in a de facto partition of the country. The case for a full-scale military intervention to liberate the whole of Iraq from his rule would surely have been as strong, if not stronger.

LIBYA. Sanctions were imposed on Libya in March 1992 in an attempt to compel the Libyan government to extradite two of its citizens accused of involvement in the destruction of a U.S. civilian airliner. These sanctions were not comprehensive, but they included an arms embargo and a ban on the sale or supply of aircraft and any services or products that were destined to be used for construction of airfields and related facilities and equipment. (A somewhat quaint attempt to "make the punishment fit the crime" in the manner of W. S. Gilbert's Mikado!) As with Iraq, a sanctions-monitoring committee was set up, and member states were required to reduce their diplomatic representation in Libya. In November 1993 the sanctions were tightened, but they still excluded petroleum and its derivatives as well as agricultural products. (The U.S. unilaterally has also frozen Libyan assets, boycotted Libyan oil, and banned U.S. investment in Libya.)

These sanctions eventually succeeded in obtaining the handover of the two suspects in 1999, but not (as some hoped) in forcing a change of regime in Libya. But, as in Iraq, they did inflict suffering on the population, contributing to a 30 percent unemployment rate. Like Saddam Hussein, Muammar Qaddafi tried to exploit this, claiming that the sanctions-induced recession obliged him to repatriate more than one million migrant laborers to neighboring countries. But inasmuch as he has pursued a less aggressive foreign policy of late, and is apparently no longer involved in sponsoring terrorism, it can be claimed that these sanctions successfully prevented conflict. It is also possible—though it cannot be proved—that they helped to deter some other states from sponsoring terrorism.

HAITI. In Haiti sanctions were used with the explicit purpose of changing the country's internal regime—or, more precisely, of restoring the elected president Jean-Bertrand Aristide who had been ousted by a military coup in September 1991. There was no obvious reason why this internal development, however unwelcome, should be held to threaten international peace and security, as Article 39 of the UN Charter requires; but the United Nations did have a kind of parental interest in Mr. Aristide's government because his election had been monitored, and certified free and fair, by the General Assembly. The United States also had an interest in preventing large numbers of Haitian refugees from arriving in Florida. But sanctions actually had the effect of aggravating this problem, because they gave Haitians economic as well as political motives for fleeing the country. Far from preventing conflict, therefore, they helped provide the United States with a motive for military intervention.

In Haiti—as in Iraq, Libya, and indeed South Africa—the brunt of sanctions was borne, at least initially, by the poor. But it was also clear, as in South Africa, that many of the poor nonetheless favored sanctions as a mark of the regime's isolation, presaging its eventual downfall. In the later stages, moreover, sanctions were targeted specifically at Haiti's economic and military elites: in October 1993 the United States froze the assets of forty-one government supporters; in January 1994 it froze those of all members of the Haitian military, and prohibited transactions with them. These sanctions, and the offer to lift them, may have helped persuade the Haitian junta to step aside in September 1994. The fact remains, however, that it did so only at the very last minute, when a U.S. military invasion was unmistakably imminent. Once again, sanctions proved at best a useful adjunct to military force, rather than a substitute for it.

YUGOSLAVIA. In Yugoslavia incentives rather than sanctions were used by the European Community and the Conference on Security and Cooperation in Europe in an attempt to prevent the conflict provoked by Croatian and Slovenian secession at the end of June 1991. It is possible that these efforts might have been more successful if accompanied by explicit threats of sanctions, though the latter would have had to be very carefully targeted so as to deter both the secessionist republics and the federal authorities from initiating the use of force (in circumstances where there was ample room for dispute over what constituted an act of force), and to oblige both sides to seek and abide by a negotiated compromise.

United Nations sanctions were introduced only after war had broken out and was raging violently in Croatia, in September 1991. They then took the form of a blanket embargo on all arms deliveries to any part of Yugoslavia. This had the effect of freezing a huge imbalance in favor of the Yugoslav People's Army (JNA), most of whose weapons passed into Serb hands as the country disintegrated. Yet the embargo at the time had near unanimous support among UN members, including the many nonaligned states that later lobbied hard for it to be lifted during the war in Bosnia-Herzegovina.

Sanctions played little part in ending the fighting in Croatia in January 1992, and no serious attempt was made to use them to prevent the outbreak of war in Bosnia two months later. It was only in May 1992, by which time "ethnic cleansing" in Bosnia was in full swing and the extent of Serbian assistance to the Bosnian Serbs was becoming clear, that the UN Security Council decided to impose a complete economic embargo and blockade on the Federal Republic of Yugoslavia (FRY—Serbia and Montenegro), as well as to order that all diplomatic, scientific, cultural, and sports relations be broken off.

These sanctions lasted for three and a half years, but for much of that time they were very unevenly enforced. As Lord Owen, the European Union Mediator, recalls, "Serbia had a virtually open border with Macedonia and Albania, both of which developed a thriving black market business, particularly in breaking oil sanctions."[3] Yet gradually the noose was tightened. The United Nations and the European Union cooperated in establishing and maintaining a network of Sanctions Assistance Missions (SAMs) of unprecedented scale, aided by a communication and cooperation center (SAM-COM) in Brussels. This slowed, but did not cut off, the flow of goods to the ruling elite and military in Serbia.

There is no doubt that, over time, sanctions had a huge impact on Serbia's economy and society. Inflation skyrocketed, and agricultural supplies and fertilizer virtually disappeared—as did fuel, spare parts, and supplies for all industries. Equally, there is little doubt that anxiety to get sanctions lifted was an important motive prompting President Slobodan Milosevic of Serbia to detach himself from his former protégés, the Serb leaders in Bosnia and Croatia. Lord Owen believes sanctions had already begun to weaken the resolve of Milosevic and other leaders of the FRY by the spring of 1993, when they accepted the Vance-Owen peace plan.[4] But Milosevic at that time was unable (or unwilling) to impose the plan on the Bosnian Serbs. (Owen blames this on lack of firm support for the plan from the West, especially the U.S. But he argues that such firmness should have included a willingness to use air power to interdict supplies to the Bosnian Serbs from the FRY.)

In any event, it was not until 1995 that peace was imposed on Bosnia through the Dayton accords, following an intensive NATO bombardment of the Bosnian Serbs and a spectacular ground offensive by the Croatian army, which, in the meantime, had been trained and handsomely equipped, with Western connivance (ignoring the arms embargo). Thus, although sanctions may be held to have shown themselves a useful tool of conflict resolution in Bosnia, they were used in conjunction with, not as a substitute for, armed force. This is not an example of conflict prevention. Later, in 1998–99, sanctions completely failed to halt the bloodshed in Kosovo, or to prevent it from escalating into a large-scale international conflict.

SUB-SAHARAN AFRICA. Similarly, in Somalia and Liberia in 1992, Rwanda in 1994, and Sierra Leone in 1998, sanctions were introduced only well after the outbreak of violence. In none of these cases did they prevent the violence from continuing and even escalating. It is possible that violence in Somalia and Liberia could have been even more destructive had there been no restriction on the type of weapons available—but probably the combatants' lack of resources, and the fact that neither country was of strategic interest to potential suppliers after the end of the Cold War, were more important limiting factors. In Rwanda the arms embargo came too late to prevent a full-scale genocide of up to one million people, carried out mostly with very low-tech weapons. Many of the factors that led to this genocide are also present in neighboring Burundi, yet no mandatory UN sanctions have been applied to that country. It appears the international community is very reluctant to employ sanctions as a genuinely preventive tool, rather than as a response to ongoing conflicts.

That is also true in Angola, where the Security Council applied sanctions—an embargo on arms and related material, military assistance, petroleum, and petroleum products—only in September 1993, nearly two years after the collapse of the cease-fire following the UN-monitored elections of 1991. These sanctions did however break new ground in being targeted specifically at one party in an internal conflict, namely, UNITA, which was held responsible for the resumption and continuation of the fighting. And they probably did play a part in bringing UNITA back to the negotiating table, leading eventually to a new cease-fire and a more carefully constructed peace process. But this did not prevent a full-scale resumption of hostilities in 1998.

Such targeting of sanctions at an internal "bad guy" is, of course, much more feasible in a conflict such as that in Angola, where UNITA controls a more or less clearly defined territory. It would have been almost impossible to apply in a situation of total anarchy like that in Somalia or Liberia. But the precedent does raise an important question about Iraq, where the Security Council insisted on applying sanctions to the whole territory, including the liberated Kurdish area in the north. It would surely make more sense to limit them to the area actually controlled by the "guilty party," namely, Saddam Hussein's regime.

LESSONS FOR THE FUTURE

Elizabeth Rogers writes: "Without sanctions it seems likely that Saddam Hussein would have withheld his concessions on weapons of mass destruction and further built up his military, the Haitian elites would not have accepted Aristide's return, and Yugoslav President Milosevic would not have pressured the Bosnian Serbs to make concessions for peace. In sum, the post–Cold War experience suggests that the future prospects for the success of serious sanctions efforts are bright."[5] Our view is that these examples do not warrant such a broad conclusion. At most, they show that sanctions are a useful tool of conflict resolution, rather than prevention, and then only when used in conjunction with, rather than as a substitute for, military force.

Sanctions probably helped prevent a major conflict in South Africa. They have helped to ensure that Saddam Hussein could not revert to his aggressive behavior pattern since 1991, and that his ability to wage non-conventional war was effectively dismantled. They secured the handover of the two Lockerbie suspects and may have deterred Libya and other states from sponsoring terrorism since 1992. They may have helped persuade the Haitian junta to step aside rather than resist the U.S. military intervention in 1994. And their use in all the cases discussed may have reinforced the credibility of international conflict prevention efforts in other contexts by demonstrating that ignoring international pressure can entail real costs.

But clearly sanctions have not as yet been systematically used for conflict prevention. As a general rule they are deployed only after a grave breach of international law, usually involving large-scale violence, has already occurred. Of the cases discussed, South Africa, Haiti, and Libya are the only ones where large-scale violence was actually avoided. In these cases sanctions could be said to have helped prevent conflict. But the precise contribution made by sanctions remains controversial. Most commentators would say it was not the main element. In both South Africa and Haiti the element of military force, or the threat of violence, was clearly present—and in the case of Haiti, at least, it was clearly decisive.

Both, moreover, were cases where the main issue was the domestic character, rather than the external behavior, of the sanctioned regime. For sanctions to be used systematically as a tool of conflict prevention, the international community would need to be prepared to generalize from these two instances. That is, it would have to agree on norms of internal behavior by which regimes could be judged and found guilty *before* their actions had led to actual conflict. The systematic monopolizing of power by a minority racial group—as in South Africa—may perhaps provide one such norm. It seems less likely that the forcible removal of an elected government—as in Haiti—will provide another, at least until such time as a popular mandate, conferred through free and fair elections, has come to be seen as an essential qualification for any government to be recognized by other states and allowed to represent its people in the United Nations. That time may be closer now than it was before the end of the Cold War, but it is still not very close. Until it arrives, Haiti is probably best regarded as a special case, the treatment of which had far more to do with its close proximity to the United States than with any universalizable norm. Even if such a norm were accepted in theory, it is far from clear that great powers would be willing to undertake the costs and risks of enforcing it, except in places where they felt their own national interests to be directly at stake. It seems probable, therefore, that sanctions will only prevent conflict by deterrence—that is, by making an example of states that engage in conflict, and so deterring others—rather than directly.

If we think of the post–Cold War era in economic rather than political terms (the global market), new forms of sanctions become possible at the subpolitical level. Loans given by or supported by international institutions like the IMF, World Bank, and EBRD have strong conditionality clauses attached to them. These are primarily directed to ensuring against commercial risk—for example, default. But political risk is part of commercial risk, so that political conditions (like respect for human rights) can be made part of the conditions, as they are in the case of loans from the EBRD. The recent practice of private credit-rating agencies, in ranking countries by political as well as commercial risk, points in the same direction. Similarly, the deepening and widening of world trade rules, together with the establishment of a monitoring organization (the WTO), offers a theoretical possibility of linking trade issues to legal conditions, including human rights guarantees, on a multilateral basis. Thus the process of economic integration can be used to promote a common set of standards for doing business which spill over into political standards.

But it remains to be considered how far sanctions of this type are cost-effective. Economic sanctions start with negative connotations for liberals. Historically, embargo and blockade have been instruments of war, and liberals have deplored their use outside the special circumstances of war. More generally, economic sanctions contradict the principle of nondiscrimination in trade. They are instruments of "trade war," which can lead to hot wars. Economic liberals have traditionally preferred nondiscriminatory trade as a means of promoting both prosperity and international harmony.

The League of Nations made the first attempt to detach economic sanctions from their war, or war-inducing, setting and to promote them as instruments for maintaining peace. It introduced the concept of penalizing unacceptable behavior by measures that fell short of war and provided an alternative to war. The UN extended the concept of acceptable (peaceful) behavior to the maintenance of human rights within states, breach of which could call forth economic sanctions. But the use of economic sanctions to uphold "civilized values" carries the danger of increasing interference in free commerce between nations where no issue of war arises. This begins to look like imperialism or protectionism decked out in the language of "rights." Economic liberals instinctively see sanctions as a cover for reasserting state control over economic life.

From this perspective, sanctions can be seen as one arena of the contemporary struggle between liberal and statist forces. The end of the Cold War exposed two potentially conflicting concepts of universalism:

global unification through capital and trade flows on the one hand, and the establishment of a law-based world order, sometimes called New World Order, on the other. The first offers a trade dividend (faster growth through increased trade), the second a peace dividend (reduction in military establishments and arms expenditures). The two are partly connected: a trade dividend is an important precondition of the peace dividend, as trade growth reduces the conversion costs of the military sector; conversely trade growth is damaged by a weak legal environment. However, they are based on different philosophies of pacification, and if carried to extremes, each can damage the other. For example, economic sanctions imposed on countries that fail to conform to norms of human rights impede economic intercourse and thus damage any pacifying effects of such intercourse. Moreover, it is far from obvious that human rights will fare better in a country isolated and impoverished by sanctions than in one with a growing middle class and rapidly thickening international links. In general, the opposite seems more likely to be true.

Insofar as the peace dividend means reduced reliance on military means, it implies increased use of economic sanctions to secure law-based behavior. This threatens the trade dividend. The use of economic instruments to support political goals carries the familiar risk of political trade wars, and the possible breakup of the emerging world economy into political trade blocs. Bergeijk points out that a move to a "better" world in terms of human rights carries costs. The "opportunity costs of the New World Order may be summarized as the potential gains from trade that might have to be foregone in the course of defending the international legal order." Bergeijk argues that only "very serious infractions" of international rules should be considered as potential cases for use of sanctions.[6]

CONCLUSION

The health metaphor undoubtedly has dirigiste implications. If you know what health is, you have a duty to promote and maintain it—the doctor's duty to his patient or to the world. But the application of this metaphor to political life is dangerous. Hitler likened Jews to germs and bacilli that had to be eliminated to restore healthy races. The communists called their opponents vermin. Because we have only a very imperfect idea of what political health is and what the conditions for its maintenance are, we ought to err heavily on the side of freedom and experiment, reserving our medical interventions for cases of clear and present danger to the survival and well-being of the human race, or large parts of it. Clearly, the question of how much freedom needs to be sacrificed in the interests of global health will be dominant in the next century.

RECOMMENDATIONS

1. When sanctions are used they should as far as possible be targeted at the decision makers whose policy or behavior they are intended to punish or influence, rather than at the general population of the state.
2. Sanctions should not be thought of as a humane alternative to the use of force. They are themselves a way of using force, and their human consequences, if they are sustained over a long period, can be as bad as, or even worse than, those of direct military action. They should be seen as a method of waging war rather than preventing it.
3. It should not be assumed that regimes targeted by sanctions will cooperate in shielding the general population from their most painful effects. On the contrary, a regime of the type that incurs sanctions is likely to be quite unscrupulous in its treatment of the population and quite willing to exploit human suffering for its own political ends.
4. More attention should be given to ways of compensating innocent victims of sanctions, both in the target state and in neighboring states whose commerce is disrupted.
5. Isolating or pillorying a state will not normally bring about an improvement in its human rights performance. Discreet warnings from private investors may often be more effective in altering a regime's behavior than public ones from other governments.

PART 3
MAJOR ACTORS

As bloated bodies floated over the waterfalls and clogged Lake Kivu, as rescuers discovered churches packed with the hacked bodies of those who had unwisely sought refuge in a house of God, as a million desperate people fled across the border in a single week to overwhelm the town of Goma, those who believed in preventive diplomacy had to face the depth of its failure in Rwanda.

Warning signals of impending genocide were not heeded. The opportunity for timely intervention was shamefully missed. Early neglect allowed, like an infection gone wild, an outbreak of ethnic madness to spread through green hills and small villages until more than half a million men, women, and children were killed with clubs and machetes. And then, as so often happens in epidemics, the victors became the victims, and hundreds of thousands more perished in overcrowded and unsanitary camps where the evil seeds of hatred and ignorance allowed the festering sores of conflict to flourish.

A similar tragedy unfolded in Kosovo as the twentieth century stumbled to a close. NATO, the most powerful military alliance in the world, bombed a state into submission, but seemed surprised to realize that people flee bombs and war zones. When adequate preventive plans did not exist, a million cruelly displaced persons ended up in poorly prepared refugee camps. To care for the vast number of displaced, most, awash in a chaotic world of conflicts, turn to the United Nations.

We know that budgetary restrictions for preventive actions coupled with a lack of political will result in costly postconflict therapy—a poor choice when prevention was possible. Since the first edition of this book, only three years ago, preventive diplomacy has gradually gained a following among leaders who see no alternative. Some nations, led by Sweden, have formally endorsed the "culture of prevention" and are implementing programs based on ideas proposed in this text. Let us hope that this approach is recognized as indispensable in the new millennium.

In this section Cyrus Vance and Herbert S. Okun provide a thoughtful analysis of the strengths and weaknesses of three critical partners in international conflict prevention; the rest of the section is devoted to the United Nations. In moving medical metaphors, UN Secretary-General Kofi A. Annan discusses the importance of military forces in diplomacy, emphasizing that timing and coordination of humanitarian and political initiatives are critical in preventing the escalation of impending or existing conflicts. Former UN Secretary-General Boutros Boutros-Ghali discusses the wide range of diplomatic tools available for preventive action but cautions that states can sometimes be even more difficult than patients. Marrack Goulding reflects on the techniques of fact-finding missions and cites the very real problems faced by the United Nations in developing preventive programs in the absence of local, regional, or international political understanding. Sweden's Secretary of State for Foreign Affairs Jan Eliasson, the first UN Under-Secretary-General for Humanitarian Affairs, details the "ladder of prevention" available in promoting international peace.

10

CREATING HEALTHY ALLIANCES

CYRUS VANCE AND HERBERT S. OKUN

More than two centuries ago, Alexander Pope wrote in his philosophic poem the *Epistle on Man* that "Reason's whole pleasure, all the joys of sense / Lie in three words—health, peace, and competence." His words seem to us to be appropriate to the problem we have been discussing, particularly the last word—competence. For if health and peace remain our two goals, and they surely do, then we can go about the business of working to achieve these goals only if we do so competently. This will require a great deal of thought, effort, and goodwill from each part of the humanitarian triad—from governments, from international organizations, and from nongovernmental organizations.

Let us begin by briefly assessing the capabilities and limitations of each of the three elements of the triad. We will then suggest some ways and means of enhancing their individual strengths while improving mutual coordination in situations of emergency or conflict.

With respect to governments, only they have the financial means— derived from their tax base—to tackle the really large emergencies. There are of course private-funding sources, but they are understandably much smaller. In 1996, for example, the last full year for which figures are available, about 70 percent of the total funding for emergency humanitarian assistance worldwide came from governments; and that figure does not include military outlays in support of humanitarian operations. Governments also command other vital resources, such as surplus food stocks. Additionally, governments often have specialized civilian capabilities that they can and do put at the disposal of the international community in emergency situations. In the United States, for example, the Center for Disease Control in Atlanta, Georgia, has played a major role in cooperating with international health authorities.

Similarly, the Nordic countries, both individually and collectively, have placed qualified national institutions at the service of the international community. For example, they have offered their excellent police-training academies to instruct international civilian police in peacekeeping operations. They have also provided many election observers, as well as technical expertise in conducting free elections.

At the same time, however, governments have their limitations and drawbacks. First, no government is large enough—or often willing enough—to take on a tough emergency or conflict situation all by itself. No matter how they may be defined, "national interests" will come into play, and such interests will often be insufficient to move national authorities to take action. Governments, especially representative governments, also must pay attention to their domestic political base. Therefore, it should not be an object of either surprise or scorn that they want to keep casualties as low as possible when they deploy their troops into conflict situations. Nor is it unusual for taxpayers to want their tax monies to be spent at home. In addition, we must always remember that, when they do take action, governments are rarely disinterested; their actions will not be determined by humanitarian instincts alone. Finally, individual governments cannot by themselves create new international standards, such as additional rules for protecting refugees or limiting the use of land mines. So, essential as they are, governments are not the sole answer.

When the need arises, governments and citizens alike rely on the second leg of the triad, international organizations. These exist both within and outside the UN system. The United Nations and its agencies, of course, play an essential role. As a universal organization, unlike governments and NGOs, the United Nations possesses international legal authority recognized by 185 member states. UN humanitarian agencies can also mobilize resources and pool the collective financial contributions of individual governments when collective action is called for. In the last four years UN agencies have become increasingly proficient at meeting the escalating number of complex emergencies. For example, the United Nations High Commission for Refugees (UNHCR) now has eight emergency-response teams available at all times to deploy to the field, and the World Food Programme (WFP) prepositions food stocks in order to be able to respond promptly to crises.

But the United Nations has its limitations, and there are restrictions on the actions it can undertake in dealing with conflicts and emergency situations. It is the creature of governments and, unless it is operating under Chapter 7 of the UN Charter in a matter involving international peace and security, the United Nations must gain the acquiescence of local authorities in order to operate on their territory. For example, there is no meaningful UN role in Sri Lanka where a civil conflict has been in progress since 1983. Just as UN agencies cannot go where they are not wanted, so too the United Nations cannot do what major governments deny. For example, the Secretary-General in 1994 made urgent, unprecedented appeals to the Security Council for action on the developing genocide in Rwanda, but for several months very little was done. Likewise, the UN has difficulty in staying the course in conflict situations where its major members and donors are either uninterested or have changed their priorities. Afghanistan, where the UN role is now declining, provides an example. As an intergovernmental organization, the United Nations cannot go beyond what governments are willing to permit.

Besides the UN, there are other international or regional organizations that also play an important role in emergency or conflict situations. Three organizations stand out because of their size or mandates: the International Red Cross and Red Crescent Movement, led by the International Committee of the Red Cross (ICRC); the International Organization for Migration (IOM); and the European Community Humanitarian Office (ECHO).

The ICRC is the world's oldest international—and independent—humanitarian institution, and it is the largest outside of the UN system. It operates in more than fifty countries and has an annual budget approaching a billion dollars. The world community over the years has entrusted the ICRC with unique legal capabilities and responsibilities: it is the guardian and implementing agency of the Geneva Conventions, and it is authorized to bring protection and assistance to victims of both international and noninternational armed conflict. Thus, for example, the ICRC is active inside Chechnya where no UN agency is present.

But, like the United Nations, the ICRC must obtain the agreement of governments before it can work in a particular country. The ICRC also cannot undertake any overt political action to resolve an emergency or conflict situation, because of the role it plays as a neutral intermediary. Although the ICRC can and does call upon governments and others to live up to their commitments in times of conflict, it cannot compel compliance with international humanitarian law. Only governments can do that.

With respect to the third leg of the triad—nongovernmental organizations—they have come to play an increasingly important role in conflict situations. Some fifteen to twenty large international NGOs deliver all sorts of aid in large-scale emergencies and often dominate humanitarian operations. Dozens of other smaller and more specialized NGOs are selectively involved in crisis situations. Numerous NGOs are also active in seeking to build civil societies, monitoring human rights, providing informal mediation services, and doing developmental work to prevent further outbreaks of violence. In addition to outside NGOs, many local NGOs are, of course, active in their own societies in economic development, in preventive diplomacy, and in emergency situations when such occur.

The strengths of NGOs are multiple and varied. Many of them embody the pluralist values of democratic societies. They often advocate human rights where governments might be reticent to do so. Operationally, the large international NGOs provide the arms and legs for UN agencies and national governments by actually delivering the bulk of humanitarian aid. In order to do this, they receive official funding, and they have the ability to spend such funds flexibly. Along with rapid growth in recent years, the major NGOs have become increasingly professionalized: military officers, some recently retired, have been recruited from national armies. Large NGOs are also specializing—for example, CARE in logistics, OXFAM/UK in water and sanitation, and Catholic Relief Services in food distribution. Finally, NGOs often show a commendable commitment to economic development activities as well as to emergency actions, thereby linking their short-term relief work to longer-term development priorities.

But NGOs also have weaknesses and shortcomings, and it would be unrealistic not to recognize them. First, while espousing broad humanitarian principles, some have their own partisan religious or political agendas. Rather than promoting peaceful settlements of conflict or working to prevent potential conflicts, such agendas can continue or even stimulate violence. In addition, as NGOs grow they tend to become increasingly dependent on official governmental funding. This results in their not being able to go where the need for prevention is paramount or where a humanitarian need is great, but rather where governments want them to go. The old proverb "He who pays the piper calls the tune" is still operative.

Increasing competition for funds also means that NGOs must be visible in crises that draw the attention—and especially the cameras—of the media. If an NGO is not present in Bosnia, or in the southern Sudan or in Goma, its funding government and its board of directors are likely to ask why. Another danger, inherent in the well-intentioned activism of most NGOs, is that of dominating a situation so that the indigenous people (and even local NGOs) lose the will to solve their own problems. Creating a culture of dependency is in nobody's interest and must be guarded against. Last but not least, one of the great virtues of NGOs lies precisely in their freedom of action—in their marching to the beat of their own drummer. But this free-spirited attitude, desirable as it is, makes coordination with other NGOs and with official institutions difficult to achieve.

Before turning to specific recommendations, we must remember one fundamental principle: a first commandment, if you will. Each element of the humanitarian triad—governments, international organizations, and NGOs—has a valid, legitimate role to play. Thus it falls to governments to initiate the political or military actions that may prove decisive in conflict resolution. It falls to international organizations to initiate concerted international efforts. And it falls to NGOs to execute rapid and effective responses and to mobilize the resources of the public at large. Each must take the lead in its own domain and each has the right to count on the understanding and support of the others.

Turning to specifics, we would recommend first that major governments ensure that adequate resources are made available not only to respond to current crises, but also to support financially the prevention and management of incipient conflicts. At a time of budget-cutting in most industrialized nations, it is hard for governments to avoid prioritizing and earmarking funds for emergencies of particular interest. But the imperatives of emergency humanitarian action also require that governments maintain the means to respond to new or rapidly deteriorating situations through administrative and budgetary mechanisms, such as standby reserve funds, prepositioned humanitarian stockpiles, joint civilian-military training exercises, rosters of specialized personnel, and the like. It is essential that governments also ensure that international organizations are equipped to develop such standby capabilities, so that they too can respond quickly and effectively to new conflict situations. In short, governments must invest in humanitarian capacity building— not only by funding urgent demining projects, but also by funding a comprehensive mine-clearance database, so that future demining projects can be well designed.

Second, it is important to recognize that in recent years progress has been made in improving coordination among humanitarian organizations, both within the UN system and in the field. Thus, for example, responding to the difficulties confronted in Northern Iraq in the aftermath of the Gulf War, the UN General Assembly in 1992 established a Department of Humanitarian Affairs (DHA). It was given the critical task of coordinating the delivery of humanitarian aid in future emergencies. Shortly thereafter, DHA established an Inter-Agency Standing Committee—composed of the heads of UNICEF, UNHCR, WFP, FAO, WHO, UNDP, as well as representatives of the ICRC, the International Federation of Red Cross and Red Crescent Societies, and three consortia of international NGOs. DHA took this essential step in order to engage the major actors delivering humanitarian relief in ongoing policy coordination. In the field, the international community since 1992 has also experimented with a number of different mechanisms—giving responsibility for coordinating humanitarian response variously to a "lead agency," such as UNHCR in Bosnia; to Special Representatives of the Secretary-General; to a Disaster Management Team under the UN's Resident Coordinator; and to DHA's own appointee as Humanitarian Coordinator.

There is, however, no textbook solution for optimal coordination in all emergencies. What is now required is the further strengthening of policy-coordinating mechanisms at the headquarters level and clearer lines of authority in the field. Policy-planning functions now exist at UN headquarters. They include the Consolidated Emergency Appeals mechanism, the Central Emergency Revolving Fund, the Special Representative of the Secretary-General on Internally Displaced Persons, and the new databases on early warning, antipersonnel land mines, and the like. These need to be available immediately in specific emergency or conflict situations.

In the field, the international community must ensure that, whatever the organizational arrangements may be, there should be a clear focal point and individuals responsible for coordination of humanitarian and other civilian assistance operations in crisis situations. Such a focal point should interface with NGOs as well as with military forces in the area. Someone must clearly be in charge. Moreover, field operations will be improved to the degree that specialized agencies develop their own memoranda of understandings for better coordination with each other.

Third, although the numbers are inexact, internally displaced persons (IDPs) have increased from less than five million in 1983 to about nineteen million in early 1999. Their number now exceeds the thirteen million refugees in the world. The large number of IDPs has created a new and serious international humanitarian dilemma. Internally displaced persons often flee to dangerous, exposed locations or areas vulnerable to hostile combatants, making them hard to reach or help. In addition, governments are often unwilling for political reasons to admit the existence of internally displaced persons and to consent to the delivery of external assistance to them.

In this connection, we note that several humanitarian organizations—including UNHCR, the ICRC, and the IOM—have general mandates that permit them to assist internally displaced persons. Yet no organization has a specific mandate to attend to their needs. It is important, therefore, that the international community develop new, uniform, and practical policies to protect and assist internally displaced persons. It is important both to strengthen the ability of the international relief agencies and to strengthen international humanitarian law and human rights statutes governing the treatment of internally displaced persons.

Finally, measures need to be taken to ensure the safety of civilian aid providers, as humanitarian workers are increasingly being caught up in fighting associated with internal conflicts. International humanitarian law already calls for the protection of humanitarian workers and institutions, but much more needs to be done. Sanctions should be seriously considered against governments or combatant groups that target or permit the targeting of civilian humanitarian workers. We have seen these selfless men and women in action, and they deserve our fullest support.

11
THE PEACEKEEPING PRESCRIPTION
KOFI A. ANNAN

If I were a doctor examining the health of the world today, I would be greatly alarmed at the state of my patient. The international community, vibrant in its resolve to achieve a strong, stable, and healthy political environment as the post–Cold War era began, was drained and weakened by one bout after another of conflict during the last decade. In Somalia, Bosnia, Rwanda, Sierra Leone, Kosovo, and elsewhere, it has had to weather the massive displacement of people, extensive loss of life, and irreparable damage which are conflict's concomitants. Clearly, this is a pattern that must be broken.

Ideally, each of these bouts of conflict would either have been prevented completely or nipped in the bud. Prevention is—and would have been—by far the best medicine. But the practice of prevention, in both medicine and politics, is uneven. Some diseases resist early treatment. Some patients resist treatment until their condition becomes critical—or even longer. In many cases, the disease spreads beyond the area of its inception. Because of this, it often becomes necessary to address conflicts fully blown, to treat the bout of conflict at or near its height.

Even at this stage, the efforts undertaken, while hopefully curative and sometimes palliative, also have a preventive aspect to them. They can prevent the escalation of conflict or the resumption of it. As in the case in which a primary tumor is discovered, intervention of this kind can prevent metastasis and hopefully bring the disease into remission. Thus, when we speak here of the "peacekeeping prescription" or the "treatment" it entails, we must always be clear that, while we have one eye on the crisis of the moment we have the other on protecting the future and preventing the threat now posed against it from becoming a reality. Prevention is a great part of the goal of peacekeeping, and, in many instances, has constituted a large (and too often overlooked) part of its success.

Many of the conflicts of the last ten years have had, for various reasons, to be treated using the peacekeeping prescription. And, as with any other ailment, the disease has manifested itself differently in each instance, and the treatment has had to be adapted to those variations. Peacekeeping has proved itself a flexible remedy. Since the first edition of *Preventive Diplomacy*, we have deployed new United Nations peacekeeping operations in Haiti, Guatemala, the Balkans, Sierra Leone, the Central African Republic, and the Democratic Republic of Congo. While these have been adapted to differing circumstances, the main themes I enumerated in this volume in 1996 remain valid today. As Secretary-General, I remain committed to enhancing the Organization's capacity to understand conflict and to respond in a meaningful and timely way.

If we are to strengthen the international community, if we are effectively to confront the conflicts before us and those which await, if we are to prevent their spread or resumption, we need to understand three things as clearly as possible: the disease we are addressing, the treatment we are applying, and the changes to both of them which are occurring. It is to those points that I wish to turn here.

DIAGNOSIS

In the context of peacekeeping, how do we define and diagnose the disease of conflict? What are its symptoms? Technically, peacekeeping is prescribed for conflicts that constitute a threat to international peace and security. The civil strife in the former Yugoslavia was identified as constituting this kind of threat, as were the genocide that ravaged Rwanda in 1994 and the interclan warfare that engulfed Somalia in the early 1990s.

A quick cross section of these conflicts alone can highlight two of the most important characteristics of current conflicts for which peacekeeping has recently been prescribed: most of them are intrastate wars, and many of them have been identified as ethnic conflicts.

Peacekeeping through the first forty years of its over-fifty-year history was devoted primarily to the treatment of conflicts between clearly delimited armed forces on either side of a cease-fire line; missions were deployed to separate antagonists, verify cease-fires, and promote accord. Following the fall of the Berlin Wall and the dissolution of the bipolar system, however, a seminal change occurred. Increasingly, the conflicts for which peacekeeping was prescribed were internal in nature. More than two-thirds of the operations deployed since the end of the Cold War—and more than two-thirds of those currently in the field—have been sent to respond to internal conflicts. These recent wars, which include the former Yugoslavia, Somalia, Rwanda, Sierra Leone, and Kosovo, share other traits. These conflicts have displaced hundreds of thousands or even millions of people, riven entire societies, devastated economies, caused irreparable physical and psychological damage, and risked involving or have actually involved other countries.

Many of them have also been perceived as showing strong symptoms of ethnic conflict. Ethnic conflict as a symptom is, at best, extremely difficult to assess. Looking at any of the internal conflicts we have mentioned, most of us would be hard-pressed to say exactly where ethnic differences were the cause of conflict and where they were the result of it. Ethnic differences are not in and of themselves either symptoms or causes of conflict; in societies where they are accepted and respected, people of vastly different backgrounds live peacefully and productively together. Ethnic differences become charged—conflictual—when they are used for political ends, when ethnic groups are intentionally placed in opposition to each other. Of the conflicts we have mentioned, it has been said that they are not really ethnic conflicts, but political conflicts in ethnic clothing. It is a point that we will have to continue to observe and consider.

The broader range of symptoms which it has become necessary to address have created what are basically new strains of conflict. Although the kinds of conflict to which peacekeeping traditionally responded are still very active—and even still virulent in certain areas—the kind of conflicts that occupy us principally today (and that would probably do so well into the future) constitute more of a complex or syndrome in nature. They display many different but connected symptoms and usually require multiple medications.

PRESCRIPTION

In developing and prescribing treatments for these conflicts, the United Nations has attempted to focus upon and reflect the complexity and individuality of the cases before it. We have attempted to better identify and understand both the new strains of conflict appearing and the possible responses to them. We have reconfirmed the necessity of the core elements of the treatment. We have expanded its range of application. And we have improved our understanding of when it should be applied, in what dosages, and when it should be withdrawn.

In response to the new symptoms and strains just mentioned, mandates prescribed in the last few years have far exceeded the traditional supervision of truces and separation of antagonists; they have expanded to include elements as diverse as monitoring free and fair elections, guaranteeing the delivery of humanitarian aid, overseeing land reform, observing and reporting on human rights abuses or violations, maintaining presence in towns and villages under attack to prevent loss of life, establishing safe and secure environments, assisting in the strengthening or rebuilding of social and political structures, and even acting to save failed states.

We have found, however, that regardless of the symptoms of the conflict, their variety, or the other elements of our treatment, three core components of the peacekeeping prescription remain crucial: humanitarian, political, and security. The common element of all the cases that we have confronted is that each of them has required treatment for the individuals and groups who have suffered the consequences of conflict, for the political structure that has been either shaken or broken, and for the social environment that has been drained of trust, confidence, and any semblance of stability.

We have learned painfully that even in the case of an active civil war, a purely humanitarian response is both dangerous and impractical. The treatment we attempted in Somalia confronted the national community with the grim reality that it is sometimes not enough to unload aid and expect a problem to right itself. When the United Nations entered Somalia, it faced a situation in which thousands of people were dying daily. As time went on and the effects of the famine were countered, it became patently clear that the continuing high death rate was being caused not so much by the absence of food and the presence of natural disaster as by a group of ambitious armed men who prevented food from reaching the needy.

To allow ourselves the simplistic response of funneling aid into a port, only to have it sequestered and sold on the black markets by men controlling that port, would have been less than inadequate—it actually would have worsened the problem. Alain Destexhe, the former Secretary-General of Medicins sans Frontieres, referred to this kind of prescription as "the humanitarian placebo," explaining that, when it is applied, "aid becomes the pretext for political inaction, which leads only to catastrophe."

We have learned that the linkage of the humanitarian, political, and security components, handled well, can ensure the mission's progress.

And we have realized that, handled poorly, this linkage creates only a vicious cycle. Where security is present, humanitarian aid reaches those who need it, political instability is diminished, and restoration can move forward. Where security is absent, humanitarian aid is blocked, violence increases, political stability is weakened, and the situation is exacerbated. All three elements are essential.

Rwanda, Somalia, and Bosnia have also reinforced the lesson that we must not only prescribe the right elements, but prescribe them in the right dosages. Because of this, there has been movement, both within the United Nations and outside it, toward peacekeeping with a credible deterrent capacity. The easiest way to see the extent of the change in dosage is to compare the United Nations mission in Bosnia in 1992–95 to two other missions: its NATO-led successor and the UN operation in neighboring Eastern Slavonia.

For nearly four years, the United Nations Protection Force (UNPROFOR) in the former Yugoslavia spanned not only Bosnia and Herzegovina, but Macedonia and parts of Croatia as well. Its mandate included guaranteeing the delivery of humanitarian aid, observing cease-fires, aiding the evacuation of displaced persons, remaining present in towns under siege to deter attacks upon them and prevent loss of life, and keeping Sarajevo airport open throughout what became the longest humanitarian airlift in history. All this it did with little over thirty thousand people (of which only roughly twenty thousand were in Bosnia and Herzegovina), at an annual cost of roughly $1.7 billion.

The NATO Implementation Force (IFOR), which was deployed in Bosnia and Herzegovina alone, was considered robust in comparison to UNPROFOR. Within a narrower area, a far more restricted mandate, and with far more equipment, it deployed sixty thousand troops for a period of one year, after which it was replaced by the smaller, but still robust, Stabilization Force (SFOR). This was in addition to the United Nations International Police Task Force, the UN Civil Affairs and Human Rights teams, UNHCR, the OSCE staff present to support the election process, and other international actors who took on various tasks within the mission area. Beyond these, the operation in Macedonia continued to be run by the United Nations until 1999. IFOR, with fewer tasks, a smaller mission area, three times the personnel, at three to five times the cost, constituted a stronger, and no doubt more potent, prescription for peace in the Balkans. Similarly, when the United Nations deployed a multinational peacekeeping operation to Eastern Slavonia, it arrived with a strong, well-equipped force that provided credible deterrence against violations. Partly as a result of this, the operation was able successfully and peacefully to provide the transitional administration for what had been a highly volatile region of the former Yugoslavia. The UN brought another advantage as well. By deploying a well integrated, multidimensional operation under sole UN authority, the Organization was able to implement a comprehensive strategy to address the conflict in its various manifestations, thus laying the groundwork for a lasting peace.

The concept of a stronger presence, a critical mass, has in fact long been supported by the United Nations. When the six Safe Areas in Bosnia were being mandated, the United Nations asked for 34,000 troops to "provide deterrence through strength." The Security Council agreed to allow it only 7,600, and the UN's Member States took nearly a year to provide them. There was also concern expressed within the Organization regarding Somalia when UNITAF, the U.S.-backed coalition operation, was replaced by UNOSOM II. UNITAF, a well-armed and well-trained coalition force of 37,000, was deployed in southern Somalia alone, with a mandate limited to the establishment of a secure environment for the delivery of humanitarian assistance. When UNO-SOM II, the United Nations Peacekeeping Operation in Somalia, replaced it, it was deployed throughout the country with a nation-building mandate that included pursuing disarmament, repatriating refugees, establishing a national police force, and fostering national reconciliation. But it was given a force of only 28,000 to achieve it. In other missions at other times, the same kind of problem has occurred.

It is important that we realize at this point (and remember as future crises arise) that, if we want an intervention to succeed—if we want to counter the symptoms that are present, halt their spread and prevent their recurrence—two things are necessary. First, its mandate must be practicable. Second, it must be provided resources adequate to achieve it.

These recent years, when internal conflict has been so prevalent, have brought us a number of late, expensive, large-scale operations. But they have also broadened the other end of the spectrum with the first United Nations preventive deployment operation. The United Nations Preventive Deployment Mission (UNPREDEP) in the former Yugoslav Republic of Macedonia, though in the same theater of operations with UNPROFOR, and later IFOR, played a very different role in the treatment of the region. As the Balkan situation worsened, many worried that it would also spread laterally, involving or enveloping one country after another. Those working to address the conflict in 1992 had the conflict of 1914 in the back of their minds. For that reason or others, as the situation in the former Yugoslav Republic of Macedonia grew increasingly unstable and the Balkan conflict threatened to spread through and beyond it, the United Nations' first preventive deployment mission was mandated. With a strength of 11,225, UNPREDEP monitored activities at the country's border and worked to contribute to the maintenance of peace and security within it. By applying the right elements in the right strength over the right period, the international community created what might well be a paradigm for future preventive deployment missions and what was certainly a highly successful element of its treatment in the Balkans.

In 1999, United Nations peacekeeping missions are treating different variants of the same disease worldwide. A number of them are classical peacekeeping missions, whose mandates consist primarily of observing cease-fires and separating antagonists. The others are, as Cambodia was, more complex and multidimensional in nature, treating the abuse of human rights through the deployment of observers to monitor the human rights situation; treating the presence of mines with the implementation of demining programs; treating the need to return both military and guerrillas productively to the civilian sector with demilitarization and demobilization programs; treating the absence of broadly representative, legitimate government with the administration and supervision of fair and free elections; treating the absence of effective administration by building the capacity of newly legitimated authorities and addressing a wide range of other symptoms. In each case, as in the missions just examined, the questions of the proper diagnosis and prescription, correct medication and dosages are essential. So, for all of them, are two other parameters: When should the treatment be begun? How long should it run?

The beginning point of treatment is, perhaps, the most difficult decision of all. We have learned that peace can be neither coerced nor enforced. There must be a genuine desire for peace amongst the warring parties. No system can achieve peace when leaders use negotiation not to end conflict but merely to prolong it to advantage. And no agreement, no matter how well-intentioned, can guarantee peace if those who sign it see greater benefit in war. The patient must embrace the treatment fully and willingly.

Yet, can we always wait for a conflict to ebb and the will for peace to emerge before we intervene? Recent experience has shown us that, if anything, urgent intervention is sometimes necessary at the very height of the conflict, even if only to keep the disease and its symptoms from

raging completely out of control. It is preferable—and more prudent—
to intervene at a moment of relative stability, but situations like
Rwanda, and more recently East Timor, have made us realize that emergency measures might first be required simply to stabilize the patient
enough so that treatment can be administered. Measures of this kind are
not likely to lead to recuperation on their own, but they can help the
patient to survive until the tumor of conflict is ripe for removal. And, as
we have seen in Rwanda, they are far preferable to the devastation which
is their alternative. Along with preventive deployment, it is this kind of
intervention that constitutes the preventive element of peacekeeping. It
is preventive not in the prophylactic sense, but rather in the sense that,
given a conflict in progress, it can help avoid the worst.

Intervention of this kind, however, is risky, is costly, and is not
always effective. Where the will to pursue treatment and cure cannot be
mustered, where the patient has not responded—as in Somalia and
more recently in Angola—there is, beyond a point, no real alternative to
curtailing the treatment and hoping that the body proves capable of
treating itself. These are the cases that are the most frustrating for us,
the cases where we realize that what we have are imperfect instruments
at best, even if the only ones available. They highlight the fact that our
approach to violent conflict is very similar to our approach to cancer or
AIDS: an incomplete understanding of the nature of the disease means
that our response to it will have to follow the law of successive approximations, requiring us to learn from failure as well as success.

But even where a treatment is effective, should it be limited in time?
Long-term therapy is never popular with those who have to pay for it.
It is often difficult to see progress, and it is nearly always impossible to
prove the benefit achieved by avoiding further deterioration. In this
context, the call for quick cures and sunset clauses has become nearly
clamorous. This is dangerous for a number of reasons. First of all, in situations like Cyprus, where the United Nations has had an operation for
over thirty years, political accord has proven frustratingly elusive, but
armed conflict has been halted. The dynamics of the situation are such
that there is little doubt that conflict could quickly rekindle were the
mission withdrawn. With roughly $44 million a year, we are able to
keep the Cyprus conflict in check. Is it worth risking having to spend
far more in the wake of new devastation and bloodshed to avoid that
preventive investment? Second, the larger missions, the international
coalitions, partly because of their large size and cost, usually deployed
with very firm and tight deadlines. In each case, however, they went into

situations where the problems that plague the patient are deeply embedded and where more than a symptomatic treatment will most probably require more time than they allow. In this context, the great hazard of an arbitrary deadline is that it can actually subvert the process of reconciliation and recovery rather than move it forward. We need to understand and acknowledge that for a treatment to be effective it must run until it has achieved what it can and needs to do, not just until the insurance coverage runs out. We have applied this lesson in Kosovo, where no arbitrary time limit has been imposed on the international presence. Furthermore, in 1999, the UN mission in Sierra Leone has been expanded due to the increasing demands of the situation. And a mission has been sent to the Democratic Republic of Congo, following movement in the peace process there. These cases reveal a determination not to be swayed by pressure for quick and conclusive results. Long-running, deeply-rooted conflicts cannot be resolved overnight.

The efforts we have made have improved our sense of what we are dealing with and how we must handle it. They have allowed us to respond to the complexities of the crises that have faced us and to broaden the range of our response to them. They have refined our sense of what dosages should be applied when and for how long. And they have reminded us that peacekeeping as a therapy is valuable (sometimes vital) in both its curative and preventive capacities.

PROGNOSIS

Stepping back from all of this, however, we realize that the outcome of our efforts will and must depend upon other things as well. An effective response to conflict, as to cancer, must nourish the body as best it can, giving particular attention to organs within it that are vulnerable. We must ensure that the circulatory system allows nourishment to move throughout every limb; we must prevent and treat blockages and dysfunctions. We must use the presence of peacekeepers like a form of chemotherapy, to contain the spread of the tumor and, hopefully, to reduce it to an operable size. We must do what we can to bring about a remission and move toward a cure. Above all, we must be patient and persistent. We must not allow hope to be lost, and we must not lose it ourselves.

Hope, the desire of the people on the ground to cure the conflict that afflicts them, is the single most essential factor in determining its probable outcome. This becomes eminently clear to us when we reflect upon the definition of an epidemic—an agent that acts literally "against the people." The participation of the people is necessary to mount and sustain conflict. They, ultimately, bear in greatest part its consequences. Without their support it is impossible to bring it to a halt.

A number of other factors, however, are also crucial in developing a prognosis. Generally, they fall into two categories: those relating to the patient's general health and will to live, and those relating to the level of care received. Strength and hope alone are not enough. Perseverance and dedication to the course of treatment prescribed are vital. Like the diabetic who takes an intentionally liberal interpretation of his dietary restrictions, the government whose commitments to peace are honored more in the breach than in the making, the group that uses a peace process not so much to end conflict as to prolong it to advantage, is undermining its own future and perhaps foretelling its own doom. The will to sustain life or peace needs to be accompanied by the commitment to do what is necessary to sustain it.

But what of the factors that are not within the direct control of the patients? When we consider the level of care received, a number of important criteria come quickly to mind. The most immediate is the rapidity of response. A clear diagnosis and practical prescription are also essential. The presence of a treatment team that is unified in its approach, consulting and working closely, is also vital. Adequate resources, technology, training, and equipment are indispensable.

Rapid response is vital, particularly from a preventive perspective, because in cases like Rwanda, the conflict's worst effects are often felt in its earliest stages. A rapid response is thus essential if we are effectively to limit the range, extent, and momentum of a conflict. Of the million lives lost in the Rwandan genocide, the vast majority occurred in the first three months of the conflict, between the deaths of the presidents in an air crash on April 6, 1994, and the installation of the new government on the following July 19. We must be clear, however, that a rapid response means more than simply examining or diagnosing the problem early. It means establishing an adequate presence on the ground as quickly as possible. In the case of Rwanda, Member States of the United Nations passed a resolution in the Security Council five weeks after the crash, authorizing a mission of 5,500 to treat the conflict. Four months later, only 550—10 percent of that number—had been contributed and deployed. The mission did not reach its full strength until October, nearly half a year after the crash and months after the bulk of the killing had occurred. Rwanda is clear proof that, as a number of people have said, "we shouldn't wait until we hear a fire alarm to begin putting a fire department together."

Closely tied to this point is the need for adequate resources, personnel, equipment, and training. In the context of public health and medicine, where the fragility of the organism with which we are dealing is understood, the importance of proper training and equipment should need no emphasis. What could 550 peacekeepers do at the height of the Rwandan genocide when they were surrounded by armed factions that totaled over fifty thousand? What good can a contingent do when deployed to the Balkans in winter if its government sends it without winter clothes and other supplies, untrained and unprepared? To mount and sustain an effective operation, appropriate resources are required.

Even where we have the will and the resources to react rapidly, however, an additional element is required. For treatment to be effective in and beyond its initial stages, a clear understanding and unified approach among all involved in the treatment is vital. This means that the mandates passed by the Security Council must be clear, pointed, and practicable; that member governments and troop contributors must be willing to provide and sustain the support necessary to implement them; that ongoing consultations between the Security Council and the troop contributors address and surmount the obstacles and difficulties that arise as the mission pursues its tasks; that unified command must be observed and respected both within the mission and by all who support it from outside; and that agencies and organizations cooperate maximally. This is no small task, but we are making substantial and encouraging progress toward it. My reform programme has placed great emphasis both on clean lines of authority as well as effective mechanisms to ensure that all parts of the UN system that can contribute to the success of a mission can work together in a single, integrated effort.

But if the international community is truly to become more effective, whatever steps we take within the Secretariat must be complemented by corresponding action from Member States. The unfortunate reality up to now has been that the will to act differs greatly from case to case. It is important for the Security Council to respond with consistency and for governments to follow up those decisions by making troops available, when necessary, to help implement them.

Clear and achievable mandates are also vital if we are to respond adequately to the needs of a situation, present a credible and effective response, and maximize the safety and productivity of those who have gone to serve. Initial international intervention in the former Yugoslavia was hampered by both vague and limited mandates. The Security Council must, thus, identify the right medications and the right dosages. And "right dosages," in this context, need to be determined not only in the light of the needs on the ground, but also in the light of support that will be available (or be made available from member governments). The strength and structure of a peacekeeping operation must permit it to do two things: carry out its mandate and defend itself. Determining the right dosage is the first step toward achieving this; ensuring that governments promptly provide adequately trained and equipped troops is the second. Our ability to respond more rapidly, preventively, and effectively depends very much on this.

Further actions will need to be taken if we are to intervene more effectively in either a preventive or curative capacity. We must have adequate information sharing. Many countries possess information facilities far beyond anything available to the United Nations. Enhanced information sharing by those governments could be of significant use in addressing the conflicts that face us. It would have a direct impact upon our capacity to analyze situations and the ways in which they are likely to develop, another factor that is crucial to a rapid and effective response.

Beyond the Secretariat, beyond its Member States, however, there lies one other step to be taken. As we approach each crisis, we must ensure that the public at large has the firmest possible understanding of what lies before us. Strong, sustained support on their part is absolutely vital. For this reason and others, we must above all work to mobilize and optimize understanding. The health profession realized long ago that there are a number of benefits in pursuing this goal: it helps those who are ill better understand what they are dealing with; it helps those who are concerned better understand how they can best contribute; and it helps each of us understand how we can best stave off the disease or recognize it early. The heart disease and breast cancer campaigns are admirable models of this.

We are slowly learning the same lessons in the area of conflict, but there are a number of obstacles impeding our progress. The first of these is that the general public has come to misunderstand to a great degree what peacekeeping missions are meant to do and could do. Second, too few of us are aware of the positive side of the peacekeeping prescription—what it can achieve and has achieved. To take a few examples, what have most of us read of Namibia, Mozambique, or El Salvador? And how many realized, when the UN was under fire from public opinion for failing to stop the fighting in the former Yugoslavia, that our troops had not the mandate, much less the means, to do so? At the same time, the successful facilitation of the delivery of humanitarian aid received precious little coverage. Last, it is true that today we hear, see, and read far more of conflicts in various parts of the globe than we did during the Cold War. Full-blown crises are news, nascent conflicts are not. In an age when international intervention is decided by governments, and governments are propelled by public opinion, this means that effective and preventive rapid reaction is remarkably difficult. Neither do ongoing conflicts concern the media unless there is a reason for renewed interest. In many countries, the nuclear tests by India and Pakistan were followed by revived media coverage of the Kashmir dispute. Apparently of no direct concern to other parts of the world, the conflict between Eritrea and Ethiopia floats in and out of the media.

When global attention reaches a conflict at its height, a number of problems occur. Acting at this point is the costliest and most dangerous way to intervene. It is also the least likely to succeed. Without any doubt, media coverage has generated in recent years a degree of attention and response that the conflicts examined here would otherwise never have known. But it has also shown that the public needs to be made aware earlier of what is happening and could happen in a conflict area. Technology has made it possible for governments (and often the media) to know about many conflicts very early on, yet this information often takes far too long to reach the public at large. The problem is one of focus, priorities, and, once again, political will. If our efforts are indeed to become more preventive, if they are to limit more tightly the incidence and escalation of violent conflict, that focus must shift.

The steps that we have taken and the problems that we have identified show us that, while we have made substantial progress developing and applying the peacekeeping prescription, our understanding of both conflict and its cure are far from complete. As with AIDS and cancer, each step brings us closer, but the disease itself changes even as we work, making a cure even more evasive. This, however, must not daunt us. We realize today that peacekeeping is not a wonder drug, that it is not applicable to every situation and not guaranteed to cure every case. But, as we struggle to understand better the disease of conflict, the most intractable that humanity has known, we cannot help but be encouraged by the inroads we are making.

CONCLUSION

Having looked at the developments of both the disease of violent conflict and the peacekeeping prescription, having examined the prognosis of both the patient and the treatment, we have given a clearer context and direction to our efforts. In closing, I would like to broaden it.

As I reflected on the idea of the peacekeeping prescription, on the concept of peace as an integral and essential component of international public health, I recalled a speech in a similar vein given more than sixty years ago by the former U.S. president Franklin D. Roosevelt. In October of 1937, as the first shadows of World War II gathered, President Roosevelt delivered what has since become known as the "Quarantine the Aggressors" speech, in which he warned that "the epidemic of world lawlessness is spreading." Taking the public-health perspective that we have adopted here, he asserted that

> War is a contagion, whether it be declared or undeclared. It can engulf states and peoples remote from the original scene of hostilities. We are determined to keep out of war, yet we cannot insure ourselves against the disastrous effects of war and the dangers of involvement. We cannot have complete protection in a world of disorder in which confidence and security have broken down. If civilization is to survive, the will for peace on the part of all peace-loving nations must express itself to the end that nations that may be tempted to violate their agreements and the rights of others will desist from such a course. There must be positive endeavors to preserve peace.

Sixty years later, these words are both sobering and encouraging. They are sobering because they reemphasize the depth and breadth and length of the challenge before us; they remind us that violent conflict is as old as humankind itself. They are encouraging because they show us very clearly and tangibly the recent progress that we have made in addressing it.

Roosevelt's necessity of quarantining the aggressors is no longer the only option. Even in instances where conflict is advanced, the peacekeeping prescription does not simply quarantine the victim and leave him to his fate. The new tools and approaches that we have developed have allowed us to remedy cases where the patient would otherwise have been lost. As in medicine, we have developed techniques for detecting problems earlier. Through research and experience, we have honed our understanding and our methods. New tools and technologies have made it possible for intervention to be more targeted, separating, identifying, and correcting specific symptoms and improving the prognosis. We have, as Roosevelt urged us, undertaken "positive endeavors to preserve peace."

In doing so, we have achieved a great deal. In places like Namibia, Mozambique, El Salvador, and the Aouzou Strip, cures have been achieved. In other areas we have been able to bring the conflict into remission. In yet others we have halted its growth. Some areas—like Somalia—have proven resistant to treatment, and the international presence has had to be withdrawn, with the hope that the body's own defenses would help to stabilize it. But these are the exception, not the rule. What will develop in Iraq and Kosovo remains to be seen. In Africa we continue to respond to ever more complicated and distressing situations.

I admitted earlier that, if I were a doctor examining the world today, I would be greatly alarmed at the state of my patient. And indeed I would. But what I did not tell you is that I would not be pessimistic about his prognosis. My work, and particularly those aspects of it which are discussed in this book, has given me a keen sense of what we can achieve together—and what we should. I believe that we have made great progress in this treatment in the last fifty years. I believe that we will continue to do so. And I believe that the challenges ahead will demand nothing less of us.

12

REFLECTIONS ON THE ROLE OF THE UN AND ITS SECTRETARY-GENERAL

BOUTROS BOUTROS-GHALI

One system of metaphors that I have recently used extensively is the comparison between peace and health. . . . Peace research and health research are metaphors for each other, each can learn from the other. Similarly, both peace theory and medical science emphasize the role of consciousness and mobilization in healing.

—Johan Galtung[1]

INTRODUCTION AND DEFINITIONS

In matters of peace and security, as in medicine, prevention is self-evidently better than cure. It saves lives and money and it forestalls suffering. Since the end of the Cold War, preventive action has become a top priority for the United Nations. From the beginning, a preventive role had been envisaged for the Organization. Article 1 of the UN Charter had stated that one of the purposes of the United Nations was "to take effective collective measures for the *prevention* [emphasis added] and removal of threats to the peace." But the Cold War reduced almost to zero the Organization's capacity to take such measures collectively.

When the Cold War began to thaw in the mid-1980s, two consequences followed. First, it became possible at last for the UN Member States to act collectively in matters of peace and security. Second, the need for preventive action was made brutally clear to them. The Cold War might be over but the world was still plagued by a number of wars that it had spawned, almost all of them wars within states. These were the so-called proxy wars in which each of the protagonists was backed, politically and in *matériel*, by one of the Cold War power blocs. The United Nations Security Council was now able to take effective action to end most of them. But the cost was high. Major peacekeeping operations had to be established in Namibia, Angola, and Mozambique, between Iran and Iraq, in Afghanistan, in Cambodia, and in Central

America. At the same time, the collapse of communism in the Soviet Union and Eastern Europe was creating a new set of conflicts, one of which was to bring about the deployment in the former Yugoslavia of the United Nations' largest ever peacekeeping operation.

In the eight years from 1986 to 1993 the annual cost of peacekeeping to the United Nations increased more than twelvefold from $234 million to $2,984 million, without counting the peacekeeping costs borne directly by the countries that contributed troops to those operations. It is not surprising, therefore, that the Member States began to look for more economical ways of maintaining peace and security. On December 5, 1988, the General Assembly adopted a "Declaration on the Prevention and Removal of Disputes and Situations Which May Threaten International Peace and Security and on the Role of the United Nations in this Field." Through that instrument, the General Assembly declared that states should act so as to prevent in their international relations the emergence or aggravation of disputes or situations. It encouraged the Secretary-General to approach the states directly concerned with a dispute in an effort to prevent it from becoming a threat to the maintenance of international peace and security; to respond swiftly by offering his good offices if he were approached by a state directly concerned with a dispute; to make full use of fact-finding capabilities; and to use at an early stage the right accorded to him under Article 99 of the UN Charter (namely to bring to the attention of the Security Council any matter that in his opinion may threaten the maintenance of international peace and security). This decision represented a marked departure from the Cold War culture in which the legitimacy of a political initiative by the Secretary-General had usually been challenged if it was not taken explicitly under Article 99.

On January 31, 1992, at the end of the first ever meeting of the Security Council at the level of Heads of State and Government, the Council adopted a statement that *inter alia* invited me to prepare an analysis and recommendations on ways of strengthening and making more efficient the capacity of the United Nations for preventive diplomacy, for peacemaking, and for peacekeeping. As I worked on the resulting report, which was later published as *An Agenda for Peace*,[2] it quickly became clear that preventive diplomacy is in fact a portmanteau term for a range of prophylactic measures that can be taken by states, groups of states, or international organizations to help maintain peace and security between and within states. Since that report was published, the United Nations has gained experience not only of preventive diplomacy, strictly defined, but also of preventive peacekeeping, preventive humanitarian action, and preventive peace-building. Let me define these four main types of preventive action.

Preventive diplomacy is the use of diplomatic techniques to prevent disputes from arising, prevent them from escalating into armed conflict if they do arise, and, if that fails, prevent the armed conflict from spreading. Article 33 of the UN Charter requires parties to disputes that could endanger peace and security to seek a solution by negotiation, inquiry, mediation, conciliation, arbitration, judicial settlement, resort to regional agencies or arrangements, or other peaceful means which the protagonists may choose. To those techniques can be added confidence-building measures, a therapy that can produce good results if the patients, that is to say, the hostile parties, will accept it. Central, of course, to the idea of preventive diplomacy is the assumption that the protagonists are not making effective use of these techniques on their own initiative and that the help of a third party is needed if the threatened conflict is to be prevented by diplomatic means.

The techniques employed in preventive diplomacy are the same as those employed in *peacemaking* (which, in United Nations parlance, is a diplomatic activity, not the restoration of peace by forceful means). The only real difference between preventive diplomacy and peacemaking is that the one is applied before armed conflict has broken out and the other thereafter. But in the world today there are many endemic situations where the causes of conflict are deeply rooted and chronic tension is punctuated from time to time by acute outbreaks of virulent fighting. Examples of such situations are those arising from the conflict between India and Pakistan over Kashmir, Israel's occupation of parts of southern Lebanon, the conflict in southern Sudan, recurring problems in the Great Lakes area of Africa (Rwanda, Burundi, and neighboring Congo) and, clearly, throughout the former Yugoslavia. In such cases it may be artificial to make a distinction between preventive diplomacy and peacemaking or indeed between preventive and postconflict peace-building. Those who want to help control and cure such chronic maladies need to maintain their efforts over a long period of time, varying the therapies they prescribe as the patients' condition improves or deteriorates.

One is sometimes asked to give examples of successful preventive diplomacy. It is not always easy to do so. Confidentiality is usually essential in such endeavors. Time may have to pass before one can say with confidence that success has been achieved. Many different peacemakers may have been at work, and it can sound presumptuous for just one of them to claim the credit.

A conspicuous success, which history now permits us to claim for the United Nations, was the good offices mission undertaken in great secrecy in 1969/1970 by Under–Secretary-General Ralph Bunche, on behalf of U Thant, to resolve an Iranian claim to Bahrain before that country achieved full independence. U Thant said of it: "The perfect good offices operation is one which is not heard of until it is successfully concluded or even never heard of at all."

Another example, whose success cannot yet be predicted, was my appointment of a Special Envoy at the end of 1994, in response to a request from the government of Sierra Leone, to facilitate the opening of negotiations between that government and the Revolutionary United Front (RUF), which has for several years been fighting the government forces. At the same time I lent the United Nations' political and technical support to the electoral process in Sierra Leone. On both the diplomatic and the electoral fronts, the United Nations has worked closely with regional organizations and interested Member States.

Preventive peacekeeping involves the deployment of international military and police personnel to perform a variety of possible functions: to deter aggression, to help maintain security, to build confidence, to create conditions favorable to negotiations and/or to assist in the provision of humanitarian relief. As with all peacekeeping, a wide range of tasks can be considered, but it is essential that each mandate should specify with absolute precision what tasks the force will actually perform. The only such operation so far deployed by the United Nations is the one in the former Yugoslav Republic of Macedonia, which has, at least to some degree, helped to protect that country from being infected by the contagious ills that have caused so much suffering and destruction elsewhere in the former Yugoslavia.

Preventive humanitarian action is action that, in addition to its humanitarian purpose of bringing relief to those who suffer, has the *political* purpose of correcting situations, which, if left unattended, could increase the risk of conflict. A wide range of measures can be required. They can include planning for the humanitarian action that will be required if a crisis breaks, such as the stockpiling of relief goods in certain places. But they can also include action to create conditions that would help persuade refugees or displaced persons to return to their homes, for example, improvements in security, greater respect for human rights, creation of jobs, and so on.

Preventive peace-building is the application to potential conflict situations of the idea of postconflict peace-building, which I set out in *An Agenda for Peace*. Like its postconflict cousin, preventive peace-building is especially useful in internal conflicts and can involve a wide variety of activities in the institutional, economic, and social fields. These activities usually have an intrinsic value of their own because of the contribution they make to democratization, respect for human rights, and economic and social development. What defines them as peace-building activities is that, in addition, they have the political value of reducing the risk of the outbreak of a new conflict or the recrudescence of an old one.

An example in the context of potential interstate conflict is the offer in 1951 by the then International Bank for Reconstruction and Development (now the World Bank) to provide its good offices to India and Pakistan to help them resolve their dispute over the waters of the Indus River by approaching it as a technical and engineering problem rather than as a legal and political one. The Bank's offer was accepted and after nine years of negotiation, the parties signed the Indus Waters Treaty, which became the basis of the biggest water power and irrigation project in the world at the time. In due course it made the two countries independent of each other in the operation of their water supplies, thereby removing the risk of conflict on that set of issues.

THE SECRETARY-GENERAL'S ROLE IN DIAGNOSIS AND IN THE PRESCRIBING OF PREVENTIVE THERAPY

None of these preventive treatments need exclude use of any of the others. Indeed, a fully integrated international response to an impending conflict could prescribe them all. Nor does the United Nations have— or claim—an exclusive right to prescribe and administer these treatments. The most effective prophylaxis may be achieved through coordinated teamwork by the United Nations, various of its specialized agencies, one or more regional organizations, individual Member States, and nongovernmental organizations.

There are five generic conditions that have to be fulfilled if the Secretary-General of the United Nations is to be able to apply the preventive treatments effectively. They are discussed in the following paragraphs with particular reference to examples of the most pressing situations, which, during my tenure as Secretary-General, demanded preventive action by the international community. One was the internal crisis in Burundi. It is worth recording in this context that the Minister of Human Rights of Burundi, in a statement to the United Nations Human Rights Commission, described her country as being "a patient on the operating table" and appealed to the international community to help in finding "a permanent cure."

Fulfillment of the conditions becomes more difficult when, as is so often the case today, the potential conflict is an internal one. More than 60 percent of the actual or potential conflicts in which the United Nations played an active peacemaking or peacekeeping role during the 1990s related to disputes within states, though several of them also had a significant international dimension too. As is well known, Article 2(7) of the United Nations Charter provides that the United Nations should not intervene in matters that are essentially within the jurisdiction of a state, or require its Members to submit such matters to settlement under the Charter. The General Assembly's declaration of December 5, 1988, to which I have already referred, provided that "States should act so as to prevent *in their international relations* [emphasis added] the emergence or aggravation of disputes or situations."

Since the end of the Cold War, however, there has been a growing readiness by the Member States to accept, or even insist, that the United Nations' preventive, peacemaking, peacekeeping, and peace-building services should not be denied to a conflict simply because it is a conflict within a state and not one between states. At the same time, Member States have continued to insist on the inviolability of their sovereignty and strict respect for Article 2(7). Because the sovereign state is the basic building block of the international system and will so remain, it is not possible to resolve this contradiction on a generic basis; Member States will continue to defend their sovereign rights. But in practice the contradiction will continue to be resolved on a pragmatic basis in certain situations where there is broad agreement within the international community that an internal conflict is so dangerous and/or so cruel that international efforts have to be made to control and resolve it.

As a result, however, the United Nations cannot take preventive action without a specific request from, or at least the consent of, the Member State or states concerned. From the Secretary-General's point of view the ideal is that he should receive a request from the government. But sometimes, when the threat of imminent conflict is evident, he feels compelled by his general mandate for preventive action to take the initiative in suggesting a course of preventive therapy. Even when such an idea is put forward tentatively and confidentially, it can be taken as a slight to the sovereignty of the state concerned and the Secretary-General is blocked from further action.

The Secretary-General also has to be ready to propose preventive action in cases where a country no longer has a government capable of exercising sovereignty in an effective way—the so-called failed state syndrome epitomized by Somalia. In such cases the Security Council may decide that the state of war is so threatening to the country's neighbors, or is causing so much suffering, that the Council is obliged to establish a UN operation to bring it under control without seeking governmental consent. But the United Nations will still need the consent and cooperation of those who actually control the situation on the ground in the various parts of the country. As has been demonstrated in Somalia, Bosnia, and Kosovo, the lack of such consent and cooperation can prevent the United Nations operation from carrying out the tasks entrusted to it by the Security Council, even when the Council's decision has been taken under Chapter VII of the UN Charter.

The first of the five conditions for preventive action is that the Secretary-General should have the necessary capacity for the collection and analysis of information. One of the main reasons for my decision in 1992 to bring all the Secretariat's political work into a single Department of Political Affairs was to create this early-warning capacity. That department, working with the Department of Humanitarian Affairs (now retitled the Office for the Coordination of Humanitarian Affairs), which had its own early-warning system to detect impending humanitarian emergencies, and with the Department of Peacekeeping Operations, created a "Framework for Coordination," which is essentially a set of procedures for ensuring that the three departments review at regular intervals all information relevant to a potentially threatening situation and institute, in good time, consultations with other elements in the United Nations system that may have information to contribute and/or a role to play in a concerted preventive action.

It is sometimes said that the United Nations is handicapped in its peace efforts by the lack of an intelligence service of its own. I do not believe that this need be the case. Much information is available to the Secretariat from the media and from academics and nongovernmental organizations, who often contribute their own interesting perspectives to the analysis. Above all, Member States responded generously to my request in *An Agenda for Peace* that they be ready to provide the information needed for effective preventive diplomacy. Of course, the information they provide may sometimes reflect their own national interests and their own preferences for action by the United Nations. But if information on the same situation is sought from several Member States it is not difficult to form an accurate picture.

That said, the United Nations, like the rest of the international community, was caught unawares by the assassination of the president of Burundi in 1993, as it was by the shooting down of the aircraft carrying the presidents of Burundi and Rwanda in Kigali six months later, and by the horrors that followed both incidents. There will always be acts of extreme political violence which cannot be predicted with precision. But the United Nations needs both to be sensitive to the conditions that can lead to such acts and to be able to contribute to contingency planning for an adequate response by the international community when they occur.

The second condition is that the Secretary-General should have the clinical capacity to prescribe the correct treatment for the condition diagnosed. To fulfill this condition, he needs to be able to assess both the factors that have created the risk of conflict and the likely impact on them of the various preventive treatments that are available. Making those judgments in an interstate situation is easier than in an internal one. In the first case, much can be learned from consultation with the states concerned and their neighbors, friends, and allies. In the second, the crisis is often due to ethnic or economic and social issues of an entirely internal nature and of great political sensitivity, and the potential protagonists may include nonstate entities of questioned legitimacy and with shadowy chains of command. If in such circumstances the Secretary-General probes for the information needed to identify the right treatment, he can find himself accused of professional misconduct by infringing the sovereignty of the country concerned.

Another potential source of difficulty for the Secretary-General at this stage of the process is the need for triage. His analysis of the symptoms may lead him to conclude that there is no preventive action that the United Nations can usefully take. This could be because he judges that, contrary to the general impression, conflict is not actually imminent and that what is being observed is posturing or shadow-boxing rather than serious preparations for war. Or he may judge that there is no effective treatment that would be accepted by the parties or even that there is no effective treatment at all. Such conclusions will not always be welcome to the Member States. They rightly want the Secretary-General to do everything possible to prevent conflicts. But the reality is that not all—perhaps not even many—actual or potential conflicts are susceptible to the United Nations' treatment at all times. Selectivity and careful timing are necessary, especially when Member States are so reluctant to make resources available for the Organization's peace efforts.

In Burundi, the ethnic massacres of October 1993, to which reference has already been made, led me to dispatch a Special Representative to that country with instructions to inform himself about the situation, to help prevent it from deteriorating further, to facilitate national reconciliation, and to recommend to me further preventive measures that the United Nations could take. His initial advice was that the situation was so threatening that the United Nations' efforts should be concentrated on stabilizing the patient and that, for the moment, the modalities for longer-term treatment were a matter of second priority.

After my Special Representative's efforts and those of other peacemakers had brought about a certain stabilization, notably through the signature by almost all the political parties of a "Convention of Government" in September 1994, attention was turned to longer-term therapy. This required action on two fronts: promotion of a political dialogue and national reconciliation, for which a countrywide "National Debate" was the chosen remedy; and measures to improve security. For the latter, I had already proposed to the Security Council at various times a number of possible remedies. These had included the establishment of a humanitarian base, manned by United Nations troops, at Bujumbura Airport; the maintenance in a neighboring country of a military presence capable of intervening rapidly if the situation in Burundi should deteriorate rapidly; and the deployment of a contingent of United Nations guards to protect humanitarian activities. However, these ideas had not found favor either with the government of Burundi, whose armed forces were strongly opposed to the stationing of any foreign troops in the country, or with the members of the Security Council.

In the second half of 1995 the situation in Burundi began to deteriorate further. When I visited the country in July of that year, I warned its leaders and parliamentarians that they could not count on continuing support from the international community unless they produced convincing evidence that they were ready to reconcile their differences. In other words, I told them that unless the patients took their physicians' advice seriously, the physicians would turn elsewhere. The country's condition did not improve, and in December 1995 I reaffirmed to the Security Council my conviction that the international community should prepare for the possibility of a humanitarian emergency so severe that foreign forces would have to intervene. I again put forward the ideas of United Nations guards and/or a preventive deployment of foreign forces in a neighboring country. This proposal again proved unacceptable to the government of Burundi and to the Security Council. In February 1996 I urged that Member States should at least undertake contingency planning so that troops could be quickly deployed to Burundi if the worst happened and a humanitarian intervention became imperative. The Security Council responded by inviting me to pursue consultations with Member States to this end. It was not possible to reach any agreement on the various proposals. As a result, the international community witnessed a counter genocide which killed two hundred thousand Hutus who had left the refugee camps.

The third condition for preventive action is that the parties to the potential conflict (the patients) should accept the action proposed by the Secretary-General. This is a sine qua non because he has no power to impose any remedy on them and can act only with their consent. In any case, the remedy will have no effect unless the patients have confidence in it. Sadly, this is usually the most difficult condition to fulfill. There are, of course, at least two patients in every potential conflict. Usually one of them is more favorable than the other to international involvement; indeed, the very fact that Party A wants it is often cause enough for Party B to oppose it. Sometimes also there exist earlier agreements committing the governments concerned to give priority to bilateral means; for instance, the Simla Agreement of July 1972 by which India and Pakistan agreed "to settle their differences by peaceful means through bilateral negotiations or by any other peaceful means mutually agreed between them." At other times powerful countries in the region concerned may object to United Nations involvement and may insist that the parties have recourse to regional mediators.

In internal conflicts sovereignty is an added complication. A government faced with an opposition that is threatening to take up arms is understandably reluctant for an international organization to come onstage professing its impartiality and apparently treating government and opposition as equals. The Secretary-General has to proceed with great delicacy and finesse in such circumstances if he is to succeed in persuading both patients to consult the doctor and to take the medicine he prescribes.

Returning to the example of Burundi, the parties had very different views about the desirability of United Nations—or any other foreign—

intervention. The main political party representing the Hutu majority welcomed my proposals for contingency planning for a possible humanitarian intervention. But the main party representing the Tutsi minority reacted very negatively, as have the Burundi Armed Forces, which are largely recruited from the minority.

The fourth condition for action is that the Secretary-General, having prescribed a preventive treatment and got the patients to accept it, must persuade the other Member States, and especially the members of the Security Council, to give him steady political support. Unless they are ready to use their influence in a concerted effort by the international community as a whole, the efforts of the Secretary-General alone are unlikely to produce the desired results. The reactions of the Security Council to my various proposals for preventive action in Burundi have already been described.

The Secretary-General must also—and this is the fifth and final condition for success—persuade the Member States to provide the necessary resources to finance the agreed preventive action. The mandates given to him by Article 99 of the UN Charter, by the Security Council statement of January 31, 1992, and by the resolutions and statements adopted by the General Assembly and the Security Council, respectively, in response to *An Agenda for Peace* provide the Secretary-General with considerable freedom of maneuver in diagnosis and prescription, as will be evident from the foregoing description of my own initiatives related to Burundi. But he has no power to commit funds without the authority of the General Assembly, which will have to be convinced of the legitimacy, feasibility, and likely efficacy of the prescribed treatment. If it includes the deployment of military personnel, more than financial authority will be needed. The political authority of the Security Council also will be necessary, as well as a readiness on the part of Member States to contribute the troops and equipment required, whether as a UN peacekeeping operation or as a multinational force authorized by the Security Council but under national command.

To sum up, the salient fact that emerges from this analysis is that the Secretary-General's ability to take effective preventive action depends most critically on the political will of the parties to the potential conflict. In international politics, as in human medicine, the physician cannot impose treatment that the patient is not prepared to accept. Important improvements have been made in the Secretary-General's capacity to diagnose and prescribe. Failure to take effective preventive action is, in any case, only rarely due to lack of early warning; the symptoms usually are there for all to see. What too often is lacking at present is a predisposition by the parties to accept third-party assistance in resolving their dispute. Ways have to be found to persuade them, without infringing on their sovereignty or other rights, that it is in their own interests to accept the help of the United Nations and other international players rather than to allow their dispute to turn into armed conflict. And the Member States of the United Nations have to be persuaded to pay the costs of providing that help.

THE SECRETARY-GENERAL'S ROLE IN THE APPLICATION OF PREVENTIVE THERAPY

Once a course of therapy has been defined and agreed upon by all concerned, decisions have to be taken on the modalities for its application. There is no fixed pattern. Specific modalities have to be worked out for each case. The Secretary-General's role can take many different forms. He can do the work himself, directly or through his Secretariat. He can refer the patients to specialists, such as specialized agencies of the United Nations system, regional organizations, individual Member States, or nongovernmental organizations, and work with them to apply the therapy. He can coordinate the work of others or simply provide them with political and moral support.

The Secretary-General often performs his role through a senior United Nations official or outside personality, appointed as his Special Representative or Special Envoy, who takes up residence in the country or region concerned or visits it on a regular basis. The mere appointment of a Special Representative or Envoy can have a political impact. It alerts the Member States of the United Nations to a possible new conflict and alerts the potential protagonists to the international community's concern. There are other conspicuous actions available to the Secretary-General that can achieve similar results—the dispatch of a goodwill or fact-finding mission, a public offer of his good offices, briefing of the media, a report to the General Assembly or Security Council, or a formal notification to the Council under Article 99 of the UN Charter.

Such public manifestations of the Secretary-General's concern can sometimes have a useful therapeutic effect. But more often he will prefer to provide his good offices quietly, especially where the looming conflict is an internal one. Quite apart from sovereignty-related sensitivities, it is easier for parties to make concessions when it is not publicly known that they are being urged to do so by the Secretary-General of the United Nations who can guarantee little or nothing in return. As already mentioned, preventive diplomacy is usually best done behind closed doors, which can make difficulties for the Secretary-General if the world is clamoring for the United Nations to do something but he knows that to reveal what he is actually doing would impair his chances of success, as well as being the diplomatic equivalent of violating the Hippocratic oath.

Where preventive peacekeeping takes the form of a United Nations operation, the Secretary-General's role is more clearly defined and more exclusive. It is he who designs the operation; obtains the Security Council's authority to establish it; assembles the necessary troops and equipment from Member States; deploys, commands, and manages the operation; and reports on it to the Council. But even in this situation the Secretary-General can find himself exposed to considerable pressure from countries directly or indirectly involved in the conflict.

It is not, however, to be assumed that preventive peacekeeping will always be done through a United Nations operation. In the case of Burundi, I believed that the peacekeeping therapy would be so demanding militarily that it could be provided only by Member States capable of responding with the necessary rapidity to a crisis in a distant theater, and that the correct prescription would, therefore, be a multinational force authorized by the Security Council under Chapter VII of the UN Charter. In such a case the Secretary-General's role is likely to be less than if the operation were under United Nations command.

In the case of preventive humanitarian action, one aspect of the Secretary-General's role is to establish adequate arrangements for the coordination of relief activities. Another is to take, or support, the political action required to persuade the governments concerned to create the conditions that will permit resolution of the humanitarian crisis. As already noted, these can include a wide range of measures in the fields of security, law and order, human rights, institution building, reconstruction, restoration of economic activity and social programs, and may, therefore, require the Secretary-General to play a coordinating role in this field also.

Peace-building is perhaps the preventive therapy where the Secretary-General's role is least well-defined. In the case of preventive diplomacy and humanitarian action he has the necessary authority to administer the therapy that he has agreed upon with the parties. For preventive peacekeeping he has to obtain the authority of the Security Council, but well-established procedures exist for him to do so and for the operation to be deployed once authority has been obtained.

But peace-building is more complicated. It can require a wide range and variety of actions not all of which will fall under the direct executive responsibility of the Secretary-General. His functions in this context are essentially those of a general practitioner. He can diagnose the patients' condition and advise them that certain general measures of a political, economic, or social nature will help reduce the risk of conflict. Such therapies can include confidence-building measures, increased respect for human rights, more just law enforcement, strengthening democratic institutions, improving social services, addressing gross economic injustices, sharing natural resources more fairly, and so on. But for a detailed prescription and for help in administering the therapy, the general practitioner will have to refer the patients to various specialists inside and outside the United Nations system, including nongovernmental specialists.

This gives the Secretary-General three roles in the implementation of preventive peace-building, all of them delicate. The first is to persuade the specialists to apply the therapy that he has prescribed and the patients have accepted. The best way of doing this, of course, is to associate the specialists with the earlier consultations and make them a part of the diplomatic process through which the parties are brought to accept the desirability of preventive action and the nature it should take.

The Secretary-General's second role is to coordinate implementation of all the agreed upon peace-building actions. In some cases this can be done through the standard arrangements for coordinating the United Nations system's operational activities for development through a United Nations Resident Coordinator. But usually wider coordination will be necessary, especially if the overall prescription includes diplomatic, peacekeeping, and/or humanitarian elements. In that case, the normal arrangement is for the Secretary-General to appoint a resident Special Representative, who should have not only diplomatic skills but also sufficient experience in the economic and social fields to give him or her credibility with the specialists in those fields.

The Secretary-General's third role is to monitor the political impact of the agreed peace-building measures, so that he can assess how well the patients, or the parties to the potential conflict, are responding to the therapy and whether the prescription needs to be modified—or, of course, discontinued if the risk of conflict has been sufficiently alleviated. Obviously, the Secretary-General will depend to a considerable extent on the advice of his Special Representative; but this is an area where visits by the Secretary-General himself or by his senior officials to the country or region concerned, and direct contacts with their leaders, can be of great value.

EPILOGUE

Prevention is indeed better than cure. And the Secretariat has given high priority to improving the United Nations' capacity in the preventive field, as desired by the Member States for well-founded political, humanitarian, and financial reasons. But this chapter also should have shown that preventing the malady of conflict is even more difficult than preventing the diseases that afflict the mind and body of human beings.

There are no guaranteed vaccinations to prevent conflicts from starting and no miracle cures to end them once they have started. The best prevention is for the region or country concerned to follow a strict and healthy regimen of democratization, human rights, equitable development, confidence-building measures, and respect for international law, while eschewing indulgence in such unhealthy practices as nationalism, fanaticism, demagoguery, excessive armament, and aggressive behavior. Most of the elements of such a regimen are prescribed in the United Nations Charter and in the corpus of international law.

The difficulties of prevention in the field of peace and security do not arise because the warning signs of conflict are more difficult to detect than those of human disease; on the contrary, they are usually more obvious. Nor is it that the therapies are less effective; many effective therapies have been devised over the years. The United Nations dispensary is well stocked and many experienced consultants and specialists are on call.

The problem is with the patients and with the friends and enemies of the patients. Human beings may be full of phobias and superstition about disease but they can usually be relied upon to respond fairly rationally to the diagnoses and prescriptions of their physicians. The same cannot, alas, be said of governments and other parties to political conflicts. Many general practitioners would have been tempted to retire in despair long ago if their advice had been disregarded by their patients as consistently as the advice of the United Nations has been disregarded by those to whom it prescribes therapies to avert imminent conflict. But the Secretary-General of the United Nations cannot abandon his principal duty any more than a conscientious physician can abandon a difficult case. The Secretary-General's duty is to use all the means available to him, be they political, military, economic, social, or humanitarian, to help the peoples and governments of the United Nations to achieve the goal, emblazoned in the first paragraph of its Charter, of saving succeeding generations from the scourge of war.

13

OBSERVATION, TRIAGE, AND INITIAL THERAPY

MARRACK GOULDING

> Now what I want is Facts. . . . Facts alone are wanted in life.
> —Charles Dickens, *Hard Times*

The utilitarian strictures of Charles Dickens's Mr. Gradgrind may seem restrictive and unimaginative, but facts, and effective methods of collecting them, are instruments that are as indispensable to the peacemaker as the thermometer and the stethoscope are to the physician. Establishing the facts plays an important part in the second phase of the process described by Dr. Boutros-Ghali in chapter 12. In this chapter let us assume that the early warning has worked; the symptoms of what could be an impending conflict have been detected. What can and should the international community do next?

The answers to that question are given here in a United Nations context, reflecting the writer's own experience. But other international actors—regional organizations, governments, nongovernmental organizations, distinguished individuals—can undertake the tasks described. None of them will have the legitimacy and authority that resides in the unique world body that is the United Nations; but often they will have a capacity to take initiatives and run risks that are not available to the United Nations Secretary-General. He is answerable to 185 Member States that often have differing views about the rights and wrongs of a particular dispute and about how it should be resolved.

The first task to be performed after analysis of early-warning information has indicated that a conflict may be brewing is to verify the diagnosis. If it is confirmed, then other tasks will be required. The main ones are:

1. to establish whether the patients are ready to accept international therapy and whether their dispute is likely to respond to it;
2. if the dispute passes this triage, to stabilize the patients and devise a longer-term therapy;
3. to enlist the help of other therapists.

The urgency with which these tasks have to be undertaken will vary from case to case as in human medicine.

Sometimes the crisis will not be detected until conflict is imminent, as was the case recently with the near-hostilities between Greece and Turkey over the islet in the Eastern Aegean that is known to one side as Imia and to the other as Kardak, or has already begun, as was the case with the recent hostilities between Eritrea and Yemen over the Hanish Islands in the Red Sea.

In other cases the analysis will have identified disputes where there has so far been no hint of the possibility of armed conflict but where the analysts conclude that conflict will occur at some time in the future if the root causes are not addressed: "Unless something is done about the land problem in Ruritania, there will be an armed uprising there within a decade"; or, "If Ruritania continues to abuse the human rights of its Urbanian minority, the Urbanian Government will feel obliged to do something forceful before the next election."

These are particularly difficult cases for the United Nations to handle. Its interest in possible preventive action, when the risk of impending conflict is not self-evident, can affront governments, which, jealous of their sovereignty, ask what right the United Nations has to meddle in their internal affairs or their relations with their neighbors. Public mention of a possible future conflict can exacerbate the situation on the ground and strengthen resistance to preventive action by the international community (which is why the examples in the preceding paragraph are imaginary ones). In such cases, the United Nations is often told politely that its services are not needed. But when the armed insurgency breaks out or there are skirmishes on the Ruritanian-Urbanian border, it can be the United Nations that is held responsible for the lack of preventive action and asked to help restore the peace. As Kipling said of the British soldier's lot in peacetime,

it's "Tommy this," an' "Tommy that," an' "Tommy, fall behind,"
But it's "Please to walk in front, Sir" when there's trouble in the wind

But few of the situations with which the United Nations is asked to deal are either totally unforeseen or totally predictable. Most of them result from chronic disputes that from time to time create spasms of heightened tension and the threat of armed conflict. The existence of a complex of disputes between Greece and Turkey in the Aegean is well-known; the sudden military confrontation over the islet Imia-Kardak occurred for fortuitous reasons and was unpredictable. In Rwanda in 1994 the interethnic hatreds were only too well-known and reports had been received of possible plots by Hutu extremists. What could not be foreseen was that the president's aircraft would be shot down on April 6, and that this would be the incident that would unleash the genocidal forces. In such cases a preventive strategy needs to combine long-term efforts to resolve the underlying dispute with an emergency capacity to control the unpredictable but dangerous crises that will occur.

One of the most frequently employed responses to early warning of an impending conflict is the dispatch of a goodwill or fact-finding or good-offices mission to the area where the threat exists. Whether the mission is labeled goodwill, fact-finding, or good-offices may not make much practical difference, but it can be important presentationally. "Goodwill" can sound less threatening to the governments concerned; it implies concern by the Secretary-General and a desire to be helpful, but it does not necessarily imply subsequent action by him. "Fact-finding" sounds more purposeful and does imply, at the least, the likelihood of further involvement by the United Nations. "Good-offices" suggests that the parties have already agreed in principle to preventive action by the United Nations.

Whatever label the mission is given, it cannot, of course, be dispatched without the prior consent of the government or governments concerned. The Secretary-General's first step normally is to contact governments confidentially, by letter or telephone, to establish that they would be ready to accept a mission sent by him and to give it the access and other facilities needed for it to accomplish its tasks. In some cases this initial confidential contact is the end of the matter; the government indicates that it would find it difficult to receive the mission and does not want the United Nations to become involved.

It should be added parenthetically that the Secretary-General has a very extensive correspondence with the governments of Member States. Letters and telephone calls to heads of state and government are a standard instrument he uses in the discharge of all his responsibilities, including those relating to preventive action. When, therefore, a threat of conflict is diagnosed, one of the first things he does is usually to establish contact with the governments concerned, without necessarily proposing the dispatch of a mission.

When he does propose a mission, the Secretary-General can face a difficult decision if, as often happens, one party says yes and the other says no. Is it better to send his mission to one party only or to wait in the hope that with the passage of time the reluctant one will change its mind? In a recent case, the Secretary-General proposed the sending of a small mission to establish the facts relating to a threatened resumption of hostilities between Cameroon and Nigeria over the Bakassi Peninsula. One government gave immediate consent; the other did not send a substantive reply. The Secretary-General decided that little purpose would be served by sending a mission to one side only.

Governments may also expect to be consulted about the leadership of a mission and sometimes about its composition more generally. The Secretary-General's policy is to do what he can to accommodate governments' preferences but not to an extent that would impair the mission's ability to do its job or that would compromise its credibility. The level and composition of missions varies greatly. Sometimes they are led by the Secretary-General himself, for instance his goodwill mission to the two States on the Korean Peninsula in 1993, or by one of the Under-Secretaries-General. At other times the Secretary-General will entrust the mission to a distinguished person from outside the Secretariat; examples are the several missions led by Cyrus Vance to the former Yugoslavia in the second half of 1991. In other cases the leader may be the official with primary responsibility in the Secretariat for the region concerned; most of the missions sent to Georgia, Moldova, Nagorno-Karabakh, and Tajikistan when conflict erupted or threatened to erupt there after the breakup of the Soviet Union were led by one of the directors in the Department of Political Affairs.

Another point of importance to governments can be the duration of the proposed mission, especially if they have accepted it rather reluctantly and would like to see it come and go as quickly as possible. Again, the Secretary-General does his best to accommodate governments' wishes but not at the expense of the mission's efficacy and credibility. Normally, however, the Secretary-General himself does not want a mission to linger. Missions cost money and their purpose normally is to make recommendations for preventive therapy rather than to apply the therapy themselves.

That said, the very dispatch of a mission can have a valuable therapeutic effect. Indeed, this can be one of the reasons for deciding to dispatch a mission. It is a public act that tells the parties to the conflict that international concern has been aroused by their failure to resolve their dispute peacefully and that may, therefore, induce them to handle it more responsibly. At the same time the decision conveys the message that international help is available if the parties want to take advantage of it. The dispatch of a mission also alerts the Member States of the United Nations to a threat of conflict and puts them on notice to expect recommendations from the Secretary-General on how it should be controlled.

Sometimes a fact-finding mission can by itself make considerable progress in preventing a conflict. In 1989, for instance, violations by the then government of Bulgaria of the human rights of its Turkish minority caused a flow of over three hundred thousand refugees into neighboring parts of Turkey and created the risk of confrontation between the two countries. The Secretary-General offered his good offices; they were accepted by both parties (though with a stipulation by Bulgaria that they should be exercised in a discreet way); and the Secretary-General dispatched a mission whose mandate included both fact finding and good offices. In the event it proved impossible to conceal the mission's activities from the media, the presence of a host of journalists at the first refugee camp it visited could have caused the Bulgarian government to withdraw its consent. But after two weeks work the mission submitted a confidential report to the Secretary-General, who conveyed its recommendations to the two governments. Meanwhile the very presence of the mission in the region had eased tensions and had caused some of the refugees to return home.

In other cases, a fact-finding mission can have a very specific mission. A recent example is the International Commission of Inquiry that was established by the Security Council to investigate reports relating to the alleged supply of arms to former Rwandese government forces in the Great Lakes region of Central Africa. One of the main purposes of the mission was the preventive one of easing tension between Rwanda and Zaire. Another recent example is the mission to Sudan and its neighbors undertaken early in 1996 by one of the Secretary-General's Special Advisors in connection with alleged Sudanese support for international terrorism. In these two cases the mission itself can be said to have been the therapy.

More often, however, the focus of a mission's mandate is to prepare the way for therapeutic work by others. This can involve a number of functions. Their scope will depend on the complexity of the dispute, on the extent to which the facts about it are already known in New York and on whether the Secretary-General has already developed some ideas about the treatment to be applied.

The first function is to verify that the Secretariat's analysis has correctly diagnosed a threat of conflict. As the Secretary-General has said in his chapter of this book, actions that look like preparations for war may in reality be no more than shadow-boxing or posturing to impress domestic audiences. A mission, therefore, needs to examine the situation on the ground and sound out the views of as wide as possible a spectrum of informed opinion.

Assuming that a mission's inquiries confirm that there is a real risk of conflict, its second function is to discuss with the parties whether they would like, or would accept, United Nations help in trying to resolve their dispute. For reasons already described by the Secretary-General, this is often the point at which the application of preventive therapy is blocked by the reluctance of one of the patients to accept external involvement. There is then a delicate judgment to be made about how far the mission should go in trying to persuade the reluctant party to accept United Nations help. Should it insist on Member States' obligations under the UN Charter to settle disputes peacefully? Should it argue that the party's own interests will suffer if it demands absolute respect for its sovereignty? Should it appeal to the party to acknowledge that the Secretary-General has a duty to do everything possible to prevent conflict? Is it wise to appear to plead with a party to accept United Nations help when the Organization is so stretched elsewhere and its financial base is so insecure?

A mission's third function is to make a judgment about whether, assuming the cooperation of the parties, the dispute is susceptible to treatment by the United Nations. Cheering though it may be to be optimistic in this business, it is more important to be realistic. If the major hurdle of the parties' cooperation has been cleared, it is tempting to assume that there must be *something* useful that the United Nations can do. That temptation must be resisted. The mission should rigorously analyze the patients' condition and the relevance to it of the various therapies available to the United Nations. It should not be afraid to conclude that there is nothing, for the moment, that the United Nations can do. Such a conclusion can be justified by the intractability of the dispute, by the damage to the credibility of the United Nations that will result if it tries but fails to cure a hopeless case, or by a judgment about timing (for example, that the malady will be more susceptible to treatment when it has matured a little and its lethal potential is more evident to the parties). One of the lessons learned from the United Nations' intensive experience of peace operations in recent years is that it is a mistake to believe that it can intervene usefully in every crisis. Effective triage is necessary if the physician's credibility and sources of funding are to be preserved.

A mission's fourth function is to make recommendations about immediate and longer-term therapy. If it judges that conflict is imminent, it must identify immediate measures that can be taken to stabilize the situation. A wide range of options is available: the appointment of a senior person as the Secretary-General's Special Envoy (who normally works on a part-time, visiting basis) or Special Representative (who normally resides in the country or region concerned); the dispatch of further missions of a technical nature, for example, a military mission or experts in the subject under dispute; a good-offices mission to initiate and facilitate discussions between the parties; a commission of inquiry to investigate the parties' allegations against each other; confidence-building measures on the ground (mutual withdrawal of forces, and so on); a proposal for the preventive deployment of military observers or a peacekeeping force; and so on.

The main purpose of such measures is to calm tempers, to create space and time for longer-term therapy, and increase the price that will be paid by a party who, despite the international community's concern, decides to open hostilities; but they should also, of course, be of a kind that will facilitate and contribute to the longer-term treatment.

A mission's fifth function is to make recommendations about what that treatment should be. Again, there are many options but they go beyond the initial therapy that is the subject of this chapter, and, therefore, they are not discussed further here.

The above is a very schematic analysis of the functions of fact-finding and goodwill missions. Real diplomacy is rarely so neat and tidy. As already observed, most preventive action is required in the context of chronic disputes that may suddenly look as though they are going to degenerate into armed conflict. It is rather rare for a crisis to come completely out of the blue. For these reasons, no actual mission known to this writer has ever proceeded in such an orderly way from (a) verification of the diagnosis to (b) confirmation of the parties' acceptance of United Nations help to (c) the judgment that the dispute will be susceptible to United Nations treatment to (d) immediate confidence-building measures and finally to (e) recommendations for longer-term peacemaking. In reality, the initial stages of United Nations preventive action tend to proceed in fits and starts, as opportunities for forward movement open and close. It is usually only when the longer-term peacemaking has been launched that a continuous process begins—and that too can be susceptible to unforeseen setbacks and delays.

Another important point that has been obscured in this analysis of the work of an imaginary mission is the continuous interaction between the Secretary-General and the other therapists. These include other organs of the United Nations system, regional organizations, individual Member States, and various nongovernmental actors.

Foremost amongst the United Nations bodies are the Security Council and the General Assembly. The Secretary-General has considerable powers of political initiative these days and has been encouraged by the Member States to take the lead in early-warning and preventive action. But the effectiveness of his efforts depends critically on the political support of the Member States, expressed not only in resolutions and statements of the Council and the Assembly but also in diplomatic action by individual Member States in support of the Secretary-General's own initiatives. His success is also dependent on the General Assembly's readiness to make the necessary resources available. He, therefore, takes care to keep the Member States informed of what he is doing, once the initial confidential contacts have confirmed that there is at least a possibility that the United Nations will be able, and permitted, to take preventive action.

Cooperation is growing fast between the United Nations and regional organizations in all aspects of the prevention, management, and resolution of conflicts. Regional organizations themselves often dispatch fact-finding missions with the same sort of objectives as the United Nations. It is also possible for the United Nations and a regional organization to field a mission jointly.

In some cases, the Secretary-General may decide to invite a small group of Member States with special interest and influence in the country or region concerned to constitute themselves informally as "the Friends of the Secretary-General for Ruritania." The announcement that such a group is being informed can itself be a useful public manifestation of the United Nations' concern and readiness to help.

Others who can help the Secretary-General in devising and applying preventive remedies are scholars and nongovernmental organizations who often have information and perceptions different from those of governments. If our imaginary mission was working properly, it would have taken care to consult such sources both inside and outside the region of potential conflict.

This chapter, responding to the theme of this book and of the symposium that gave birth to it, has discussed fact-finding missions mostly in the preventive context. But it is necessary to point out, in conclusion, that fact-finding missions can be used at other stages in the efforts of the international community to manage and resolve conflicts. Such missions can be fielded not only by the Secretary-General but also by other principal organs of the United Nations, especially the Security Council, and by a variety of governmental and nongovernmental therapists.

Burundi, already much referred to in the Dr. Boutros-Ghali's chapter, shows how fact-finding can play a part in peacemaking efforts to resolve a conflict that has already erupted. In 1994 the Secretary-General sent a mission to try to establish the facts relating to the assassination of the President of that country in October 1993 and the massacres that followed. The work of that mission led eventually to the establishment of an International Commission of Inquiry, which after several months' work submitted a report to the Security Council. As has been demonstrated in El Salvador and other countries where truth commissions have worked, establishment of the facts relating to past horrors can have a detoxifying and cathartic effect and thus help to reduce the risk of the resumption of conflict.

In the case of Bahrain, also referred to by the Dr. Boutros-Ghali, the fact finding came at the end of the process, when a way had to be found to implement the agreement that Ralph Bunche had negotiated with the parties. In accordance with that agreement, Iran and the United Kingdom asked the Secretary-General to appoint a Personal Representative who would, in effect, find facts by ascertaining the true wishes of the Bahraini people. After thorough consultations, the Representative reported the facts to the Secretary-General: the overwhelming majority of the people of Bahrain wished to gain recognition of their identity in a fully independent and sovereign state.

With the use of a number of examples, this chapter has attempted to demonstrate the importance of fact finding in the prevention of conflict. Whether the American writer Henry Adams was right when he said that "practical politics consists in ignoring facts" (and I do not myself think he was), it is undoubtedly true that practical peacemaking depends on establishing them.

14

ESTABLISHING TRUST IN THE HEALER: PREVENTIVE DIPLOMACY AND THE FUTURE OF THE UNITED NATIONS

JAN ELIASSON

Prevention of conflicts is a moral imperative in today's world. It is a humanitarian necessity in order to save innocent lives. It is an economic necessity both for the countries immediately involved and for the international community, because of the exorbitant price of war and postwar reconstruction. It is a political necessity for the credibility of international cooperation, in particular for the United Nations. Past events in former Yugoslavia, not least in Kosovo, have once again shown the need for conflict prevention and prompt action in response to early warning. A failure to respond to early warning, such as aggressive nationalist behavior and violations of human rights, lead ultimately to increased violence and conflict. Early action should be the natural reaction to early warning.

This chapter begins with an examination of how the pattern of conflicts has changed in the post-Cold War period, and how these conflicts can involve the United Nations in all stages, from early warning, fact finding, the peaceful settlements of disputes and peacekeeping to action under Chapter VII of the UN Charter. Given the recognition that priority should be given to the earliest possible action, the chapter then discusses how and when preventive diplomacy is a practical possibility, and in particular the role of the United Nations in this context. The chapter considers how mistrust of the Organization—both due to its abilities and disabilities—can hinder its preventive work. Important issues to examine are related to the principles of national sovereignty and the impartiality of the United Nations. My conclusion is that the United Nations has an essential role in preventive diplomacy, by virtue of its mandate, legitimacy, and wide-ranging capabilities. By accepting and playing that role to the fullest extent, the United Nations will also gain the credibility needed to bring it out of its present crisis.

In the chapter I outline a number of essential elements in a program to strengthen the United Nations by enhancing its capacity for preventive action. The elements deal with getting the United Nations' own house in order through financial and other reform, establishing a division of labor with regional organizations, NGOs, and others, getting to the root causes of conflicts, and utilizing and sharpening the various preventive means provided by its Charter.

I focus on the opportunities of preventive diplomacy, although I am aware of the obvious difficulties. Grieving parties will often feel that their cause is just and will be hesitant to enter into a process that may imply the need for compromise. They may feel that they can prevail on the battlefield. External actors will often be hesitant to invest political, financial, and human capital in order to find peaceful solutions.

The way to overcome these difficulties is, in my view, twofold. First, we must emphasize the broad nature of preventive diplomacy. Conflict prevention is—and should be—an integrated aspect of other political and humanitarian action. A very wide range of instruments is at the disposal of parties and the international community. If we consider this range in its entirety, we will be in a better position to identify realistic means acceptable to all. Second, we must continue to make the moral and political case that in today's world conflicts must be prevented and not fought. The suppression of war has been the first objective of the United Nations for half a century. It is time to recognize that this objective applies equally to conflicts between and within states. All have a right to enjoy peace and the fruits of democracy, sustainable development, and a life in dignity.

STEPS TO PREVENT AND HANDLE POST–COLD WAR CONFLICTS

The end of the Cold War radically reduced the risk of large-scale interstate war, in particular nuclear war. At the same time it was followed by the emergence of a number of serious conflicts, notably in the former Yugoslavia and Soviet Union.

The pattern of conflicts has changed worldwide, and internal conflicts have taken prominence over international conflicts. It is, however, not an absolute tendency. International conflicts continue to occur, and there are risks for serious interstate confrontations in many parts of the world. It is also an obvious, albeit sometimes ignored, fact that internal conflicts in the developing world also were rampant during the Cold War period. Much of the change is that these conflicts are more often dealt with by the international community.

The end of the Cold War brought new possibilities to resolve long-standing conflicts and to tackle new threats to peace and security. This occurred in Southern Africa, Central America, Cambodia, Afghanistan, the Gulf, and even the Middle East. In all of these areas a key role was played by the United Nations.

The two Gulf Wars were in many respects turning points. In dealing with the Iran-Iraq war, in which the late Swedish Prime Minister Olof Palme and I acted as UN mediators, the Security Council developed new and cooperative working methods that were applied on a full scale from the early 1990s. Iraq's occupation of Kuwait demonstrated that, where the international community had failed both in preventive diplomacy and attempts at peaceful settlement, the UN could—in the spirit of Article 48 of the UN Charter—provide international authority and legitimacy to a peace enforcement coalition.

In contrast to the relatively limited role of the United Nations with respect to the actions of the Desert Shield and Storm coalition, and in the recent NATO-led operation in Kosovo, the United Nations took on a central role in the difficult operations in Somalia, the former Yugoslavia, and Haiti. It tragically failed to avert catastrophe in Rwanda, with neighboring Burundi still at the brink of disaster. The United Nations was relatively successful in promoting peace in Central America, as it has also been in nation building in Namibia and Mozambique, largely in Cambodia, and hopefully in Angola. More recent examples where the UN has the potential of making a difference are Eastern Timor, Sierra Leone, Eritrea-Ethiopia, and the Democratic Republic of Congo.

The cases mentioned illustrate the present broad spectrum of UN involvement in crisis management. It ranges from actions before a crisis has materialized to actions to limit conflicts and intervention to bring them to an end, with varying degrees of consent from the parties directly affected. These actions can, as a conceptual tool, be seen as different steps on a ladder of prevention,[1] ranging from

- early warning,
- fact finding,
- peaceful settlement of disputes,
- peacekeeping operations,
- to actions under Chapter VII.

The different steps on the ladder obviously will not always occur in this strict sequential order. Informal fact finding, for example, through nongovernmental organizations, may well be a source of early warning. Measures of early warning and prevention, fact finding, and peaceful settlement of disputes often will be even more important after a peace-keeping operation has been launched; conflicts sometimes quickly reignite, as tragically seen for example in Angola. Peacekeeping can also be a crucial means of prevention.

My focus here is on preventive diplomacy[2] and I will not detail my views on UN peacekeeping or peace enforcement. It will suffice to note the growing understanding of the need to move away from the later steps on the ladder to the earlier—an understanding that needs to be translated into concrete action.

IS PREVENTION POSSIBLE—AND WHEN?

History and recent experiences tell us of the enormous destructive strength and built-in automaticity of violence. Once an armed conflict erupts it is like the genie escaping from the bottle—it is almost impossible to put it back. A heavy toll in human lives and material and financial costs is the obvious, tragic result. It has become all the more apparent that both the UN and the international community need to focus on preventing conflicts before they occur.

If there is broad international consensus that conflict prevention is desirable as such, there is certainly a debate over whether, when, and to what extent it is possible. Skeptics have no difficulties in pointing at the inability of foreign-policy experts to predict important political changes, as well as the inability of politicians to act upon troublesome advice. Some critics maintain that only after violence has become manifest will the international community be motivated to invest political and other resources to promote a settlement. They also maintain that the same conditions are needed for the parties to accept the need for external involvement.

There is certainly no lack of situations that fit this pattern. Opportunities for preventive diplomacy are often missed and attempts are often in vain. The 1994 genocide in Rwanda—in which between five and eights hundred thousand people were killed—is a tragic example. An international study[3] points particularly at the failure of the international community, including the United Nations, to draw appropriate conclusions from available warning signals, for example from human rights mechanisms. The lack of early political response, in fact, emboldened those who were planning for genocide. The study identifies as its most important finding that humanitarian action cannot substitute for political action. Its specific conclusions deal with strengthening policy coherence in the Organization, developing more effective mechanisms for early warning and prevention, making better use of regional and subregional organizations, and strengthening the human rights machinery. Past failures must be thoroughly analyzed and conclusions drawn. But there is no reason to allow them to define the pattern for future action.

There are several current and recent cases of successful preventive diplomacy. They are, however, easily neglected; a war or an epidemic that did not break out is seldom considered news. An example from Europe is the preventive deployment of UN peacekeepers in the former Yugoslav Republic of Macedonia.[4] In an area of instability and rampant violence this force substantially diminished tensions. Another example is the Organization for Security and Cooperation in Europe (OSCE),[5] which has carried out a number of important and often successful missions to prevent conflict and diffuse tension, for example in South Ossetia (Georgia), Moldova, and the Baltic Area.

The border dispute between Libya and Chad over the Aouzou Strip is an interesting example of how various means of preventive diplomacy can combine to produce a successful result. Twenty-one years of border dispute ended peacefully in 1994 after a process of bilateral negotiations, support by a regional organization (the Organization of African Unity), a judgment by the International Court of Justice, and a short UN peacekeeping operation to assist the parties in implementing the judgment.[6]

Inaction in the face of threatening conflicts goes against the interest of states to try to avert developments that are potentially dangerous for their own well-being. This is particularly true in a period of growing interdependence and ever more complex international cooperation. Isolationism may still be a temptation for some, but it is likely to come at a high price. It is also becoming an ever more unacceptable option from a moral point of view.

To recognize the necessity of preventive diplomacy does not mean to disregard the primary responsibility of the parties to any dispute or conflict to settle their differences between themselves. The obligation to do so, as stated in Article 2 (3) of the UN Charter, is a cornerstone of international law. The increasing importance of internal factors in conflicts underscores the centrality of this obligation. There is a limit to the possibilities of external actors to provide lasting solutions to conflicts. There is also a limit to the willingness of external actors to make human and financial sacrifices to bring about such solutions. Rwanda, Bosnia, Somalia, and former Zaire may be the clearest examples of these limits.

The key question for the international community in the face of potential conflicts is not if preventive diplomacy is an option, but by whom, how, and when it should be exercised. I will revert to the question of finding a realistic and rational division of labor in this domain, and discuss the regional organizations, nongovernmental actors, and others. I may underline at this stage that such a division is needed for preventive diplomacy to be effective, and also to avoid overstraining the UN system.

The methodology is determined by the availability of various instruments and by an assessment of how they are likely to affect the situation at hand. A decisive factor is whether they will be seen as desirable or even acceptable by the parties directly involved and by major actors in the region and elsewhere. A very broad range of preventive instruments is, in principle, at the disposal of the international community. It includes traditional bilateral diplomacy, from discrete inquiries to more heavy persuasion. Multilateral diplomacy has added an almost boundless number of carrots and sticks—political, economic, and others.

Correct timing is, of course, essential, as always in diplomacy. A useful distinction could be made between early and late prevention.[7] Late prevention occurs when warning signs indicate an imminent risk for armed conflict. It involves situations that are brought to the attention of the Security Council, often through reports given at informal consultations. Actions to be considered involve summoning the Permanent Representative of the state(s) concerned, presidential statements exhorting restraint, fact finding, and possibly deployment of UN personnel or missions.

Early prevention focuses on assisting parties to find solutions to potentially dangerous situations, in accordance with Article 33 of the UN Charter. In organizational terms, the role of the Security Council is less dominant in early prevention, whereas the Secretariat, in particular, has a key function. Whenever possible, early prevention has distinctive advantages. It occurs before positions have hardened and grievances have multiplied through the escalation of the dispute. Early prevention offers better chances to resolve the fundamental problems, thereby reducing the risk that the outbreak of a conflict is postponed rather than averted. Conflict prevention is a global responsibility and a challenge to the international community facing a new millennium. Sweden has taken on this challenge through its Action Plan *Preventing Violent Conflict*, which was introduced in May 1999 and welcomed by Secretary-General Kofi Annan. The Action Plan aims toward encouraging new attitudes in governance and diplomacy, finding new and efficient methods of conflict prevention, and developing new universally held norms that support a global culture of prevention.

THE ROLE OF THE UN IN CONFLICT PREVENTION

"WE THE PEOPLES OF THE UNITED NATIONS DETER-MINED to save succeeding generations from the scourge of war ..."— the well-known opening words of the UN Charter establishes the suppression of war as the first objective of the United Nations.

Article 33 obligates Member States to seek peaceful settlements of any dispute that may endanger international peace and security. The Security Council is empowered by Article 34 to investigate not only such disputes, but "any situation which might lead to international friction or give rise to a dispute." Any State can, according to Article 35, bring disputes or situations to the attention of both the Security Council and the General Assembly. Once a concrete threat has materialized, far-reaching powers are granted to the Security Council in accordance with Chapter VII. The Secretary-General has an important independent right of initiative through Article 99, whereas the function of the International Court of Justice comes into play after an initiative by a Member State or a so empowered organ of the United Nations.

The Cold War constrained the ability of the United Nations to involve itself in preventive missions. The superpowers were equally uninterested in what they considered UN meddling. A well-known illustration is that the war in Vietnam was never even on the agenda of the Security Council. Among the few noteworthy exceptions is the important behind-the-scenes role played by Secretary-General U Thant in helping to defuse arguably the most dangerous episode of the Cold War, the Cuban missile crisis.

The end of the Cold War brought about a dramatic reactivation of the Security Council. A number of new peacekeeping operations were launched, and considerable interest arose in strengthening the preventive capacity of the Organization. In retrospect, the Security Council summit on January 31, 1992, appears as the peak event in a period where confidence in the possibilities of the UN was higher than at any time since 1945. The presidential statement read out by Prime Minister John Major of the United Kingdom specifically invited the Secretary-General to give his recommendations on ways of strengthening the capacity of the Organization for preventive diplomacy, peacemaking, and peacekeeping.

At the request of the summit, Secretary-General Boutros-Ghali presented his report *An Agenda for Peace* in June 1992. The report draws attention to practical measures to strengthen the preventive capacity of the Organization in five areas: confidence-building, fact finding, early warning, preventive deployment, and demilitarized zones. The 1995 Supplement to *An Agenda for Peace*—prepared for a second, but canceled, summit—draws some necessary lessons from UN successes and failures after the original report. It concludes that the greatest obstacle to successful UN preventive diplomacy is not lack of information or ideas but the reluctance of parties to accept UN assistance. The Secretary-General speaks in favor of "creating a climate of opinion, or ethos, within the international community in which the norm would be for Member States to accept an offer of United Nations good offices."[8]

CAN THE HEALER BE TRUSTED?

The potential of the UN system in conflict prevention is underutilized. This is clear from the Secretary-General's observations on the difficulties the UN system is facing in this area. Lack of trust by Member States is an important factor. It would seem that two contradictory, even paradoxical, forms of mistrust frustrate the preventive work of the Organization: concern that the UN may be effective, and concern that it may be ineffective.

The first concern, as related by the Secretary-General, deals largely with the issue of national sovereignty. Respect for national sovereignty must be a key element in the choice of preventive approach. Prevention will fall into disrepute if it is used only as a pretext for external intervention.

Respect for the sovereignty of states nevertheless cannot be an absolute bar against preventive diplomacy in dangerous situations; instead it should be a major consideration in the choice of its means. Preventive diplomacy is thus infinitely more likely to be successful when it is carried out with not only the consent but also the cooperation of the parties directly concerned.

It should be added that the UN Charter principle of nonintervention, as expressed in Article 2 (7), is very much a topic under discussion[9] The meaning of both "intervene" and "matters which are essentially within the domestic jurisdiction of any state" has evolved. The tendency has been particularly clear, though by no means uncontroversial, in human rights work. The importance of access and the responsibility of governments for their own populations in humanitarian crises has been recognized by General Assembly Resolution 46/182 of December 19, 1991.

The United Nations has in practice replied positively to the question of whether it has a role in internal conflicts. This is in line with its Charter, which makes no distinction between different threats to international peace and security and which, with foresight, made peoples and individuals objects of international concern.

It must be recognized, however, that the issue of sovereignty is particularly sensitive because of the strong powers granted by Chapter VII of the UN Charter. A State may—with or without reason—fear that, if it accepts even an initially uncontroversial UN role, for example, in an internal conflict, it will be faced with gradually more intrusive demands. This is an additional reason to emphasize early prevention and support for the efforts of regional and other organizations. It is also a consideration that underscores that the Security Council must avoid the trappings of "creeping mandates." There is a fundamental difference between Chapters VI (peaceful settlement of disputes) and VII (action when peace is threatened or broken, including sanctions and the use of force) of the UN Charter, and the leap should only be taken after a well-considered decision.

The second concern, over the inefficacy of the United Nations, relates to the crisis in which the Organization today finds itself. Whereas the political damage done to the UN by recent setbacks in peacekeeping will fade with time—as new problems come to the fore and require UN action—that will not be the case with the financial and structural crisis. If resolute action is not taken without delay, the crisis will instead soon escalate to a point of no return where long-term damage will be done.

An Organization preoccupied with its own survival is a less likely candidate for countries to approach with their own fundamental problems. The financial crisis will inevitably harm the professional qualifications of the Secretariat and the broad competence of the UN system in economic, environmental, humanitarian, legal, and other affairs—also of major importance in conflict prevention.

Trust and confidence are a *conditio sine qua non* for UN preventive diplomacy. The United Nations must be seen not only as a capable, but also as an impartial actor. The principle of UN impartiality goes back to the 1956 UNEF operation in the Suez. It has, at least conceptually, been fairly uncomplicated in classic peacekeeping, but less so in situations of lacking or loosening consent and in confronting parties responsible for violations of humanitarian law and human rights. It is also more difficult for the UN to be recognized as being impartial when the mandate for its actions is unclear, which is often the case in preventive situations.

Can the UN be impartial between good and evil? This almost existential question certainly arises in the preventive context. A related question is whether efforts to prevent conflicts in some extreme situations may run counter to other fundamental objectives of the Organization. There are no easy answers to such questions. In some instances—such as the antiapartheid struggle in South Africa—the United Nations qualified injustice itself as a threat to international peace and security. In less clear-cut cases a difficult balance has had to be found between competing objectives.

The need to prevent conflicts in the international system should also be borne in mind when interpreting UN Charter objectives. Whereas, for example, the principle of the self-determination of peoples once spearheaded the historic process of decolonization, it should not be allowed to justify dangerous current tendencies of micronationalism or tribalism.

The UN has to gain trust and respect for its actions not only from opposing parties but from all of the international community. In order to do this, impartiality cannot denote a requirement to be equidistant in all situations. Likewise, in preventive diplomacy the United Nations must be true to all its purposes and principles, both those on the prevention of conflicts and those that establish other norms for the behavior between and within states. Impartiality should, therefore, signify predictability and lack of ulterior motives, rather than moral indifference.

The dominant position in the Organization of the major world powers is both a potential asset and a liability for trust in its political integrity. The superpower rivalry of the Cold War was, to a certain extent, a guarantee for evenhandedness, although, more often, it meant paralysis. The improved cooperation between permanent Security Council members hopefully has brought this to an end. But it makes it no less important to act to ensure that the Council is perceived as legitimate and as acting equally on behalf of all UN Member States.

BEYOND THE CRISIS: A PROGRAM FOR PREVENTIVE ACTION

Prevention has been called a good cause in search of a program. The statement highlights the need to move decisively in the direction of early response by developing means of concrete action for prevention. Responses to crises, including conflict prevention, will have to emanate from an ever wider group of actors. There is a growing role for regional organizations and other international actors, including nongovernmental organizations. This may change the role of the United Nations to some extent, but it will become no less crucial.

Effective UN preventive action requires more than organizational improvements to develop methods to collect information and sound the alarm bells. It can only come about through a mobilization of the manifold resources of the entire UN system. It requires a flexible utilization of a broad arsenal of diplomatic, political, economic, and other instruments. The program here outlined does not deal with UN preventive action in a restricted sense. Many of the measures are also needed for reasons that have little to do with prevention.

A United Nations that is more effective at the core task of preventive diplomacy and conflict prevention will also be a stronger organization moving beyond the present crisis. Conversely, without major reform the UN role will also fail its task in preventive diplomacy. The following aspects must, in my view, be part of a program to strengthen the United Nations by strengthening its capacity for preventive action.

CARRY OUT FINANCIAL AND STRUCTURAL REFORM

A stronger and more effective United Nations requires fundamental financial and structural reform. It is an exceptionally grave occurrence when the Secretary-General has to admit that the financial crisis has brought the United Nations to the brink of insolvency. He is, furthermore, hardly erring when concluding that without a solution to the financial crisis, other reform efforts cannot succeed and the very future of the Organization is in jeopardy.[10]

The major reason for the financial crisis is the failure of some of its Member States to pay their contributions in full, on time, and without spurious conditionality—in accordance with the legal obligations of the Charter. The foremost responsibility rests with the United States because of its level of assessment and arrears. The United States will have to face this responsibility, or the consequences will be grave both for the United Nations and for the very idea of multilateralism.

The European Union, which more and more is assuming a central role in the United Nations, has presented a comprehensive proposal to resolve the financial crisis of the United Nations. It comprises four main elements: clearing the arrears of all Member States, adoption of a new scale of contributions, introduction of a system of payment incentives and penalties, and steps to control administrative expenditure and rationalize structures.[11]

While stressing the need for financial reform we should stay clear of the common trap of seeing the United Nations simply as a vast money-spending bureaucracy. The United Nations is not only a good investment; it is inexpensive and modest in size. The regular annual budget is only around $1.25 billion. The Secretariat in New York employs less than 4,500 staff members, and the entire system (including field staff of the specialized agencies, funds, programs, and the international financial institutions) employs less than 52,000. At the recent peak of United Nations peacekeeping, only about 1 out of 5,000 armed service personnel worldwide carried the blue UN helmet.

Financial reform must go hand in hand with structural reform to make the Organization more efficient. Reform should be pursued throughout the UN system as a whole. Only such a broad review will allow for a rational discussion of functions, mandates, policy formulation, and funding of the various institutions. Consolidation and coordination must be substituted for competition and duplication.

From the point of view of Sweden, the primary purpose of financial and structural reform is not to bring about savings, but to get a global multilateral system that is better than the present one at doing its work. We must identify the comparative advantages of the United Nations and set the priorities and direction in important areas, such as the new generation of peacekeeping operations, the UN role in the economic and social fields, and, most certainly, the prevention of conflicts.

DEFINE A RATIONAL DIVISION OF LABOR WITH REGIONAL AND OTHER ORGANIZATIONS

The UN Charter gives the Organization itself, and in particular the Security Council, a paramount role in the maintenance of international peace and security. The Charter nevertheless recognizes the role of regional organizations, particularly in the peaceful settlement of disputes. Through Article 52 (2) they are given precedence: Member States are under an obligation to try to achieve peaceful settlements through regional organizations before they approach the Security Council. Several regional organizations have defined peaceful settlement of disputes as a key task.[12] It is, however, only during the last few years that major attention has been given to the potential of regional organizations both in conflict prevention and settlement.

A pioneering role has been played in the 1990s by the Organization for Security and Cooperation in Europe (OSCE). The OSCE has carried out important preventive missions (in Estonia, Latvia, the former Yugoslav Republic of Macedonia, Moldova, Georgia, Kosovo, Sandjak, and Vojvodina) and mediation, for example, in the Nagorno-Karabach conflict, where I, as OSCE representative for dealing with this conflict, also reported to the United Nations Security Council. The OSCE has developed forward-looking institutions such as a High Commissioner on National Minorities, an Office for Democratic Institutions and Human Rights, as well as a Court within a Convention on Conciliation and Arbitration. The OSCE approach is a cooperative one, based on the required consent of the state(s) affected.

Conflict prevention is also a key issue under discussion in other European organizations, particularly in the European Union and the Western European Union (WEU). A part of the background to the increased interest in regional prevention and peacekeeping is obviously the inability of an overstretched world body to address the multitude of potential and actual conflicts. There are at the same time other compelling reasons for a stronger regional role in conflict prevention. Given the importance of cultural, ethnic, and religious factors in current conflicts, regional organizations often would be in a better position both to assess risks and to devise resolution strategies.

Many situations will, however, continue to occur where UN preventive action will be preferable to that of a regional organization, or where joint ventures should be undertaken. One or more of the protagonists may consider the regional organization to be partial, or may resent it because of the role played by powerful regional members.[13] In other cases there may be no regional organization available (for example, in major parts of Asia), or none that is able or willing to act, or strong enough to do so, on its own.

The United Nations and regional organizations thus have complementary rather than competing roles in preventive diplomacy. Close coordination is often beneficial. It is also increasingly recognized that the United Nations should assist regional organizations in developing their capacity for prevention. Practical support should also be provided directly between the regional bodies. The EU has for its part decided to give support specially to the work of the Organization of African Unity (OAU) to prevent and resolve crises in Africa. What should emerge is a global security architecture, in which the efforts of the UN, regional, and other organizations are mutually reinforcing.

WORK TOGETHER WITH NGOS AND CIVIL SOCIETY

The last few decades have seen the rapid growth of a vital international civil society.[14] In much the same way as domestic politics the world over is no longer an exclusive domain for politicians and officials, international affairs are today the affairs of everyone. Contemporary diplomacy is largely public; states and multilateral organizations act in a constant interplay with media, international and national nongovernmental organizations, trade unions, business, and civil society at large.

Civil society is an important factor in preventive diplomacy in at least two ways. It is often a part of the crises that preventive diplomacy aims at de-escalating. It can also be an instrument in finding appropriate solutions. It would be futile to engage in conflict prevention without taking careful account of the effects of various measures not only on governments but on all actors in societies. The United Nations and other practitioners of preventive diplomacy must, therefore, have access to the viewpoints and concerns of civil society, through formal or informal channels.

Many civil society organizations are today actively involved in conflict prevention. Particularly in difficult internal situations, governments are often unwilling to accept intergovernmental involvement, be it by the United Nations, regional organizations, or other states, because of the legitimacy it may seem to bestow on insurgents or opposition groups. NGOs, academic institutions, or prominent individuals may instead have unique possibilities to gain access and to try to defuse conflict. They have, furthermore, an advantage in being better suited to work not only with political leaders and officialdom but with all levels of society.

Nongovernmental entities are of course under no formal obligation to be neutral or impartial. In some cases their chosen role is instead to manifest solidarity with the suppressed. It should, however, be recognized that this may considerably limit their possibilities to take on functions that require the confidence of all parties.

The United Nations should work together with civil society in both the analysis and action phases of preventive diplomacy. It should look at civil society as an important partner also in prevention, as it has recognized it in dealing with human rights, the environment, and humanitarian relief.

ADDRESS THE ROOT CAUSES OF CONFLICT

It is possible to identify a number of political, social, economic, environmental, and other factors that typically increase the risk for conflicts. To identify such risk factors in concrete situations is the role of any early-warning system designed to trigger a preventive response.

Effective preventive action, however, implies that root causes for conflicts are addressed not only when warning lights flash. To promote democracy, respect for human rights, protection of refugees, and sustainable economic development—worldwide—must be part of a comprehensive preventive strategy. The same goes for international cooperation in response to humanitarian emergencies. The United Nations is in a unique position as the only global organization that incorporates all these aspects in its work.

"Democracy" is not mentioned in the UN Charter.[15] The Declaration adopted at the commemoration of the fiftieth anniversary of the Organization stresses the need to "create new opportunities for peace, development, democracy, and cooperation." Furthermore, the promotion of democracy has been a key objective of recent complex peacekeeping operations, such as UNTAG in Namibia and UNTAC in Cambodia, and a number of missions in Latin America. The United Nations has provided various forms of electoral assistance to over sixty Member States during the last few years, including the first democratic elections in South Africa and the popular consultation on the future status of Eastern Timor.

Promotion of democracy is directly related to the protection and full enjoyment of human rights. The UN Charter itself recognizes, in Article 55 (c), the importance of universal respect for human rights for "the creation of conditions of stability and well-being that are necessary for peaceful and friendly relations among nations." In spite of this recognition, human rights issues have been one of the most contentious fields of UN activity.

The General Assembly has played a pivotal role by not shunning such controversy. This has made it possible to establish the UN both as a forum for the development of an entire international treaty system for human rights, and for the implementation of established norms. The new international situation has also facilitated a useful cooperative role for the Organization: to give advice and assistance to states in setting up national human rights infrastructures.

Respect for the rights of persons belonging to national and other minorities is particularly important to conflict prevention. The Declaration on the Rights of Persons Belonging to National or Ethnic, Religious, and Linguistic Minorities has set high standards and confirmed that this—in the same way as human rights in general—is a matter of legitimate international concern.

Poverty and underdevelopment is the root cause of many conflicts. Multilateral as well as bilateral development cooperation can, under the right circumstances, be preventive. A distinction should be made at the same time between general conditions that may pose long-term risks—and should be addressed through an overall policy for sustainable development—and specific developments or abuses that may trigger violence and conflict in the short term.[16] This was recognized in the crucial discussions in the General Assembly on an Agenda for Development. It aims at reaching agreements both on the setting of objectives for development and development cooperation, and on how this work can institutionally be made more effective in the UN system.

Natural and man-made disasters often can combine to menace the very foundations of society, as seen, for example, in Somalia or Mozambique. Apart from the immediate suffering, they often are the harbingers of serious conflict. International relief in humanitarian emergencies is, therefore, not only a moral obligation as such, but an important preventive action.[17]

Addressing the root causes of conflict must also involve dealing with weaknesses of the international system as such. The codification of the Law of the Sea, which has been a major endeavor under UN auspices throughout the last two decades, is just one example of how the development of legal norms can help avert future conflicts.

Thus, effective preventive action must begin by addressing the root causes of conflict. There is a medical analogy: in order to raise public health you must begin by looking at living conditions, how people live and work, what they eat and drink, which environmental risks they are exposed to, and other such factors. We should recognize that the dietitian is no less important than the surgeon in fighting heart disease.

INTEGRATE DISARMAMENT INTO PREVENTIVE ACTION

The debate over the relationship between armaments and military conflict is old. One side of the debate tends to consider military strength as the best way to prevent conflict. Others point at excessive accumulation of armaments and military imbalances as a prime source of friction and war between states. Both can legitimately point at important historical cases to prove their points. From the outset, disarmament became an arena for East-West confrontation at the UN. For others, such as the neutral and nonaligned states, the United Nations served as a useful, although often frustrating, forum for international opinion building. Although much of the real negotiating work was carried out elsewhere, some important results were achieved, such as the Treaty on Non-Proliferation of Nuclear Weapons (NPT), agreements on biological and other weapons, and negotiations that paved the way for a ban on chemical weapons.[18]

Throughout the Cold War period disarmament and arms control was, however, seen as a political pursuit rather separate from other international efforts to strengthen peace and security. Even firm advocates of far-reaching disarmament in reality sometimes treated it as a distant goal rather than an immediate possibility. This obviously changed dramatically with the new international situation.

Substantial nuclear disarmament took place earlier in the 1990s, including the signing of START II and the indefinite extension of the NPT. Nuclear proliferation has come to the fore—with the breakup of one of the nuclear superpowers, concern over illicit trade in nuclear materials, the debate leading up to the indefinite extension of the NPT, and in worrisome developments in Iraq and in the Democratic People's Republic of Korea, and nuclear testing in India and Pakistan. How to implement the ban on chemical and biological weapons is on the agenda in many countries. Various measures have been taken with respect to conventional weapons; in particular, the Ottawa Convention, which prohibits the use and production of land mines. The new concept of microdisarmament covers useful efforts, particularly in Africa, to assist in the collection of small arms and light weapons that actually are killing people by the thousands. These developments make it all the more obvious that disarmament must be seen as a top item on the international security agenda.

Disarmament and related measures are directly linked to conflict prevention and management. Confidence-building measures (CBMs), openness, and transparency on military matters are important in avoiding dangerous miscalculations of the intentions of states. The UN Register of Conventional Arms could, especially with broader participation, become a useful tool for early warning and preventive diplomacy.

The Middle East peace process provides an interesting example of an integrated approach to arms control, in spite of difficulties mainly linked to nuclear issues. Progress has been made in areas such as maritime CBMs, and exchange of information and notifications. The participants have agreed to establish three regional conflict-prevention centers (in Jordan, Qatar, and Tunisia).

To halt proliferation of weapons of mass destruction is essential in order to prevent future conflicts. So is continued international cooperation for environmentally sound destruction of such weapons and for conversion of military facilities. The longer-term goal should be an agreement to ban all weapons of mass destruction, including nuclear weapons. The indefinite extension of the NPT is a good basis for pursuing this goal; it highlights the fundamental obligations of the present nuclear powers to conclude a nuclear test ban and, eventually, to eliminate nuclear weapons.

REFORM THE SECURITY COUNCIL

Security Council reform is urgently needed in order to strengthen confidence in the United Nations in general, and, in particular, to enhance the perceived legitimacy of the Council and its actions. This is essential in order to strengthen the ability of the Security Council to perform its role in preventive diplomacy. A more representative Council will, thus, gain in efficacy and political authority. This concern must at the same time be balanced against the need to maintain the efficiency of Security Council decision making.

The setup of the Council has remained unchanged for thirty-five years,[19] whereas the number of UN Member States during this period has risen from 113 to 185. The geographic balance is lopsided, with, for example, the Asian states competing for the same number of nonpermanent seats (2) as the group of Western European and other states, with half as many members.

In spite of a number of initiatives, beginning almost at the previous enlargement, it was only in January 1994 that the General Assembly began a concrete discussion of Security Council enlargement and other aspects of Council reform. A large number of proposals have been presented, by the state members of the Non-Aligned Movement, the Nordic countries, and a number of individual states. Regrettably, the working group appears to be facing at least a temporary stalemate, particularly over the issue of new permanent members.

Additional political impetus and high-level discussions are needed in order to give direction to the enlargement discussion. It would also be important to consider an enlargement not as a single historical occurrence—not to be reevaluated again for another thirty years—but as a step in an ongoing process. Hence the idea that a reform should be revisited in a not too distant future.[20]

Equally important is to continue the efforts to reform the working methods of the Council. Excessive secrecy and lack of consultation with concerned nonmembers runs counter to the spirit of Article 24 (1) of the UN Charter. As the Security Council acts on behalf of all the members of the United Nations, it should be seen as doing so. Since the establishment of the General Assembly group, much has been done to improve the working methods of the Security Council. Although all steps that have been taken (regular briefings to nonmembers, publication of the agenda of informal consultations, and so on) are the result of decisions in the Council itself, it has been admitted that they have been inspired by criticism and proposals made in the General Assembly working group.

Further steps are needed to improve openness and transparency in the workings of the Security Council, and thereby to improve trust and confidence in its actions. A case in point is the need for more formalized consultations with troop-contributing countries. A subsidiary organ could be set up for this purpose in accordance with Article 29 of the UN Charter. Directly affected non-Council members should be heard to a greater degree in the crucial informal consultations. Sweden has, with Nordic support, suggested the possibility of a Charter amendment to make the implicit in Article 24 explicit: the Security Council shall inform and consult interested Member States on its work.

STRENGTHEN THE CAPACITY OF THE SECRETARIAT IN PREVENTIVE DIPLOMACY

The UN Secretariat has a crucial role in preventive diplomacy. Whereas this was originally seen as very much a personal task for the Secretary-General, a practice developed of assigning representatives and senior staff members for special missions. Primary responsibility for preventive diplomacy and peacemaking now rests with the Department for Political Affairs (DPA), whose responsibilities include analysis of political developments, identification of potential conflicts, and policy implementation. The total number of staff members dealing with preventive diplomacy and peacemaking in this department is today less than 150. An increased priority to preventive diplomacy would require allocating increased resources to this function, and setting up a specific conflict-prevention unit to deal with analysis and the preparation of proposals for action. Such a unit could serve as the nucleus for small field teams for preventive purposes.[21]

A number of possible measures in order to improve the capacity and coordination of the Secretariat in preventive diplomacy have been proposed both in the *Agenda for Peace*, its Supplement, and connected General Assembly resolutions and Security Council presidential statements.[22] Many important proposals specifically deal with how Member States can assist the United Nations in all stages of prevention: early warning (politico-military as well as socioeconomic), analysis, and action. They involve the sharing of information and assessment of dangerous situations, provision of high-level personalities for fact finding, good offices, and mediation, as well as financial and other support to UN missions for preventive diplomacy.

The Secretariat itself has taken useful steps to improve coordination between the Departments for Political Affairs (DPA) and Peacekeeping Operations (DPKO) and the Office for Coordination of Humanitarian Affairs (OCHA),[23] especially to interpret early-warning signals from humanitarian and other systems. Support should be given to further initiatives by the Secretary-General to strengthen structures for such coordination and regularize their standing within the Organization.

Other parts of the Secretariat could also usefully pay more attention to conflict prevention. Information gathered, for example, by the High Commissioner for Human Rights must not be neglected. A comprehensive information system should be developed, which should take into account information and capacity available in the field, not least among nongovernmental organizations.

It is equally essential to develop Secretariat coordination beyond the relatively easier task of information gathering and analysis; early warning is of little use if it is not followed by early action. Indeed, using the medical analogy, predicting disease can only help the patient if a cure is available.

MAKE BETTER USE OF ARTICLE 99

According to Article 99 of the UN Charter, the Secretary-General may bring to the attention of the Security Council "any matter which in his opinion may threaten the maintenance of international peace and security." Although this Article has been formally invoked only twice (Congo 1960, U.S. Embassy occupation in Teheran 1979), it has been the basis for the development of one of the most dynamic aspects of the UN system: the independent role of the Secretary-General in the maintenance of international peace and security. This important task presupposes an effective system of information, and also a fact-finding capacity. Such a capacity is needed not only for information but also to serve as a catalyst for potentially conflicting parties to identify peaceful solutions. A UN "preventive presence," even if it does not involve peacekeeping, may help to avert conflict.[24]

The Secretary-General has and should make use of his/her considerable freedom in deciding to dispatch fact-finding and other missions. In some cases, such missions can and should take place discretely and may not necessarily lead to action, if successful. In other cases, a reporting mechanism to the Security Council may need to be established. In other instances, written reports to the Security Council and/or the General Assembly may serve a useful purpose by giving the conflict public exposure. The practical possibilities for the Secretary-General to make proper use of the role given by Article 99 need to be developed. Funding must be adequate and flexible. The costs involved are minimal, especially compared to the stakes involved.

DEVELOP THE INSTRUMENTS FOR PEACEFUL SETTLEMENT OF DISPUTES

Article 33 of the UN Charter lists a whole range of instruments for states to settle their disputes: negotiation, enquiry, mediation, conciliation, arbitration, judicial settlement, resort to regional agencies or arrangements, or other peaceful means of their own choice. It represents, in my view, an untapped diplomatic resource. Many of the means listed are important UN tasks that the Secretary-General, Special Representatives, and the Secretariat are engaged in, for example, mediation and conciliation. An important part of strengthening the capacity of the Secretariat in preventive diplomacy should be to develop its ability to serve Member States by providing such assistance.

Strengthening the international legal system is essential to conflict prevention. With the establishment of a permanent International Criminal Court (ICC) in July 1998, the international community, in Secretary-General Kofi Annan's words, "took a giant step forward in the march towards universal human rights and the rule of law." That the international community now has the capability to try individuals for serious offences such as genocide, war crimes, and crimes against humanity will help to deter atrocities that sow the seeds for future strife. Furthermore, the Permanent Court of Arbitration should be encouraged in its efforts to revive this neglected instrument for peaceful settlement. And, the International Court of Justice (ICJ) must be fully utilized and strengthened. A study of old case lists of the ICJ provides concrete proof of successful prevention—a rarity, given that conflicts avoided are otherwise so easily forgotten.

All States, not least the permanent Security Council members, should accept the compulsory jurisdiction of the ICJ according to Article 36 (2) of its Statute. Resort to the Court should be accepted as a remedy in new international conventions. It should be encouraged by measures to shorten and facilitate the Court procedures.

KEEP OPEN THE POSSIBILITY OF PREVENTIVE DEPLOYMENT OF PEACEKEEPERS

Peacekeeping is in one sense also a preventive measure since its purpose is to prevent hostilities from reigniting. In classic peacekeeping, troops are interpositioned between opposing forces along a border or a cease-fire line in order to act as a tripwire or shield. An identical role obviously can be played from an operational point of view, before hostilities have erupted.

An Agenda for Peace made the case for a more systematic use of preventive deployment of peacekeepers to discourage internal as well as interstate conflict. The idea was welcomed by the General Assembly, although with some caution. A particularly sensitive point in the General Assembly was whether such deployment should be possible on only one side of a border, and on the request of only one adjacent state.

The UN operation in the former Yugoslav Republic of Macedonia (originally a part of UNPROFOR, from March 31, 1995, to February 28, 1999, UNPREDEP) was a successful example of preventive deployment in a volatile area. A Nordic battalion, which was reinforced by a U.S. contingent, was deployed on the Macedonian side of the border to Albania and the Federal Republic of Yugoslavia (Serbia-Montenegro). By its presence, it demonstrated the commitment of the international community not to allow a spillover of the conflicts of the former Yugoslavia.

It is not likely that the Security Council will look to preventive deployment as a regular means of forestalling conflicts. The financial situation of UN peacekeeping today will add to a certain reluctance in this regard. It would, nevertheless, be a mistake not to realize the potential of preventive deployment of UN peacekeepers. A small-scale and rather inexpensive international presence could be contemplated in a number of cases in which conflicts could escalate to a point where large-scale and costly interventions would be the remaining option.

DEVELOP CONCRETE PREVENTIVE TASKS FOR THE GENERAL ASSEMBLY

Any viable strategy for strengthening the preventive role of the United Nations should take account of the significant role of the General Assembly. The Assembly has the budgetary power of the Organization and exercises also, in spite of the prerogatives of the Secretary-General, considerable influence over how the Secretariat deals with its tasks. The General Assembly is not only the engine of the normative work of the United Nations, it is the highest forum for expressing the common concerns of the international community. The powers of the General Assembly give it a responsibility to act and take initiatives to ensure that proper priorities are set.

The Assembly also has a role in helping prevent specific conflict. This is recognized in the UN Charter, especially through the right that Article 35 gives states to bring disputes to the attention of the General Assembly. The Assembly can deploy preventive missions, send observers and mediators, and mandate representatives to carry out various tasks. Current examples of how the General Assembly has actually made use of these possibilities include Afghanistan, Guatemala, and Haiti.

The General Assembly has both advantages and disadvantages in preventive action compared to other principal organs. Its composition and legitimacy give it a high political and moral weight when acting in unison. The fact that it does not dispose of Chapter VII powers can be an advantage in the eyes of a party concerned about avoiding a too-potent intervention. Among the drawbacks of the General Assembly would count its unsuitability for performing more discreet functions in sensitive situations. It lacks the ability of the Security Council to respond to changing circumstances by quickly considering adjustments in mandates.

The General Assembly should be able not only to support preventive diplomacy in general but actually to exercise it itself in certain types of situations. To do so would contribute to revitalizing this main political body of the Organization.

MOBILIZE ALL OF THE UN SYSTEM

Preventive diplomacy—in the broad sense of the term—should engage all parts of the UN system, including specialized agencies, funds, programs, regional and field offices, and the international financial institutions. By combining the knowledge and capacities of all these actors, the system will be vastly better both at analyzing warning signals and at devising options for preventive action.

Many of the activities of the United Nations have, at least indirectly, a conflict-prevention dimension. There is a growing awareness that more needs to be done to consider developmental, humanitarian, and other activities from a conflict perspective. Of course, this should not mean that development policy is subordinate to political considerations. A country that is at peace with itself and its neighbors is no less entitled to benefit from international cooperation than a country in less peaceful circumstances.

Coordination is a difficult problem—but also a necessary task—in the United Nations, with its 185 members and its wide array of agencies and activities set up under different circumstances and for diverse purposes. The first condition for consolidation and coordination is that the Member States themselves take charge of the Organization. Member States have to show the ability to set priorities. The role of bodies such as ECOSOC and the Administrative Committee on Coordination (ACC) should be reviewed, and the Secretary-General should be supported in taking on a stronger coordinating role together with his closest collaborators. Secretary-General Kofi Annan certainly has taken a step forward by presenting comprehensive reform proposals in order to strengthen the organization.

CONCLUSION

Prevention of conflicts will be a defining and fundamental task for international cooperation in the years to come. It will be so because of the multitude and destructive force of contemporary conflicts, where the international community cannot stand by as a passive observer.

There has been much doom and gloom around the United Nations over the last years. It is preoccupied by its own housekeeping problems. The financial situation will impose difficult decisions and hard choices. In the latter respect the United Nations is no different from many of its Member States, including my own. But it is in difficult times particularly that clear visions and distinct priorities are needed.

The United Nations is at a crossroads. It can attempt to muddle through by piecemeal reform and internal crisis management. Or it can set priorities and demonstrate that it is able effectively to deal with the most important challenges.

The United Nations was born out of the horror of World War II. The face of war has, if possible, become even uglier. I have seen it in the empty stare of a refugee child in Somalia and mine amputees in Angola and Cambodia. It counts sound economic development, democracy, human rights, and tolerance among its many victims. At the same time experience tells us that this plague is preventable. Our goal must be a world where war and armed conflict is recognized by all as what it is: a primitive and repugnant anachronism.

The United Nations has the mandate, legitimacy, and capacity to take on a leading role in developing modern preventive diplomacy. It can play such a role by bringing together the efforts of the UN system itself and by encouraging an equally active involvement by other actors. Preventive diplomacy is an imperative for the international community. It is difficult, but it is possible. It should be a moral and political priority for the United Nations.

PART 4

POTENTIAL PARTICIPANTS IN
PREVENTIVE DIPLOMACY

In this final section I present examples of some of the other—but certainly not all—potential participants in preventive diplomacy. The scholarly contributions of academia may seem, at first blush, far removed from the coarse realities of conflicts. But that would be similar to viewing nuclear physics as only a classroom discipline, forgetting that the basis for the development of the atomic bomb were the equations, theories, and formulae of scientists who irrevocably changed modern warfare. Ted Robert Gurr details the absolute necessity for adequate early-warning systems and links an academic approach to preventive diplomacy problems. Salim Ahmed Salim notes the significance of regional organizations in preventing and mediating conflicts throughout Africa. Kenneth Hackett discusses the role of international voluntary agencies and spiritual leaders in traumatized areas where traditional initiatives have failed. Finally, Dr. Scott R. Lillibridge, the Chief of the U.S. Office of Bioterrorism and a world famous epidemiologist, reminds us that, to a poorly prepared world, new diseases may pose political, diplomatic, as well as health threats that can make armed conflict appear like a child's game.

15

EARLY-WARNING SYSTEMS: FROM SURVEILLANCE TO ASSESSMENT TO ACTION[1]

TED ROBERT GURR

The idea of early warning is simple and widely accepted in the international community. Officials and NGO activists who must deal with the consequences of local conflicts and humanitarian disasters need early warnings of impending crises to buy time—time to build political support for action, time to design and implement proactive strategies, time to plan for assistance and rescue.[2] Dr. K. M. Cahill has made the point elsewhere: the thrust of international policy "should be on long-term foreign assistance, conflict resolution and development programs that could prevent many disasters from happening in the first place."[3]

The task undone is to translate the early-warning idea into systems, like those used to monitor threats to public health, that provide and help interpret information on emerging conflict situations on a global scale. The key concept is *system*, as distinct from an unstructured flow of public and private reports from observers who happen to be on the ground in places that are ripe for conflict. Early-warning systems are no longer needed to call attention to ongoing and potential conflicts in the Caucasus, the Balkans, or the Greater Horn of Africa. These regions are the focus of close international scrutiny and preventive efforts. The challenge for early-warning systems is to search beyond the time horizon to identify latent and low-level conflicts that have not yet attracted CNN crews or fact-finding missions.

Ethnic repression and warfare within states are now the leading challenges to security in most of the world.[4] Recent findings from the Minorities at Risk project suggest the dimensions of the problem. At the beginning of 1999 thirty-eight communal (national, ethnic, religious) groups were enmeshed in armed rebellions against governments over issues of autonomy and collective rights. International bodies were committed to containing some of them, as in Kosovo and Iraq, but most were ignored. Another forty communal groups throughout the world were targeted by discriminatory public policies that substantially and selectively limited their political, economic, or cultural rights. In a handful of instances the victimized groups, like Hutus in Burundi and the Lhotshampas of Bhutan, have benefitted from preventive international efforts. Most, however, are of serious concern only to human rights observers. Farther beyond the time horizon are an equally large number of latent or low-level conflicts, about 110 of them, in which ethnic groups have mobilized to promote or protect their collective interests but have not yet rebelled openly or precipitated repressive responses.

International attention to these situations is selective. Ethnopolitical conflicts in Western democracies are not usually of international concern because, it is assumed, the conflicts are likely to be worked out through the democratic process. Other conflicts are ignored because of triage decisions, based on a tacit consensus that little or no international leverage can be brought to bear on them, as in southern Sudan and Burma. And there is the problem of attention deficit: the sheer number and diversity of ethnopolitical conflicts, open and potential, overwhelms the capacity of international officials to monitor, assess, and respond.

Enter early-warning systems. In which of the present and future ethnic rebellions will large-scale humanitarian assistance be needed, where will political pressures build for international responses? In which latent ethnic conflicts are the risk factors highest? Where and when are the openings for early, low-cost preventive measures? Which preventive strategies have been used in the past, and with what effects? A global system for conflict, early warning is a means to efficiently monitor such situations. Analysis is the essential component to monitoring: analysis provides assessments of risks and openings. An early-warning system cannot answer fundamental policy questions about optimal preventive measures, but it should be able to provide increasingly reliable information and assessments that will help decision makers answer those questions.

This chapter addresses some specific issues raised in this preamble. It begins with a survey of organizations working to develop early-warning systems and concludes with evidence from early-warning research about ethnic conflict situations at high risk of escalation at the beginning of the twenty-first century.

WHO IS WORKING ON EARLY WARNING?

A potent impetus for research on early warning of conflicts with grave humanitarian consequences came from the UN Secretary-General's

Agenda for Peace of June 17, 1992. Dr. Boutros Boutros-Ghali focused attention on threats to international security arising from "ethnic, religious, social, cultural or linguistic strife" (par. 11) and called for strengthening early-warning systems that incorporate information about natural disasters and "political indicators to assess whether a threat to peace exists and to analyze what action might be taken by the United Nations to alleviate it" (par. 26).[5] Efforts to design and employ early-warning systems for international policy planning are being undertaken by three UN agencies.

(1) In New York the UN's Office for the Coordination of Humanitarian Affairs (OCHA) maintains the Humanitarian Early Warning System (HEWS), a database of quantitative and qualitative information on countries vulnerable to humanitarian crises. HEWS is used to support interpretive analyses and reports for decision makers in UN operational agencies. (2) The OCHA's Geneva office maintains ReliefWeb, an Internet-based compendium of current information and assessments on complex emergencies. Unlike HEWS, ReliefWeb's information is publicly accessible and thus is widely used by humanitarian organizations and private activists. (3) Also based in Geneva is the UN High Commission for Refugees' Center for Documentation and Research. This Center provides structured assessments of country situations likely to generate refugee flows and provides situation assessments for UN interagency meetings. Its assessments also are open and available on an Internet site.

A fourth UN-related early-warning project focuses on food crises rather than the civil conflicts that cause most humanitarian crises. The Global Information and Early Warning System (GIEWS), run by the Food and Agricultural Organization in Rome, monitors demand and supply for all basic foods throughout the world and provides alerts of imminent food crises. It is an exemplar of what could be done for conflict early warning given sufficient resources and political support from the UN's Member States.[6]

The European states also support a number of early-warning and preventive-action programs. The Organization for Security and Cooperation in Europe maintains the research-oriented Conflict Prevention Center in Vienna, while the OSCE's High Commissioner on National Minorities (Max van der Stoel, based in the Hague) has responsibility for reporting on and planning diplomatic responses to emerging ethnonational conflicts.[7] The European Commission supports the work of the Conflict Prevention Network of academic institutions and NGOs designed to provide analytic and operational input to the

EU system. The Organization of African Unity also has initiated an early-warning system, based at OAU headquarters in Addis Ababa— the first such effort by a regional organization outside Europe.

A number of Western governments are developing risk-assessment and early-warning systems to support post–Cold War policies of developmental and humanitarian assistance. The long-run planning question for development administrators is how to design programs to forestall future crises; the short-run question is whether impending crises will destroy the gains of ongoing programs. The U.S. Agency for International Development makes such assessments, so does the Swiss Foreign Ministry (under contract with the Swiss Peace Foundation), and the Foreign Ministry of the Netherlands (at its Clingendael center). Beginning in the early 1990s the U.S. Department of Defense and the American intelligence community began to shift their early-warning efforts from the interstate conflicts with which they were preoccupied during the Cold War to communal conflicts and humanitarian crises that may call for U.S. rescue, assistance, and peacekeeping operations.[8] A vivid illustration of the shift in U.S. concerns toward humanitarian issues was the establishment, early in 1999, of an interagency Genocide Early Warning Center, based in the Department of State.

Parallel to these national and international efforts at early warning are the research and action programs of numerous nongovernmental organizations. Some are umbrella organizations like the London-based Forum on Early Warning and Early Response. FEWER is a consortium of NGOs and academic research institutions that is building a global network for information exchange and action partnerships with governmental and private organizations. It has working links with regional early-warning networks in Africa and the CIS, for example the Moscow-based Network of Ethnological Monitoring on Early Warning of Ethnic Conflict, and distributes information from organizations doing early-warning research, such as the Swiss Peace Foundation and the University of Maryland's Center for International Development and Conflict Management.

The next link in the chain that begins with early warning is prevention, which is the focus of a great many NGOs. One very active umbrella organization is the Utrecht-based European Platform for Conflict Prevention and Transformation, which exchanges information and advocates prevention activities by participating NGOs. Its publication projects include a handbook that inventories conflict prevention centers worldwide and a series of regional Conflict Prevention Surveys.[9]

A major program of action research is carried out by the Center for Preventive Action, supported by the New York–based Council on Foreign Relations. The Center uses expert teams for in-country early-warning assessments and advocates preventive actions.[10]

A great many other bodies doing research related to early-warning and preventive action might be cited. Annual tracking of armed conflicts are reported by university-based researchers in Sweden, the Netherlands, and the United States. Periodic human rights assessments are prepared by Amnesty International, Human Rights Watch, the Human Rights Internet (Canada), and the U.S. Department of State. Political risk analyses are prepared for corporate clients by applied-research groups in the United States and London. Refugees and the crises that generate them are assessed by university researchers and NGOs in North America, Europe, and Japan.[11]

It is obvious from this overview that early warners have diverse objectives and methods and work in different kinds of environments. The specific "bads" they warn about include ethnic wars, massive rights violations, and refugee flows. Some collect and report data, others do case studies, some disseminate information. Some prepare rigorous risk assessments, others try to focus preventive efforts on impending crises. Some work in NGOs and university research programs, others provide staff support to national and international policy makers. But some issues cut across this diversity. These are dealt with in the sections that follow.

THE CONNECTION BETWEEN EARLY WARNING AND EARLY ACTION

Advocates of early warning assume that credible warnings of impending conflict, however derived, will make it possible to initiate preventive action and plan for humanitarian assistance. Skeptics point to the collapse of the Yugoslav federation and the onset of the new Balkan wars, which were anticipated by many local observers and the U.S. Central Intelligence Agency, among others, as an example of early warning that failed. What failed in this instance was not "early warning" but the governments and international organizations that should have responded more quickly and coherently to the emerging crisis. The warning signals were present in prospect as well as in retrospect. Either they were ignored, or the preventive actions were inadequate to the crisis.

Effective early responses are by their nature less visible, and less often analyzed, than failures. An antidote to skepticism about early warning is to cite briefly some recent cases in which early warnings led to international responses that have thus far checked the escalation of crises into humanitarian disasters.[12]

Early warning of drought in southern Africa in spring 1992 prompted a concerted international program of relief and rehabilitation that forestalled significant loss of life.[13] Information networks that provide early warning of ecological disasters are better developed than the conflict early-warning programs discussed in this chapter. The international community also is predisposed to respond to them. The example calls attention to what in principle should be possible in the political realm. It also illustrates the role political factors play in preventive responses: the international response depended on cooperation of governments in southern Africa with relief agencies. The successful outcome contrasts sharply with the Horn of Africa, where similar conditions in the 1980s and early 1990s caused enormous suffering, population displacement, and loss of life. Most contenders in civil wars in the region, both governments and their opponents, refused to cooperate fully with international relief agencies and as a consequence humanitarian efforts were crippled.[14]

Early warnings of a Bosnian-type civil war in Macedonia were widely echoed, and heeded, by the international community after the country seceded from the Yugoslavian federation in 1992. The major threats have included ethnic rivalries between the Macedonian majority and Albanian and Serbian minorities; diplomatic and economic sanctions by a hostile Greek government; and serious economic deterioration. Among the responses were intensive diplomatic efforts by international, regional, and U.S. diplomats directed at the Macedonian government and its neighbors; the stationing of Scandinavian and U.S. troops as "trip-wire" peacekeepers; and initiation of grassroots conflict resolution efforts by a U.S.-based NGO, Common Ground. The conflict was contained, and in one significant respect lessened: in autumn 1995, in response to U.S., European, and UN pressure, the Greek and Macedonian governments reached an accord that led Greece to suspend its embargo and to open their common border.[15] The influx of refugees from Kosovo in spring 1999 was a severe test of the delicate ethnic balance in Macedonia and of its relations with its neighbors, but intensified international engagement helped diffuse tensions.

The Congo Republic in late 1993 was in a state of incipient civil war between rival political groupings following disputed elections. The

Organization of African Unity and the government of Zaire provided mediation that led to a peace accord in early 1994. The peace accord checked the escalation of conflict, though it did not end it.[16]

In Burundi the assassination of the newly elected Hutu president in October 1993 by elements of the Tutsi military precipitated a series of massacres and contributed indirectly to the Rwandan genocide in spring 1994. Since late 1993 Burundi has been the focus of intensive efforts by the United Nations, the OAU, the U.S. and West European governments, and NGOs to check further communal and political violence. Serious massacres have occurred and the situation is very tense, but orchestrated violence on the scale of Rwanda has been prevented, as of this writing.

The nationalist leaders of a number of postcommunist states have proposed and imposed restrictions on the rights of national minorities, seeking in some instances to encourage them to emigrate. The targets have included Magyars (Hungarians) in Slovakia and Romania, Russians in the Baltic states, and Gagauz and Russians in Moldova. All these situations have been the focus of diplomatic and political initiatives by the UN, the OSCE, the Council of Europe, and West European governments (and the Russian government, in the case of Russian minorities in the near abroad). The governments in question have been encouraged to abide by international standards for the protection of national minorities. These efforts have included reminders about the political and economic costs of rights violations as well as inducements (especially assistance programs). In all the instances cited the nationalist governments in question have modified their policies and threats of ethnic warfare have subsided.[17]

Most of these successes of preventive diplomacy occurred in regions that have been the subject of intensive international scrutiny and concern. Regional organizations as well as the UN and European powers have been actively engaged. Detailed information about emerging crises usually was available to all interested parties, and except in the case of the Congo, major international actors had stakes in checking the escalation of conflict.

Two critical questions are raised by these examples. One is whether the collection, dissemination, and assessment of information on prospective violence and humanitarian disasters can be done systematically and in a timely fashion. From the perspective of the research community there is little doubt that the answer is yes, given some modest but sustained investment of resources in information technology, data analysis and display, and the further testing of forecasting models of internal conflict. The second question is whether the results of such assessments are credible enough that they help guide policy makers and activists about where to invest efforts in prevention. On this question the jury is out. Most diplomats, desk officers, and activists are accustomed to relying on their own fly-by-wire understanding of a situation and often are skeptical of outsiders using new information technologies and lists of risk factors. The value of the systematic approach may be most appreciated by high-level decision makers who are responsible for planning regional and global strategies of prevention. They are most acutely aware of the value of long-range risk assessments and systematic monitoring.

DESIGN CRITERIA FOR EARLY-WARNING SYSTEMS

The capacity to collect and disseminate information on emerging crises has vastly increased since the mid-1980s, due especially to electronic networking, the widespread availability of personal computers, and advances in technology for data management and analysis. It is fair to say, however, that the capacity for assessing this information's policy implications has developed much more slowly. Discussions of early-warning systems too often ignore the implications of the growing gap between the capacity of observers to generate information and the capacity of analysts and policy makers to interpret it. The point can be highlighted by contrasting three different approaches to early warning.

Early warning as field monitoring: This is the long-established practice by which diplomats and local representatives of international organizations report any event or intelligence they receive that suggests an imminent escalation of conflict. The Human Rights Watch organizations and other NGOs have carried out this kind of monitoring and reporting for a number of years. UN agencies concerned with humanitarian issues have done so for decades. In early 1993, after years of planning, the UN's Office of Humanitarian Affairs held its first "consultation" to synthesize such information as it related to potential flows of refugees. On the basis of these assessments ten countries, such as Zaire and Cambodia, were identified as being at risk of escalating conflicts and refugee flows.

Field monitoring is of great potential value because the information it generates on emerging crises is generally of high quality and immediacy. Three further steps are needed if field monitoring is to make an optimal contribution to a systematic early-warning system. First, standard protocols are needed to increase the consistency in the kinds of information reported by field representatives. Second, those who assess field information need explicit models to guide its interpretation. Third, those who plan and carry out preventive diplomacy, humanitarian assistance, and peacekeeping operations must be committed to the early-warning process and give close attention to its signals and assessments—even if in specific instances they choose to discount them.

Early warning as monitoring of indicators: Much discussion and planning for the establishment of early-warning systems in the early 1990s focused on using indicators to assess risks and monitor trends. Planners envisaged systems based on available statistical indicators and construction of new indicators that would be easily accessible to desk officers and policy makers. The concept is that when decision makers confront or anticipate crises, they will turn to the system for background data and for indicators that enable them to track the situation over time. The UN OCHA's Humanitarian Early Warning System, referred to above, was designed beginning in summer 1993 with this in mind. It consists of an electronic database of statistical indicators on more than one hundred countries plus "headlines" on recent political, humanitarian, and other developments in a smaller number of countries. The system is regularly used to prepare assessments of emerging crises in response to requests from senior UN officials, but there are no concrete plans for systematic analysis of information. In its present form HEWS is, in short, a system for managing information on potential humanitarian crises, not for its analysis.

Systems that rely mainly on indicators have great potential value for systematizing information and making it readily available but also have two general limitations. First, conflicts evolve through phases. The transitions among phases, for example from disputes to armed violence, usually are abrupt and not predictable from analyzing trends.[18] Indicators are more suitable for tracking country situations than for anticipating rapid changes in them. Analyses based on indicators are more likely to lead to "late warning" or to quantified description that lags behind events than to "early-warning." Second, reliance on indicators may help regulate the flow of information to planners, analysts, and policy makers but does not give them tools to interpret it. Conversations with UN and U.S. officials suggests they often are skeptical about indicator-based, early-warning systems for two reasons: first, they are already flooded by more information than they can cope with, and second, what they need most are filters to guide them in screening and interpreting that information. Their own "filters" tend to be the presuppositions and policy orientations of the bureaucratic and political contexts in which they work.

Systematic, model-based early warning: The essential complement to field monitoring and indicator construction is the development of explicit frameworks, or models, that analysts and policy makers use to interpret the flow of information. Models for systematic early warning should meet three general design criteria:

• Specify what "disease" is to be warned about. Ethnic warfare, regime failure, massive human rights violations, and refugee flows are the result of different combinations of factors, hence require somewhat different models.

• Specify the combinations of risk factors and sequences of events that are likely to lead to crises. Lists of variables or indicators are only a starting point; models should identify which measurable conditions, in what combination and relative importance, establish a potential for which kinds of crisis.

• Distinguish between remote and proximate conditions of crises. This may be done in either of two ways. One is to specify the conditions associated with each phase in the development of crises (see note 18). The second is to distinguish between background conditions, intervening processes, and the accelerators or triggers that lead to rapid escalation. Such distinctions are essential for analytic clarity, and for planning long-term versus short-term responses.

It should be evident that early-warning models that meet these design criteria not only structure analysis, they help determine the kinds of information sought. That is, they stipulate what kinds of information is especially needed as well as how to interpret it. They are thus information-management tools as well as analytic tools.

THE CHALLENGE OF DEVELOPING AND TESTING MODELS FOR EARLY WARNING

To design and test valid models of the etiology and epidemiology of crises is a demanding task. Substantive knowledge about a number of cases of humanitarian crises is a necessary condition. Once outlined, models need to be validated: that is, they require testing against the empirical reality of a large number of conflict situations to ensure that they identify the potential for escalation with acceptable levels of accuracy.[19] And significant resources need to be invested to collect and test such models. These activities are interdependent. To test models adequately requires extensive data and sustained research effort. If early warnings are to be credible to those who might act on them, they should be based on good data that is analyzed by tested models. But if organizations that want early warnings fail to give adequate support to this research, "early warnings" are likely to include too many "false negatives" (unanticipated crises) and too many "false positives" (predicted crises that did not happen). If early warnings are too often inaccurate, early-warning research may be discredited in the eyes of skeptical policy makers.

A number of social-science models have been developed with early warning of civil conflict and humanitarian crises in mind. For example, forecasting refugee flows is the objective of early-warning models developed by Akira Onishi at Soka University (Tokyo) and by Susanne Schmeidl and Craig Jenkins at Ohio State University.[21] The author of this chapter has developed and statistically tested models that can be used to forecast magnitudes of ethnic rebellion.[22] Since 1994 the U.S. government has supported the work of a task force that uses empirical techniques to identify the conditions linked to the onset of episodes of "state failure" worldwide. The purpose is to identify risk factors of ethnic and revolutionary war, regime collapse, and humanitarian disasters that might be susceptible to influence using developmental assistance and diplomacy.[23]

The use of statistical analysis of indicators on large numbers of cases is one approach to developing and testing early-warning models. This "large n" approach should be complemented by comparative case studies in which sequences of events can be examined in much greater detail. Case studies can focus on less tangible factors as cultural context, the significance of ideology, the role of leaders, and the impact of preventive actions—factors that rarely can be measured precisely in broad statistical studies. Especially recommended is what Alexander George calls "structured, focused comparison." Such studies ask a specific theoretical question and seek answers through comparative examination of cases that resemble one another in a number of respects, but differ on one or a few theoretically significant factors. A hypothetical example of a "structured, focused comparison" of communal conflict is a comparison of Sri Lanka and Malaysia; the theoretical question is why Tamil-Sinhalese conflict escalated into protracted communal war in the 1980s, contrasted with the largely successful management of Chinese-Malay conflict. A not-so-hypothetical example is a comparative study of Rwanda and Burundi that asks what conjunction of internal conditions and international events led to genocide in the first country and more limited political massacres in the second.[24]

DESIGN CRITERIA FOR A GLOBAL EARLY-WARNING SYSTEM

Embedded in the foregoing discussion are suggestions about the steps needed to institute a global early-warning system in support of international efforts at preventing ethnic warfare and humanitarian disasters. The criteria are similar to those used in monitoring potential epidemics. These are seven guidelines:

- Highest priority should go to identifying and monitoring latent and emerging crisis situations, long before the onset of armed conflict and massive human suffering.
- Information should be gathered and reported using standard protocols, designed to ensure that assessments are comprehensive and precise. Prototypes exist: they use various combinations of text and quantitative indicators, not only statistical data.
- Information should be interpreted by reference to risk factors known or thought to be associated with the occurrence of specific kinds of conflict and crises. This implies using simple etiological models for related phenomena such as ethnic warfare, regime instability, and massive human rights violations. At a minimum, distinctions need to be made among remote, intermediate, and proximate conditions.
- Risk assessment and early warning are distinct but complementary activities. Risk assessments are based on the systematic analysis of remote and intermediate conditions. Early warning requires near-real-time assessment of events that, in a high-risk environment, are likely to accelerate or trigger the rapid escalation of conflict.
- The monitoring and analysis of conflict situations should be done independently of political control and considerations so that its results are, and are seen to be, as objective as possible.
- Risk assessments and early warnings should get close attention from officials with operating responsibilities for preventive diplomacy and humanitarian assistance. There is little point in establishing early-warning systems if their results are not communicated in a timely way to officials who give them some degree of credibility.

• Risk assessments should be widely circulated to international, regional, and nongovernmental organizations as well as activists, journalists, and scholars. No effort should be made to shield potential contenders from knowing that they are under international observation. On the other hand, it may be necessary to limit the publicity given to close-to-real-time early warnings because, if they become known to contenders, preventive efforts may be compromised.

RISK ASSESSMENTS: HOW TO IDENTIFY POTENTIAL COMMUNAL CONFLICTS

A first step toward global early warning of communal conflicts and humanitarian crises is to inventory ethnic, religious, and national groups that are at risk from latent or ongoing conflict. This final section reports the results of such an inventory. The Minorities at Risk project has identified 275 politicized ethnic groups with a total population of about one-sixth of the world's population. They are present in 116 of the world's larger countries, as table 1 shows (see end of chapter). Each group meets one or both of these criteria:
• They are, or have been, subject to discriminatory or invidious treatment by other groups because of their cultural, ethnic, or religious traits.
• They are mobilized for political action to promote or defend their common interests.

The critical questions for early warning are: How great are the future risks of conflict for these groups? and, What are the risk factors that point toward intensified conflict and humanitarian crises? Some have been victimized by past discrimination and repressive state policies that in two dozen previous episodes reached genocidal proportions. As noted at the outset of this chapter, 38 are engaged in armed conflicts in 1999. Others, like Québécois separatists and indigenous activists throughout the Americas, are using conventional political means to pursue collective ends.

The theory and data of the Minorities at Risk project provide a means for systematically identifying groups at high risk of future rebellion. Risk models are developed along the lines used by medical researchers to assess the risks that individuals will suffer from heart disease. Risk factors are measured for cases of protest and rebellion by ethnic groups during the early to mid-1990s, then the 275 groups in the study are profiled on these factors in 1998, and statistical models are used to assess each group's probability of new or escalating conflict in 1999 and later. The risk models include five key factors, indicators of which are discussed below.[25]

RISK FACTOR 1: SALIENCE OF GROUP IDENTITY. The more important group identity is for people with shared descent and culture, the more likely they are to define their interests in ethnocultural terms and the easier it is for leaders to mobilize them. We assume that collective identity is most important for people who experience discrimination and who recently have been involved in conflict. Five indicators of these conditions were tested for the risk-of-protest and risk-of-rebellion models. Results are described below, with special attention to models that predict rebellion.

- *Persistent protest during the previous decade* proves to have a consistent leading relationship with rebellion and is one of the six factors in the final model of risks of future rebellion.
- *Persistent rebellion during the previous decade* correlates with future rebellion but is not used in the risk models because it tells us only what we already know—that once rebellions have begun they tend to persist.
- *Economic and political discrimination* are correlated with future increases in protest but do not contribute independently to risks of rebellion.
- *Cultural restrictions* prove to be a significant risk factor in the model for protest but not for rebellion.

RISK FACTOR 2: GROUP INCENTIVES FOR COLLECTIVE ACTION. The greater the disadvantages imposed on a people and the greater their sense of injustice, the easier it is for group leaders to convince them that they have something to gain from rebellion. Opposition to new discriminatory policies (cultural restrictions are an example), anger about state repression, and hopes for redress of past wrongs such as loss of collective autonomy therefore are among the precursors of sustained political action by ethnopolitical groups. Three such conditions are tested as risk factors.

- *Lost autonomy* is correlated with ongoing rebellions and is one of the domestic conditions that facilitate future rebellions.
- *Government repression* is a very strong leading indicator of both protest and rebellion. Any inhibiting effect repression might have on ethnopolitical action is more than offset by the mutually reinforcing spiral of

attack and counterattack. Repression is one of the highest-weighted risk factors in the rebellion model.

- *Increased political restrictions* is a leading indicator of rebellion, probably for the same reason as repression. The indicator has no independent effect on risks of future rebellion and is not included in the model used.

RISK FACTOR 3: GROUP CAPACITY FOR COLLECTIVE ACTION. The greater a people's sense of common identity, the greater their potential for joint action. But identity alone is not sufficient, it needs organizational expression. Two structural indicators of ethnopolitical groups' capacity for political action were tested as well as two indicators of change in capacity.

- *Territorial concentration* has been established in other etiological studies as a precondition for most ethnorebellions. It proves to be the second-strongest risk indicator in the risks-of-rebellion model.
- *Group organization* is the third-strongest risk indicator in the rebellion model.
- *Increased support for conventional and militant ethnopolitical organizations* are two of the time-sensitive indicators tested in an effort to forecast imminent changes in collective action. We found that increased support for conventional organizations, other things being equal, reduces the likelihood of future rebellion. This implies that strengthening conventional ethnopolitical organizations makes strategies of protest more attractive than rebellion. Therefore this indicator is one of five domestic facilitating factors (inversely, because it reduces the risks of rebellion).

RISK FACTOR 4: DOMESTIC OPPORTUNITIES FOR COLLECTIVE ACTION. Group leaders make strategic decisions about when to initiate, escalate, and terminate political action. They do so in the context of changing political environments that shape the chances of successful political action. A great many factors affect the opportunities for successful ethnorebellion. We tested how characteristics of political systems affect the likelihood of protest and rebellion.

- *Democratic, autocratic, and incoherent polities*: Democratic states have above average protest but below average rebellion, therefore the existence of democratic institutions proves to be a significant risk factor for protest. By contrast, autocracies and incoherent polities (regimes with a mix of democratic and autocratic features) have less than average protest. Incoherent regimes are especially susceptible to increased rebellion, therefore the incoherence indicator is one of five domestic facilitating factors.

• *Regime instability*: The statistical risk analysis showed that ethnic protest and rebellion increase during the first five years after an abrupt change in political regime. Regime instability is the strongest risk indicator in the protest model and also enters the rebellion model.

RISK FACTOR 5: INTERNATIONAL OPPORTUNITIES FOR COLLECTIVE ACTION. We distinguish between direct and diffuse international factors that encourage ethnopolitical rebellion. Direct support includes diplomatic, material, and military assistance from kindred groups, sympathetic states, and international organizations. Diffuse factors include the effects of armed conflicts being fought in adjoining countries. Their spillovers—arms, refugees, militants looking for safe havens—may give ethnic contenders incentives and opportunities to press their claims. They also contribute to a general climate of insecurity that can provoke governments into taking preemptive action.

• *Support from kindred groups*: Ethnopolitical groups that get support from kindred in neighboring states are more likely to rebel than to protest. This indicator appears in the protest risk model as a factor that significantly enhances the chances of protest. It also is one of four international factors that facilitate future rebellion.

• *Support from foreign states*: Support from foreign states predicts future rebellion in the risk model.

• *International political support*: Whereas bilateral support for ethnopolitical groups (from kindred or states) increases the risks of conflict, our statistical analyses show that in the 1990s sustained engagement by international organizations reduced the risks of future rebellion. Therefore, international political support is included as a factor that inhibits future rebellion.

• *Spillover effects of regional conflicts*: Protest is significantly less likely and rebellion is more likely in countries in "bad neighborhoods." Two indicators of regional conflict are used as external facilitating factors.

GROUPS AT RISK: A WATCH LIST FOR THE TWENTY-FIRST CENTURY.

When the risk models are applied to 1997–98 data about the 275 groups in the Minorities at Risk study we find that about 90 of them, including those already fighting ethnic wars, are at medium to high risk. These 90 groups are the most likely protagonists in new and escalating ethnic wars early in the twenty-first century. The risk assessments come in two parts. One is a probability estimate for each group generated by a statistical risks model; the numbers of high and medium risk groups in each region are shown in the first column of table 2 (see end of chapter). The second is a data-based set of indicators that show whether domestic and external factors that facilitate rebellion, described in the previous section, are increasing or decreasing. The highest-risk groups in each region are listed in the second column of table 2; the net escalating and dampening effects for each group are summarized in the pluses and minuses.

The broad picture is that the largest numbers of at-risk groups are situated in the postcommunist states, West and South Asia, and in Africa south of the Sahara. Risks of ethnic war are minimal in the Western democracies and only slightly greater in Latin America and the Caribbean. Following are the specifics by world region.

In Europe risks are highest in the Balkans. Spillover from the Kosovo conflict is likely to increase them, especially for groups already at some risk like the Sandzak Muslims and Vojvodina Hungarians in Serbia. A new democratic government in Serbia is the best antidote for these risks. Our analysis also points to medium potentials for renewed fighting among Serb, Muslim, and Croat contenders in the Yugoslav successor states. In the Caucasus preventive diplomacy and peacekeeping efforts have paid off in the containment and settlement of most ethnic wars of the early 1990s. Risks remain high, however, for intensification of warfare over the status of Nagorno-Karabakh and armed conflict by the Ingush, who live on Chechnya's western border.

Outside Europe prospects for ethnopolitical peace are best in Latin America. Almost all domestic and external facilitating factors indicate a dampening of risks in this region. Most high-risk protagonists are indigenous peoples whose demands for recognition and local autonomy are being substantially addressed by democratic governments. The Nicaraguan and Mexican governments face the greatest risks of rebellion. In Nicaragua this is due to lack of resources for implementing an autonomy agreement for the coastal peoples, in Mexico because of lack of political will to respond with real reforms to political action by indigenous peoples in Chiapas, Oxaca, and elsewhere.

Four other zones of ethnopolitical conflict pose greater present and future challenges. One is the Middle East, where the central issues are the unsatisfied ethnonational aspirations of Palestinians and Kurds.

Further east is the West and South Asia zone, characterized by communal contention for power in Afghanistan and Pakistan and ethnonationalist rebellions by Kashmiris and Sri Lankan Tamils. The largest number of ongoing and prospective ethnic wars anywhere in the world occur in the Central Asian uplands, stretching from the hill country of Bangladesh, Assam, and Burma to Tibet and China's Xinjiang province.

Africa's situation is the most grave. Twenty African groups are at medium to high risk of future rebellion, half of whom live in or on the periphery of the Eastern and Middle African conflict zone (or two zones) ranging from Sudan and Ethiopia through the Great Lakes region to the Congo basin and the Angola highlands. There is also a less threatening West African conflict zone, where revolutionary and ethnic wars have been brought under control in Niger, Mali, and Liberia but continue in Sierra Leone and Chad. The greatest risk in this region has been the possibility of internal war in Nigeria along the north-south, Muslim-Christian divide. The Ogoni minority of the Niger delta and the much larger Yoruba both are high on the factors that elsewhere predict ethnic war. The prospects of ethnic war in Nigeria are very much dependent on the ongoing transition to democracy. Civil war in Nigeria would have spillover effects far beyond its borders.

The primary purpose of the risk analysis is to highlight situations that should have the highest priority for remedial and preventive action. By whom and how? The answers depend on which actors have the will, the political leverage, and the resources to act. International and regional organizations are more likely to pursue effective preventive strategies in areas where the Western powers have vital interests, which means Europe, Latin America, and the Middle East. Asian and African conflicts are more remote and resistant to external influence. When preventive strategies fail, or are not made in the first place, the international challenges are different: how to provide humanitarian aid and how to contain the regional dispersion of conflict.

TABLE 1. MINORITIES AT RISK IN THE 1990S BY WORLD REGION

World Region	Number of Countries with Minorities at Risk	Number of Minorities at Risk			Total Group Population as Percent of Regional Population
		National Peoples	Minority Peoples	Total	
Western democracies and Japan (21)	15	17	13	30	11.8
Eastern Europe and NIS (27)	23	49	10	59	13.8
East, Southeast, and South Asia (24)	20	36	23	59	13.3
North Africa and the Middle East (20)	13	15	13	28	27.9
Africa south of the Sahara (45)	27	14	53	67	36.1
Latin America and the Caribbean (24)	18	20	12	32	24.5
Total Countries (161)	116	151	124	275	17.4

Note: Politically significant national and minority peoples greater than 100,000 or one percent of country population in countries with 1998 populations greater than 500,000. The list is based on current research by the Minorities at Risk Project, Center for International Development and Conflict Management, University of Maryland. Changing political circumstances and new information lead to periodic updates in the inclusion and exclusion of groups under observation. Numbers of countries above the 500,000 threshold in 1998 are shown in parentheses in the World Region column. The population estimates for national and minority peoples are approximations. Population percentages are calculated from 1998 estimates for all countries in each region.

The Western democratic region includes Canada, the United States, Australia, New Zealand, and Japan, in addition to Western Europe. The Middle East including

TABLE 2. RISKS OF NEW AND ESCALATING ETHNIC WARS IN THE TWENTY-FIRST CENTURY

Region and Groups	Groups in Ethnic Wars in 1998 and at Future Risk	Highest Risk Groups and Facilitating Factors in 1998
Western democracies: 31 ethnopolitical groups	0 groups in ethnic wars 5 groups at medium risk	Basques in France + + Basques in Spain +
Eastern Europe and Former USSR: 59 ethnopolitical groups	2 groups in ethnic wars 8 groups at high risk 7 groups at medium risk	Armenians in N-K - - Kosovars in Yugoslavia - Russians in Estonia - Crimean Tatars + Crimean Russians + Bosnian Serbs +
Southeast and Pacific Asia: 34 ethnopolitical groups	5 groups in ethnic wars 3 groups at high risk 12 groups at medium risk	Uighers in China + + Timorese in Indonesia - Aboriginal Taiwanese 0
West and South Asia: 25 ethnopolitical groups	11 groups in ethnic wars 6 groups at high risk 13 groups at medium risk	Hazaras, Tajiks, and Uzbeks in Afghanistan 0 Kashmiris in India + + Tripuras and Scheduled tribes in India +
North Africa and Middle East: 28 ethnopolitical groups	3 groups in ethnic wars 6 groups at high risk 2 groups at medium risk	Kurds in Turkey 0 Shi'a in Iraq + Shi'a in Lebanon + Palestinians in Gaza and the West Bank 0 Kurds in Iraq + + Arabs in Israel 0
Africa south of the Sahara: 67 ethnopolitical groups	11 groups in ethnic wars 12 groups at high risk 8 groups at medium risk	Ogani in Nigeria + + Tutsi in Congo-Kinshasa 0 Ovimbundu in Angola + Yoruba in Nigeria + + Hutu in Burundi + + Afar in Ethiopia + +
Latin America and Caribbean: 32 ethnopolitical groups	0 groups in ethnic wars 1 group at high risk 11 groups at medium risk	Miskitos in Nicaragua - - Maya in Mexico 0 Indigenous highlanders in Ecuador - -

Note: Ethnic wars in 1998 are conflicts between rebels and states with rebellion magnitudes of 4 or greater. No more than six highest-risk groups in each region are listed here. For details see Gurr, *Peoples versus States*, chapter 7 and Appendix B.

16
LOCALIZING OUTBREAKS
SALIM AHMED SALIM

The Organization of African Unity (OAU) has developed a systematic approach to localizing and resolving conflicts on the African continent. Its premise is that the original conception of the United Nations with regard to regional diplomacy, as expressed in the UN Charter, involved permissive concession to regionalism. Chapter VII of the UN Charter does not explicitly involve fundamental reliance upon regional organizations as important pillars of the world system. However, within the context of the UN Charter, regional organizations were to handle frontier disputes and other issues of regional concern. Disputants in a regional conflict were to exhaust local remedies in accordance with Article 33 and were encouraged to resort to regional arrangements for peaceful settlement of conflict before approaching the UN. Relations between regional organizations and the UN system were, therefore, envisioned to complement and not necessarily to supplement each other.

Although the UN Charter provides that intra- and interstate disputes and conflicts of a regional character should be settled within the framework of Articles 33, 51, and 52, it is generally acknowledged that some regional organizations, such as the OAU, have modest constitutional powers and limited financial, material, and political resources that allow them to handle only intra- and interstate conflicts of low intensity. This is not to suggest that the OAU should not have a built-in capacity to relieve the UN of the burden of handling intraregional conflicts, especially in promoting the doctrine of "Try the OAU first." Significantly, at the inception of the OAU, there was no specific mention of specialized regional institutions for security concerns as envisioned in both Articles 51 and 52 of the UN Charter. The OAU, however, conforms to both Chapter VII and Article 51 of that Charter.

BASIC ASSUMPTIONS

Several assumptions need to be stated to explain the approach taken by the OAU. These may be summarized as follows:

1. Regionalism as a sustainable framework for containing outbreaks of conflict depends primarily upon the nature of the conflict to be dealt with.
2. As in medicine and public health, the concept of prevention also underpins the philosophy of preventive diplomacy.
3. Regional organizations have a comparative advantage over global organizations in localizing outbreaks within their specific region, assuming regional organizations have the necessary capacity and mechanisms to confine specific outbreaks.
4. Localization is essentially a management function related to the containment of a specific conflict to a particular locality. This approach conforms with the role of the OAU Mechanism for Conflict Prevention, Management, and Resolution (MCPMR), which was created to prevent the outbreak of conflicts through early warning followed by early political action.

The Mechanism for Conflict Prevention, Management, and Resolution was set up by the OAU Assembly in 1993. The localizing mandate of the MCPMR has assisted the OAU in preventing the outbreak of conflicts or in containing them where they have occurred. The objectives of the MCPMR are to foster collective action authorized by regional organizations within the meaning of the UN Charter.

FROM GLOBAL PERSPECTIVE TO REGIONAL CONTEXT

The concept of preventive diplomacy has its origin in the UN system. It first appeared in the Annual Report of United Nations Secretary-General Dag Hammarskjold. Preventive diplomacy is currently defined as any action to prevent disputes from arising between parties, to prevent existing disputes from escalating into conflicts, and to limit the spread of the latter when they occur. It may involve preventive deployment.

In the African context, conflict, as a state or condition characterized by the absence of social harmony, has been a major concern of the OAU since its inception, in May 1963. Its founding fathers specifically stated in the preamble of the OAU Charter that they were inspired by a common determination to promote understanding among the African peoples and cooperation among African states. This declaration was a clear manifestation of their desire to work collectively and to coordinate their efforts in localizing outbreaks in order to promote the aspiration of the African peoples to brotherhood and solidarity, and to a larger unity transcending ethnic and national differences.

Since the inception of the OAU, African leaders have resorted to various techniques of preventing and/or localizing outbreaks. Some of the techniques have been used on an ad hoc basis whereas others have been institutionalized. All the techniques applied, traditional or nontraditional, have been initiated largely on the basis of "Try the OAU first." It was in recognition of the need to develop an African approach to preventive diplomacy that the founding fathers of the OAU made a provision in Article XIX of its Charter for the establishment of the Commission for Mediation, Conciliation, and Arbitration (CMCA).

COMMISSION FOR MEDIATION, CONCILIATION, AND ARBITRATION

Between 1963 and 1990 issues of conflict in Africa were, on the whole, treated on an ad hoc basis, without recourse to the CMCA, despite the fact that this body had been conceived as the sole permanent organ of the OAU, specifically and exclusively charged with the settlement of disputes. The CMCA has remained virtually dormant since its establishment, though there have been some suggestions and unsuccessful attempts to use it.

It was obvious that the CMCA had certain limitations that inhibited its ability to address conflict situations in Africa. First, its jurisdiction was limited to intervention in interstate rather than intrastate conflicts; second, it was an organ concerned exclusively with conflict resolution rather than conflict prevention. Moreover, the dormancy of the commission could also be attributed to the preference of Member States for diplomatic rather than judicial means of conflict settlement.

AD HOC MODALITIES FOR CONFLICT RESOLUTION

Because Member States were reluctant to invoke any of the provisions of the Commission, the Assembly of Heads of State and Government, as the supreme organ of the OAU, employed other means of conflict resolution. The Assembly set up ad hoc commissions and/or committees from among its members to deal with conflicts. Similarly, the OAU Council of Ministers also appointed ad hoc commissions or committees when the need arose, and this practice became prevalent in the 1960s and 1970s. The use of Elder Statesmen and Good Offices were also common during the period.

Although some conflicts were resolved through ad hoc arrangements, the imperative still existed to create a more permanent mechanism for conflict resolution because of the proliferation of both inter- and intrastate conflicts on the continent. Moreover, the importance of introducing a new political approach and institutional dynamism into the way Africa dealt with conflicts became increasingly evident. A new regional arrangement was required, therefore, to enhance the capacity of the OAU to meet the challenges.

THE OAU MECHANISM FOR CONFLICT PREVENTION

At its meeting in Cairo in June 1993, the OAU Assembly took the opportunity to shift from the ad hoc modality of conflict resolution of the past to a more permanent arrangement for the anticipation and resolution of conflict by setting up the MCPMR. The establishment of the MCPMR marked, within Africa, a new institutional dynamism that put the OAU at the center of all efforts of conflict prevention, management, and resolution when and where they occurred. In circumstances where conflicts had occurred, it would be the MCPMR's responsibility to undertake peacemaking and peace-building functions in order to facilitate conflict resolution, and it could mount and deploy civilian and military missions of observation and monitoring of limited scope and duration.

During the seven years that the MCPMR has been in operation, it has made significant strides in addressing conflict situations on the continent. As required by the Cairo Declaration establishing it, the Central Organ of the Mechanism has been able to meet at summit, ministerial, and ambassadorial levels, in regular and extraordinary sessions, to adopt various decisions and resolutions, empowering the MCPMR to function fully.

The MCPMR is built around a Central Organ with the Secretary-General and the secretariat as its operational arm. The Central Organ of the Mechanism is composed of the state members of the Bureau of the Assembly of Heads of State and Government, elected annually. The countries of the outgoing OAU Chairman and the Chairman (designate) are also members of the Central Organ.

The Central Organ functions at the level of Heads of State as well as that of Ministers and Ambassadors accredited to the OAU or a duly authorized representative. It may, where necessary, seek the participation of other OAU Member States in its deliberation, particularly the countries neighboring those involved in the conflict. The OAU is expected to cooperate and work closely with the United Nations about issues relating to conflict resolution, peacemaking, and peacekeeping.

Since the adoption of the Mechanism in Cairo in 1993, the OAU has been deploying military and political electoral observers as well as Special Representatives to many conflict situations in Africa, including Burundi, the Democratic Republic of the Congo (then Zaire), Comoros, Ethiopia/Eritrea, Gabon, Ghana, Liberia, Malawi, Mozambique, South Africa, and Zambia. In the case of electoral missions, the OAU has officially observed over sixty electoral processes, and some of the countries where those electoral processes have taken place are now on their third rounds of holding elections.

More specifically, the ascendance of South Africa from an apartheid regime to a multiracial democratic government was an issue which remained a preoccupation of the OAU since its inception in 1963. Following the historical agreements of the date of the democratic and nonracial elections and the establishment of transitional structures as part of the preparations for the holding of free and fair elections, OAU Member States moved speedily to reinforce the OAU Observer Mission which, under Ambassador Joseph Legwaila of Botswana as OAU Special Representative to South Africa, had been deployed in that country for one year to monitor the electoral process. The successful conclusion of those elections, which took place in April 1994, was the culmination of OAU full support of not only the peace process in South Africa, but also of the protracted struggle and sacrifices of the people of that country with which the OAU collective membership in particular, together with friends outside the continent, had always identified.

In Rwanda, even before the OAU Mechanism officially came into existence in 1993, the OAU had already deployed efforts toward resolving the conflict in that country. The OAU initiative was in the form of helping in the mediation of the Arusha Peace Agreement for Rwanda, and the deployment by the OAU of a Neutral Military Observer Group in Rwanda during the time the political solution to the Rwanda conflict was being negotiated. Subsequently, and partly for lack of resources, the responsibility for implementing the Arusha Peace Agreement was entrusted to the United Nations, whose force incorporated the officers and men who had been serving under the OAU Neutral Military Observer Group. It is true that ultimately, in 1994, Rwanda witnessed a genocide that the international community failed to avert, but the achievement of the OAU in the form of negotiating the Peace Agreement for Rwanda up to a point when the OAU passed it on to its operational partner, the United Nations, a body with more resources and greater experience in peacekeeping operations, deserves recognition.

A special fund has been established for the purpose of providing financial resources to support the OAU operational activities relating to conflict management and resolution. This special fund is allocated 2 percent of financial appropriations from the regular budget of the OAU (about \$30 million), voluntary contributions from Member States, as well as other sources from within and outside of Africa.

TYPOLOGY OF CONFLICTS IN AFRICA

The typology of conflicts in Africa consists of the following major classifications: boundary and territorial conflicts, such as those that existed between Algeria and Morocco and between Ethiopia and Somalia, as well as the ongoing Ethiopia/Eritrea conflict over those two countries, disputed areas along their common border; civil wars and internal conflicts having international repercussions, such as the civil wars in Nigeria, Chad, and Congo; succession conflicts in territories being decolonized such as Angola, Mozambique, and Western Sahara; political and ideological conflicts; and other types of conflicts including those related to transhumance and irredentism.

These types of conflicts can also be reclassified into two major categories. The first relates to interstate conflicts that characterized the period following the creation of the OAU. During this period African leaders were, essentially, preoccupied with conflicts arising out of territorial claims or other disputes, such as Algeria/Morocco, Ethiopia/Somalia, Somalia/Kenya, Chad/Libya, and Uganda/Tanzania. The second classification relates to intrastate conflicts. Such conflicts include the Congo crisis, the conflicts in Angola, Mozambique, Somalia, Sudan, Liberia, Nigeria, Sierra Leone, Rwanda, Burundi, Comoros, and others.

But we are also having a rather unique conflict on the African political landscape which started off as largely a civil/internal conflict, only later to draw into national borders six other African states. This is the conflict in the Democratic Republic of Congo (DRC) involving that country's government and its rebel outfits on the one hand, and, on the other hand, Rwanda, Uganda, Zimbabwe, Angola, Namibia, and Chad coming in as external entities.

On the question of interstate conflicts, the legacy of the Berlin Conference on the partition of the African continent and the subsequent arbitrary division of countries and demarcation of African boundaries has, despite the principle of the intangibility of African boundaries adopted by the 1964 OAU Summit in Cairo, remained a major source of conflict in Africa. Indeed, conflicts arising out of territorial disputes were endemic to Africa for over a decade, especially in the postindependence period. Most African boundaries were drawn by the colonial powers without taking into consideration issues related to ethnicity, language, or common cultural values. The colonial boundaries arbitrarily separated tribes and families; they transferred territory along with resources. But it must be noted that the principle of the sanctity of African boundaries inherited at the time of independence has contributed significantly to the evolution of a relatively stable regime governing African interstate relations. The good sense of respecting inherited boundaries has averted numerous conflicts, kept broad unity in place, and allowed the continent to direct its energies to more pressing issues, such as economic development.

Another source of interstate conflicts is the ownership and sometimes control and/or management of transboundary resources. This particular type of conflict is often subsumed under the broader classification of territorial disputes and frequently involves petroleum or mineral deposits on or around common border areas.

Ideological differences among neighboring states, particularly during the Cold War, have also been a major source of interstate tension and conflicts. Ideological differences tended to compound and exacerbate existing tensions and often led to open hostility. However, with the end of the East-West ideological divide, conflicts related to ideology seem to have subsided.

In recent years, Africa has experienced few interstate conflicts. However, because there is a strong possibility for the resurgence of these types of conflict, there is a need for the OAU to strengthen its preventive capacity to ensure that many outbreaks are localized.

On the issue of intrastate conflicts, these have become prevalent in Africa, especially in the 1980s and 1990s. In slightly over three decades, the continent has experienced a total of seventy-eight unconstitutional changes of government as a result of intrastate conflicts. Some eighty-eight government leaders have been deposed during that same period. Changes of government as a result of internal conflicts took place in thirty-one countries of which twenty experienced this kind of change more than once.

Internal conflicts are ongoing in Angola, Burundi, DRC, Sudan, Somalia, Republic of Congo, Central African Republic, Guinea-Bissau, and Sierra Leone. Many other African countries are also facing conflict situations in one form or another, and the OAU has been closely following such situations of potential conflict. There are clear indications to suggest that, of all regions, Africa has had the highest number of conflicts in recent years and has borne a terrible burden of war. It is estimated that in the 1980s, 2 to 3 million people lost their lives in wars and 150 million, about 27 percent of Africa's population outside Egypt, covering one-third of the continent's land area, were living in countries seriously affected by war. Although the OAU has not yet developed sufficient indicators to test sensitivity to conflicts, it is clear that ethnicity has of late been one of the major sources of internal conflicts.

In Africa there are many states in which ethnic and religious groups have historically been living together in harmony; some are currently experiencing antagonistic tendencies between these diverse groups. These developments require careful monitoring. Religion is increasingly becoming a potential source of internal conflict in Africa. In Somalia, where the population is united by language and religion, internal conflict has been demarcated and fueled by clan-based division and rivalry. In a number of states, cultural intolerance has created divisions between different ethnic groups and has led to internal strife and turmoil.

Quite apart from those intrastate and interstate conflicts, Africa is also afflicted by other types of conflict. The experience of recent years has confirmed that mass unemployment among the young creates a politically explosive situation that is almost bound to result in violence and anarchy. Towns and cities in Africa have grown beyond the capacity of local governments to deliver even basic essential services. Urbanization in Africa has also given rise to potential conflict situations. Structural adjustment programs have resulted in depressed incomes in urban areas, unemployment, and reduced social services, thereby generating situations with the potential for conflict. Policies to promote universal primary education have been dropped with serious impact on functional literacy programs.

Similarly, programs for primary health care and human settlement have been seriously affected. Average labor earnings in the urban public sector of Africa declined by 30 percent during the first half of the 1980s, and the number of workers employed in the private sector fell by 16 percent. Africa's rapid population growth and the corresponding growth in the labor force means that there will be a need for six million new jobs each year at the beginning of the next century to absorb the new entrants into the workforce. Rapid population growth, without a parallel increase in opportunity for employment, has created pressure for population movement, which threatens to become a serious source of conflict. Indeed, as societies have become more liberal, ethnic and religious conflicts among groups seeking to capture political power by exploitation of these differences are more likely to erupt. Preventive measures must be initiated.

Conflicts often occur when human rights and human needs are repeatedly denied, threatened, or frustrated, especially over long periods of time. Grievances and feelings of injustice accumulate, particularly when one identified group within a state is perceived to be unfairly disadvantaged in relation to other identified groups. In Africa some of these grievances and feelings of injustice have resulted in open hostility between different ethnic groups and have become a serious threat to physical security.

The concept that prevention is better than cure, originally coined by public health activists, is being accorded wider acceptability, and its usage is rapidly spreading into many other fields—social, political, and scientific. But although prevention in public health relates to the physical security and well-being of the population, that of preventive diplomacy relates to the national security of states. Key actors in public policy have become increasingly aware of the need to formulate and support policy measures and structures that have built-in preventive devices. The African experience demonstrates the disastrous impact that armed conflicts and political strife have on the social well-being of nations and the physical security of their citizens.

As a result of those conflicts, millions of people in Africa have been forced to flee their countries and become refugees, and even greater numbers are without potable water and adequate health and sanitation services. More still have been forced to abandon their education and economic activities, and this has had serious impact on their livelihood. Apart from the deaths of hundreds of thousands of innocent people, conflicts in Africa have devastated vast areas, caused food and health emergencies and widespread disruption of economic activities, social services, and productive use of resources. Efforts to address issues related to physical security, especially in combating the outbreak of epidemics, including that of AIDS, have been seriously constrained by the prevalence of conflicts in the affected region. Moreover, conflicts have undermined efforts by African governments toward the elimination of hunger and malnutrition, the provision of primary health care as well as safe drinking water, sanitation, and adequate shelter. The lack of epidemic preparedness and control plans, the increase in social unrest, drought, and difficult economic situations in many African countries continue to cause an increase in the number of refugees and internally displaced persons, thereby creating ideal conditions for cholera and dysentery epidemics.

In Africa in the mid-1990s there were 17.5 million internally displaced persons and over 6.5 million refugees; about 4.7 million of these two groups were reported as being at immediate high risk of malnutrition, micronutrient deficiencies, and associated mortality. The overall outcome is a general increase in illness and death that extends well beyond the immediate areas of conflict.

Given Africa's population structure, these figures speak mostly of women and especially of children. According to the WHO Center for Emergency Preparedness and Response in Addis Ababa, Ethiopia, these figures encompass a vast range of public health issues. Although it is difficult to estimate with any accuracy the number of people wounded in the wars now ravaging Africa, it is possible to provide a general picture of the impact of such conflicts on the public health infrastructure in the areas of conflict. Among the most dramatic effects of conflict on health are those where epidemics force the migration of people and transhumance across international boundaries. Poor sanitary conditions have resulted in increased spreading of cholera, and tuberculosis has resurfaced with renewed ferocity in urban centers, especially those centers in areas of conflict.

Epidemiological studies have shown that mass displacement has caused an increase in the infant mortality rate up to twenty times normally recorded for children in the same population. In other cases entire populations are held hostage by armed groups and are deprived of vital resources needed to maintain their health. Since the 1960s, African governments and peoples, through sustained policies and concerted efforts, have managed to improve infrastructure, build more schools, increase literacy, construct more hospitals, and provide better social services. Tragically, all these efforts have been undermined by the prevalence of recent conflicts in Africa.

INTERNATIONAL NGOS IN PREVENTING CONFLICT

KENNETH HACKETT

By their nature and mandate, many nongovernmental organizations (NGOs) have an obligation to work to prevent and transform conflicts, overcome injustices, and promote values of dignity and empowerment. Working cooperatively at times with governments and at times independently of them, and effectively using the resources that governments can provide, international NGOs can maximize and personalize assistance during times of conflict and disaster. By implementing programs that emphasize holistic development and the growth of civil society, NGOs can play a critical role in preventing future violent conflicts.

Today's world conflicts are proving difficult to resolve through traditional methods. Instead of wars between nation states, conflict often appears as struggles for power and dominance within states; pitting elite, ethnic, and religious groups against one another, often amid the breakdown of government. New kinds of preventive action, referred to in this chapter as peace-building, need to be redefined precisely because many of these situations are, and likely will remain, charged by ethnic, religious, and nationalistic motives. The nature of these conflicts has led NGOs to place increased emphasis on conflict prevention and has raised awareness that their roles and programs must be more integrally involved in addressing the causes, not only the symptoms, of conflict.

Peace-building is a process rather than a technique or outcome. It is a commitment to justice rather than temporary results or agreements. The pursuit of justice often involves standing with the oppressed and changing oppressive systems or relationships. For many NGOs, a focus on justice requires that humanitarian assistance and development serve to lay the foundation for more just relationships in society across lines of class, gender, ethnicity, area of origin, age, and religion. Peace-building as a process assists all people—especially the disenfranchised and oppressed—through solidarity, assistance, and opportunities whereby they may become full participants in the decisions that affect their lives and relationships.

Conflict is often the product of inequity and injustice. Preventive action requires a shrewd understanding of the interest of all parties and of the emotional stakes, deeply rooted in history, culture, social divisions, and actual and perceived injustices—issues that tend to impassion and motivate people. In the West, spiritual lives are generally separate from public ones. Consequently, we have not always understood the level of interaction between traditional leaders—be they religious or cultural—and politics, and how this interaction shapes the motivations of individuals and communities in other societies. Leaders operating from a nongovernmental, particularly an ethical or religious point of view, may have an advantage as politically nonpartisan agents who can evoke trust and reach people at an individual and group level to address emotional and ethical issues. It is at these levels where much of today's conflicts are felt and where transformation and healing need to occur, and where inequities and insecurities are often manifested most strongly.

It is the thesis of this chapter that many international NGOs by their mandates and by their access to communities, societal structures, and traditional and moral leaders, have a unique role to play in preventing conflict. Economic development is not sufficient to build a cohesive society. Integral human development—which includes social, political, cultural, psychological, intellectual, spiritual, physical, and economic development—helps people find an alternative to violent conflict. Many international NGOs facilitate this process by strengthening indigenous institutions and supporting their role in civil society to work toward the common good, and by carrying out integral human development as a means to eradicate poverty and injustice. Civil society can be a stabilizing force, acting as a buffer and providing the possibility for civil dialogue to de-escalate local tensions.

This chapter reviews the nature of today's conflict and the roles that NGOs can play in developing civil society, promoting human development, working toward justice, and building peace.

THE NATURE OF TODAY'S CONFLICT

As circumstances in Bosnia, Liberia, Sierra Leone, Sudan, and Rwanda attest, complex local and regional power struggles have proven difficult to end. Such conflicts lead to massive suffering and the need for humanitarian assistance. In today's world, the horror is conveyed in the faces of the victims whose voices are not heard and whose rights are not respected. The numbers we hear about only objectify the suffering they represent.

As strategic and economic interests of First World countries change and as resources available to the international community to exercise influence or control over conflict situations become limited, adherence to and enforcement of internationally accepted conventions that reflect normative values, including human rights, are less respected. Leaders of developing nations cannot depend on playing off superpowers or on the distribution of external aid within their countries to promote their priorities. In an effort to give substance to their causes, less scrupulous leaders resurrect long-suppressed issues. They use ethno-nationalist, tribal, or religious platforms to gain or maintain their power, as evidenced in the current situations in the Democratic Republic of Congo, Rwanda, Liberia, Sudan, and Kenya.[1]

In threatening or unstable environments, people search for security and identity, making them vulnerable to manipulation by local power elites. In these situations, lines of violent conflict are often drawn along the lines of group identity, with fighting aimed at achieving collective rights in opposition to groups of differing ethnicity, religion, race, class, or geographic affiliation. These confrontations threaten each groups' collective identity, indeed their very survival, and can lead to the breakdown of whatever degree of civil society exists. Deep-rooted, longstanding animosities breed high levels of violence and atrocity, and the resulting psychological and cultural factors drive and sustain the conflict. Conflict prevention depends not only on addressing the causes of the tensions but, more fundamentally, on repairing relationships and changing systemic problems in society.[2]

THE PEACE-BUILDING ROLE OF NGOS

It will be useful here to identify the particular group of NGOs that is the subject of this chapter. International nongovernmental organizations encompass a wide range and diverse group of organizations, which include private sector associations, interest groups, and private voluntary organizations, among others. International NGOs have a rich diversity of objectives and functions, many united by a commitment to improving conditions around the world. Some have objectives that are solely charitable, whereas others shape their efforts in a more political fashion.

There are those that are fundamentally concerned with supporting development initiatives expressed by indigenous constituency groups. The focus of this discussion is on the subset of NGOs that includes both secular and faith-based or religious-affiliated organizations, whose mandates include emergency relief and development assistance to refugees and displaced persons, human rights monitoring and advocacy, sustainable development programs, building democratic institutions, conflict resolution, and combinations of these.

The level of development achieved by efforts of the international development community hand in hand with indigenous governments and organizations over the last thirty years—through programs in education, agriculture, health, small business, political pluralism, promotion of women, and protection of the environment—has undeniably provided a degree of stability in developing societies, and remains a fundamental ingredient to peace. Nonetheless, from Bosnia to Burundi, we have learned that something more is required in the formula for sustainable development and lasting peace.

The nature of today's humanitarian crises and their long and everevolving understanding of the development process has led these NGOs to begin to redirect their resources to programs that address the interdependence of relief, development, and conflict prevention. A great number of them see their traditional paradigm of moving assistance through a continuum, from relief to rehabilitation to development, as patently insufficient. They realize that if they are not consciously engaged in a process that integrates reconciliation and the promotion of justice in their programs, nothing lasting will be accomplished.

Many of these NGOs are placing greater emphasis on efforts to build and repair relationships and to address systemic problems. These include:

- raising awareness of the public and officials to human suffering and abuses, and calling for justice;
- advocating for increased resources for development and debt relief for developing countries;
- strengthening local groups and organizations in civil society, enabling them to critically analyze their problems, take action to address them, and learn from those actions;
- carrying out relief and development in a manner that builds and sustains indigenous capacities;
- promoting gender-responsive social, economic, and cultural development and relief programs;

- facilitating mechanisms in civil society for dialogue, relationship building and healing;
- identifying the status of conflict and early-warning indicators to the international community; and
- standing in solidarity with moderate elements in troubled societies.

These NGOs are taking a hard and critical look at the manner in which they undertake relief and development activities to ensure they are not creating conflicts or barriers to reconciliation. There is a recognition that the act of providing assistance can have either positive or negative impacts on civil society and community harmony, and that, in the past, some international NGO assistance, whether economic, technical, financial, or in kind, may have exacerbated tensions. Aid provided by international NGOs can also have a positive impact on conflict.[3] For example, in southern Sudan, persistent dialogue between humanitarian relief groups and the Sudan Relief and Rehabilitation Association has led to improved accountability for resources as well as opportunities for training on humanitarian concerns and development approaches among the front-line military.

Many NGOs have become much more conscious of opportunities for positive impact as well as mindful of when their actions have negative consequences.[4] For example, in Liberia in 1996 some international NGOs drew back into a reflective mode to assess what had been done and what had not been done to build peace and to analyze the impact of their assistance in that disintegrating society. They sought to instill respect for humanitarian principles by defining a joint policy of operations through which they committed themselves to work to avoid the potential negative effects of aid on the conflict, to provide only essential inputs in order to minimize the risk of fueling the conflict, and to support local capacities for peace.

The challenge for international NGOs in collaboration and coordination with United Nations agencies, donors, governments, military, civil society, and each other is to move toward a more coherent and concentrated effort to build indigenous institutional capacity to manage conflict. There is strong consensus that multifaceted approaches at all levels simultaneously are required.[5] Action is needed that supports institutions at various levels—regional, national, and civil society—and that involves all levels of society and creates linkages among these levels and between groups.

These international NGOs increasingly engage and support actions of a range of individuals and groups who may not have always been factored into the process of peace-building. In collaboration with indigenous partners, they can identify and enhance actions and processes within society, at the grassroots and intermediate levels, that are working for peaceful resolution to societal tensions. They have capacity to understand communities and can encourage community leaders, women and men, to identify local capacities to build peace.

Peace-building of this kind depends largely on middle-range actors such as local NGOs, religious leaders, and community elders. The best way to promote long-term peace is to work at the intermediate and grassroots levels to build capacity to promote nonviolent options to resolving conflict, undercutting the capacity of those who manipulate and perpetuate it. Quick answers and quick fixes will not work. Part of the task of building peace is to rewrite the historical narratives of intrasocietal conflict. This rewriting occurs in settings where people interact in new ways and where individual transformation can occur.[6]

International NGOs have an important role to bring people together in polarized societies through cross-ethnic community projects that have mutually beneficial results. In Sarajevo during the war, the provision of humanitarian relief brought to the table four faith-based groups: Dobrovtor, representing Orthodox Serb communities; Merhamet, representing Bosnian Muslims; Caritas, representing Catholic Croats; and, La Benevolencija, representing Jewish communities. Through dialogue and planning the use of resources to ensure that all people in need were served, these groups came to identify with the suffering and acknowledged the needs of each others' communities. What is important is that the relationships created have a potential to transform and prevent future violent conflict.

Looking at development with a peace-building lens at the conception and design of a project places the emphasis on the building of relationships through dialogue and action toward a mutual goal. An example of this was a project to strengthen parent-school partnerships in Macedonia that brought together Albanian Muslim and Macedonian Orthodox parents to plan the improvement of schools for all their children. For Macedonia it was an effort to establish communication between the lines of community conflict. Such nonpolitical activity, promoted by NGOs, opened the lines of communication between diverse communities in a politically neutral and safe environment.

The destruction of homes and community buildings was extensive during the 1994 genocide in Rwanda. International NGOs with indigenous organizations encouraged and supported collaborative reconstruction of homes. Families from different ethnic groups participated in this program. Over the long term, this rehabilitative program has the potential to increase respect, tolerance, and reconciliation in Rwanda while meeting the basic need of shelter and while preventing conflict by settling disputes of ownership as increasing numbers of refugees return home.

A Liberian health association integrated therapeutic psychological counseling and conflict resolution approaches within their broader community development and public health programs to address postwar trauma. Skills of public health officials, conflict resolution trainers, and counselors are developed through workshops to enable these professionals to assist their clients and communities.

In the current environment in Burundi, the absence of a guarantee that development projects begun today will not be destroyed tomorrow does not mean these projects should be discontinued. International NGOs witness many instances in which communities of mixed ethnic backgrounds in Burundi continue to work together for the betterment of all members of the community. Without these projects there may be little opportunity for people to come together around a unifying and shared need or concern. Searching for a degree of normalcy and stability, community leaders and local groups call on international NGOs not to withdraw or give up. This kind of dedication to peace and development deserves to be supported.

What stands out in these examples are the efforts being made toward peace and conflict prevention by local leaders and individuals working at community and intermediary levels in civil society. These programs work through existing networks, such as churches, schools or health care systems. Health and religious institutions are places where people might look for healing, because these are two places where trusting relationships can be built. International NGOs can naturally support the psychological healing role of these institutions.

These examples demonstrate that there is not one approach to peace-building; each situation has to be assessed and analyzed in its own context. Patient work at the level of the community, work with and through leaders with a measure of moral suasion, and an open partnership with those engaged in peace-building can make a long-term difference. Practitioners must be willing to be self-critical, to reflect on directions taken or not taken, and to make the task of systemic transformation, increasing justice and equality, a priority.

INTEGRAL HUMAN DEVELOPMENT AND STRENGTHENING CIVIL SOCIETY: FUNDAMENTAL TO PEACE-BUILDING

Impoverishment and conflict are the basic economic and political forces that underlie suffering. Structural adjustment programs of international lending institutions assumed that the growth of civil society and other aspects of human and social development would follow economic and physical development. This has not proven to be the case, as people need more than physical resources to transform conflict and overcome poverty.

A sustainable peace presupposes a foundation of justice. The full meaning of peace includes not only nonviolence but development, respect for the human rights of all, and ecological balance. Human rights includes not only civil and political rights but also economic, social, religious, and cultural rights and the right of people to participate in decisions that affect their lives.[7]

Development in a sustainable peace involves economic and physical aspects and the equally important social, cultural, psychological, intellectual, political, and spiritual aspects of human development. This more holistic development—known as integral human development—is a process that includes the ingredients of a just, equitable, and cohesive society, because it builds self-esteem, respect for others, and a sense of responsibility. This kind of development provides people with tools to gain control over their lives and obtain resources required to reach their potential. Without such a holistic process of development, people may not have the skills and attitudes to reject violence and strive for the common good.

One process which fosters integral human development is the Development Education for Leadership Teams in Action (DELTA) training program. DELTA, which began in Kenya in the 1970s and has spread to all regions of the world with international NGO support, integrates the insights of Paulo Freire, organizational development, community development, and the concept of transformation from the great religions. Paulo Freire, a Brazilian philosopher, in the early 1970s provided seminal education and development ideas (for example, the link between emotion and motivation to act and the importance of participants choosing the content of their education, and practical methods of breaking through apathy), involving groups and developing critical awareness of causes of problems.[8]

Built on the recognition that people are already involved on a day-to-day basis in their own development, the DELTA program seeks to facilitate community groups' active involvement in addressing problems that affect their lives by developing critical awareness skills. An animator assists groups within the community to reflect critically upon a problem and its causes and what is currently being done to address the problem, identify any new information or skills needed, get the information and training, and then plan action. Often the first action will solve some aspects of the problem but not deal deeply enough with its root causes.[9]

Within this process, a cycle of reflection and action is continued by the group, where successes are celebrated and causes of mistakes analyzed so that individuals become more capable of addressing problems and transforming their lives. The groups in a community are essential for forming relationships based on shared values. The critical reflection-action process brings the group to consider cleavages in society, such as inequity, and ultimately empowers them to work toward social change. Community self-reliance, fostered by this process, has resulted in numerous community-initiated sustainable development efforts in agriculture, water, agroforestry, health, literacy, and credit for small enterprise that are supported by international NGOs. International NGOs work with indigenous groups and organizations not only because it is ethically right to allow people affected by the problems to participate in making decisions and taking actions that affect their lives, but because it is an effective process to build people's skills and institutional capacities to prevent conflict and bring about social change.

Support to local organizations that promote participation and pluralism is part of the process to ensure lasting peace. Local NGOs bring a particular advantage to peacemaking efforts. They are knowledgeable about the complexity of local conflicts, and, when they enjoy the confidence of local communities and leaders, they are more able to effect change that national, regional, or international organizations cannot. By effectively strengthening local NGOs in civil society, constituencies can be created that hold governments accountable to adopting policies that minimize conflict.

Civil society encompasses informal groups at local levels; formal organizations and institutions; groups such as productive and commercial associations; religious institutions that defend beliefs, rights, and values such as trust, inclusion, dignity, and subsidiarity; interest-based or educational associations; developmental organizations to improve the

quality of life of communities; issue-oriented movements like environmental protection and women's rights; and civic groups seeking to
improve political systems. Civil society involves citizens acting collectively to express their interests and ideas, to exchange information, to
achieve mutual goals, to make demands on the state, and to hold the
state accountable.[10]

Research from the Joan B. Kroc Institute for International Peace
Studies suggests that NGOs have strengthened the resiliency of societies to their structural, cultural, and political tensions. As the case of
South Africa illustrates, a strong civil society, supported by committed
transnational movements and networks, can mitigate violent conflict
and hold a country together as it undergoes social transformation. The
interaction between local and international NGOs helped to organize
communities in South Africa around national grievances, to put the
issue on the international agenda, and to carry out the conflict resolution program of the National Peace Accord. States with strong civil
societies also have greater capacity to rebound from disaster and widespread social strife, which can make all the difference between recovery
and collapse.[11]

Kenya is another example. The level of development achieved in
Kenya has often been heralded as impressive. Indeed, Kenya has
attained a certain degree of economic and social development. It is also
one of the strongest civil societies in East Africa with a significant number of political and cultural associations, development NGOs, and
active women's groups, all of which have received international NGO
investment over the years. Although cultural and political tensions have
been severe in Kenya, these have not erupted in widespread civil unrest.
Most altercations have been manipulated and perpetuated by corrupt
leaders, and have been short-lived. Having assessed that violent conflict
will not produce beneficial results, many Kenyans are hopeful that eventual political pluralism will improve the state of affairs. In contrast with
its northern and central African neighbors, Kenya has not exploded,
although, considering its societal and political tensions, it could have.

In most countries, civil society collaborates with the state respecting
their separate but connected roles and functions. Within pluralistic societies, capacities exist to mediate and address causes of conflict. The
assumption is that without a well-developed civil society there are few
to no mediating institutions.[12] Civil society is credible in playing a role
of protector and mediator between government and the citizenry, and as
such, should be the locus for peace-building.

A U.S.-sponsored NGO program, for example, supported rural peasant associations in providing farmers with basic inputs on credit or at reduced prices to mitigate the suffering experienced as a result of the commercial embargo on Haiti in 1994. Built on traditional forms of sharing work, Haiti has had an active voluntary association sector in the rural areas since the early 1980s. This U.S. program strengthened the local associations and their role in the community during a period of distress. It demonstrated a practical method of preventive diplomacy.

NGOs strengthen civil society by supporting communities and organizations to guarantee personal and collective rights and liberties and protection of vulnerable groups, increasing their sense of security, and offering opportunities for participation in constructive development processes. Increasingly, NGOs are working at developing ways to shift from development projects to process, that is, more emphasis on solidarity support for movements for self-determination and less on specific project outcomes. Donor and public demands for quantifiable results provide contrary pressures, making this shift a challenging one.

There has been an upsurge in the creation of NGOs around the globe. This growth is even more dramatic in the developing world, where some 4,600 international NGOs are now active, providing support to hundreds of thousands of indigenous organizations.[13] Indeed, international NGOs have helped to populate the institutional landscape in developing countries, and in so doing their impact has not purely been in terms of economic growth and social welfare but in strengthened societies. The increase in indigenous organizations has brought about social change through civil movements and has acted as a stabilizing influence in the developing world.[14]

The exponential growth of local organizations is not, in and of itself, a positive trend. For example, in the United States, the growth of ethnocentric groups has been fueled by the promotion of individualism where concern for the common good has been replaced by fear of those who are different almost solely because of economic interests. International NGOs, and particularly faith-based organizations and religious institutions, can help in addressing feelings of hate, violence, and self-interest within civil society by making explicit mutually agreed values, such as trust, reciprocity, and respect, and by providing an ethical framework for the pursuit of the common good that helps to diffuse the power of individuals to perpetuate conflict. When the common good is defined by the people who are confronted with the problems and then supported by international organizations, actions that follow will more likely address the structural and cultural tensions in society.

FUTURE CHALLENGES

As NGOs take on the challenge of supporting development in a manner that builds lasting peace, they must look for transformative processes that repair and strengthen relationships and resolve societal tensions, as well as those that increase equity and establish just structures. They must become more proficient in supporting these processes. International and indigenous NGOs operating in partnership in this way should be widely supported by governments and the international donor community. NGOs offer a unique, effective, and efficient opportunity to prevent future conflicts in an environment of decreasing resources because of their experience, access to local structures, and an improved development or peace-building practice. At the same time, these NGOs must coordinate their efforts well with the full range of players in this process, UN agencies, governments, and each other.

As the international community does this, it must look at a new diplomatic paradigm for peace just as it looks for new paradigms for humanitarian and economic assistance before and after situations of conflict. It is imperative to look outside the foreign service or international banks for solutions to such emotionally charged problems. For it is not in the language of statecraft or economic models or in transplanted Jeffersonian democracy that lasting solutions will be found. It may be in solutions that flow from dialogue with mullahs, with bishops, or with community leaders and individuals who live deeply in the emotions that often fuel the problems. The challenge is to build on existing traditions of social organization, not purely those that are externally conceived. If one searches, the right individuals and processes will be identified, and if those concerned are smart, they can help these individuals and processes work toward peace.

The role of both international and indigenous NGOs in conflict prevention can no longer be ignored. Although there is no quick fix, there are connections to the community and trust of the society which can be nurtured, and there are actions from which we can learn. NGOs, through their development programs, must continue to strengthen the resiliency of societal groups and organizations to structural, cultural, and political tensions. Peace-building presents both a significant opportunity and a major challenge to NGOs, spiritual leaders, their religious communities, governments, and the international community.

In accepting and participating in this challenge, the international community is responsible and will be held accountable by future generations to look critically at the extent to which it worked toward a just and peaceful world. Everyone involved must start by examining the ways they, as individuals and as parts of institutions, are seriously doing this. Courage is required to take a stand against injustice, to make tough decisions, to embrace difficult tasks, to prevent violent conflict, and to challenge traditional or Band-Aid actions and push for social change. Societies that respect the dignity of all persons must be built. The synergism of effective NGOs, governments, and the international community operating in a dynamic and credible way to prevent conflict and injustice can contribute to dramatically reduced violence and suffering in the world today.

18

EMERGING INFECTIOUS DISEASE:
THREATS TO GLOBAL SECURITY

SCOTT R. LILLIBRIDGE, M.D.

Despite armed conflict in many quarters of the world and continued concern for the proliferation of weapons of mass destruction, infectious diseases remain the major cause of death worldwide.[1] Although we have made great strides in medical science, the spread of many of these diseases continues to defy political boundaries and our efforts for permanent control. For example, in the 1990s the resurgence of diseases such as tuberculosis in the United States and the former Soviet Union have led us to reassess our prospects for long-term success in this contest.[2] The Ebola hemorrhagic fever virus outbreak in 1995 in Kikwit of the former Zaire provided an example of how a highly fatal infectious disease can descend suddenly, seemingly from the unknown, to disrupt local health services and kill critical medical staff, and cause panic within the population.[3] Although some of the best international laboratories quickly confirmed the diagnosis, why the disease reemerges and how the virus is sustained between outbreaks remains a mystery.

Diseases that are increasing or emerging de novo to threaten the health of populations have been termed Emerging Infectious Diseases (EIDs).[4] In an age when national borders provide little solace against the spread of disease, EIDs challenge our parochial notions of disease control. Inadequate resources and deterioration of the public health infrastructure, the development of resistance to common antimicrobial therapies and a false sense of security that infectious diseases have been conquered have left us unprepared to deal with the intrusion of infectious diseases into our populations. While stories of mass migration, economic collapse, and armed conflicts fill the news media, at the same time deadly diseases are, with little notice, proliferating or gaining a foothold in populations throughout the world. Unexpected infectious disease threats have emerged from factors like increased global travel, greater human contact with wilderness, the loss of habitat through deforestation, and the development of areas that promote human interaction with insects and animals harboring disease.[5]

Only a small percentage of the world's viral and bacterial populations have been thoroughly evaluated, or even discovered, suggesting that many potential infectious disease threats may remain as obstacles in the path of human development.

Once new diseases have emerged, as in the case of Dengue fever, the process of continued global urbanization greatly facilitates their spread. In the new millennium more than twenty cities of the world will have a population of over eight million. Moreover, urban migration is continuing at an unprecedented scale. The resulting population collections, called megacities, are growing most rapidly in the poorer countries of the world that are least able to cope with the need for expanded disease control services. The lack of sanitation, inadequate documentation of residents, and lack of basic public health services, even at the most basic level, make these locations ideal for person-to-person transmission of disease. Our lack of knowledge concerning diseases that may be smoldering or emerging within these populations challenges our notions that we are winning the effort to improve global health. Cities like Karachi and Calcutta are examples of this trend and each year new cities are added to the list. Infectious disease concerns in these populations run the gamut of potential EID concerns and include tuberculosis and malaria.

As new health challenges threaten populations, lack of adequate resources, poor disease control policies, ineffective therapy, or merely the lack of knowledge concerning the extent of the spread of a disease within a population can lead to delayed response to a mounting problem. Such a delay can mean that disease control will be more difficult and the costs can rise to precipitous levels. For example, vast global control programs now exist for diseases that were either unknown or thought to be insignificant only ten or fifteen years ago. Human immunodeficiency virus (HIV) is among the best known in this category.

HIV infection weakens the immune system making it difficult for stricken individuals to fight infections; in some cases, infections that would be termed as relatively mild for individuals with healthy immune systems can be fatal. Despite billions of dollars spent on research, there is still no known cure and a new vaccine appears years away. Until recently, the prospect for long-term survival for those infected was practically nil, until new medications were discovered that can slow the progress of this disease. However, the cost of these regimens is enormous to individuals as well as nations. Unfortunately, countries that have high HIV prevalence rates, such as many African nations, are also among the countries least able to support the costs of new drugs. The implementation of programs to prevent disease within these countries presents a humanitarian dilemma. Without external assistance to support expanded prevention services, the burden of disease related to HIV in the population will continue to increase in many of these less developed countries, laying waste to some of the most productive segments of their workforce and posing a burden on their overall development.

Ironically, if attention and resources had been directed at developing rapid international responses for the identification and control of infectious diseases several decades ago, we might have found ourselves in a better position to control this epidemic. Such preparedness measures would have involved expanded viral disease detection activities, coordinated and highly focused laboratory research, and the rapid collection of information detailing the means of transmission at an earlier stage of the epidemic. Such a path would have required serious geopolitical leadership, resource allocation, and new methods of international health cooperation. It is disconcerting to learn that recent laboratory evaluations of banked specimens suggest that HIV may have been present in the human population as far back as the late 1950s. That was long before the HIV virus was conclusively isolated, clinically appreciated, and before specific control measures to protect populations were instituted. It is hard to know if other diseases, yet to be discovered, are moving silently through the population and might eventually be as devastating in impact to the world as has the HIV epidemic. Response to such threats to our global health security must follow a more rapid path from the first alarm to the point when coordinated global public health mobilization ensues.

To further develop the way the international community must collaborate to effectively deal with EID threats in the future, we should consider the example of a disease that continues to evolve and threaten the world's population in a more rapid and pressing way. This infectious disease culprit is the influenza virus. Each year, when a new flu strain emerges from the wild, there is concern over its potential impact on the world's population, given that certain strains can be expected to result in relatively more deaths and hospitalizations. Worldwide vigilance to quickly discern the emergence of a super lethal strain that could be the harbinger of the next global episode of the "killer flu" is our paramount concern related to this exercise. Such an event was last seen in 1918–19, when a global flu epidemic killed more than twenty million people.

The more recent 1997 outbreak of avian influenza (bird flu) in Hong Kong challenged our complacency and suddenly demonstrated how a single infectious disease threat could galvanize global action from countries, health organizations, and multinational bodies.[7] For example, this outbreak was initially thought to portend the next serious flu epidemic and for a short period the world's attention was focused on this emergency public health investigation. The media was thoroughly engaged, as daily press releases documented the progress of an investigation that largely centered in Asia. International follow-up on potential cases ensued, along with a greater emphasis on case reporting and patient tracking. A global contingency plan was needed more than ever. Under the advice and consultation of international experts, the local political leadership moved quickly to implement control measures focusing on birds (such as, ducks and chickens), thought to harbor a new flu virus that was beginning to move into the human population. Control measures included the slaughter of large populations of potential disease-carrying fowl in and around Hong Kong.

The adverse economic consequences resulting from the destruction of these domestic livestock and wild fowl populations were enormous. As the international community prepared for what they thought was the next global epidemic of flu, close cooperation between the World Health Organization (WHO), various ministries of health and their laboratories, and the Centers for Disease Control and Prevention (CDC) were required as we prepared for a possible catastrophe. Governments at odds on issues ranging from trade to national security engaged their public health communities to facilitate the movement of consultants and laboratory samples. Throughout the world, vaccine manufacturers from the private sector waited to learn more about the characteristics of the new strain.

Fortunately, a worst-case scenario did not ensue. Still, global disease tracking must continue to monitor and report critical information related to the seasonal rise and ebb of the influenza virus and its effect on the world's population. Clearly, this limited mobilization required new partners and involved both preventive medical, diplomatic, and intergovernmental measures in an attempt to protect the world's population. On a global scale, disease tracking, decision making, and laboratory capacities need to be strengthened. Had this event culminated in the confirmation of a new "killer flu" virus, it would have become clear that our emergency capacities for a global epidemic response are not fully in place. In the future, our survival against deadly microbes may depend on these ready capacities, along with the political mechanisms necessary to facilitate the rapid implementation of such a response. Efforts like the "Pandemic Influenza" plan developed by the CDC will need to be expanded and further developed.[8]

EMERGING INFECTIOUS DISEASES AND THE PUBLIC HEALTH INFRASTRUCTURE

It is extremely important to realize that threats to populations from infectious disease are directly related to the functional capacities of the supporting public health infrastructure. The overall health status of a population can be viewed through the lens of various health measures such as life expectancy, infant mortality rates, and the prevalence of infectious diseases. A favorable health status of a population results from the sum of all the disease treatment programs, clinical services, preventive health activities (such as childhood immunizations), and hundreds of other public health measures that work toward improving a community's health. A healthy population is essential to continued economic development and is reflected in the strength of a nation's workforce, a longer life expectancy, and many other health indices tracked with regularity by organizations like UNICEF, the World Bank, and many others. Invariably, such populations are served by a pharmaceutical system, a trained public health workforce, and a functioning network of clinics and hospitals.

During civil or ethnic conflict and conventional warfare essential health services of all types are often destroyed. Public health safeguards such as vaccine programs, disease control, and sanitation services quietly evaporate. The effects on the populations can be dramatic, as exemplified in the Rwandan civil war in 1994. During the ensuing mass refugee exodus thousands of refugees died on the shore of Lake Kivu, near Goma, Zaire, from cholera, dysentery, and vaccine-preventable diseases. Unfortunately, vulnerable populations like women and children, who may be already weakened by the effects of the malnutrition so often associated with civil conflict, will suffer disproportionately in these episodes.

The history of warfare is associated with many examples of serious epidemics whose burden is often borne by both the civilian and the military populations. The recent situation in war-torn Liberia aptly demonstrates how controls to infectious disease are eroded during conflicts, to the point where diseases once contained begin to reemerge.[9]

After nearly seven years of intermittent civil conflict, a site visit in 1997 revealed mere remnants of a health system that had once been an amalgam of private, public, religious, and developmental organizations. At this point in the conflict, nearly all public health safeguards to prevent the spread of common infectious diseases had been destroyed. No national or regional disease surveillance activities existed and the country lacked a functional ministry of health. The resurgence of vaccine preventable diseases, the lack of an effective national drug system, and the overwhelming collapse of the public health infrastructure, including laboratory and hospital services, were readily demonstrated. Visits to outlying areas revealed destroyed hospitals and thoroughly looted clinic sites. In many cases the workers had moved on along with the dislocated populations or had often been hired away by the growing relief industry. In some cases critical health staff had been killed.

The consequences for the health of the remaining embattled population were clear. The incidence of malaria, which had once been reasonably well controlled, had exploded. Rumors of Lassa hemorrhagic fever, a deadly virus transmitted by rodents, could not be confirmed but were given credence due to the presence of other infectious disease outbreaks, such as measles, that were more readily apparent. Liberia's situation was not unique. Examples of infectious disease outbreaks in other countries plagued by ongoing armed conflicts are easy to find. The resurgence of trypansomiasis (sleeping sickness) in Southern Sudan and measles in Kosovo among war refugees and internally displaced populations are just a few recent examples of conflict-related outbreaks.

In some regions of the world, armed conflicts are destroying the public health infrastructure faster than it can be repaired. These lost capacities may take a generation to rebuild and will require a completely new skilled public health workforce. Unfortunately the United Nations reports that, worldwide, there are more than forty countries or regions where such armed conflicts are in progress. Many of these conflicts persist for decades and often destroy all components of a society until little of the original fabric remains. As a result, conditions that favor disease transmission throughout the population increase dramatically, and infectious diseases are quick to reclaim their previous domains and extract their human toll. It is ironic that in an age of unparalleled scientific progress many areas are continuing to slide backward from a public health perspective and present giant gaps in our global disease control efforts.

There are additional factors in the struggle against deadly infectious disease that are related purely to the internal nature of the organisms, even in countries at peace and with good economies. Take the tragic case of malaria. The malaria organism is transmitted to humans by the bite of an infected Anopheles mosquito. In the past, prevention measures included efforts to control mosquitoes and reduce human exposure to them. Half a century ago public health efforts pushed this disease to low levels throughout the world. In the past, inexpensive antimalarial drugs were able to control the disease in those portions of the population unfortunate enough to contract malaria. Insect control efforts, using chemical agents to kill adult mosquitoes and larvae, were widely used to reduce the mosquito population. For a period, malaria rates decreased in many areas, depending on the level of effort and resources applied to this task. However, in nature the quest for survival is strong and, over time, adult mosquitoes and their larvae developed resistance to certain chemicals, and malaria organisms have developed resistance to key drugs such as chloroquine and mefloquine at an alarming speed.[10] Consequently, there has been a resurgence in malaria and prospects for control are increasingly difficult and ever more expensive. Worldwide, the incidence of malaria has quadrupled in the past five years and continues to increase despite advances in environmental health and medical science.[11] As a consequence, today more than 270 million people still suffer from malaria each year and 1–2.5 million will die.

The experience with resistance of the malaria organism to certain drugs is not an isolated event in medical science. Most therapies, particularly antibiotics, have a limited life expectancy against infinitely adaptable microbes. Our ability to mount a global attack on a particular disease with an inexpensive drug may be seriously challenged by the development of antimicrobial resistance during the course of a control campaign. For example, the drug penicillin, once a powerful agent in our fight against bacteria, is no longer effective against many infectious agents for which it was originally used. It is clear that bacteria are able to develop resistance to antibiotics and are adaptable to an extent unforeseen by medical sciences, leaving some to question whether we may not return to a preantibiotic era. If medical therapies lose their effectiveness, we could experience a reversal in our collective public health fortunes and could be at greater risk of epidemics on a vast scale.

Apart from infectious ravages due to drug resistance, historically, whole populations have been decimated by common diseases, such as measles or smallpox. Such populations were characterized as having little or no previous experience with these diseases and, subsequently, no acquired or natural immunity against them. Such situations could be repeated today if populations were challenged by infectious diseases that have been eradicated and for which immunization programs have been discontinued. These populations would be immunologically "naive," and the public health community would be unprepared.

Unfortunately, smallpox continues to present such a challenge to our collective public health security. Since the late 1970s no new cases of naturally occurring smallpox have been detected due to the global eradication effort. Since the 1980s routine immunization against this disease has been discontinued. Immunity among the last cohort vaccinated begins to wane after about four or five years. No source of commercially available smallpox vaccine exists at this time, and the effective vaccine programs that succeeded in eradicating this disease no longer exist. The status of the remaining smallpox virus stocks is surrounded by controversy.

Officially, the smallpox virus is authorized by the WHO to be contained only in two laboratories, one in Russia and one in United States, and is slated for review for destruction in the near future. However, there is growing concern that stocks of virus that have the potential of being used in offensive biological warfare or terrorism may exist outside of this framework.[12] In the case of a laboratory accident involving smallpox the human impact would likely be limited and controllable. However, consider for a moment the result of a deliberate introduction of smallpox into a large, mobile urban population. The disease is transmitted from person to person through respiratory droplets in coughs and sneezes. The disease is highly contagious. The fatality rate is reported to be as high as 30 percent. The consequences of such an outbreak are almost difficult to imagine. Even in a developed country with an intact public health system the reintroduction of smallpox would quickly demonstrate a vulnerable population. The disease might spread beyond the borders of any one nation and could reemerge as a global killer. Rationing of limited stocks of vaccine and dealing with the unvaccinated medical workforce would be among the major issues confronting national leaders. Commerce and travel would be disrupted on an unprecedented scale.

PREVENTIVE DIPLOMACY CHALLENGES RELATED TO EID

Although biotechnology continues to offer many new methods to diagnose and treat populations stricken by infectious diseases, it also provides the potential for unparalleled harm. For example, given adequate resources and time to build the proper scientific staff, virtually any organization in the world could set about, through a process of genetic manipulation, or even through more basic methods, to create deadly or contagious strains of microbes. Such organisms could be released into an unsuspecting population for political, ethnic, or military purposes. While this seems unimaginable, we know from experience that nations with tremendous resources once approached this task in earnest. The United States program for biological weapons development was unilaterally discontinued after 1969 by President Nixon. There was also concern that these weapons might be uncontrollable. However, in the former Soviet Union an offensive biological weapons development program was believed to be active well into the 1990s, employing thousands of scientific staff and linking biological agents with long-range missile technology.[13]

Apart from the obvious need for vigilance against the effects of a deliberate release of microbes into a population, other gaps in our infectious disease preparedness must be addressed. These include the lack of a global early-warning system, the need for coordinated multinational response, and the recognition that in many parts of the world the public health infrastructure has been destroyed by armed conflicts. These problems cannot be fully addressed purely within a medical science perspective. Effective strategies must reflect political, economic, and diplomatic realities if we are to control diseases at an early stage when intervention can be most effective.

To do this one must develop better surveillance and outbreak responses. The key to the control of any disease is knowledge of the magnitude of the problem and of why disease rates are increasing or decreasing. In public health this information is called infectious disease surveillance. This data is obtained from clinical or laboratory facilities as a result of patient encounters. It is collated into composite reports that arise locally, then regionally, and eventually nationally to provide decision makers with critical disease trends related to the population. Such reports provide vital clues concerning who is infected, what types of microorganisms are responsible, and what specific geographic regions or populations are most affected. This information is extremely important in galvanizing support from the international community and in designing and evaluating proper public health interventions. On a global scale, if we are to seriously challenge the relatively free range of microbes, we will need to organize and expand these myriad activities into a surveillance system that is both timely and sensitive.

This endeavor will need to incorporate new technologies to match the adaptability and complexity of the microorganisms we are trying to contain. For example, the "fingerprinting" of different viruses and bacteria through new technology allows disease control staff to read specific genetic codes within individual microbes. This technology greatly facilitates the work of disease detectives in determining when new strains of microbes are emerging or whether an outbreak of disease in several locations is in fact associated with identical infectious agents. These capacities will allow health authorities to respond to outbreaks of emerging diseases that might otherwise go undetected, or are at the point before they have entered the human population.

On a global scale it will be important to harness such technologies in support of disease surveillance efforts. Currently there are insufficient funds to do the job, leaving the world's population exposed to EIDs under what would be best described as a patchwork of incomplete coverage with great technical limitations. Effective preventive diplomacy demands that we understand the relationship between our collective security and the infectious threats of today and the emerging diseases of tomorrow. We must have the resources and tools to improve and expand global surveillance, just as we have the national commitment for promotion of human rights and the prevention of genocide.

Another important issue related to disease surveillance is the flow of public health information, particularly concerning those events that unfold on a global scale. The Internet has brought reports of unverified and potentially serious disease outbreaks from nearly every corner of the world. The Internet has also permitted public health workers to communicate and share disease surveillance information on an almost instant basis. Services such as ProMED (Program for Monitoring Emerging Diseases) report rumors of infectious disease, potential biological misconduct, and provide a locus to conduct public health forums that link distant consultants to the general public. Recently, information from this service containing ongoing reports from Malaysia alerted key Center for Disease Control staff who subsequently, with local public health officials, helped isolate a previously unknown virus, the Nipah virus.

The global community can learn about potential infectious disease problems earlier than we could in the past. However, worldwide EID prevention needs better methods to monitor and act collectively on such warnings. The WHO plays a leading role in organizing this global task, but additional partners, resources, and political will are needed to realize the robust disease-tracking and response capabilities that will be required in the future.

External partners must also contribute to EID control. Organizations like the International Committee of the Red Cross (ICRC), Doctors Without Borders (MSF), and EPICENTRE have demonstrated strong public health capacities on a regional or national basis, suggesting that the key to successful global surveillance may not reside totally within United Nations agencies or any single host country. In terms of preventive diplomacy related to EID, we urgently need to involve new partners in a common effort to expand our weak global disease control capacities, particularly to strengthen disease surveillance in developing countries. Since international donors fund much of the activities of the nongovernmental and intergovernmental organizations, disease surveillance should receive greater support to assist local capacities to collect vital information at a stage when the "microbial versus human" conflict is only a potential global threat.

There are many areas where applied research is needed to hone our tools for EID control. Research to provide better drugs, better disease-tracking technology, and new vaccines is urgently needed to sustain current and future global programs. Other broad areas for applied EID research focus on further defining the relationship between changes in global climate and the spread of disease. Additional challenges confront us in learning how best to respond to EID in less developed countries, particularly those with limited economies for health services. The cost of research is also an issue. It will take a good deal of preventive diplomacy to prioritize and promote a common global infectious disease control framework, one that can be seen to benefit both the affected communities and the interests of more developed and potentially donor countries.

Globally, the international community must do a better job in defining and communicating the core public health functions related to disease control and defending these capacities when they are weakened. Our global disease control infrastructure must be seen in aggregate. Worldwide laboratory reference capacities must be enhanced, so that the development of drug resistance and new strains of disease may be detected early. Laboratory networks must be able to share technology and rapidly transfer samples through a system that operates as efficiently as international air traffic control. We must broaden preventive diplomacy to include public health components of disease control if we are to fully address the humanitarian needs of stricken populations at the local level and strategically at the global level.

Multilateral health-related organizations such as WHO must be supported to a much greater extent than in the past. In the pursuit of global EID control new partnerships are necessary. Nations with adequate resources must understand that the global disease response system is in their immediate interest, and that their quest to control diseases in other lands is far cheaper economically only when early intervention is made possible. We must realize that our vulnerability to infectious diseases, on a global scale, is a risk that is as immediate and tangible as if we were facing an invading army. Such preventive action to control EID will require significant international cooperation and leadership, actions not unlike those taken by the international community in containing the armed conflicts in the Balkans.

CONCLUSION

Despite the ebb and flow of war, changing political institutions, and new scientific achievements, infectious diseases remain the number one global killer. Trends such as antibiotic resistance, emerging new bacterial and viral strains, and the specter of bioterrorism challenge the notion that we are prepared to easily manage the task before us. To fully address these issues will require significantly more debate and political motivation. Proper resources must be allocated and EID global priorities clearly defined if we are to turn the tide. Such an effort will require the collaboration and support of those outside the traditional health community, those who control government funding and set our policies for development. A framework for global survival must include consideration for the control of EID because the history of human development and disease have always been, and will continue to be, inexorably linked.

CONCLUSION

Wars, like epidemic diseases, usually sputter to an end, and exhausted populations then try to rebuild broken societies. However, enormous numbers of lives are lost in the process, and generations suffer when basic traditions and customs, as well as the infrastructure of schools, hospitals, and homes are destroyed. Hatreds flourish in refugee camps and the seeds of new conflict take hold in fertile soil. One must break the cycle, try to prevent the recurrent tragedy—to stop wars before they start. Mankind's determination to control the threats of epidemics has resulted in a reasonably effective global system of public health with a specific methodology that can serve as a model for conflict prevention.

This book gives evidence of man's capacity to adapt, to learn from failure, to hope and work for a better world. It is possible, with effort and training and cooperation, to cultivate a new culture, one where prevention is considered, and funded, as much as reaction. This is not an impossible dream and, in fact, since the first edition of this book, has been adapted as a national policy in a major European country.

Students in courses in international relations and conflict resolution have utilized this textbook around the world. The editor and contributors to this new revised edition submit our work with the hope that a new generation will force the current political system to devote the necessary energy and funds to prevent deadly conflicts before they scar the next century.

NOTES

1. Kevin M. Cahill. *The Untapped Resource: Medicine and Diplomacy* (New York: Orbis Press, 1971); id. *A Bridge to Peace* (New York: Haymarket Doyma, 1988); id. *A Framework for Survival: Health, Human Rights, and Humanitarian Assistance in Conflicts and Disasters* (New York: Routledge and the Center for International Health and Cooperation, 1999).

CHAPTER ONE: A CLINICIAN'S CAUTION

1. W. Clarke and J. Herbst, *Foreign Affairs* 75, no. 2 (March/April 1996): 78.
2. *Rwanda: An Agenda for International Action* (UK and Ireland: Oxfam, 1994).
3. S. R. Feil, "Preventing Genocide: How the Early Use of Force Might Have Succeeded in Rwanda," a report to the Carnegie Commission on Preventing Deadly Conflict, April 1998.
4. W. Zartmank, ed., *Collapsed States: The Disintegration and Restoration of Legitimate Authority* (Boulder, Colo.: Lynne Remner Publishers Inc., 1995).
5. David Owen, *Balkan Odyssey* (London: Gollancz, 1995).
6. J. W. Honig and Norbert Both, *Srebrenica: Record of a War Crime* (London: Penguin 1996).
7. D. S. Zaidi and M. C. Smith Fawzi (Center for Economic and Social Rights, New York, and Harvard School of Public Health, Boston), "Letter to the Editor," *Lancet* 346 (December 2, 1995): 1485.
8. UNICEF, *Iraq Report*, CF/DOC/PR/1999-29.
9. Carnegie Commission on Preventing Deadly Conflict, *Preventing Deadly Conflict: Final Report*, Washington, D.C., 1997.

CHAPTER THREE: THE FUNDAMENTALS OF PREVENTIVE DIPLOMACY

1. S. Kull, *Foreign Policy* (winter 1995–1996): 185; (March–April 1996): 182.
2. Boutros Boutros-Ghali, *An Agenda for Peace*, June 17, 1992, UN Document A/47277–S/24111.
3. A. Fontaine, *L'un sans l'autre* (Paris: Fayard, 1991).
4. L. B. Pearson, *Partners in Development* (New York: Praeger, 1968).
5. R. McNamara, *One Hundred Countries, Two Billion People,* French ed. (Paris: Denoël, 1973).
6. J. Wolfensohn, "Sans progres social il n'y a pas de developement satisfaisant,"

interview given to the French newspaper *Le Monde*, February 16, 1996.

7. Preamble to the United Nations Charter, paragraph 4, 1945.

CHAPTER FOUR: THE CHALLENGE OF HUMANITARIANISM

I am more than unusually indebted to Dr. Randolph Kent's contribution to this paper.

1. The term *humanitarian network* is used throughout this text instead of *humanitarian system* or *community* or other similar expressions. It is used to encompass the wide gamut of humanitarian institutions including UN agencies, multilateral organizations, the International Red Cross system, bilateral donors, and international and national nongovernmental organizations. The reason for the use of the term is that a network is normally devoid of any institutional framework, lacks coherent goals, reflects few patterned relationships, yet points to a variety of transnational and functional linkages that have emerged probably more out of informal contacts than from binding institutional arrangements. The humanitarian network is an amalgam of nonbinding contacts, sustained by various channels of communication and by an awareness of who is around. On occasion, various components of the network will align themselves to promote particular interests, and will also work in concert to assist in relief. However, such arrangements are rarely enduring, and when they do occur, create little more than short-term dependencies.

2. Calculation of needs for Operation Lifeline Sudan in 1991 was in no small part determined by the Government of Sudan's insistence that it controlled a larger portion of population in southern Sudan than was actually felt to be the case. If, however, the position of the government was not accepted, the likelihood may well have been severe government restrictions on the overall relief effort, e.g., permission for relief flights.

3. P. Macalister-Smith, *International Humanitarian Assistance in International Law and Organization*, (Boston: Martinus Nijhoff Publishers, 1985), 17.

4. In standard texts, the terms *disaster relief* and *humanitarian assistance* have normally been used interchangeably. However, there is probably increasing reason to see the former as a subset of the latter. Disaster relief is generally associated with lifesaving assistance to populations whose lives are threatened by disasters or emergencies. Humanitarian assistance increasingly is taking on a broader meaning, encompassing a wide range of important activities, e.g., lifesaving activities as well as post-trauma care, care and maintenance activities, and family reunification.

5. "In hazards work, one can see how language is used to maintain a sense of discontinuity or otherness, which severs these problems from the rest of man-environment relations and social life. What emerges is that 'hazards' are not viewed as integral parts of the spectrum of man-environment or as directly dependent upon those," in K. Hewitt, *Interpretations of Calamity* (Boston: Allen & Unwin, 1983), 10.

6. See Chapter 6 in this volume.

7. A. Sen, *Poverty and Famines: An Essay on Entitlement and Deprivation* (Oxford: Clarendon Press, 1981), 75 f.

8. In a study conducted almost twenty years ago, Freudenhem reviewed eighty-nine natural disasters that occurred between 1972 and 1976 to determine the relationship between relief response and domestic politics, domestic corruption, rejection of aid and of international politics. In her final conclusion, she remarks that "there clearly exists evidence that political considerations on the part of national governments, donor governments, and international agencies obstruct the provision of sorely needed disaster relief, rehabilitation, and disaster preparedness assistance. The effects of this political reality, which can be as disastrous to the victim as any earthquake, drought, or epidemic, should be the urgent concern to all those interested in improving the international and national response to natural disaster situations." L. H. Stephens and S. J. Green, *Disaster Assistance: Appraisal, Reform and New Approaches* (New York: UN-USA, New York University, 1979), 244.

9. See, for example, F. C. Cuny, *Disasters and Development* (Oxford: Oxford University Press, 1983).

10. J. Fichett, "Rwanda Provides a Lesson for France," *International Herald Tribune*, August 2, 1994.

11. Although the exact number of affected remains uncertain despite considerable research, it is generally assumed that within a matter of six hours on the evening of November 20, 1970, over 250,000 people living in the area of cyclonic impact were killed. The relief operation, probably one of the largest up to that time, provided assistance to an estimated one million people. The political dissatisfaction generated by that crisis had a significant impact upon a series of events that culminated in the Indian invasion of Pakistan in 1973 and the creation of Bangladesh. It is worth considering whether a more expanded humanitarian intervention, including support for local structures and more extensive recovery efforts, might have at least mitigated some of the factors that led one year later to civil war.

12. There is often a distinction between humanitarian and human rights activities. While there is a practical field-level interrelationship, there are often reasons for humanitarian agencies to have an initial reluctance to provide anything more than functional support to counterpart human rights groups.

13. A post-conflict Multi-Donor Evaluation Study confirms this view.

14. In the words of the first UN Under-Secretary-General for Humanitarian Affairs, Mr. Jan Eliasson, "The United Nations has the moral obligation and authority, in my view, to continue to expand its role also in complex emergencies, in civil wars. This pioneering multilateralism will require institutional reform, new rules and regulations, new forms of recruitment of staff for high risk areas. Generally, more emphasis must be put on prevention: prevention in the deepest sense of attacking the root causes of conflict" (J. Eliasson, "The United Nations in a Changing World," a speech presented to the Columbia University School of International and Public Affairs, May 18, 1993).

15. W. Clarke and J. Herbst, "Somalia and the Future of Humanitarian Intervention," *Foreign Affairs* 75, no. 2 (March/April 1996).
16. International Colloquium on Post-Conflict Reconstruction Strategies, "Stadschlaining," June 23–24, 1995, p. 4.
17. A recent study prepared by the Université de la Sorbonne makes this very evident in its inventory of Security Council resolutions.
18. The Inter-Agency Standing Committee was established by the General Assembly in Resolution 46/182. The IASC, chaired by the UN Emergency Relief Coordinator/USG for Humanitarian Affairs, is composed of the main UN operational agencies as well as the International Organization for Migration, the Red Cross movement, and the NGO consortia, InterAction and ICVA. The basic objective of the IASC is to ensure more effective policy and field coordination for humanitarian activities.
19. United Nations, Department of Humanitarian Affairs, *Protection of Humanitarian Mandates in Conflict Situations: Draft* (rev. April 13, 1994), 1.

CHAPTER FIVE: DEVELOPING PREVENTIVE JOURNALISM

1. For more about this concept and its relationship to the communications revolution, see Michael J. O'Neill, *The Roar of the Crowd: How Television and People Power Are Changing the World* (New York: Times Books/Random House, 1993). The connection between preventive journalism and preventive diplomacy was first discussed by the author in a paper for the Council on Foreign Relations in 1986.
2. A. Eban, *The New Diplomacy: International Affairs in the Modern Age* (New York: Random House, 1983), 345.
3. W. H. McNeill, *A World History* (New York: Oxford University Press, 1979), 537.
4. For a fuller discussion of this argument, see Michael J. O'Neill, "Hold the 21st Century! The World Isn't Ready" (paper given at Symposium on the Legacy of McLuhan, Fordham University, March 27, 1998).
5. Discussed in Lewis A. Coser, *Masters of Sociological Thought* (New York: Harcourt Brace Jovanovich, 1977), see especially p. 388 ff.
6. R. Holbrooke, *To End a War* (New York: Random House, 1998), 21.
7. Quoted by Holbrooke, *To End a War*, 24.
8. Ibid.
9. Ibid., 27.
10. Ibid., 360.
11. For a marvelously detailed vivisection of media coverage of famines, genocides, and wars, from Ethiopia to Bosnia, see Susan D. Moeller's *Compassion Fatigue* (New York: Routledge, 1999). She argues that sensationalism, formulaic reporting and the Americanization of stories promote public apathy and, in the process, contribute to a dangerous failure of international reporting.
12. H. Kissinger, *Diplomacy* (New York: Simon & Schuster, 1994), 26.
13. J. S. Nye, Jr., and William A. Owens, "America's Information Edge," *Foreign*

Affairs 75, (March/April 1996): 20ff.

14. Max Frankel, *Media Madness: The Revolution So Far* (Washington: The Aspen Institute, 1999), 14.

15. H. A. Grunwald, "The Post–Cold War Press," *Foreign Affairs* 72 (summer 1993): 15.

16. A. Shuster, "Global News: Changing Views," *IPI Report* (February/March 1996): 4.

17. J. F. Hoge, Jr., "How the Media Will Change World Politics" (draft manuscript, January 3, 1995).

18. B. Kovach, "Tom Carlson or His Dog" (from an address at Washington and Lee University, March 15, 1996).

19. M. Kakutani, "Is It Fiction? Is It Nonfiction? And Why Doesn't Anyone Care," *New York Times*, July 27, 1993.

20. R. Lambert, "Business News and International Reporting," *Media Studies Journal* 13 (spring/summer 1999): 80.

CHAPTER SIX: WOMEN AS PARTNERS FOR PEACE

1. Gereth Evans, *Cooperating for Peace—The Global Agenda for the 1990s and Beyond* (St. Leonards: Allen & Unwin, 1993), 62.

2. United Nations Development Programme, *Human Development Report 1998* (New York, Oxford: Oxford University Press, 1998), 36.

3. Noeleen Heyzer, "A Women's Development Agenda for the 21st Century," in *A Commitment to the World's Women: Perspectives on Development for Beijing and Beyond*, ed. Noeleen Heyzer, with Sushma Kappor and Joanne Sandler , (New York: UNIFEM, 1995), 3.

4. United Nations, "Nairobi Forward-Looking Strategies for the Advancement of Women," in *The United Nations and the Advancement of Women 1945–1996* (New York: United Nations, 1996), Document 84, par. 13, 313.

5. Fourth World Conference on Women, Beijing, China, September 4–15, 1995, *Platform for Action and the Beijing Declaration* (New York: United Nations, 1996), par. 23, p. 25.

6. Ibid., par. 134, pp. 83–84.

7. Edward E. Azar, *The Management of Protracted Social Conflict: Theory and Cases* (Aldershot, England: Dartmouth, 1990), 9.

8. Heyzer, "Women's Development Agenda," 2–3.

9. United Nations Development Programme, *Human Development Report 1998*, 31–32.

10. Lourdes Arizpe, "Women and Conflict in a Changing World," in *Commitment to the World's Women*, ed. Heyzer, 213.

11. Boutros Boutros-Ghali, *Building Peace and Development: 1994 Annual Report on the Work of the Organization* (New York: United Nations, 1994), par. 316, p. 113.

12. Report of the Commission on Global Governance, *Our Global Neighborhood* (New York: Oxford University Press, 1995), 1.

13. Frene Ginwala, "Discrimination Not the Problem," in *The Process of Nations* (New York: UNICEF, 1995), 37.

14. Fourth World Conference on Women, Beijing, *Platform for Action*, par. 146, p.90.

15. Karin Sham Poo, "Why Gender Balance Matters," in *Women in the United Nations* (New York: Franklin & Eleanor Roosevelt Institute, 1995), 55–59.

16. Inger Skjelsbæk, *Gendered Battlefields: A Gender Analysis of Peace and Conflict* (Norway: Peace Research Institute [PRIO], 1997), report 6/97, p. 37.

17. Alida Brill, introduction to *A Rising Public Voice: Women in Politics Worldwide*, ed. Alida Brill, (New York: The Feminist Press, 1995), 3–4.

18. Skjelsbæk, *Gendered Battlefields*, 37.

19. Hikka Pietilä and Jeanne Vickers, *Making Women Matter* (London and New Jersey: Zed Books, 1994), 65.

20. *Our Global Neighborhood*, 17.

21. "Nairobi Forward-Looking Strategies for the Advancement of Women," par. 258, p. 345.

22. United Nations, *Women: Challenges to the Year 2000* (New York: United Nations, 1991), 67.

23. Ibid.

24. Ibid.

25. Ibid.

26. Ibid., 74.

27 United Nations Development Programme, *Human Development Report* 1998, 35.

28. Roberta Cohen, *Refugee and Interanally Displaced Women: A Development Perspective* (Washington: The Brookings Institution, Refugee Policy Group Project on Internal Displacement, 1995), 1.

29. United Nations Development Programme, *Human Development Report* 1998, 35.

30. Ibid., 20.

31. *Our Global Neighborhood*, 22.

32. Cohen, *Refugee and Internally Displaced Women*, 9.

33. Martha Alter Chen, "The Feminization of Poverty," in *Commitment to the World's Women*, ed. Noeleen Heyzer, 23.

34. Heyzer, *Commitment to the World's Women*, 5.

35. Chen, "The Feminization of Poverty," 23.

36. United Nations Development Programme, *Human Development Report* 1995 (New York, Oxford: Oxford University Press, 2995), 1.

37. United Nations, *Women: Challenges to the Year 2000*, 16.

38. *Our Global Neighborhood*, 22.

39. Elizabeth Jelin, "Towards an Engendered Democracy," in *Building a Democracy with Women: Reflecting on Experience in Latin America and the Caribbean*, ed. Ana María Brasileiro (New York: UNIFEM, 1996), 26.

40. Report of the Secretary-General of the United Nations, *Priority Themes, Peace: Women in International Decision-Making—Participation of Women in*

Political Life and Decision-Making, presented at the thirty-ninth session of the Commission of the Status of Women in New York, March 15–April 4, 1995 (New York: United Nations, 1995), 3.

41. *Our Global Neighborhood*, 36.

42. Fourth World Conference on Women, Beijing, *Platform for Action*, par. 186, p. 111.

43. United Nations Development Programme, *Human Development Report 1998*, 131–136.

44. United Nations, Division for the Advancement of Women, Department for Policy Coordination and Sustainable Development, *The Role of Women in United Nations Peacekeeping* (New York, 1995), 1.

45. Ibid.

46. Dorota Gierycz, "Women in International Decision-Making: Peace and Security Areas," prepared for the Expert Group Meeting on Gender and the Agenda for Peace, United Nations, New York, December 5-9, 1994.

47. Lilly Rivlin and Ilana Bet-El, "Israeli Women in Two Voices: Myth and Reality," in *A Rising Public Voice*, ed. Alida Brill, 97.

48. *Our Global Neighborhood*, 13.

49. David Hecht, "Women in Sierra Leone Risk Lives to Bring Peace," *Christian Science Monitor*, April 25, 1996.

50. "Peace is Now Taking Root in Sierra Leone," *New York Times*, May 5, 1996.

51. Rose Styron, "The Right to be Safe," *New York Times* (op-ed), May 1, 1996.

52. Marjorie Agosím, "The Dance of Life: Women and Human Rights in Chile," in *Rising Public Voice*, ed. Alida Brill, 234.

53. Lynne O'Donoghue, "Women Expanding the Reach of UN Missions," *Secretariat News*, January–February, 1999.

54. Judith Hicks Stiehm, "Peacekeeping: Men's and Women's Work," prepared for the Expert Group Meeting on Gender and the Agenda for Peace, United Nations, New York, December 5–9, 1994.

55. Ibid.

56. Antonia Cubeiro, "Women as Agents of Change in Peace-Keeping Operations: A Voice from the UN Peace-Keeping Mosaic (A UNOMSO Perspective)," prepared for the Expert Group Meeting on Gender and the Agenda for Peace, United Nations, New York, December 5–9, 1994.

57. Stiehm, "Peace Keeping," 14.

58. James C. McKinley, Jr., "Asmara Journal—In Peace, Warrior Women Rank Low," New York Times, May 4, 1996.

59. United Nations, Commission on the Status of Women, *Report of the Forty-second Session*, March 2–13, 1998, (E/1998/27. E/CN.6/1998/12), 19–20.

60. Ibid.

61. Ibid.

62. Ibid.

63. Ronald J. Fisher, "The Potential for Peacebuilding: Forging a Bridge from Peacekeeping to Peacemaking," in *Peace and Change: A Journal of Peace Research* 18, no. 3 (July 1993): 249.

64. Ibid., 250.

65. United Nations, Division for the Advancement of Women, *The Role of Women*.

66. Stiehm, "Peace-Keeping," 14.

67. United Nations Development Programme, *Human Development Report 1995*, 1.

CHAPTER SEVEN: NEUTRALITY OR IMPARTIALITY

1. H. Dunant, *Un souvenir de Solférino* (Geneva, 1862).

2. A. Destexhe, *L'humanitaire impossible ou deux siècles díambiguité* (Paris: Armand Colin, 1993).

3. J. C. Favez, *Une mission impossible? Le CICR, les déportations et les camps de concentration nazis* (Lausanne: Éditions Payot, 1988).

4. J. de Saint Jorre, *The Nigerian Civil War* (London: Hodder and Stoughton, 1972).

5. A. Destexhe, "Why Famine?" in *Populations in Danger*, ed. F. Jean and A. M. Huby (London: John Libbey/Médecins Sans Frontières, 1992).

6. R. Lemkin, *Axis Rule in Occupied Europe* (Washington, D.C.: Carnegie Endowment for International Peace, 1994).

7. United Nations Convention on the Prevention and Punishment of the Crime of Genocide, approved December 9, 1948, in effect since January 12, 1951.

8. A. Destexhe, "The Third Genocide," *Foreign Policy* N°97 (winter 1994–95), and *Rwanda and Genocide in the Twentieth Century* (New York: New York University Press, 1995).

9. The Shorter Oxford English Dictionary, 1992.

10. Ibid.

11. W. Shawcross, *The Quality of Mercy: Cambodia, Holocaust and Modern Conscience* (Simon & Schuster, New York, 1984).

12. On several occasions, Bosnia's leaders made it known that if they were given the choice between humanitarian aid and arms (or the lifting of the arms embargo), they would prefer the latter option.

CHAPTER EIGHT: CHANGING CONCEPTS OF DISPLACEMENT AND SOVEREIGNTY

1. The working definition of the internally displaced used by the 1992 analytical report of the UN Secretary-General considers them "persons who have been forced to flee their homes suddenly or unexpectedly in large numbers, as a result of armed conflict, internal strife, systematic violations of human rights or natural or man-made disasters; and who are within the territory of their own country" (*Analytical Report of the Secretary-General on Internally Displaced Persons*, E/CN.4/1992/23(1992), pp. 4–5). IDP figure cited in 1999 GA report at par. 1. Refugee figure (actual figure is 11,491,710) cited in UNHCR's *Refugees and Others of Concern to UNHCR—Statistical Overview* (Table 1.4, "Indicative number of Refugees, 1989–1998").

2. The definition of the internally displaced used in the Guiding Principles on Internal Displacement defines them as "persons or groups of persons who have been forced or obliged to flee or to leave their homes or places of habitual residence, in particular as a result of or in order to avoid the effects of armed conflict, situations of generalized violence, violations of human rights or natural or man-made disasters, and who have not crossed an internationally recognized State border." Report of the Representative of the Secretary-General, Mr. Francis M. Deng, submitted pursuant to Commission Resolution 1997/39. Addendum. *Guiding Principles on Internal Displacement*, E/CN.4/1998/53/Add.2 (1998).

3. Statement by Mrs. Sadako Ogata to the World Conference on Human Rights (Vienna, June 15, 1993), 3.

4. UNHCR, *The State of the World's Refugees: In Search of Solutions* (London: Oxford University Press, 1995), 8–10.

5. Ogata, Statement to the World Conference on Human Rights, 3.

6. M. Toole, Centers for Disease Control, Department of Health and Human Services, testimony before the U.S. Senate, April 3, 1990, as quoted in Refugee Policy Group, "Internally Displaced Women and Children in Africa" (1992).

7. Boutros Boutros-Ghali, *Report of the Secretary-General on the Work of the Organization*, A/50/60; S/1995/1, 3

8. Ibid., 5. Evidently, as there are no reliable statistics, estimates for both refugees and internally displaced vary considerably.

9. L. Minear, and T. Weiss, *Humanitarian Politics* (Washington, D.C.: Foreign Policy Association, 1994).

10. Statement by Mrs. Sadako Ogata on the occasion of accepting the Human Rights Award from the International Human Rights Law Group, Washington, D.C., June 8, 1994.

11. Ibid.

12. Ibid.

13. B. Boutros-Ghali, *Report of the Secretary-General*, par. 27, pp. 7–8.

14. H. Hannum, *Autonomy, Sovereignty, and Self-determination: The Accommodation of Conflicting Rights* (Philadelphia: Univ. of Pennsylvania Press, 1990); G. M. Lyons and M. Mastanduno, *Beyond Westphalia?* (Philadelphia: Univ. of Pennsylvania Press), 6; and T. G. Weiss and J. Chopra, "Sovereignty Is No Longer Sacrosanct: Codifying Humanitarian Intervention," *Ethics and International Affairs* 6 (1992): 95.

15. J. Austin, *Lectures on Jurisprudence*, ed. Campbell, 1885, 225–26. Extracts reproduced in D. Lloyd, *Introduction to Jurisprudence* (London: Stevens and Sons Limited, 1959), 134–37; and W. M. Reisman and A. M. Schreiber, *Jurisprudence: Understanding and Shaping Law* (New Haven, Conn.: New Haven Press, 1987), 270–80. See also W. Friedmann, *Legal Theory*, 4th ed. (London: Stevens and Sons Limited, 1960), 211–13.

16. Friedmann, *Legal Theory*, 211.

17. L. L. Fuller, "Positivism and Fidelity to Law: A Reply to Professor Hart," *Harvard Law Review* 71 (1958): 634; see also H. L. A. Hart, "Positivism and

the Separation of Law and Morals," *Harvard Law Review* 71 (1958), 593–629.

18. Weiss and Chopra, "Sovereignty," 103. See also, Hinley, *Sovereignty*, 2d ed. (Cambridge, England: Cambridge University Press, 1986).

19. W. M. Reisman, "Through or Despite Governments: Differentiated Responsibilities of Human Rights Programs," *Iowa Law Review* 72, no. 2 (January 1987): 391–99.

20. Lillich, "Sovereignty and Humanity: Can They Converge?" in *The Spirit of Uppsala* 406-407, ed. Grahl-Madsen and Toman (Hawthorne, N.Y.: De Gruyter, 1984). Quoted in Lewis Henkin et al., *International Law: Cases and Materials*, 3rd ed. (St. Paul, Minn.: West Publishing Co., 1993), p. 19.

21. Lyons and Mastanduno, *Beyond Westphalia*, 6.

22. W. M. Reisman, "Humanitarian Intervention and Fledgling Democracies," *Fordham International Law Journal* 18, no. 3 (1988): 794–805, 795. See also W. M. Reisman in "Coercion and Self-determination: Construing Charter Article 2(4)," *American Journal of International Law* 624 (1984): 78; and "Sovereignty and Human Rights in Contemporary International Law," *American Journal of International Law* 866 (1990): 84.

23. W. M. Reisman, "Haiti and the Validity of International Action," *American Society of International Law* 89, no. 1 (January 1995): 82–84, 83.

24. UN press release SG/SM/4560, April 24, 1991. Cited in Lyons and Mastanduno, *Beyond Westphalia*, 2. Portions of the statement also cited in Chaffer, "Toward a Modern Doctrine of Humanitarian Intervention," *University of Toledo Law Review* 23 (1992): 262.

25. J. Perez de Cuellar, *Report of the Secretary-General on the Work of the Organization* (1991), 12, 13.

26. Ibid.

27. B. Boutros-Ghali, *An Agenda for Peace,* June 17, 1992, UN Document A/47277–S/24111, p. 5.

28. B. Boutros-Ghali, "Empowering the United Nations," *Foreign Affairs* (Winter 1992/93): 91–101, 99.

29. D. J. Scheffer, "Toward a Modern Doctrine of Humanitarian Intervention," 262–63.

30. Council of Ministers, *Report of the Secretary-General on Conflicts in Africa: Proposals for an OAU Mechanism for Conflict Prevention and Resolution,* CM/1710 (L. VI)(Addis Ababa: Organization of African Unity, 1992).

31. Ibid.

32. United Nations, Note by the President of the Security Council, S/25344 (February 26, 1993).

33. United Nations, *Analytical Report of the Secretary-General on Internally Displaced Persons*, E/CN.4/1992/23.

34. See R. Cohen and J. Cuenod, "Improving Institutional Arrangements for the Internally Displaced," the Brookings Institution/ Refugee Policy Group Project on Internal Displacement, October 1995.

35. Ogata, statement to the World Conference on Human Rights, 3.

36. See Economic and Social Council, Commission on Human Rights, *Internally*

Displaced Persons: Report of the Representative of the Secretary-General, Mr. Francis M. Deng, E/CN.4/1995/50 (United Nations, 1995); and Chris J. Bakwesegha, "The Role of the Organization of African Unity in Conflict Prevention, Management and Resolution," paper prepared for the Organization of African Unity/United Nation High Displacement in Africa, Addis Ababa, September 1994.

37. Statement by Mrs. Sadako Ogata, United Nations High Commissioner for Refugees, to the 52nd Session of the United Nations Commission on Human Rights, Geneva, March 20, 1996, p. 5.

38. See Economic and Social Council, Commission on Human Rights, *Internally Displaced Persons: Report of the Representative of the Secretary-General, Mr. Francis M. Deng,* E/CN.4/1995/50 (United Nations, 1995); and Chris J. Bakwesegha, "The Role of the Organization of African Unity in Conflict Prevention, Management and Resolution," paper prepared for the Organization of African Unity/United Nation High Displacement in Africa, Addis Ababa, September 1994.

39. Statement by Mrs. Sadako Ogata, United Nations High Commissioner for Refugees, to the 52nd Session of the United Nations Commission on Human Rights, Geneva, March 20, 1996, p. 5.

CHAPTER NINE: ECONOMIC SANCTIONS AS A MEANS TO INTERNATIONAL HEALTH

1. M. P. Doxey, *International Sanctions in Contemporary Perspective* (London: Macmillan, 1987), 91.

2. This section draws heavily on two unpublished papers: J. Stremlaul, "A Draft Report to the Carnegie Commission on Preventing Deadly Conflict" (January 1996), and E. S. Rogers, "Using Economic Sanctions to Control Regional Conflict" (March 1996).

3. D. Owen, *Balkan Odyssey* (London: Gollancz, 1995), 363.

4. Ibid., 125.

5. E. S. Rogers, "Using Economic Sanctions to Control Regional Conflict."

6. P. A. G. van Bergeijk, *Economic Diplomacy, Trade and Commercial Policy* (Cheltenham, England: Edward Elgar, 1994), 4, 6.

CHAPTER TWELVE: REFLECTIONS ON THE ROLE OF THE UN AND ITS SECRETARY-GENERAL

1. *Choose Peace: A Dialogue between Johan Galtung and Daisaku Ikeda* (London: Pluto Press, 1995).

2. B. Boutros-Ghali, *An Agenda for Peace,* June 17, 1992, UN Document A/47277–S/24111.

CHAPTER FOURTEEN: ESTABLISHING TRUST IN THE HEALER

1. J. Eliasson, "Responding to Crises," in *Security Dialogue,* 26, no. 4 (1991): 405 ff.

2. Preventive diplomacy has been given a broad definition in, e.g., Secretary-General Boutros-Ghali's report *An Agenda for Peace*, UN Document A/47277–S/24111, par. 20: "Action to prevent disputes from arising between parties, to prevent existing disputes from escalating into conflicts and to limit the spread of the latter when they occur." This term, or simply *prevention*, is used in the same sense in this chapter.

3. Steering Committee of the Joint Evaluation of Emergency Assistance to Rwanda, *The International Response to Conflict and Genocide: Lessons from the Rwanda Experience*, Odense, Denmark, 1996. The Steering Committee of the study included representatives of nineteen bilateral donor agencies and a number of international government and nongovernmental organizations and agencies. The respective study teams and consultants engaged are responsible for the content of the reports included in the study.

4. See p. 238.

5. Formerly CSCE, see p. 229.

6. The United Nations Aouzou Strip Observer Group (UNASOG) was established on May 4, 1994, and the mandate was terminated on June 13, 1994. See UN Document A/1994/512 and 672.

7. This distinction is clearly made in, e.g., G. Evans, *Cooperating for Peace* (Victoria: Allen & Unwin, 1993), 65 ff.

8. UN Document A/59/60-S/1995/1, par. 28.

9. A selected bibliography of the academic debate on this issue is provided in B. Simma, ed., *The Charter of the United Nations* (New York: Oxford University Press, 1994), 139 ff.

10. Statement by the Secretary-General to the General Assembly's High Level Group on the Financial Situation of the United Nations, February 6, 1996.

11. Statement on behalf of the EU by the Deputy Permanent Representative of Italy in the above-mentioned working group, January 24, 1996.

12. A good overview of this is given in United Nations, *Handbook on the Peaceful Settlement of Disputes*, UN Publication Sales No. E.92N.7 (1992), pars. 239–71.

13. Note, e.g., statements by a number of states that the granting of observership in the General Assembly for the Commonwealth of Independent States (CIS) must not imply that it should be considered a regional arrangement within the meaning of Chapter VIII (A/48/PV.91).

14. The importance of international civil society has been particularly highlighted by the Commission on Global Governance in *Our Global Neighborhood* (New York: Oxford University Press, 1995), 32 ff and elsewhere.

15. A proposal in San Francisco by Colombia to include such a reference was actually defeated by a majority vote. See *Documents of the United Nations Conference on International Organization*, UNCIO VI, p. 373, Doc. 817,1/1/31.

16. This point was emphasized by the Commission on Global Governance in *Our Global Neighborhood*, 97.

17. On this topic, see various contributions in K. M. Cahill, ed., *A Framework for Survival: Health, Human Rights, and Humanitarian Assistance in Conflicts and Disasters* (New York: Routledge and The Center for International Health and

Cooperation, 1999), including my own, "The World Response to Humanitarian Emergencies."

18. The principal multilateral negotiating body in this field, the Conference on Disarmament (CD), is formally independent of the United Nations but serves in practice as its disarmament organ.

19. The Charter amendment to increase the number of nonpermanent seats from six to ten was adopted on December 17, 1963, and enforced on August 31, 1965.

20. The Nordic countries have proposed such a reexamination ten to twenty years after the enforcement of changes presently considered (UN Document A/49/965, p. 1040 f). The Commission on Global Governance proposed a two-stage enlargement including a new class of "standing members," where the second review would take place around 2005 (see note 14).

21. This point is also made by a report of the Joint Inspection Unit. See UN Document A/50/853, especially pars. 90 and 113.

22. General Assembly resolutions and statements by the President of the Security Council have been collected in Boutros-Ghali, *An Agenda for Peace.*

23. The DHA has established a Humanitarian Early Warning System (HEWS) to identify potential complex emergencies and crises with humanitarian implications, covering the socioeconomic, environmental, and human rights fields.

24. Burundi is an interesting current example, albeit still with uncertain results, of such efforts.

CHAPTER FIFTEEN: EARLY-WARNING SYSTEMS

1. This chapter incorporates materials from T. R. Gurr and B. Harff, *Early Warning of Communal Conflict and Genocide: Linking Empirical Research to International Responses* (Tokyo: Monograph Series on Governance and Conflict Resolution, GCR 05, United Nations University Press, 1996) and from Ted Robert Gurr, *Peoples versus States: Minorities at Risk in the New Century* (Washington, D.C.: United States Institute of Peace Press, 2000).

2. A compelling argument about the connection between early warning and action is made by B. Harff in "Rescuing Endangered Peoples: Missed Opportunities," *Social Research* 62 (spring 1995): 23–40.

3. In his introduction to K. M. Cahill, ed., *A Framework for Survival: Health, Human Rights, and Humanitarian Assistance in Conflicts and Disasters* (New York: Basic Books for the Council on Foreign Relations, 1993), 7.

4. The following paragraphs draw on new evidence developed by the Minorities at Risk (MAR) project, directed by the author and based at the University of Maryland's Center for International Development and Conflict Management. The project compiles systematic information about 275 politically active ethnic groups' cultural and religious traits; where they live, their status and inequalities; their past and present involvement in conflict; and many other variables. Publications that report previous findings from the study include T. R. Gurr, *Minorities at Risk: A Global View of Ethnopolitical Conflict* (Washington, D.C.:

United States Institute of Peace Press, 1993) and T. R. Gurr, "Peoples Against States: Ethnopolitical Conflict and the Changing World System," *International Studies Quarterly* 38, No. 3 (1994): 347–377. Current findings are reported in Gurr, *Peoples versus States* (note 1 above) and on the projectís web site at www.bsos.umd.edu/cidcm/mar. The MAR project has been supported by the United States Institute of Peace, the National Science Foundation, the Hewlitt Foundation, the Korea Foundation, and the University of Maryland.

5. Boutros Boutros-Ghali, *An Agenda for Peace*, June 17, 1992. Report of the Secretary-General pursuant to the statement adopted by the summit meeting of the Security Council on January 31, 1992. New York: UN General Assembly/Security Council Document A/47/277.

6. For descriptions of these early-warning systems, written by UN officials who have managed them, see J. L. Davies and T. R. Gurr, eds., *Preventive Measures: Building Risk Assessment and Crisis Early Warning Systems* (Lanham, Md.: Rowman & Littlefield, 1998), chaps. 15, 17, 18, and 19.

7. An example of the Conflict Prevention Center's work is Heinz Vetschera and Andrea Amutek-Riemer, "Early Warning: The Case of Yugoslavia" (paper presented at the World Congress of the International Political Science Association, August 1994). Max van der Stoel describes the OSCE's preventive activities in "The Role of the OSCE High Commissioner in Conflict Prevention," in *Herding Cats: Multiparty Mediation in a Complex World*, ed. Chester A. Crocker, Fen Osler Hampson, and Pamela Aall (Washington, D.C.: United States Institute of Peace Press, 1999).

8. The concept of early warning was first widely used during the Cold War by U.S. military and intelligence analysts who sought to anticipate East-West flashpoints. Two accounts of empirical early-warning research during this era are Gerald W. Hopple, "The Rise and Fall of Event Data: From Basic Research to Applied Use in the U.S. Department of Defense," *International Interactions* 10 (1984): 292-309; and Edward Laurence, "Events Data and Policy Analysis: Improving the Potential for Applying Academic Research to Foreign and Defense Policy Problems," *Policy Sciences* 23 (1990): 111–32.

9. *European Platform for Conflict Prevention and Transformation, Prevention and Management of Violent Conflicts: An International Directory*, 1998 Edition, compiled by T. R. Gurr (Utrecht, 1999). The first in the regional series is *Conflict Prevention in Africa*, compiled by T. R. Gurr (Utrecht, 1999).

10. The Center for Preventive Action issues country-specific reports and comparative assessments, such as Barnett R. Rubin, ed., *Cases and Strategies for Preventive Action: Preventive Action Reports Volume 2* (New York: Century Foundation Press, 1998).

11. See "List of Open Access Early Warning Projects," in *Preventive Measures*, ed. Davies and Gurr, 268-280 (note 6 above) for sketches and access information on fifty-five public, private, and academic projects on early warning, risk assessment, and preventive action projects, including most of those cited in the foregoing text.

12. A comprehensive discussion of the modalities of preventive diplomacy and

their actual and potential applications in a variety of contemporary cases is Michael S. Lund, *Preventing Violent Conflict: A Strategy for Preventive Diplomacy* (Washington, D.C.: United States Institute of Peace Press, 1996). Also see the reports of the Center for Preventive Action (note 10 above).

13. J. Dedring, "Early Warning and Preventive Diplomacy" (paper presented to the International Peace Research Association meetings, Kyoto, July 1992).

14. The region is the focus of a recent U.S. government early-warning initiative. In 1995 the Clinton administration established the interagency Greater Horn of Africa Initiative, aimed at conflict prevention and food security in that region. One of its tasks was to put in place an electronic early-warning system to connect governments in the Horn, donor countries, international organizations, and NGOs. This task is the focus of intensive efforts by a working group in the Department of State called RADARS (Reporting, Analysis, Decision-making and Response System).

15. See Steven L. Burg, "Nationalism and Civic Identity: Ethnic Models for Macedonia and Kosovo," chap. 2 in *Cases and Strategies for Preventive Action*, ed. Rubin (note 10 above).

16. This was a short-term success only, since in 1997 the country was devastated by civil war. For other examples of preventive diplomacy by the OAU, see the chapter by Salim Ahmed Salim in this volume.

17. A study of successful preventive diplomacy in the Baltic states is reported in Bruce W. Jentleson, ed., *Opportunities Missed, Opportunities Seized: Preventive Diplomacy in the Post–Cold War World* (Lanham, Md.: Rowman & Littlefield, 1999).

18. Lincoln P. Bloomfield and Amelia Leiss identify five phases: dispute, pre-hostilities conflict, hostilities, cessation of hostilities, and settlement (in *Controlling Small Wars: A Strategy for the 1970s*, New York: Knopf, 1969). I use a more precise set of phases to analyze the management of ethnic wars: conventional mobilization, militant mobilization, low-level hostilities, high-level hostilities, talk fight, cessation of open hostilities, posthostilities, and settlement. See T. R. Gurr and Deepa Khosla, "Domestic and Transnational Strategies for Managing Separatist Conflicts: Four Asian Cases," in *Journeys Through Conflict: Narratives and Lessons*, ed. Hayward Alker, T. R. Gurr, and Kumar Rupesinghe (Lanham, Md.: Rowman & Littlefield, forthcoming).

19. No models of social phenomena generate perfect predictions. Economists' models of national economic performance yield forecasts with a substantial range of indeterminacy. Pollsters' forecasts of electoral outcomes have error margins that make it difficult to predict reliably the winners in close elections. Results of the State Failure project, referred to in note 23 below, suggest that early-warning research using macro-indicators can correctly classify at best 75 percent of state failures vs. nonfailures.

20. "False negatives," or crises that are not anticipated, usually are thought to be the most serious challenge for early warning. On the other hand, a system that identifies too many "false positives" may prompt efforts at conflict prevention that are diffused too widely rather than focused on the highest-risk situations.

21. A. Onishi, "The FUGI Model as a Global Early Warning System for Refugees," chap. 12 in *Preventive Measures*, ed. Davies and Gurr, (note 6 above); Susanne Schmeidl, "Exploring the Causes of Forced Migration: A Pooled Time-Series Analysis, 1971–1990," *Social Science Quarterly* 78, no. 2 (1997): 284–308.

22. T. R. Gurr, and Will H. Moore, "Ethnopolitical Rebellion: A Cross-Sectional Analysis of the 1980s with Risk Assessments for the 1990s," *American Journal of Political Science* 41 (October 1997): 1079–1103.

23. The first public account of the project is Daniel C. Esty et al., "The State Failure Project: Early Warning Research for International Policy Planning," chap. 2 in *Preventive Measures*, ed. Davies and Gurr (note 6 above). A full report of recent findings is Daniel C. Esty, Jack A. Goldstone, T. R. Gurr, Barbara Harff, Marc Levy, Geoffrey D. Dabelko, Pamela T. Surko, and Alan N. Unger, *State Failure Task Force Final Report: Phase II Findings* (McLean, Va.: Science Applications International Corporation, July 31, 1998).

24. See Alexander L. George, "Case Studies and Theory Development: The Method of Structured, Focused Comparison," in *Diplomatic History: New Approaches, ed. Paul Gordon Lauren* (New York: The Free Press, 1979). Barbara Harff reports a comparative empirical study of the causes and accelerators of genocide in Rwanda and Burundi in chapter 3 of Gurr and Harff, *Early Warning of Communal Conflict and Genocide* (note 1 above).

25. This section summarizes the results of detailed statistical risk analyses by M. G. Marshall and T. R. Gurr that are reported in Gurr, *Peoples versus States* (note 1 above), chaps. 7, 8, and appendix B.

CHAPTER SEVENTEEN: INTERNATIONAL NGOS IN PREVENTING CONFLICT

1. Discussion led by Janie Leatherman at Catholic Relief Services, March 22, 1996, based on source Janie Leatherman et al., "Early Warning and Conflict Prevention: Training Implications," a report on research findings, University of Notre Dame, Joan B. Kroc Institute for International Peace Studies, Notre Dame, Indiana, 1996.

2. Ibid.

3. M. B. Anderson, *Do No Harm: Supporting Local Capacities for Peace through Aid* (Cambridge, Mass.: Local Capacities for Peace Project, The Collaborative for Development Action, 1996). Ideas later expanded and updated in id., *Do No Harm: How Aid Can Support Peace—or War* (Boulder and London: Lynne Rienner Publishers, 1999).

4. L. Minear, and Thomas G. Weiss, "Development and Prevention of Humanitarianism," in *Humanitarianism Across Borders: Sustaining Civilians in Times of War* (Boulder and London: Lynne Rienner Publishers, 1993), 23–29.

5. J. Leatherman, et al., "Preventive and Inventive Action in Intrastate Crises," draft manuscript, University of Notre Dame, Joan B. Kroc Institute for International Peace Studies, Notre Dame, Indiana, 1996. Later published as *Breaking Cycles of Violence: Conflict Prevention in Intrastate Crises* (West

Hartford, Conn.: Kumarian Press, 1999).

6. J. P. Lederach, *Conflict Transformation Across Borders* (Syracuse: Syracuse University Press, 1995).

7. R. A. Coate, Chadwick F. Alger, and Ronnie D. Lipschultz, "The United Nations and Civil Society: Creative Partnerships for Sustainable Development," *Alternatives* 21, no. 1 (January–March 1996): 93–122.

8. A. Hope, and Sally Timmel, *Training for Transformation: A Handbook for Community Workers*, 3 vols. (Gweru, Brazil: Mambo Press, 1984).

9. Ibid.

10. L. Diamond, "Rethinking Civil Society: Toward Democratic Consolidation," *Journal of Democracy* 5, no. 3 (July–August 1994): 3–17.

11. Leatherman et al., "Preventive and Inventive Action," 37-38.

12. Diamond, "Rethinking Civil Society."

13. L. Salamon, "The Rise of the Non-Profit Sector," *Foreign Affairs* (July–August 1994): 109–15.

14. M. Bratton, "The Politics of Government: NGO Relations in Africa," *World Development* 17, no. 8 (1989): 569–87.

CHAPTER EIGHTEEN: EMERGING INFECTIOUS DISEASE

1. S. Binder, A. M. Levitt, J. M. Hughes, "Preventing Emerging Infectious Disease as We Enter the 21st Century: CDC's Strategy," *Public Health Reports*, 114 (March/April 1999): 130–135.

2. L. B. Reichman, "How to Ensure the Continued Resurgence of Tuberculosis," *Lancet* 347 (1996): 175–77; "Diphtheria Epidemic B New Independent States of the Former Soviet Union, 1990–1994," MMWR (Morb Mortal Wkly Rep) 44 (1995): 177–81.

3. A. S. Khan, T. F. Kweteminga, D. L. Heymann et al., "The Reemergence of Ebola Hemorrhagic Fever, Zaire, 1995," *Journal of Infectious Diseases*, 179, Supplement 1, S76–86 (1999).

4. Binder et al., "Preventing Emerging Infectious Disease."

5. Institute of Medicine, *Emerging Infections: Microbial Threats to Health in the United States* (Washington, D.C.: National Academy Press, 1994).

6. S. Nimmannitya, "Dengue and Dengue Haemorrhagic Fever," in *Manson's Tropical Medicine*, 20th edition, ed. G. C. Cook (London: WB Saunders Company Ltd., 1996), 1721-729; Centers for Disease Control and Prevention, *Dengue/Dengue Hemorrhagic Fever*, http://www.cdc.gov/ncidod/dvbid/dhfacts. htm, Nov. 1999.

7. Centers for Disease Control and Prevention, *Emerging Infectious Diseases: A Public Health Response* (Atlanta, Ga., 1998).

8. Centers for Disease Control and Prevention, *Preparing for the Next Influenza Pandemic*, FluAid 1.0 (Beta Test Version), National Vaccine Program Office, National Center for Infectious Diseases, Atlanta, Ga.

9. Office of Foreign Disaster Assistance, United States Agency for International Development, *Report of Health Assessment of Liberia*, 1997.

10. N. J. White, "Malaria," in *Manson's Tropical Medicine*, ed. Cook, 1087–1151.

11. E. R. Shell, "Resurgence of a Deadly Disease," *Atlantic Monthly* (August 1997): 1–23.

12. R. Preston, "The Demon in the Freezer," *New Yorker*, July 12, 1999, 44–61.

13.J. C. Davis, "Nuclear Blindness: An Overview of the Biological Weapons Programs of the Former Soviet Union and Iraq," *Emerging Infectious Diseases* 5, no. 4 (July/August 1999): 509–12.

KOFI A. ANNAN is Secretary-General of the United Nations. He previously served the Organization as Under-Secretary-General for Peacekeeping Operations and as Assistant Secretary-General for Personnel, Controller, and as Special Representative to the former Yugoslavia.

MOHAMMED BEDJAOUI is the President of the International Court of Justice (The World Court) at the Hague. He had been Dean of the Faculty of Law, Minister of Justice, and Ambassador of Algeria to the United Nations.

BOUTROS BOUTROS-GHALI is Secretary-General of the Francophonie. He had been Secretary-General of the United Nations and was Professor of International Law and International Relations at Cairo University, and Deputy Prime Minister for Foreign Affairs of Egypt. He is a Director of the Center for International Health and Cooperation (CIHC).

KEVIN M. CAHILL, M.D. is the President of the CIHC, Professor of Tropical Medicine at both New York University Medical School and at the Royal College of Surgeons in Ireland, and is Professor of International Humanitarian Affairs at Hunter College of the City University of New York, and the author of numerous books and articles on the relationship of medicine and diplomacy.

FRANCIS DENG is the United Nations Special Representative for Internally Displaced Persons. Formerly an Ambassador and Minister of

State for Foreign Affairs of the Sudan, he is now Senior Fellow at the Brookings Institution.

ALAIN DESTEXHE, MD, is a Senator in the Belgian Parliament and President of the International Crisis Group. Previously, he was Secretary General of Médecins Sans Frontières. His most recent book is *Rwanda and Genocide in the Twentieth Century*.

JAN ELIASSON, a Director of the CIHC, is Sweden's Secretary of State for Foreign Affairs. He was the first United Nations Under-Secretary-General for Humanitarian Affairs and had been his country's Ambassador to the United Nations.

MARRACK GOULDING is the Warden of St. Antony's College, Oxford University. He was United Nations Under Secretary-General for Political Affairs. A career officer in the British Diplomatic Service, he had served in the Middle East, at the UK Mission to the United Nations, and as Ambassador to Angola.

ROSARIO GREEN is Mexico's Secretary of Foreign Relations and was a United Nations Assistant Secretary-General, and Senior Advisor to the Secretary-General for women's issues. She was formerly the Vice Minister of Foreign Affairs of Mexico and a professor of international economic and political affairs at the National University of Mexico.

TED ROBERT GURR is Distinguished Professor at the University of Maryland, where he directs the Minorities at Risk Project. His most recent book is *Preventive Measures: Building Risk Assessment and Crisis Early Warning Systems* (with John L. Davies). He is senior consultant to the U.S. government's State Failure Task Force and has been Olof Palme Visiting Professor at the University of Uppsala.

KENNETH F. HACKETT is the Executive Director of Catholic Relief Services (CRS). For the past quarter century Mr. Hackett has worked as regional and program director for CRS in Africa and Asia. CRS is one of the largest international relief and development agencies in the world.

JOHN HUME is a Nobel Peace Prize Laureate. He is a Member of both the British and European Parliaments. He is also the leader of the

Social Democratic and Labor Party (SDLP) in Northern Ireland. SCOTT R. LILLIBRIDGE, M.D. is the Director of the U.S. Office of Bioterrorism. A career public health service officer, he had been Chief of Global Epidemiology for the U.S. Centers for Disease Control.

EDWARD MORTIMER is Chief Speech Writer to the Secretary General of the United Nations. He was Senior Foreign Affairs Editor for the *Financial Times* in England. He is Honorary Professor of Politics and International Studies at Warwick University and the author of *Faith and Power: The Politics of Islam.*

HERBERT S. OKUN is a member of the United Nations International Narcotics Control Board and a lecturer at the Yale Law School. He was formerly U.S. Ambassador to the United Nations and Germany.

MICHAEL J. O'NEILL is the author of *The Roar of the Crowd: How Television and People Power are Changing the World* and *Terrorist Spectaculars: Should TV Coverage Be Curbed?* He was formerly Editor of the *New York Daily News* and President of the American Society of Newspaper Editors.

LORD DAVID OWEN, a Director of the CIHC, is Chancellor of the University of Liverpool. He had been both Minister of Health, Minister of the Navy, and Foreign Secretary of the United Kingdom, and served as the European Union's Mediator to the former Yugoslavia.

SALIM AHMED SALIM is the Secretary-General of the Organization of African Unity. Prior to that he had been the Ambassador to the United Nations and Defense Minister and Prime Minister of Tanzania.

LORD ROBERT SKIDELSKY is Professor of Political Economy at Warwick University. He is Fellow of the British Academy and Chairman of the Social Market Foundation. His numerous books include the definitive biography of Keynes.

CYRUS VANCE, a Director of the CIHC, was Secretary of State and Secretary of the Army of the United States of America and Special Advisor to the United Nations Secretary-General.

THE CENTER FOR INTERNATIONAL HEALTH AND COOPERATION

The Center for International Health and Cooperation was founded by a small group of physicians and diplomats who believe that health and other humanitarian endeavors sometimes provide the only common ground for initiating dialogue, understanding, and cooperation among people and nations shattered by war, civil conflicts, and ethnic violence. The Center has sponsored symposia and published books, including *Silent Witnesses; A Framework for Survival: Health, Human Rights and Humanitarian Assistance in Conflicts and Disasters; A Directory of Somali Professionals;* and *Clearing the Fields: Solutions to the Land Mine Crisis,* that reflect this philosophy. The Center and its Directors have been deeply involved in trying to alleviate the wounds of war in Somalia and the former Yugoslavia. A CIHC amputee center in northen Somalia was developed as a model for a simple, rapid, inexpensive program that could be replicated in other war zones. In the former Yugoslavia the CIHC has been active in prisoner and hostage release, in legal assistance for human and political rights violations, and has facilitated discussions between combatants. The Center directs the International Diploma in Humanitarian Assistance (IDHA) and has offered courses in New York, Geneva, and Dublin.

The Center has been accorded full consultative status at the United Nations. In the United States, it is a fully approved public charity.

Africa, regional organizations in, 241, 263-72
African National Conference (ANC), 13, 151
Agenda for Peace (Boutros-Ghali), 122-23, 128-29, 190-91, 193, 199, 222, 236, 245
Angola sanctions, 156-57
Annan, Kofi A., xvi, 164, 238
Arafat, Yasser, 27
Aristide, Jean-Bertrand, 154, 157-58
Armenians, genocide against, 104, 110
Arusha Peace Agreement, 267-68
Austin, John, 125-26
Aouzou Strip, 219

Bahrain conflict prevention, 213
Bedjaoui, Mohammed, xv, xix, xx, 2
Benevolencija organization, 278
Bengal famine 1943, 57
Berlin Conference on partition of Africa, 269
Biafra crisis, 105
biological weapons, xxiii-xxiv, 294-96, 298
Bosnia-Herzegovina: failure of prevention in, 31-32; media role in, 69-70; NATO in, 14-16, 109; and neutrality concept, 105-8; sanctions in, 155-56; tribunal on, 116-17; UN in, 7, 9, 11, 13, 15, 177-78; women in, 92
Boutros-Ghali, Boutros, xv-xvi, 122-23, 128-29, 164, 190-91, 193, 199, 205, 208, 210, 213, 222, 236, 245
Brezhnev doctrine, 146
Bunche, Ralph, 192, 213
Burundi, preventive action in, 32, 156, 194, 196-199, 213, 249, 279
Bush, George, 70-71

Cairo Declaration, 266
Cameroon/Nigeria mission, 208
capitalism, global, xix, 33-34, 43-44, 69, 146-47, 159-60
capital movement, tax on, 49
CARE, 168
Caritas organization, 278
Carnegie Commission on Preventing Deadly Conflict, 10
Catholic Relief Services, 168
Center for Preventive Action, 247
Centers for Disease Control, 165, 290-91, 296
Chechnya war, 9, 20, 133
Churchill, Winston, 108
civil society, strengthening of, 274-75, 280-84
Clinton, Bill, 7, 10
CNN, xxiii, 6, 19, 73, 243
Cold War, end of, 4, 33-34, 101, 189-90, 216-17, 221-22, 246
command theory, 125-26
Commission for Mediation, Conciliation, and Arbitration, OAU (CMCA), 265
Common Ground group, 248
Commonwealth of Independent

faith-based organizations, 241, 273-85
field monitoring, 250-52
food: as aid, 14; covenant on, 40
Forum on Early Warning and Early Response (FEWER), 246
Fourth World Conference on Women 1995, 84-86
Frankel, Max, 74
free trade, 147
Freire, Paulo, 280

General Assembly, 109-10, 194, 212, 229-30, 232-33, 237
Geneva Conventions: on sexual violence, 90; on wounded soldiers, 103-5
genocide, 9, 101, 104-12, 246
Genocide Early Warning Center, 246
Global Information and Early Warning System (GIEWS), 245
Goma refugee camps, 61, 110, 163, 291
Gorbachev, Mikhail, 72
Goulding, Marrack, xvi, 164
government role: in assistance, 55-56; in partnerships, 165-69
Greece/Turkey preventive actions, 206-7
Green, Rosario, xvii, 81
group identity, 256-58, 275-79
groups at risk, listed, 258-62
Grunwald, Henry A., 74
Guiding Principles on Internal Displacement, 132-33, 141-42
Gulf War, 70-71, 217
Gurr, Ted Robert, xviii, 241

Hackett, Kenneth, xxi-xxii, 241
Haiti: intervention in, 127; NGOs in, 283; sanctions, 154, 157-58
Hammarskjold, Dag, 264
Hansen, Peter, xviii, xx, 2
healing: and peace, 17-27; women and, 93-99
Hitler, Adolf, 104, 108, 149, 160
HIV-AIDS, xxiv, 92, 271-72, 288-89

Holbrooke, Richard, 69-70
Holocaust, the, 101, 104-5, 108-09, 112
humanitarian assistance: manipulation of, 106, 110-14; in political context, 51-66; preventive, 192-93; shortcomings of, 102-117
Humanitarian Early Warning System (HEWS), 245, 251
human rights: and displacement, 119-24; international law on, 126-27; and NGOs, xxi, 250-51; vs. sovereignty, 126-27; and TV, 71; UN on, 41, 45, 66, 131-39, 229-30; and underdevelopment, 39-44; as Western, xvii-xviii, 41-42; and women, 85-88
Human Rights Watch, 250-51
Hume, John, xvi, 2
Hussein, King, 71
Hussein, Saddam, 152-53, 157-58
Hutu, the, 7-8, 110-12, 198-99, 207, 244

impartiality vs. neutrality, 115-17
Implementation Force, NATO (IFOR), 177-78
indigenous constituency groups, 276
Industrial Revolution, 69
Indus Waters Treaty, 193
infectious diseases, emerging (EIDs), 241, 287-299
influenza, 289-91
"information power," 72-77
information technology, xv, 67-79
"integral human development," xxi-xxii, 280-84
Inter-American Commission on Human Rights, 135
International Bank for Reconstruction and Development, 193
International Bill of Rights, 141
International Coffee Agreement, 8
International Committee of the Red

States (CIS), 135
Communaute Financiere Africaine (CFA) Zone, 57-58
"complex emergencies," 54
Conference for Security and Cooperation in Europe (CSCE), 46
Conference of Plenipotentiatries on the Establishment of an International Criminal Court 1998, 90
Conference on Security and Cooperation in Europe, 154-55
conflict: changing patterns of, 216-17, 273-85; civil, xviii-xix, 7; and displacement, 140-42; and gender, 84-99; and health, 271-73; guerilla-style, 105-6; as illness, 3-16; internal, 174-75, 194; inter-state, 268-70; models of, predictive, xviii, 251-54, 256; root causes of, 229-30
Conflict Prevention Network, 245-46
Congo Republic, preventive action in, 248-49, 268-69
Congress of Vienna, 47
Consolidated Emergency Appeals mechanism, 170
country visits, 137-39
Cyprus conflict prevention, 180-81

Dayton accords, 16, 109, 156
"Declaration on the Prevention and Removal of Disputes..." (UN General Assembly), 190
"Declaration on the Rights of...Minorities" (UN General Assembly), 230
de Klerk, F. W., 26-27, 151
democracy, xix, xxi, 34-35, 74, 88, 98, 126-27, 144, 229-30, 257-58
Deng, Francis, xvii-xviii, 81
Dengue fever, 288
Destexhe, Alain, xviii-xix, 81, 176
development, xix-xxiii, 34-40, 48-50, 85-93, 144, 230, 276, 280-84
Development Education for Leadership Teams in Action (DELTA), 280-81
difference, acceptance of, 22-23
Diplomacy (Kissinger), 71-73
diplomate role, 48
disarmament, 230-32
disaster: cycle of, xv, xix-xx, 53-57; vs. prevention, 52-58
Disaster Management Teams (DMTs), 136
displacement: and human rights, xvii-xviii, 120, 131-37; and infant mortality, 272-73; and NGOs, 133-39, 170-71; and sovereignty, 119-42
Dobrovtor organization, 278
dominant culture, Western, 43-45
Downing Street Declaration, 25
Dunant, Henry, 103

early warning, 123-24, 217-18, 243-60
education, 40-42, 86, 91-94, 270, 280-81
Eliasson, Jan, 164
"emergency ethic," 102
EPICENTRE, 297
epidemics, xxiii-xxiv, 3-4, 92, 120, 241, 271-72, 287-298
Ethiopia: Italian invasion, 148-49; war with Eritrea, 96-97, 185
ethnic cleansing, 113, 115
European Community (EC), 106-7, 151, 154-56, 245-46
European Community Humanitarian Office (ECHO), 167
European Parliament, 38
European Platform for Conflict Prevention and Transformation, 246-47
European Union (EU), 15-16, 23, 26, 226-28
fact-finding misssions, 164, 208-13, 217-18

Cross (ICRC), 103-5, 134, 167, 170-71, 297
International Court of Justice (ICJ), 219, 221, 236
International Criminal Court (ICC), 90, 235-36
international law: and conflict prevention, 203; on displacement, 131-33; on human rights, 126-27; on neutrality, 103-5, 115; on sovereignty, xvii; UN Charter in, 219-21, 223; in world order, 159-60
International Monetary Fund (IMF), 34, 159
International Organization for Migration (IOM), 134-35, 167, 171
Internet, the, 296
intervention: humanitarian, 15-16, 60-64, 126-27; military, 14-15, 173-87; political, 60; and UN, 7-11, 16, 167, 194-95, 217, 221-23; widening scope of, 144-61
Iraq: in Gulf War, 70-71, 217; sanctions on, 12-13, 152-54, 157-58; war with Iran, 217
isolationism, 29

Jenkins, Craig, 253
journalism, "preventive," 67-79
justice: vs. neutrality, 112-13, 116-17; vs. sovereignty, 126-27; violence as means to, 144-45

Kardak-Imia dispute, 206-7
Kenya, civil society in, 280-82
Khmer Rouge, 111
King, Martin Luther, Jr., 18, 27
Kissinger, Henry, 71-72
Kosovo: NATO in, 11-12, 14-15, 32, 163; spillover from, 249; UN and, 215

League of Arab States, 148

League of Nations, 29, 147-49, 159
Legwaila, Joseph, 267
Lemkin, Raphael, 109
Lenin, V. I., 104
liberalism, 48-50, 146-47, 159-60
Liberia: disease in, 291-92; NGOs in, 277, 279; sanctions on, 156-57
Libya: dispute with Chad, 219; sanctions on, 153-54, 157-58
Lillibridge, Scott R., xxiv, 241
Lincoln, Abraham, 17

Macedonia, conflict prevention in, 177-79, 192-93, 219, 236-37, 248, 278
Major, John, 71
malaria, 292-93
Mandela, Nelson, 26-27
Marshall Plan, xx
McNamara, Robert, 36
Mechanism for Conflict Prevention, Management, and Resolution, OAU (MCPMR), 135, 263-66
media role in diplomacy, 67-79, 184-85
Medicins sans Frontieres, 176, 297
Merhamet organization, 278
Metternich, Klemens von, 47
Milosevic, Slobodan, 14, 108-9, 115, 156
Minorities at Risk project, 243-44, 255-60
models, predictive, xviii, 251-54, 256
Mortimer, Edward, xviii, xxii, 81
Mugabe, Robert, 150
Mussolini, Benito, 104, 148-49

NATO: in Bosnia, 109; in Cold War, 4; in Kosovo, 11-12, 14-15, 32, 163
neutrality, critique of, xviii-xix, 101-17
Neutral Military Observer Group, OAU (NMOG), 8-10

"new humanitarianism," 102-17
Nipah virus, 296
Nixon, Richard, 295
nongovernmental organizations
    (NGOs): agendas of, xxi; burden
    of prevention on, xx-xxi; and dis-
    placement, 133-39; and early
    warning, 246-47, 250-51; faith-
    based, 241, 273-85; and govern-
    ments, 108, 166; and neutrality,
    113-14; in partnerships, 166-69;
    peace-building by, 273-85; and
    UN, 212-13, 228-29; weaknesses
    of, 168-69; women and, 93-98
Non-Proliferation of Nuclear
    Weapons Treaty (NPT), 231-32
Northern Ireland, peace process in,
    18, 21-25
North-South economic gulf, 34-40

Ogata, Sadako, 120-21, 123
Okun, Herbert S., xxi, 164
Omdurman, battle of, 103
O'Neill, Michael J., xxiii, 2
Onishi, Akira, 253
Organization for African Unity
    (OAU), xix-xx, 8-10, 129, 135,
    148, 219, 228, 246, 248-49, 263-
    72
Organization for Security and
    Cooperation in Europe (OSCE),
    134-35, 177-78, 219, 227, 245-46
Organization of American States
    (OAS), 135, 148
Ottowa Convention, 231
overpopulation, xix-xx, 34-35, 39-40,
    271-72
Owen, David, xv, xxii-xxiii, 2, 155-56
OXFAM/UK, 168

Palme, Olof, 27, 217
partnerships in conflict prevention,
    164-69
peace: defined, 36-38; development
    and, 35-40; and healing, 17-27;
women and, 83-99
peace-building, 201-3, 273-85
peacekeeping, 173-87, 215
peacemaking, 191-93
Pearson, Lester B., 35-36
Peres, Shimon, 27
Permanent Court of Arbitration,
    235-36
political health, problem of defining,
    144-46, 160-61
political participation, 88, 95, 98
population movements, 20
postconflict recovery, 62-64, 190
postmortem investigations, xxii-xxiii,
    10-12
poverty: militarization of, 37; women
    in, 91-92
prediction, xviii, 10
preventive diplomacy: aims of, 29-32;
    analysis and strategy in, 205-13;
    development and, 35-40, 49-50,
    280-84; and disease, 294-298;
    early warning in, 123-24, 217-18,
    241-60; and economic assistance,
    8, 51-66; and education, 40-42,
    280; and geopolitics, 32-35; idea
    of, xiii-xv; vs. intervention, xxiv,
    4-8; media role in, 67-79, 184-
    85; as peacemaking, 191; regional
    organizations in, 263-72;
    resources for, 6-7, 190; sanctions
    in, 143-61; security issues in, 46-50
Preventive Diplomacy, first edition
    (Cahill), xiv, xvi
ProMED service, 296
"Protection of Humanitarian
    Mandates in Conflict Situations"
    (IASC), 64-66
proxy wars, 106, 189-90
public health: infrastructure of, 287-
    299; as model, xiii-xxvi, 1-27,
    120, 144-46, 160-61, 173-87,
    271-72, 299

Qaddafi, Muammar, 153-54, 157-59

Rabin, Yitzhak, 27
racism, 116-17
Rambouillet Conference, 11
rape, 89-90
Reagan, Ronald, 151
Red Cross and Red Crescent movement, xviii, 103-5, 113, 115, 167, 170-71
refugees: armed elements and, 106, 110-14; and disease, 271-72, 291-92; displacement and, 81, 271-72; forecasting flows of, 253; numbers of, 144; women as, 89-93, 272
regional organizations, 212-13, 226-28, 263-72
Register of Conventional Arms, 231-32
Reisman, Michael, 127
Revolutionary United Front (RUF), 192
Rhodesian sanctions, 149-51
risk assessment, 254-62
Rivlin, Lilly, 94
Roosevelt, Franklin D., 186
Rwanda: failure of prevention in, 32, 57, 60-61, 63, 163, 196, 207, 218-19; genocide in, 110-12, 115; neutrality concept and, 109-13, 115; NGOs in, 278-79; OAU and, 267-68; UN and, 7-11, 109-12, 182-83, 267-68; women in, 90, 94-95; and Zaire, 209
Rwandan Patriotic Front, 8, 110, 115
Rwanda War Crimes Tribunal, 10

"safe haven" policy, 11
Salim, Salim Ahmed, xix, 241
sanctions, economic: on capital, 143-46; and mortality, 11-13; and sovereignty, 126-27, 144-47; use in preventive diplomacy, 143-61
Sanctions Assistance Monitoring (SAMs) teams, 13, 155
"sans frontieres" organizations, 105-6, 176

Schmeidl, Susanne, 253
security issues, 46-50
sexually transmitted diseases, 92
Shuster, Alvin, 76
Sierra Leone mission, 192
Simla Agreement, 198
Skidelsky, Robert, xviii, xxii, 81
smallpox, 3, 292-93
Smith, Ian, 150
Solferino, battle of, 103
Somalia: aid to, 52-53, 62; intervention in, 7-9, 57, 194; media role, 71
South Africa: civil society in, 280; OAU and, 267; peace agreement in, 26-27; sanctions on, 13-14, 126-27, 147-48, 151, 158
sovreignty: as basis of order, 146; definitions of, xvii; erosions of, 126-28, 144-47; and neutrality, 105; origins of concept, 125-26; UN and, 222-23
Special Representative role, 202, 211
Srebrenica massacre, 11, 70
stability, assistance and, 60-64
Stabilization Force (SFOR), 177
Start II, 231-32
states: failed, 57, 195, 253; norms of behavior, xviii, 145-47, 160
Stoel, Max van der, 245
Sudan Relief and Rehabilitation Association, 277
Swiss Peace Foundation, 246
systems, worldwide, 30-31, 243-61

Talleyrand, Charles-Maurice de, 47
technological revolution, xv, 67-79
Thatcher, Margaret, 151
Treaty of Westphalia, 125-26
triage, 6-7, 205-13
Truman, Harry, 39
Turkey: and Armenians, 104, 110; and Bulgaria, 209; and Greece, 206-7
Tutsi, the, 7-8, 110-12, 116-17, 198-99
TV images, xxiii-xxiv, 6, 9, 69-72, 75

UN, the: costs of, 190; credibility of, 215-16, 222-39; and displacement, 131-39; and early warning, 244-45, 250-51; and economic institutions, xxii-xxiii; and education, 41; financial crisis of, xx, 49, 223, 225-26, 238; future of, 215-41; and genocide, 109-10; humanitarian system of, 64-66, 170-71, 232-39; and human rights, 41, 45, 66, 131-39, 229-30; intervention by, 7-11, 16, 167, 194-95, 217, 221-23; and neutrality, 114-15; origins of, 4, 101; in partnerships, 165-69; peacekeeping role, 173-87; and prevention, xv-xvi, 18, 189-204, 225-39, 264-65; reform of, 225-26, 232-39; and sanctions, 148, 151-59; and sovereignty, 222-23; women in, 93, 96, 98; as world society, xxiv

UN Assistance Mission in Rwanda (UNAMIR), 8-9

UN Charter: and development, 38-40; on displacement, 141-42; on General Assembly, 237; on human rights, 229-30; and international law, 219-20; and intervention, 16, 167, 194-95, 217, 221-23; on member disputes, 210, 235-36; on peacekeeping, 215; and prevention, 189-91, 203, 215-16; on regional organizations, 226-28, 263-64; on sanctions, 13, 148, 154; on Secretary-General, 200-1, 234-35; on Security Council, 233-34; on war, 30, 221

UN Commission on Human Rights, 120, 130-36

UN Commission on the Status of Women, 97-98

UN Department of Humanitarian Affairs (DHA), 64, 170-71, 195

UN Department of Peacekeeping Operations, 195, 234

UN Department of Political Affairs (DPA), 64, 134, 136, 139, 208, 233-34

UN Development Programme (UNDP), 49, 85-93

UNEF Suez operation, 224

UN High Commissioner for Refugees (UNHCR), 14, 106-7, 121, 133, 135, 136, 166, 170-71, 177, 245

UNICEF, 134-35, 170

UN Inter-Agency Standing Committee (IASC), 64-66, 170

UNITA, 157

United Task Force, Somalia (UNITAF), 178

Universal Declaration of Human Rights, 41

UN Office for Coordination and Humanitarian Affairs (OCHA), 234, 245, 251

UN Operations in Somalia (UNO-SOM), 178

UN Preventive Deployment Mission (UNPREDEP), 178-79, 236-37

UN Protective Force Yugoslavia (UNPROFOR), 107-8, 177, 236

UN Secretary-General role: xxii-xxiii, 10; in analysis and decision making, 205-13; on displacement, 120; and NGOs, 212-13; in peacekeeping, 183-84; powers of, 212; in prevention, 189-204, 220-21; and Security Council, 199-202, 212

UN Secretary-General's Representative on Internally Displaced Persons, 120-21, 130-34, 137-39, 170

UN Security Council: Cold War role of, 221-22; and displacement, 129-30; and humanitarian system, 64, 232-39; and ICJ, 236;

lack of economic role, 38-39; member relations, 224-25; and peacekeeping, 178, 182-85; and preventive action, 195-199, 220-21; and proxy wars, 189-90; reform of, 232-39; and sanctions, 13, 15-16, 148, 156-57; and Secretary-General, 199-202, 212; and war crimes, 90

UN Special Committee (UNSCOM), 152

urbanization, 270

USSR, disintegration of, 33-34, 72, 208, 248-49

U Thant, 192, 213, 221

values, cultural context of, 44-46, 59-60, 77, 88

Vance, Cyrus, xxi, 164, 208

Vance-Owen Peace plan, 14, 15, 156

violence: civil, 144-45; daily, 4; and development, 39-40; dialog vs., 18, 23-25, 27; and displacement, 119-24; and justice, 144-45; sources of, xv-xvii; structural, 89;

women and, 89-93

Western European Union (WEU), 227

Wilson, Woodrow, 29, 50

Wolfensohn, James, 41

"Women and Armed Conflict" (UN), 97-98

women and conflict resolution, xvii-xviii, 83-99

World Bank, xxii-xxiii, 8, 10-11, 34, 41, 57-58, 159, 193

World Covenant on Food Security idea, 40

World Food Programme (WFP), 135, 166

World Health Organization (WHO), 3-4, 14, 134, 290, 294, 296-298

Yeltsin, Boris, 72, 75

Young Turks, 104

Yugoslavia sanctions, 154-56